THE CALIFORNIA DREAM

Second Edition

(Formerly California Civilization: An Interpretation)

Monterey—Carmel Coastline

THE CALIFORNIA DREAM

Second Edition

(Formerly California Civilization: An Interpretation)

Howard A. DeWitt

Ohlone College
Fremont, California

KENDALL/HUNT PUBLISHING COMPANY
4050 Westmark Drive   Dubuque, Iowa 52002

Formerly entitled *California Civilization: An Interpretation*

Cover photo courtesy of Alan Kirshner

Copyright © 1979, 1997 by Kendall/Hunt Publishing Company

Library of Congress Catalog Card Number: 97-73456

ISBN 0-7872-3926-7

Printed in the United States of America

10   9   8   7   6   5   4   3   2

Contents

Preface, **vii**

1. California Geography and Indians, **1**

2. The Foundation of California: Spanish Exploration, **15**

3. Spanish California: Boom to Bust, 1781–1822, **33**

4. Mexican California: Triumphant Permanent Settlement and Foreign Influences, **53**

5. The Early Days of American-California, **71**

6. The Gold Rush and California Statehood, **87**

7. California: The First Decade of Statehood, **105**

8. Mining, Land and Racial Attitudes in 19th Century California, **123**

9. The Civil War, The Transportation Revolution and a New Economy, **141**

10. Forces of Change, 1850–1900, **163**

11. California Society, 1850–1915, **181**

12. The Progressive Movement, **201**

13. California Labor: The Formative Years, **223**

14. California between the Wars, 1920–1940, **241**

15. California after the War, 1945–1962, **265**

16. Reform and Reaction: California in the 1960s and 1970s, **281**

17. From Jerry Brown's Chameleon Politics to the S.F. City Hall Killings, 1970 to 1984, **293**

18. California in the 1980s: The Golden State in the Age of Reaction and Fiscal Doom, **317**

19. Pete Wilson: A Republican for the 1990s and the Roller Coaster Ride to Conservatism, **337**

Appendix, **359**

Index, **361**

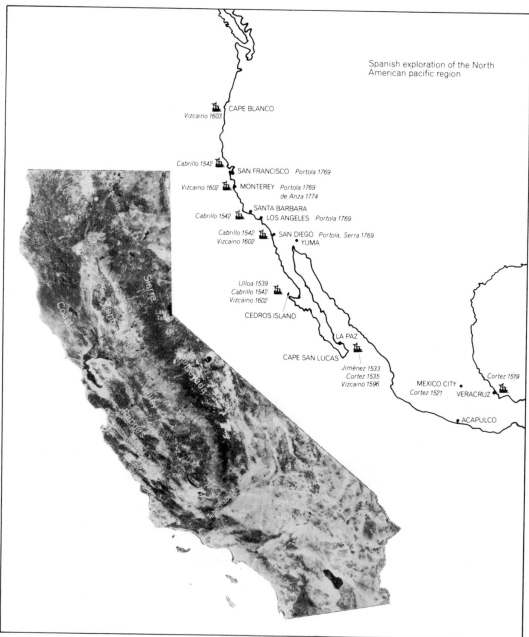

Spanish exploration of the North American pacific region

Vizcaino 1603 CAPE BLANCO

Cabrillo 1542 SAN FRANCISCO *Portola 1769*
Vizcaino 1602 MONTEREY *Portola 1769*
de Anza 1774
SANTA BARBARA
Cabrillo 1542 LOS ANGELES *Portola 1769*
Cabrillo 1542 SAN DIEGO *Portola, Serra 1769*
Vizcaino 1602 YUMA

Ulloa 1539
Cabrillo 1542
Vizcaino 1602
CEDROS ISLAND

LA PAZ

CAPE SAN LUCAS

Jiménez 1533
Cortez 1535
Vizcaino 1596

Cortez 1519
MEXICO CITY
Cortez 1521 VERACRUZ

ACAPULCO

Coast
San Joaquin
Sierra
Cascade Ranges
Lake Tahoe
Mojave
Sierra Nevada
Valley
Coast Ranges
Tehachapi Mts.

Courtesy, T. Summy

vi

Preface

The California Dream is a revision of *California Civilization: An Interpretation*, originally published in 1979. The earlier edition was one of the first textbooks to incorporate women, multicultural influences and the gay community. The changing historical climate produced the book you hold in hand. It is a volume which examines the liberal-conservative difference in California since statehood. The new chapters on the 1980s and 1990s suggest the changing pattern of California history. The confrontational politics of the last two decades are analyzed in the larger structure of the Golden State's history.

In completing this revised textbook I have had the opportunity to talk with and interview many people. I would like to thank Ronald Takaki, Dan Gonzales, Harvey Schwartz, Alex S. Fabros, Jr., the late Jesse Unruh, Willie Brown, the late Stanley Mosk, Raymond E. Frost, James Snell and Judge Richard Keller for their comments on the history of the Golden State. All errors remain mine.

My colleagues at Ohlone College Dr. Alan Kirshner, Professor Sheldon Nagel and Professor L. Stacy Cole provided a warm and intellectually stimulating work environment. I appreciate their contribution.

My wife Carolyn, my twenty-one year daughter Melanie (currently at the University of Wisconsin, Eau Claire) and my son, Darin, all helped with this book.

Former professors who influenced this volume include August Radke, Herman Batemen, Keith Murray and Earl Pomeroy. Colleagues from the past including Bradford Luckingham, Joe Gilliland, Jim Kluger, Harvey Schwartz and Manuel Sarkisyanz.

My two luncheon companions Hans Larsen and Walter Halland offered many suggestions to improve the book.

Since the publication of the earlier textbook another text, *The Fragmented Dream: Multicultural California*, has appeared to place the role of ethnic minorities and multicultural influences into the mainstream of California history.

The present text continues the tradition of interpreting the liberal-conservative split in California history. It also includes new material on the recent problems in California history over immigration, the role of women and the differences between Republican and Democratic politicians.

The California Dream introduces students to the history of the Golden State by examining the struggles for power, the manipulation of the economy and the process of institutional change. It is a journey worth taking and this volume is an attempt to suggest California's varied past.

Howard A. DeWitt
Ohlone College
Fremont, California

CALIFORNIA GEOGRAPHY AND INDIANS

Patterns of Influence

California's unique geographical setting has been an important ingredient in its history. A strange combination of isolation, an excellent climate and diverse subregions have blended into a pattern of settlement which reflects all of these elements. California has every type of climate from seacoast valleys, to desert terrain, to mammoth mountains, and they have been major influences on the historical development of the Golden State. Some sections of California receive less than an inch of rain a year and other areas face storms of over forty inches of precipitation annually. This distinct geographical quirk is an indication that there is no single means of defining California. There are some features of the Golden State which suggest why some values have become an important part of local thought.

One of the key elements in the California mind is size. As the third largest state, only Alaska and Texas are bigger, Californians proudly boast about their number one population ranking. In Los Angeles almost three million people search for the California dream. In the San Francisco Bay Area a million and a half people contribute to the local economy. Almost nine million people make up California's current work force. The present day urban-industrial complex with virtually endless suburban communities provides a sharp contrast with early California. In many respects the overwhelming concern for the environment is an indication of a continuing tie with California's geographical past.

By the late 1970s the population boom began to recede, and the number of people leaving California in 1978 and 1979 was greater than the total migrating to the Golden State. This reversal was the result of urban blight and the smoggy tinge to California life. In 1979 approximately 90% of Californians lived in urban centers, and the state's economy was in a depressed state. At the present time almost half the state's population is made up of ethnic minorities, and this serves to illuminate the Spanish, Mexican and early American past.

Geographical Areas: An Analysis

There is virtually every type of geographical form in California. The volcanic and glacial mountains are in direct contrast to the arid and fertile valleys. The desert plateaus are set off from a number of extensive river systems. The highest point in the contiguous United States, Mount Whitney, 14,496 feet is only sixty miles from Death Valley the lowest point at 282 feet below sea level. The urban setting in California is partially dictated by the fact that three-fourths of California's countryside is rolling hills and only a fourth is fertile valleys and deserts.

About half of California's land is covered by mountain ranges. The majestic shadows of Mount Shasta and Mount Lassen highlight the Cascade Range in north-central California.

Engulfing the Cental Valley are coastal mountain ranges and the legendary Sierra Nevada. To complete the circle the Tehachapi mountains extend from the California coast to the east.

The Sierra Nevada extends two-thirds of California's length, and it has acted as a natural barrier to other areas of settlement. For many years geographical isolation made overland travel very unpopular and as late as the mid-1850s most travelers preferred a lengthy sea voyage to reach California. Yet, the California climate is an exceptionally mellow one due to the influence of the Pacific Ocean and the Western winds. This has helped to foster agricultural production which has made California one of the most prosperous regions in the world. It is ironic that many of California's best agricultural areas were not developed until 1900. The mammoth Central Valley is a huge plain which is bowl-shaped and surrounded by mountain ranges. It was not until the early 1800s that Spanish explorers moved into the Central Valley. The five hundred mile valley was not an agricultural oasis as scientific farming was a prerequisite to eventual productivity. The heart of California's agricultural economy is in this area, and the agricultural yield is one of the state's most important industries.

If there is a predictability to the Central Valley, the California coastline offers a stark contrast. The large numbers of diverse bays and small anchorage spots make every few miles a new experience for the exploring mentality. Only three natural harbors of any size and economic significance dot the California coast—San Francisco bay, San Diego bay and Humboldt bay. There is an excellent man-made harbor at San Pedro just outside of Los Angeles, and the volume of trade is enormous in the present day. This was not always the case and for most of California history the coastline has been a stoic, often unexplored, giant. In the coastal areas California's climate generally does not vary more than ten degrees in a particular area during the winter and summer. The ocean currents produce a mild climate, and this is due to the California Current, a sluggish flow of water some 400 or more miles across the Pacific Ocean. It arrives to cool California in the summer and warm the Golden State during the winter months. A number of people have speculated that this current may have brought California's first settlers.

Early Spanish and Mexican explorers often believed in myths identified with climate. In fact, California weather conditions were so legendary that Spanish exploration parties were forced to place prisoners on ships as most sailors would not travel north from Acapulco. There were numerous legends of "killer storms" which led to stories of exotic whirlpools and fierce monsters. While none of these myths were grounded in fact, it was true that it was easier to sail from Acapulco to Manila Bay in the Philippines than it was to set sail from California. This helps to explain why it was 250 years before Spain settled California. While much of the state is influenced by a Mediterranean highland climate, there is still one-third of California living with other climatic conditions. This suggests the diversity of the Golden State as well as the importance of topography and climate.

Natural Resources and the Economy

California's unusual geological history has produced minerals, forests, fertile soils and an abundance of water for much of the state. The prevalence of marine, plant and animal life was an important force which allowed early explorers and settlers to survive almost anywhere in California. It is ironic that Spanish and Mexican explorers were not able to uncover local mineral wealth. California is the leading producer of sixteen separate mineral substances, and the presence of mineral deposits is located in all parts of the state. The diversity of minerals is reflected in 500 different types of soil, and this figure is an amazing one since most states possess less than 20 types of soil. Agricultural and mineral fertility are key factors in California wealth.

Much of California's economic progress can be traced to the development of water resources. In the present day water remains a serious concern to many citizens. There is also an uneven distribution of water in many parts of the state. As early as the 1770s the Spanish began irrigation projects along the San Joaquin and King rivers, but it was not until a century later that California's agricultural potential was realized. In the 1850s Mormon settlers around San Bernardino began irrigation projects which were developed for more than half a century. In 1873 the Alexander Commission was the first to report on developing a system of irrigation canals for the Sacramento, San Joaquin and Tulare Valley regions. For the next half century various irrigation projects were talked about, planned and slowly constructed in the Golden State. It wasn't until the 1920s that Colonel Robert B. Marshall proposed the Central Valley water project. As the chief geographer of the United States Geological Survey, Marshall was instrumental in developing irrigation works in the lush San Joaquin area and eventually into Southern California. It also made it possible to develop one of the most extensive irrigation systems in the world. As one travels through the Central Valley the degree of agricultural production stands as a major monument to this system.

The California economy is a major force in the modern world. Since four out of five farms use irrigation, it is possible to produce a wide variety of crops in a year-round cycle of production. There are more than 50 crops in which California leads the nation, and since 1948 the state's agricultural production has been the largest in the nation. It is in the production of fruits and vegetables that California is considered to be an agricultural oasis. John Steinbeck's writings have popularized the diversity of California agriculture, but the dollar figure is an amazing one. The marketing of lettuce and tomatoes exceeds $350 million annually. This type of production has prompted one historian to label California agriculture as "factories in the fields."

What is significant about California agricultural production are its ties to the past. The Franciscan friars introduced a number of important vegetables and fruit crops. It was this systematic attempt to bring the best plants from Europe which changed the landscape and economic nature of the California countryside. It was ironic that one of the few Spanish agricultural failures was the attempt to popularize the orange. It was not until the 1870s when the Washington navel orange was introduced that this fruit became a profitable export crop. The Mission system was filled with fruit trees, but the popularity of this type of food was not wide until the early twentieth century. The interesting point is the strong historical link between Spanish agricultural practices and those of the present day.

Perhaps the strongest link between the Spanish period and the modern day is in the production of wines. As Americans sit down to dinner each evening four of every five bottles of wine consumed are from California vintners. In France, California wines are marketed extensively, and this shows a remarkable growth for a product once considered inferior to European wines. It was in the California Missions that the best wines were produced, and it was not coincidental that many of the Franciscan secrets found their way into commercial wineries. A number of Europeans were instrumental in revolutionizing the California wine industry. The best known is Agoston Haraszthy who developed the Zinfandel grape in northern California. The wine industry is an excellent example of how European ways have been blended into a distinctive California pattern.

The Earthquake Syndrome

One of the favorite themes of modern doom forecasters is that California will slide into the sea. The list of popular works dealing with this theme are endless. While these predictions are generally designed to provide palatial estates for slick writers, there is an element of truth to the idea that California is earthquake prone. Since nine-out-of-ten earthquakes in the United States occur in California, there is a strong concern for seismographic change. A reliable historian has estimated that more than 500 earthquakes have taken place since the Spanish settled San Diego in 1769. The popularity of the San Francisco earthquake of 1906 has helped to make the earthquake syndrome a major force in the development of the California character. In a highly romanticized movie on the San Francisco earthquake, Spencer Tracy and Clark Gable stood out as heroic figures in the fight to control nature's excesses. Unfortunately, this is a romantic view of the earthquake problem. What causes an earthquake and what does it reflect about the California countryside?

The California countryside is filled with a large number of faults that vary in size from hundreds of feet to hundreds of miles. The thirteen major faults have been the reason for the large number of earthquakes. The San Andreas fault in Northern California runs through San Francisco into Central California and extends into the Gulf of California. There have been a number of important turning points in California history due to earthquakes.

In 1812, Indians around the San Juan Capistrano Mission went on the warpath as a result of the earthquake. More than a half-century later, an earthquake hit the Owen Valley in 1870 and many local citizens erroneously attributed it to the irrigation projects springing up in the area. A number of religious fundamentalists blamed the Santa Barbara earthquake of 1925 on speakeasies and illegal moonshine. In 1933 a Long Beach earthquake was explained as a reaction to population growth in Southern California. The reaction to earthquakes reflects the tendency of California citizens to blend science with a strange historical fiction. Yet, as one studies California history this is one of the humorous sidelights of the Golden State. There has been a constant tendency for more than 200 years to explain scientific change through myth and folklore.

A Touch of Archeological Madness

One of the best indications of the strange nature of California civilization is the presence of fiberglass figures depicting prehistoric mammals in Hancock Park in downtown Los Angeles. The thirty-two acre park is the site of the Los Angeles County Art Museum, and the La Brea Tar Pits. It was created during the 1920s to exploit the tourist trade. Yet, there is an important historical lesson in the La Brea Tar Pits. The oozing, sticky pitch from the pits covered the countryside, and the Indians used it for hundreds of years to waterproof their baskets. It also allowed the Indians to caulk their canoes for long journeys. Dwellings were constructed that were cool in the summer and warm in the winter due to the pitch.

In 1792 a visiting Spanish scientist, José Longinos Martínez, found fossilized animals in the tar pits. The primitive state of science prevented Martínez from realizing the paleontological treasure that he had dredged up in Los Angeles. For more than one-million years a succession of virtually unknown mammals walked into the creeping ooze of the La Brea pits. Once recovered, they provided scientists with a useful prehistory of California. In 1971, a human skull dating back 23,000 years was found in the La Brea pits, thus giving credence to the idea that human hunters were present in prehistoric California. It is ironic that the modern day hustle and bustle of Wilshire Boulevard is a few feet away from prehistoric mammals dating back thousands of years. As the automobile screeches on Wilshire, petrified relics of a former life recall the beginning of California civilization. What makes the comparison between prehistorical and present life strange is that Wilshire Boulevard was the first street to use synchronized traffic lights in the history of western civilization. If the inhabitants of the tar pits could speak would there be a strong protest against modern civilization?

Indians in Early California

The California Indian is the most enigmatic figure in the long history of the Golden State. There is every conceivable interpretation of the Indian. They have been described as "digger Indians" who failed to possess even the minor rudiments of civilization. A number of historians use the "noble savage" idea to describe a people who could do no wrong. Still others picture the Indian as possessing the faults and virtues of a primitive world. The last idea is probably closest to the truth. What is obvious is that the coming of white explorers and settlers signaled the end to Indian life and culture.

There is common agreement that early Californians were of Asiatic origin. The Indians journeyed from Asia over the Ice Age land bridge at the Bering Strait into Alaska and eventually a large number migrated into California. The dispersion of Indians throughout Western America suggests why California Indians possess such diverse physical, language and cultural patterns. The migration into California was a long and complex story and involved hundreds of tribes. The fact that more than twenty languages were brought into the area, and the presence of more than one-hundred dialects suggests a reason for the lack of early Indian unity.

Although there is general agreement on Indian isolation, there is still a raging controversy over population figures. The most recent estimate by Sherburne Cook is that more than 300,000 Indians populated the region. A. L. Kroeber, a distinguished University of California, Berkeley anthropologist, believes that 130,000 to 150,000 Indians lived in the Golden State. The debate is an insoluable one, and it suggests the difficulty in dealing accurately with early California Indian civilizations. It is commonly agreed this early civilization was Stone Age in nature. They had no knowledge of the wheel, made no use of metals, did not engage in systematic writing, and were not inspired to aggrandize material goods. These are the reasons many historians and anthropologists labeled local Indians as diggers. This term was used to describe the economic process of digging edible roots as a food source. The digger was soon looked upon as subhuman, and the term became a racial slur. This stereotype is an erroneous one, because the roots were used for a variety of purposes. It was not uncommon to see Indian women digging for root fibers for basket weaving. The diet of the Indians included roots, but they did not exist simply digging for their food. What the digger myth indicates is that hostility between whites and Indians was an inevitable condition. The digger notion also justified, in the minds of the white settlers, their right to take the land from the heathen, uncivilized Indian.

An Indian Totem in California

Photo Courtesy: Alan Kirshner

Indian Cultural Areas

One of the most convenient means of understanding California Indian cultures is to divide them into geographical-cultural areas. A cultural environment is a specific geographical area in which local Indians share a common way of life. The geographical terrain often influenced the life-style of the tribe. The presence of an abundant food supply provides a great deal of leisure which, in turn, allows basketry, jewelry, and other material goods to become a part of local culture. If a tribe is concerned with food-gathering, there is little time for craft production. In order to fully understand patterns of Indian settlement it is necessary to examine geographical settlement patterns.

HISTORY OF CALIFORNIA
EXTRA CREDIT PAPER

You can replace one test score by writing an extra credit paper. If you choose to write a paper, you must meet all of the following requirements.

1. Topic- Your paper must describe the impact of one ethnic group in California's history. (Chinese, African, Filipino, etc.)
2. Length- 7 to 10 type written pages.
3. Please include a bibliography.
4. Site your sources
5. The paper is due the night of the final exam.

Courtesy, The Bancroft Library

Inside a California Indian Temescal

In northwestern California the Yurok Indians on the Klamath River and the Hupa Indians on the Trinity River provide ample proof that rainfall and severe weather conditions were the key elements in local life. The rainy environment mandated plank dwellings and dugouts canoes. The Yurok Indians were highly individualistic, but they believed that the family was the key to a harmonious existence; however, communal living arrangements were an important part of local stability. The contradiction to this communal environment was that the Yurok's practiced the right of private land ownership. In addition, a specialized legal system was developed which provided workingmen's compensation and damages for destruction of property. Clearly, the Yurok Indians did not fit the digger stereotype.

The Hupa Indians were quite a different breed in the Klamath area. They purchased their wives from the bride's family. If the couple separated the money was returned, and this was a custom which indicated the acceptance of divorce. With a thousand people and twelve key villages the Hupa's were indigenous to the Humboldt Bay area. There was a sense of freedom in the Hupa and Yurok life due to a lack of mission influences, and the fourteen tribes in Northwest California numbered only 8,300 members. This small population base led to harmonious living in the midst of a natural rain forest.

The Central Valley contained the most numerous language groups. The eighteen tribes in this area were among the most populous Indian settlements in California. They also possessed the most divergent language patterns and the largest language family. Central Valley Indians developed rafts for river travel, instituted the use of many different foods, and practiced highly sophisticated politics. It was common for these tribes to engage in war for trade or trespass violations. The economic activity of the Central Valley Indians was not destroyed by the mission system, and it lasted until the earliest American explorers entered California in the 1840s. It is an interesting sidelight that many Central Valley tribes practiced religious ceremonies which used elaborate feasts and colorful dances to give thanks for food and peace.

In the southwest section of California there were twenty tribes which reflected the weather and environment of the San Luis Obispo to the Santa Monica area. The most important tribe was Chumash who distinguished themselves with extensive fishing, construction of elaborate housing in advanced Indian villages, and elaborate religious rituals. Early Spanish explorers, notably Juan Rodríguez Cabrillo and Gaspar de Portolá, left travel accounts praising the organization and complex structure of the Chumash tribe. With a population of eight to ten thousand people the contribution of the Chumash people to the California coastline was a major one.

The tribes of Southern California were primarily desert ones. The Shoshone, Yuma, Cahuilla and Mojave controlled the southeast desert region, and they, too, displayed a highly political civilization. These tribes are difficult to analyze because they were nomads who found it difficult to live off the land. The terrain in southeastern California would not support a permanent population with any degree of stability. There were only minimal influences from the Spanish Missions and the Church. The stark terrain and the difficulty in living on the desert fostered a high degree of Indian unity. Along the Colorado River the Yuma Indians practiced agriculture and were known to harvest corn, beans and pumpkins. The planting of crops followed a very ritualistic course which indicated these tribes were highly civilized. The most interesting aspect of the Indian agriculture of the Southwest is that it did not spread throughout California.

There were other tribes scattered throughout California. Many were unimportant to the general development of California civilization. The Modocs, for example, were a Northern California tribe of simple means and culture. They lived on roots, wild seeds and small animals, and the Modocs' struggle for survival led to a simplistic uncomplicated life without the rudiments of ceremony. In the Bay Area the Ohlone Indians were part of the larger body of Indians known as the Costanoans. A recent study by Malcolm Margolin has suggested that the Costanoans preferred to be called Ohlones. A number of academic specialists in Indian history and anthropology believe Ohlone is a word of disputed origin, and it was simply the name of a village on the San Mateo Coast. Still other academics argue that the term "Ohlone" is a Miwok word meaning "Western people." There was never a well-organized confederation of Ohlone Indians despite small tribelets from Oakland to Monterey. The mystery of the Ohlone Indians awaits future academic work. The story is important to suggest how little we know about many Indian civilizations and how tenuous our conclusions must be about a people we have failed to understand for centuries.

Indian Clothing, Food and Dwellings

The most persistent comment from the Franciscan fathers who brought Catholicism to California was the observation that the Indians believed they were in the Garden of Eden. It was common for large numbers of Indians to run naked through the countryside. On the California coast rabbit furs, fox pelts and sea otter skins were used to shield one from the elements. Many village chiefs were accorded an unusually elaborate cape to signify power. Clothing tended to be very functional. If the elements created the need for shoes or outer garments they were quickly developed. If signs of fashion existed, they could be seen in the Ohlone women who tattooed their faces and wore skirts made of tule reeds or deer skins. Dress varied according to climate, local beliefs, and the tasks required by a tribe to survive. It was a functional part of Indian life without formal rules or conventions.

The primary diet staple was the acorn. Acorns, along with dried salmon and nuts, were basic to Indian survival during the winter. There was a strong attachment to acorn groves, and for centuries Indians removed tannic acid from the acorn to produce breads and meal. While the California Indians generally were not warlike there were a number of conflicts over the acorn.

Hunting for meat was done with small bows and arrows or tipped lances. Although using primitive weapons, California Indians were highly adept as hunters, and they stalked their game with great intensity. Deer, rabbit, fox, wild pig and squirrels were the game. The coyote was not bothered because of religious beliefs. The grizzly bear was considered semi-human due to fighting skills and the Indians seldom hunted this animal. In the final analysis fish and grains provided the major portion of the local Indians diet.

Many Spanish explorers and Franciscan friars were astonished to discover that fields were set fire, and that Indians caught slugs, mice, lizards, grasshoppers, snakes, and caterpillars as food sources. Sea-snails were one of the most important Indian foods because of the special taste. It is ironic that early Spanish explorers considered the Indians subhuman due to their culinary tastes.

Most Indian dwellings were simple structures dictated by the climate. In northern and central California houses were often dug out of the ground and wood was used for weather proofing. The Yurok Indians built frame homes and thus developed a strong feeling for permanent settlement. In contrast, the Chumash Indians along the coastline near Santa Barbara used poles to construct a tent-like structure. Southern Californian Indians often used simple lean-tos to hide from the elements. Foreign intruders were critical of Indian dwellings and often pointed to them as a sign of a weak civilization.

This European criticism was not leveled at the temescal or sweathouse. Many Spaniards believed that the temescal was a sign of cultural growth, a form of social organization leading to carefully planned activity by the local tribe. Often hunting or food gathering activities were organized in the temescal. It was much like a present day sauna, and the men of a tribe were the only ones allowed inside it. The temescal was believed to have medical value as the heat drove evil spirits from the body. As an institution in Indian life, the sweathouse provided a communal meeting place for the men. The high level of socialization in the temescal suggests that it was the most advanced of all Indian institutions to European observers.

Indian Religion in California

The development of religious institutions among California Indians is an indication of the complex nature of local tribes. Each family unit clung to a legend that creation took place in their geographical area. The Ohlone Indians believed that on a small island, Coyote, the only living thing in the world, saw a feather float onto his island. Suddenly the feather turned into an Eagle, and a small Hummingbird swooped down from the sky to make a threesome. This strange trinity of animal-gods created a new race of people. For hundreds of years the Ohlone story of creation passed from one generation to the next, illustrating the continuity of emphasis on religion among California Indians.

The most important figure in the religious structure was the shaman. The medicine man or shaman was believed to cure all illness. There were many types of shamans. Some practiced dream interpretation, and a number used mysterious sucking cures. There was also body beating, manipulation of certain organs, smoking away the disease or brushing the body gently to ease out illness. The shaman had immense powers, because he was responsible for all pain and spiritual well being. In fact, Central Valley tribes looked to the shaman for signs of good weather, indications of crop successes and potential harm from other tribes. If a family or tribe lost a shaman this was often considered a sign of ill fortune.

The level of Indian myths was extensive throughout California. Most Indians believed in an afterlife. Dreams were an important means of communicating with the gods. In Spanish California the priests at San Luís Rey and Santa Ynez complained that the Indians used jimson weed with elaborate ceremonies to cure themselves of sickness. They would smoke the marijuana-type plant and dance in a staged manner to rid themselves of evil spirits. In northwest California, a "World Renewal" religious cult developed among the Yurok Indians. This miniscule cult celebrated the possession of "material goods" and it was designed to ward off earthquakes, floods and pestilence in general. This was one of a small number of cults whose existence indicated the diversity of religious experiences among California Indians.

There has been a tendency among Christians to downgrade many Indian beliefs because of the presence of figurines known as Kachinas. These pagan figurines were painted with bright colors and adorned with feathers, and they were placed in conspicuous places for daily ritualistic worship. Food offerings were common to the Kachinas, and the use of elaborate figurines is another indication of the complex nature of the Indian religious experience. The celebration of death among California Indians was another significant window into the Indian mind. The attempt to contact dead spirits suggests a reverence for life, and all Indian families practiced yearly rituals designed as a mourning exercise to highlight the importance of religion.

Indian Society: An Analysis

Most California historians believe that only the Yuma and Mojave Indians used a tribal organization. In general, California Indians practiced a system based on the family, clan or a loose confederation. Often a threat of war would bring about some form of tribal unity. Generally, local Indians were small groups of 100 to 200, and a despotic chief controlled the organization. This factor as well as multiple language use explains the general lack of unity among California Indians, and it also suggests why war was not a part of the local experience. In essence, small numbers of villages sprouted in California as social units distinct and separate from other small villages. Yet, the California Indian had a number of customs which they held in common.

There were celebrations for marriage, childbirth, the coming of puberty and the change in seasons. These different celebrations are an indication of shared values, cultural practices and social ideas. They formed a link in a civilization which was not known for its diversity in social organization. By examining these facets of California Indian life it is possible to gain extremely important insights into the nature of local Indian society.

Among California Indians marriage was a common social concept. In fact, an elaborate system of customs, rituals and mores were developed among the various tribes, including the creation of a uniform marriage code. It was common for a man to purchase a woman or for a couple to live together. All that an Indian family had to do to establish a family was to take up a permanent lodging place. Marriage was often little more than common cohabitation. There was a similar casualness to divorce. Usually an Indian couple were considered divorced if they no longer lived together. No special ritual was necessary for divorce.

When the Spanish established the mission system in California during the 1770s, the marriage institution underwent some change with a new set of rites, ceremonies and customs. Although the concept of marriage did not change radically, the Spanish did provide an elaborate Christian ceremony to highlight the moral and ethical side of the institution. There was a great change in the concept of divorce as the Spaniards no longer recognized a quick separation. Many Indians resented the changes in the marriage and divorce customs, and there were Franciscan friars who wrote puzzling accounts of the Indian's inability to understand these ideas.

The major ideas on childbirth were modern ones, because they believed in a highly structured delivery process. A large number of Indian tribes believed that the mother and father should experience the birth together. This created a strong positive feeling for childbirth. The Indians believed in a number of highly ritualistic practices. After the baby was born there was a ritual designed to dispose of the placenta. This elaborate ceremony was designed to ward off evil spirits. A number of Indian tribes buried the umbilical cord and used this process to guarantee a healthy baby. There were some tribes which believed that twins were a curse and they were generally killed. In sum, the birth process was very natural and uncomplicated.

One of the more intriguing aspects of Indian society occurred during the puberty rites. This elaborate ceremony brought both males and females into the mainstream of the local tribe. There were complicated dance rituals to emphasize the importance of reaching puberty. Young girls found that the symbolism strengthened her family responsibilities as well as the duties necessary to provide food for other tribe members. Although the girl was not yet ready for marriage, there was a great deal of stress placed upon the responsible nature of womanhood. Young boys usually reached maturity when their fathers suggested it was time to begin a family. This was at a much later time in life than when young girls experienced puberty.

The significance of puberty rites among California Indians is that it signaled the importance of all members of the community working for economic survival. The sense of local unity was reinforced during the maturescence ceremonies, thus they were utilized to further tribal loyalty. It was an honor to become a full-fledged part of the local tribe, and the emphasis upon everyone sharing the work created a strong communal spirit.

The change of seasons provided a means of keeping track of time. A large number of Indian tribes celebrated a formal New Year's feast designed to emphasize the plentiful food supply. Many rituals centered around the first salmon or acorn. These ceremonies suggested a change in mood and attitudes. Some California Indian tribes were not particularly adroit at keeping careful track of time. One season seemed to blend into another. In particular, Indians in the San Francisco Bay Area and Southern California's coastline found the mild weather conducive to ignoring seasonal changes. There were a specific number of tribes which practiced low level astronomy, and the use of twelve moons was an indication that a few Indian settlements took time seriously. Generally, there was no need to be concerned about seasons or time as the Indian lifestyle emphasized a mellow, calm approach to living.

California Indians: A Summary

Many citizens today envy the early California Indians' harmonious life. Living in a common bond with nature is one of many goals of contemporary Californians. There was also a strong identification with the communal nature of early Indian life. Values which did not create greed, selfishness and competitive zeal were among the strongest ideals held by those native Americans. The Indian lifestyle, though suited to their own needs, was viewed with condescension by the Spanish invaders and the clash between the two cultures created problems for both peoples for more than three centuries.

Perhaps the most difficult problem with the coming of the white man was the influence it had upon the Indian population. Not only were European diseases brought into California, but the Mission system created strong cultural conflict among the Indians. Many aspects of local life changed as Christianity, minimal capitalism, and a dramatic shift in the political structure confused and bewildered many Indians. These changes, coupled with personal abuses of Indian women, the violent nature of Spanish explorers, and the bewildering moralism of the Franciscan fathers, effectively dismantled early California Indian civilization. Although a large number of Indian ideas continued to attract attention, there is little doubt that the Spaniards brought in an entirely new civilization. They had neither the foresight nor the desire to utilize the more useful values and institutions which California Indians had established over centuries of settlement. The white man in his wisdom brought in a new concept of California life, and the ensuing race for material goods, political power and social status indicated that the California Dream would soon become a flourishing myth.

California Indians: Key Features of Native-Americans

Northwestern California: Main Tribes, Yurok and Hupa
   Dwellings: Sophisticated, Plank Houses, gable roofs and plank walls
   Food Sources: Acorn, Salmon
   Tools and Weapons: Precision Tools and Ornate Baskets
   Rituals: Dances and extravagant dress
   Transportation: Dugout Canoes
   Unique Feature: Precise Legal Codes
Central Valley: Pomo and Patwin
   Dwellings: Leantos and earthhouses
   Food Sources: Acorns, Berries, Vegetation
   Tools and Weapons: Simple tools but elaborate baskets
   Rituals: Colorful costumes in ceremonies
   Transportation: Tule balsa
   Unique Features: Intertribal Trade
Southwest California: Chumash and Gabrielino
   Dwellings: Domed brush earth houses
   Food Sources: Acorns, Fish, Mollusks
   Tools and Weapons: Artistic tools and baskets
   Rituals: Uncomplicated, simple ceremonies

Transportation: Plank canoes
Unique Features: Maritime Trade
Southeast California: Mojave and Yuma
　　Dwellings: Mud Houses
　　Food Sources: Beans, Corn and Pumpkin
　　Tools and Weapons: Basketry and pottery
　　Rituals: Colorful costumes
　　Transportation: Tule balsa
　　Unique Features: More agricultural than normal
Northeast California: Achomawi and Modoc
　　Dwellings: Earth huts
　　Food Sources: Roots, seeds and animal meat
　　Tools and Weapons: Simplistic basketry
　　Rituals: No important ones
　　Transportation: Log Dugout
　　Unique Feature: Preoccupation with food supply and a highly simple culture
Great Basin Eastern California: Paiute
　　Dwellings: Willow houses with domes
　　Food Sources: Small animals, seeds
　　Tools and Weapons: Simple baskets
　　Rituals: No important ones
　　Transportation: Tule balsa
　　Unique Features: Highly nomadic people with perhaps the simplest culture of California
　　　　　　　　Native-Americans

Bibliographical Essay

The best starting point for California geography is Warren A. Beck and Ynez D. Haase, *Historical Atlas of California* (1973). For an interesting article on the influence of geography upon the Golden State's history see, James J. Parsons, "The Uniqueness of California," *American Quarterly,* VII (Spring 1955), 45–55. Still useful as a historical interpretation of natural resources is John Muir's, *The Mountains of California* (1903) and Mary Austin and Sutton Palmer, *California: The Land of the Sun* (1914). An unusually perceptive analysis of a key Alameda County geographical site in the San Francisco-Oakland area is Jerome Pressler, "Landscape Modification Through Time: Coyote Hills, Alameda County," Unpublished M.A. Thesis, California State University, Hayward, 1973. The best physical and economic geography reference book is David W. Lantis, Rodney Steiner, and Arthur E. Karinen, *California: Land of Contrast* (1973). For an extensive collection of historical and geographical maps see, Robert D. Durrenberger, *Patterns on the Land* (1965–1968) and *California: The Last Frontier* (1969).

The best beginning point in studying the California Indian is Robert F. Heizer and Mary Ann Whipple, editors, *The California Indians: A Source Book* (1971). Equally important to an understanding of the changing cultural patterns of California Indians is Sherburne F. Cook, *The Conflict Between the California Indian and White Civilization* (1943) and *The Population of the California Indians, 1769–1970* (1976). For an interpretive account of the variety of Indian life see, Robert F. Heizer, "The California Indians: Archeology, Varieties of Culture, Arts of Life," *California Historical Society Quarterly,* XLI (March, 1962), 1–28.

One of the most popular accounts of the California Indian is Theodora Kroeber's, *Ishi in Two Worlds: A Biography of the Last Wild Indian in North America* (1961). Perhaps the best study of Indian agriculture is Lowell Bean, *Mukat's People: The Cahuilla Indians of Southern California* (1972). A very sympathetic look at California Indians is Jack D. Forbes, *Native Americans of California and Nevada* (1969). An extremely competent work by a non-academic scholar is Malcolm Margolin's, *The Ohlone Way: Indian Life in the San Francisco-Monterey Bay Area* (1978). Margolin's study is very important because he has broken new research ground in the controversy over whether or not an Ohlone tribe existed.

A useful collection of essays examining ecology, social organization and religious institutions is Lowell Bean and Thomas Blackburn, *Native Californians, A Theoretical Retrospective* (1976). James A. Bennyhoff's, *Ethnography of the Plains Miwok* (1977) is valuable for one particular tribe. For an excellent study of change in the Monterey Bay region since the arrival of the Spaniards see, Burton L. Gordon, *Monterey Bay Area: Natural History and Cultural Imprints* (1974).

For studies of Indian religion see Edward W. Gifford and Gwendoline H. Block, *California Indian Nights Entertainment* (1959) and Henry T. Lewis, *Patterns of Indian Burning in California* (1973). The values inherent in Indian religion are examined in James R. Moriarty, "A Reconstruction of the Development of Primitive Religion in California," *Southern California Quarterly,* LII (December, 1970), 313–34.

An obscure but excellent federal government report which is extremely useful in understanding California geography and the water problems resulting from geographical differences is Clair Engle, *Central Valley Project Documents* (1956). One of the most literate explanations of California geography is in the first chapter of W. H. Hutchinson, *California: Two Centuries of Man, Land, and Growth in the Golden State* (1969).

2

THE FOUNDATION OF CALIFORNIA: SPANISH EXPLORATION

Early Explorations

In 1519 Spain conquered present day Mexico and christened it New Spain. For the next two hundred and fifty years Spanish explorers worked toward discovering and settling California. Initially, the lure of gold and silver brought an explorer who was interested in little more than wealth. The absence of quick profit slowly changed the nature and scope of Spain's approach to California. There were other obstacles to surmount, including the presence of foreign intruders, the unpredictable nature of the Indians, the lack of precise geographical knowledge, and the inexperienced settlers who inhabited California. Considering these problems, the Spanish provided a strong foundation for Mexican and Anglo-American settlement.

Hernando Cortés, the conqueror of Mexico, landed near Vera Cruz in early 1519 where he sank his ships to prevent desertion. From 1519 to 1521 Cortés systematically led what he termed a "Christian Siege" to crush the Aztec empire. Although Cortés led a small and ill-equipped band, his inspiring leadership and the military superiority of the Spaniards led to ultimate victory. Cortés' successes were due primarily to dissension among the indians, to the military advantages of horses and sailboats, to the use of firearms by the Spaniards, and, finally, to sophisticated military strategy on the battlefield.

When Cortés arrived at the Aztec capital of Tenochtitlán, he was awed by its majestic appearance. The island city of 270,000 was connected to the mainland by four long causeways, and the gleaming masonry towers suggested a highly advanced civilization. The wealth and treasure surrounding the Aztec ruler Montezuma caused the Spanish soldiers to ponder the riches of the Aztecs. With approximately five hundred men, Cortés did not appear to have much of a chance to conquer the sophisticated Aztec civilization.

One of the primary reasons for Spanish military success was due to the welcome that the Aztec ruler Montezuma extended to his foreign visitors. After housing the Spaniards in his own personal quarters, Montezuma was taken prisoner by Cortés' forces. The Aztecs immediately selected a new leader and began to withhold food from the Spaniards. Cortés was forced to leave Tenochtitlán to fend off a Spanish force coming to arrest him. Upon his return to the Aztec capital, Cortés found that his men had attacked the Aztecs during the festival dance. When Montezuma was sent out to calm the Aztecs, they stoned him to death.

Cortés made a decision to flee Tenochtitlán. On the dark night of June 30, 1520 Cortés and his men, laden with treasure, slipped out of the Aztec capital. When the Aztecs attacked, more than a hundred Spaniards drowned some of them due to the heavy gold and silver treasure they carried on their persons. Many of his men escaped by running over the bodies of their dead comrades. It took Cortés' men four hours to fight their way down a two-mile road to freedom.

The Indian tribes surrounding the Aztecs were willing allies in the battle to conquer New Spain. With reinforcements from Cuba, and 100,000 Indian allies, Cortés began the process of systematically destroying the Aztec civilization. In 1521–1522 Cortés conquered Tenochtitlán and destroyed it block by block. On August 13, 1522 Cortés announced that all survivors could leave the Aztec capital, while the remainder of the city was destroyed.

Once Tenochtitlán fell, Cortés' men completed the conquest of Mexico. Soon the Spaniards turned to grave robbing for treasure, and it became apparent that Aztec wealth had been vastly overestimated. With Indian labor, Cortés began to rebuild Tenochtitlán. Soon Mexico City rose as the center of settlement in New Spain. European ideas were brought to the Western Hemisphere. The natives were converted to Christianity, and they were used to develop permanent agricultural production. By the mid-1520s the remnants of a new civilization had emerged as New Spain.

Establishing Spanish Governmental Institutions

King Charles V of Spain worried that Cortés was interested only in carving out a personal empire. As a result, the King began to appoint royal officials to oversee the crown's interests. In 1526 Cortés was summoned to Spain to defend his actions. An audiencia was created to govern New Spain. This body was a supreme court composed of four judges to supervise and control Spanish military officers. Soon the audiencia began to attack Cortés and to seek power for itself. Charges ranging from treason to murdering his wife placed Cortés in an awkward position. The leader of the audiencia, Captain Nuño de Guzmán, was so blatantly corrupt that the Church united with Cortés to protest the lack of governmental leadership. The end result of this internal bickering was to delay Spanish exploration in the direction of California.

Due to the chaos surrounding Mexico City, the King created the office of Viceroy. By 1535 the Viceroy acted as a governor and represented the interests of the crown. In theory, the Viceroy was the official arm of the King of Spain. The significance of the Viceroy is that he brought stability and leadership to New Spain. The use of experienced and important Spanish citizens made the position of Viceroy a powerful and profitable one. It also served to stabilize the King of Spain's control over New Spain.

As settlers moved into New Spain, a form of private enterprise capitalism began to develop on the Northern Frontier. A group of entrepreneurs, called adelantados, moved into the sparsely settled regions to develop agriculture and mining. The crown granted the adelantados political, as well as economic, privileges in New Spain. This led to the creation of a highly independent Spaniard and systematically began to undermine royal authority. While the adelantados governed in the name of the King, they frequently developed independent powers and attitudes.

The rising political and economic independence in New Spain prompted King Charles V to issue the New Laws of 1542. While the New Laws were an attempt to regain some of the lost royal prerogative, they were also instrumental in spelling out human rights. The Indians were given a bill of rights, and a plan of Spanish government was sketched out for the next two hundred years. The New Laws decreed that encomiendas, large landed estates worked by Indian slaves, could not be transferred from their present ownership. This meant that Indian slavery would vanish in the next generation.

In an enlightened statement, Charles V recognized that Indian slavery sowed the seeds of racism in New Spain. Since the Church was an important partner in the liberalization of sixteenth century New Spain, the result was a demand for Indian equality in the Western Hemishpere.

The Church and its Influence in New Spain

The role of the Catholic Church is an important factor in New Spain. Spain occupied a preferred status in the eyes of the Papacy. For more than seven hundred years Spain had fought the Moors who invaded Europe from North Africa. As a result, the Pope conferred the Royal Patronage upon the Spanish crown. This allowed the King of Spain to rule the Catholic church in Spanish settlements, and the Pope received military and financial support in times of crisis. This created a great deal of petty bickering between the church and crown, and the result was that it often delayed exploration and settlement. But it also allowed the major missionary orders, the Jesuits and Franciscans, to shape economic and settlement patterns.

Until 1767, the Jesuit order was instrumental in settling Northern New Spain and Baja California. By constructing missions, establishing permanent agriculture, building roads, engaging in mapmaking, and developing craft industries, the Jesuits set the stage for eventual settlement in California. When they were expelled in 1767 for alleged political radicalism, the Franciscan order filled the void by continuing liberal religious influences in New Spain. The Franciscans were noted primarily for educational work, and they were considered to be less politically inclined than the Jesuits.

The combination of the Jesuits and Franciscans contributions was an important facet in the settlement of California. Under the leadership of Father Eusebio Francisco Kino, the Jesuits built mission systems in Northern Mexico and Baja California. The end result was to establish the two land routes used to settle California. Perhaps Father Kino's greatest contribution was his geographical detective work which proved that Baja California was a peninsula and that Alta California was not an island.

The Myths Essential to Spanish Exploration Fever

Historians have speculated about Spain's exploration fever in the Western Hemisphere. Why did it exist without the discovery of precious metals? After the Aztec riches were exhausted, New Spain was not a profitable experience for the Spanish. The reason that Spanish explorers continued to search for wealth was due to three popular myths of the sixteenth century. The most enduring myth was the legendary fable of the Seven Cities of Cibola. In the mid-1530s Cabeza de Vaca and his Christianized Moor companion, Estevanico, appeared in New Spain with a fascinating tale. The two survivors of an ill-fated Spanish expedition to Florida in 1528, had in the course of eight years traveled more than five thousand miles, almost all of it through country never before seen by white men. In the latter stages of the journey, the travelers encountered the Pueblo culture of the American Southwest and heard of the legendary wealth of the Seven Cities of Cibola which lay to the north. This became the focal point of a myth in which hidden Indian wealth was believed to exist north of Mexico City. There was little evidence to suggest that deVaca's story was based in fact, but the increased interest in permanent exploration was due to the fable. For more than two hundred years, Spanish explorers continued to search for the wealth of mysterious Indian tribes. The search for the "Northern Mystery," or the legendary Seven Cities of Cibola, became a frantic hope.

Another important myth was the search for the Strait of Anian; this was a warm water passage way allowing quick access to the China trade. It was a myth similar to the Northwest Passage controversy which prompted early English settlers to explore the St. Lawrence seaway. The Anian myth was a reminder that Spain was more interested in Far Eastern trade than in the permanent settlement of the Western Hemisphere.

The last myth essential to continued Spanish exploration fever was the search for scientific and technical achievements lost among the ruins of the Aztec and Inca civilizations. In particular, Spain was interested in the potions, drugs, and cures for mysterious diseases which the Indian civilizations had developed. Ponce de Leon's search for the fabled fountain of youth remained an essential tenet of Spanish folklore. But many of those Spaniards with an interest in science believed that Aztec and Inca medical knowledge was the finest in the world.

A summary of these three myths indicates the varying degrees of interest in exploration among the Spaniards. Those who subscribed to the myth of the Seven Cities of Cibola were fortune-hunters and adventurers who used this tale to bolster their spirits. The search for the Strait of Anian was a popular story among the naval officers who served the Spanish crown. The learned or intellectual classes in Spain were curious as to the validity of Aztec and Inca science. Consequently, the three myths drew from every segment of Spanish popular opinion and placed subtle pressures upon the crown to continue the adventure in New Spain and expand to new areas of exploration.

The Early Spanish Thrust North to California: Baja Explorations

In 1533 Hernando Cortés was given permission to begin planning exploration parties north to the Isle of Santa Cruz. This was the name given to Baja California. But many key Spanish government officials did not trust Cortés; and he was not given permission to accompany his men. As a result of the tense atmosphere, the first expedition directed to Baja California underwent a mutiny. All the officers were killed and under the leadership of a mutineer, Fortún Jiménez, Baja California was discovered. Jiménez and twenty of his followers were killed by the Indians.

The discovery of La Paz whetted the appetite of Cortés for permanent settlement. Despite warnings that Baja California was a desolate and dreary place for a colony, Cortés founded a small settlement in 1535. It endured for two years and failed. Cortés was excited by stories of great pearl wealth off the coasts of Baja California, and this myth persisted for more than one hundred years to lure Spanish explorers northward. Part of Cortés' mania for exploration was due to his belief that New Spain was an extension of Asia. This indicated that geographical knowledge was lacking among the early Spanish explorers and suggests reasons for delays in settlement and the uncertainty of most exploration ventures.

The failure to permanently settle La Paz provided a number of lessons for future Spanish settlers. The Indians had refused to work for the Spaniards and this was a prerequisite for permanent settlement. Cortés had failed to set up a permanent agricultural base, and the early settlers were not trained as farmers. Finally, the colonists soon displayed rebellious attitudes due to their lack of preparation for frontier life.

As a result of the problems encountering Spanish exploration and the general restlessness of New Spain, the first viceroy, Antonio de Mendoza, was appointed in 1535. Mendoza's appointment was viewed as means of curing the power of Cortés, but this proved to be unnecessary as the failure of the La Paz colony seriously damaged Cortés' reputation. After careful planning, Mendoza sent an exploration party northward to search for the Seven Cities of Cibola. The results of the combined land-sea party altered many old myths concerning New Spain's geography. Francisco de Ulloa journeyed by sea up the Baja California coast. He reported that the Seven Cities of Cibola legend was nonsense, and he suggested that Baja California was a peninsula. De Ulloa's observations were ignored, possibly due to his untimely death by the sword of one of his own crewmen. Yet, he was correct in his assessment of the Cibola legend and Baja California's geography. A land party led by Fray Marcos de Niza explored northern New Spain and returned with stories of Indian wealth, agricultural plenty, and other elements necessary for successful permanent settlement. In fact, Fray Marcos reported to have glimpsed from a distance the Seven Cities of Cibola.

In the 1540s there was a strong impulse to increase Spanish exploration northward. Francisco de Bolaños was instructed to sail northward in search of the Seven Cities of Cibola. Unfortunately, the Bolaños voyage ran into a fierce storm and was driven off its course. The result was that Bolaños explored both sides of the Baja California coast and concluded that Baja was in fact a peninsula. Another significant aspect of the Bolaños voyage was the use of the term California to describe the Baja Peninsula.

The Origins of the Name California

It is impossible to pinpoint exactly when the term California became a common reference to describe Baja. Many historians believe that Francisco de Bolaños' voyage in 1541 was the first expedition to commonly use the term California. Bolaños sailed up and down both sides of Baja California. During the lengthy voyage he read an obscure chivalric novel, *The Exploits of Esplandian,* which detailed the mythical deeds of Amadis of Gaul. It was a piece of literature which extolled the virtues of Christianity and the deeds of chivalric knights. Esplandian was the son of Amadis and he met Queen Calafia, ruler of the Isle of California, in battle. The Isle of California was described as a barren, hot land with a rugged topography. It was populated by black Amazon warriors who killed the men who landed on the Isle of California. Eventually, Esplandian conquered the Isle of California and converted the Amazons to Christianity. What is intriguing about *The Exploits of Esplandian* is that it created many myths about California. Many Spaniards believed that California, like Queen Calafia's island, was desolate, barren, and largely unsuited for permanent settlement. The Latin words for California, Calida Fornax, means hot furnace, and this was precisely the definition Spaniards used in casual conversation.

The primary reason for Bolaños popularizing the term California was that he referred to the countryside as Baja California in his official reports. A number of historians have suggested that Spanish explorers showed their disgust with the California countryside by using the name. Another historian believes that "romantic fiction" has been such an integral part of California history that *The Exploits of Esplandian* is an appropriate fictional beginning for the Golden State.

The Discovery of Alta California

A Portugese navigator, Juan Rodríguez Cabrillo, discovered San Diego. The term Alta California was coined to idenify California from San Diego north of the Oregon border. In June, 1542, Cabrillo sailed north with two ships. It was not until September 28, 1542, that San Diego was sighted, and this fact suggests the rigors and uncertainty of Spanish exploration. Once Cabrillo's crew landed in San Diego they were met by hostile Indians. They described the area as desolate and barren. Cabrillo's description of San Diego harbor was an interesting one. He believed that it was an excellent port, and he surmised that Spain's influence in California might be solely to develop ports and harbors. The Far Eastern trade was the lure which brought many Spanish expeditions to California, and Cabrillo popularized the use of select California ports for refueling.

One of the most important aspects of Cabrillo's voyage was the exploration of the California coastline. Sailing north of San Francisco Bay, Cabrillo was the first Spanish explorer to experience the majesty of California's coastline. Unfortunately, Cabrillo was not able to fully explain his discoveries. On the return voyage to Mexico City, Cabrillo's crew docked in a harbor on San Miguel Island to escape a violent storm. While waiting for the storm to pass, Cabrillo fell and broke his arm. He died a short time later. A minor tragedy of the Cabrillo voyage was that a competent cartographer was not included in the expedition. Had a skilled mapmaker been present, geographical knowledge would have been significantly advanced.

European Political Problems, The Manila Galleons and California

For the remainder of the sixteenth century Spain showed little interest in California. Cabrillo's discoveries did not purport to bring riches to the Spanish empire and notions for permanent settlement were abandoned. A series of diplomatic and dynastic disputes between King Philip of Spain and Queen Elizabeth of England threatened to cause war. One of the main reasons for the strained relations between Spain and England was the rise of the Manila galleons. In 1567 trade between Acapulco and Manila opened a profitable commercial exchange between the Philippine Islands and Spain that was to last until 1815. Ocean currents allowed even the most inexperienced navigator to sail between New Spain and the Philippines. On the return trip the route led directly to fueling stops along the California coast. Manila was a natural gathering point for Far Eastern goods and the Manila galleons brought the first new wealth to Spain since the conquest of the Aztecs. Thus was the dream of Columbus finally realized sixty-five years after his death.

In 1593 the King decreed that one ship a year could sail to Manila. This decision was the result of years of harassment by English Sea Dogs. Queen Elizabeth commissioned a group of her finest navigators to search out and seize Spanish treasure. The Manila galleons were the object of the English Sea Dogs. Spain vainly protested that this was a form of legalized piracy.

The most notable English Sea Dog was Sir Francis Drake. In 1578 Drake's Golden Hind sailed into the Pacific in search of Spanish wealth. After a series of successful raids on Spanish ships, Drake sailed into Marin County in Northern California. In 1579 Drake's ship, the Golden Hind, landed in California and Spain speculated on the reasons for England's interest. Drake's landing was due to simple necessity. After a year and a half at sea, the Golden Hind, was laden with thirty tons of treasure. As a result, the one-hundred-ton vessel was on the verge of sinking, and the California landing was necessary to repair the ship. The five-week California respite was an idyllic experience for Drake's crew. Friendly Indians brought them food and entertainment, and Drake boisterously announced that he was claiming California for the English Crown. Drake often appeared uncomfortable with the California Indians, and he failed to realize that the Indians viewed the English as mystical visitors. Drake and his men did not recognize the fact that the Indians considered them either ghosts or gods.

The significance of Drake's landing is that it forced the Spanish crown to reconsider the possibility of permanently settling California. But Spain could not afford a costly settlement venture. Consequently, the viceroy of New Spain was enpowered to grant patents to explorers who desired to search for wealth in California. This was a form of private-enterprise capitalism in which the Spanish crown shared in a wealth discovered during an exploration or settlement venture.

Sebastián Vizcaíno, a merchant and explorer, approached the Viceroy with a scheme to monopolize California's pearl wealth. Vizcaíno, who had made a considerable fortune in the Manila galleon trade, had failed in the 1590s to found a colony near La Paz. He continued to petition Spanish government officials for a second chance to explore California. In 1602 Vizcaíno was given permission for an Alta California voyage. Spain was intent upon expanding geographical knowledge of California, and the Viceroy instructed Vizcaíno to take along a cartographer to chart the coastline. Vizcaíno was instructed not to rename already discovered sites. He ignored

Courtesy, The Bancroft Library

Sir Francis Drake's Plate of Brass

these orders and renamed most of the California coast. Vizcaíno defended his action by explaining that he could not identify most of the previously discovered sites.

On Sunday, May 5, 1602, Vizcaíno's crew sailed from Acapulco. It took six months to land at San Diego Bay. The Indians were friendly to Vizcaíno's crew; as a result he began Christianizing local Indians. Father Fray Antionio de la Ascensión provided the first serious religious instructions for the California Indians.

In December, 1602 Vizcaíno sailed into Monterey Bay. He promptly named it for the Conde de Monterey, the Viceroy of New Spain. In addition to appealing to the Viceroy's vanity, Vizcaíno also exaggerated Monterey Bay's economic potential. He described it as the best natural harbor along the California coast. To this day historians are puzzled why Vizcaíno wrote such a glowing tribute to Monterey and ignored the greater strength of the San Diego harbor.

Despite his personal quirks, Vizcaíno accomplished a great deal while exploring California from San Diego to Cape Mendocino. When he returned to New Spain, Vizcaíno was praised for his feats. The Viceroy Monterey planned to reward him with command of the Manila galleon and eventually with a permanent settlement party in Monterey. None of this materialized as the

Courtesy, The Bancroft Library

Sir Francis Drake meeting the California Miwok Indians, a 1599 engraving

Viceroy Monterey was transferred to Peru. His successor, the Marques de Montesclaros, disrupted the plans to settle California, and he annouced that new considerations forced the abandonment of California settlement schemes. In reality Montesclaros acted out of jealousy, because he was envious of Vizcaíno's reputation. The new viceroy hung Vizcaíno's mapmaker in an obvious attempt to discredit the expedition. But the memory of Vizcaíno's perfect harbor remained a permanent fixture in the Spanish mind. Eventually his description of Monterey Bay would lead to its settlement as the administrative center of Spanish California.

Although one hundred and sixty years elapsed between Vizcaíno's voyage and the initial settlement of Monterey, the myths surrounding the perfect harbor remained alive. This attests to the vivid symbolism his explorations evoked in the Spanish mind. Monterey was considered the natural choice for governmental and religious activity in Spanish-California.

The Jesuits and the Long Road to California

The eventual settlement of California was aided instrumentally by the work of the Jesuit order. The Jesuits never set foot in California, nonetheless, they were instrumental in establishing the two main land routes into the Golden State. Father Eusebio Francisco Kino, a brilliant Italian mathematician educated in German universities, was the driving force behind Jesuit missionary activity in Northern New Spain and Baja California. Since 1592 the Jesuit order had been in charge of christianizing the frontier regions of Northwestern New Spain. In the 1680s and 1690s Father Kino and his associate, Father Juan María de Salvatierra, constructed an extensive mission system which opened up Northern New Spain and Baja California to permanent settlement. Father Kino personally supervised the construction of 29 missions, and he baptized more than four thousand Indians.

As a scientist Kino made his greatest contributions to California settlement. After extensive exploration, Kino deduced that California was not an island. By exploring the Colorado river, Kino drew a series of maps showing that the Colorado river crossing near Yuma led directly to San Diego. Pack trains from New Spain could easily settle California. In 1702 Kino's maps ended the geographical argument that California was an island. In addition to his cartographical skills, Kino was responsible for developing the first extensive wheat crops, cattle and livestock herds, and the construction of roads which eventually brought Spanish settlers into California.

Equally important among Kino's influences upon California settlement was his persistence in keeping alive the vision of Monterey as the administrative and trade center of Spanish California. Kino suggested that the Manila galleons sail to Monterey and that wagon trains transport the goods into New Spain. They would create a bustling settlement center in Monterey. Spanish authorities in Mexico City ignored this suggestion to establish a rival administrative center. But the idea was a popular one and helped to keep alive the vision of Monterey as the center of Spanish California.

José de Gálvez and the Early Settlement Plans for California

In 1767 the Jesuits were expelled from New Spain for alleged political radicalism. José de Gálvez, a Visitor-General, was sent to Mexico City to prepare for permanent settlement in California. One reason for Gálvez' assignment to New Spain was the rumor that Russia was intent upon settling California. The reasons for King Carlos III's decision to settle California are mysterious ones. Spain had just obtained the right to settle Louisiana; thus Carlos III did not need California land settlement. At home, trade had stagnated and the treasury in Madrid was almost empty. In New Spain an entrenched bureaucracy of colonial aristocrats abused local Spaniards. But Carlos III had dreams of reviving Spanish strength in the Western Hemisphere, and the lure of California settlement proved irresistible.

Shortly after his arrival in Mexico City, Gálvez reformed the corrupt governmental bureaucracy and convinced many Spaniards to help finance the California settlement venture. The banishment and execution of more than a thousand Spaniards critical of Carlos III brought Gálvez immediate loyalty. He then subdued the troublesome Indians in Northern New Spain, and built a port at San Blas to supply California's new settlements. The Baja California missions were turned over to the Franciscan order, and the military began to play a stronger role in regulating the activities of the church.

In 1768 Gálvez journeyed to Baja California where he planned the "sacred expedition" which settled Alta California. Gálvez personally planned every detail of colonization. He pushed himself for months to insure success in reaching San Diego. Initially, Gálvez proposed three sea and two land parties to settle San Diego. But the Indians in Sonora, a state in Northern New Spain, were unruly and it was impossible to approach California at the Colorado crossing. As a result, both land parties traveled from Baja California. The tension resulting from the settlement scheme caused Gálvez to suffer a nervous breakdown. He announced to his bewildered troops that he was God. All doubts concerning his sanity were validated when Gálvez proposed importing 600 Guatemalan apes as soldiers. Some years later Gálvez regained his mental powers, but his temporary breakdown ended all thoughts of participating in California settlement.

Despite his problems, Gálvez's original scheme resulted in the settlement party which landed in San Diego in 1769. Of the five separate land and sea parties which left Baja California, two land and two sea parties landed in Alta California. A third vessel, the San Jose, was lost at sea and never heard from again. After two hundred and fifty years of Spanish settlement in New Spain, the California frontier was finally opened to permanent settlement. The obvious conclusion is that as a late addition to the Spanish frontier, California could hope to be only a marginal colony.

The First Colonies and Transitory Spanish Settlement

Spain's earliest colonies in California were not successful ones. A combination of barren terrain, uncertain geographical knowledge, and open conflict between Spanish soldiers and the Franciscans made it difficult to permanently settle San Diego and Monterey. The difficulties encountered in reaching San Diego were an omen of future problems. The two sea parties found it impossible to complete the journey, and the San Carlos landed after one-hundred and ten days at sea. The San Antonio took fifty-five days to reach Alta California. The land parties led by Gasper de Portolá, the governor of Baja California, and Captain Fernando Rivera had much easier journeys. The Portolá and Rivera parties completed their overland travels in less than eight weeks.

The Portolá settlement party included the fifty-five year old, five-foot-two Franciscan missionary, Father Junípero Serra, who became the most significant force in permanent Spanish settlement. Serra was a peasant farmer's son educated on the island of Majorca. After a brief period as a professor of philosophy at the University of Majorca, Serra announced he would seek martyrdom as a foreign missionary. At the age of 35 Serra traveled to New Spain in search of a more active religious career. After serving on the College of San Fernando in Mexico City, Serra began active missionary activity in many parts of New Spain.

It was Serra's unique personality which aided him in dealing with the rigors of frontier life. His career was one of high drama. Upon arriving at Vera Cruz, Serra announced he would walk to Mexico City. An infected foot resulted from this walk and Serra often displayed his foot to suggest that God protected him from the ravages of disease. One of Serra's favorite ploys while delivering a sermon was to beat his chest with a sharp object or to light the hairs on his chest with a candle. He whipped himself when evil thoughts entered his head. In many respects Serra's personality was a positive factor in the settlement of California, because the Indians were intrigued by his theatrics. His zeal for establishing missions, his willingness to risk anything to covert the Indians to Christianity, and his ability to blunt the negative role of the Spanish military resulted in a strong foothold for the Franciscan order in Spanish California.

On July 1, 1769, the four settlement parties were united at San Diego. Only 150 of the 300 adventurers survived the San Diego settlement. Monterey remained the focus point of Spanish settlement, and after a brief rest Portolá and Rivera set out in search of Vizcaíno's perfect harbor. While exploring California, the Portolá-Rivera party experienced a number of problems. They found it impossible to recognize most of the landmarks described by previous Spanish explorers. As they traveled north, the Portolá party christened the future site of Los Angeles. As the Portolá-Rivera party traveled north on what eventually became the El Camino Real, they found the rugged terrain much different from earlier descriptions. The El Camino Real or the King's Highway was the mission system road connecting San Diego to Sonoma. Father Serra envisioned twenty-one missions on the El Camino Real to connect the Spanish settlements. Each mission was one days travel; and this transportation system would allow supplies and settlers to permanently settle Spanish California.

An ironical episode occurred when the Portolá-Rivera party reached Monterey Bay. As they approached Monterey they failed to recognize it as Vizcaíno's perfect harbor. Quickly passing through Monterey the expedition traveled north and discovered San Francisco Bay. The best natural harbor in California was discovered by a lost and bewildered land party. Historians have speculated why San Francisco Bay was not charted by earlier Spanish exploration parties. A possible explanation is that the fog and the inland geographical location obscured San Francisco Bay from most explorers. But the members of Portolá's party were not excited over the commercial possibilities of San Francisco Bay. Only Father Juan Crespi, the Franciscan who accompanied Portolá, realized the significance of San Francisco Bay. His diary contained a passage which speculated upon the future commercial greatness of the area.

Obviously discouraged by the trek north, Portolá returned to San Diego. During the journey home Portolá's men were forced to eat some mules in order to survive. On January 24, 1770, a dejected Portolá arrived in San Diego. Twelve mules had been eaten by the motley crew that Portolá led. He had not found Vizcaíno's perfect harbor, but the idea persisted of permanently settling Monterey as the capital of Spanish California. Some measure of solace greeted Portolá when he returned to San Diego, the construction of California's first mission was underway. A crude cross supplemented a hastily constructed chapel. This was the beginning of permanent

Spanish settlement in California. A combination of Franciscan persistence and Spanish military skill had forged a transitory San Diego settlement.

San Diego was not an ideal settlement site for the Spaniards. Since the Indians did not practice permanent agriculture, there was an inadequate food supply. In addition ammunition was in short supply so the Spanish soldiers could not hunt for food. The only means of obtaining food was to trade clothing with the Indians for fish and wild fowl. This type of bartering continued until the Spanish troops were virtually naked. Captain Rivera and forty men were dispatched to Baja California to bring back some cattle and a pack train of essential supplies. For the next six weeks a precarious state of affairs existed in California, and only Father Serra's persistent arguments persuaded Portolá not to abandon San Diego. On March 23, 1770, the San Antonio arrived with corn, flour, and rice. These provisions were the key factor in the decision to settle Monterey.

On May 24, 1770, Portolá marched into Monterey Bay. Ten days later the Mission in Carmel and the Presidio in Monterey were under construction, and Monterey became the administrative center of Spanish settlement in California. Father Serra was so enthralled with the Carmel countryside that he announced he would center his mission system at the Mission San Carlos Borromeo de Carmelo.

On July 9, 1770, Gasper de Portolá sailed for Mexico never to return to California. In his brief tenure in California Portolá's accomplishments were legendary. He helped to found settlements at San Diego and Monterey. He discovered San Francisco Bay, and he provided the leadership essential in implementing a seemingly impossible settlement scheme. Portolá accepted the post as governor of the city of Puebla in New Spain and died in Spain in the mid-1780s.

The Precarious State of California Civilization in the 1770s

In the early 1770s San Diego and Monterey were settlements which the Spanish government considered semi-permanent ones. Approximately 40 settlers lived at Monterey and 23 at San Diego. Spain's hold upon Alta California was weakened further by its inability to freely transport supplies into the two settlement areas. To further complicate matters, Spain did not appoint a formal governor for California until 1777. The military commander was in charge, and he reported directly to the viceroy. When Portolá left California he selected his trusted lieutenant Pedro Fages, as military commander. The result was that Captain Rivera, who coveted the appointment, began to charge that Fages was an incompetent military leader. This was an example of the type of petty bureaucratic squabbling which characterized Spanish California.

Pedro Fages found it virtually impossible to control his men. Many of his soldiers deserted to escape the rigors of frontier California. The lack of women caused the Spanish soldiers to engage in drunken attacks upon Indian women, thereby straining relations with the various Indian tribes. To further complicate matters, Fages and Father Serra fought over the direction and scope of future California settlement. Periodically, Serra complained that Fages power was too expansive and undefined. Serra accused Fages of undermining the church's work. Fages complained that the Franciscans were not pulling their own weight in the settlement scheme, and he believed that they worked solely for the Catholic church. This unfortunate conflict between the Franciscans and Spanish military leaders surfaced periodically throughout the years of Spanish-California. This type of bickering was one of the main reasons for the transitory nature of Spanish-California settlement.

Father Junípero Serra

As a result of the disputes between military and religious authorities in Alta California, the mission site at Monterey was relocated in Carmel five miles south of the presidio. In 1771–1772, the Franciscan order began construction of three new missions. In central California the isolated mission of San Antonio de Padua, located in the Los Robles valley, reflected the Franciscans desire to escape close conflict with Spanish military authority. In September, 1771, the mission San Gabriel Archangel was founded east of Los Angeles, and the following year the mission at San Luis Obispo was constructed. These early missions were unabashed failures. In December, 1773, Father Serra reported that there had been 491 baptisms. This was a dismal figure, and it indicated that the mission system was barely able to survive the rigors of Alta California.

The power struggle between Serra and Fages was the primary reason for California's weak settlement patterns. One example of Fages' misuse of power was revealed when he halted construction of the mission San Buenaventura. The proposed mission, located halfway between Monterey and San Diego, would have aided overland travelers. Instead Fages demanded that the mission be established in the San Francisco Bay region. This unreasonable attitude prompted Father Serra to return to Mexico City to plead for a revision in settlement plans. The new viceroy, Antonio de Bucareli, agreed with Serra that changes were needed in Alta California. Pedro Fages was removed from his command and Captain Rivera was placed in charge of the Spanish frontier in Alta California. Equally important, Viceroy Bucareli decreed that Spanish soldiers who raped Indian women could be removed at the request of the Franciscans. As a result, Spanish soldiers assigned to Alta California were married soldiers who brought their families with them.

As Father Serra and Viceroy Bucareli reformed the organizational structure of Spanish California, Captain Juan Bautista de Anza requested permission to open a new land route from Northern Sonora to Monterey. The Baja California land route was no longer a useful route due to the neglect of the mission system. As a result of Anza's lengthy experience on the Sonoran frontier, he proved to be an excellent explorer. In January, 1774, he rode from Tubac, a presidio near Tucson, and crossed the Colorado river into California. After visiting the mission at San Gabriel and Monterey, Anza returned to Mexico City to report on his travels to Viceroy Bucareli. The information contained in Anza's expedition convinced Bucareli to authorize a settlement party to found a mission and presidio at San Francisco. The San Francisco settlement party was unique, because it consisted of thirty soldier-colonists who volunteered for the expedition since they desired to settle permanently in California. This marked a major turning point in Spain's approach to California settlement and future settlement ventures emphasizing colonization. The explorer mentality had given way to a notion of permanent settlement. As a result it was necessary to establish formal governmental institutions. In addition the development of trade and permanent agriculture were also important items in the future of Spanish California. Consequently, in 1776, governmental reorganization took place in Spanish California.

The Reorganization of Alta California and Governor Felipe de Neve

The reorganization of Spanish government was necessary to implement permanent settlement. A governor would be named for Alta California, and would direct Spanish interests from Monterey. The governor's office was implicit recognition of Alta California's importance in imperial politics. Felipe de Neve was appointed governor of both Californias. What set de Neve apart from the typical Spanish military officer was his penchant for administrative efficiency. From the moment of his arrival in Monterey in 1777 until his departure in 1782, de Neve was a vigorous and energetic governor. Entering California, de Neve found neither cooperation nor communication between Spanish settlements. The troops were sparse, lacking in equipment, and they had difficulty coping with Alta California.

The main problem facing Spanish settlers was the inability to produce a surplus food supply. Permanent agriculture had not developed in California. The missions were reluctant to allow government officials to requisition supplies and this dispute publicized the problems of supplying food to Alta California. Consequently, the result was to discourage new settlers. In 1777, in order to attract settlers, Governor de Neve announced that a lay pueblo would be established at San Jose. The sixty-six settlers who founded San Jose were given unusual opportunities in Spanish California; since neither military nor religious influences dominated the cities. A new class of leadership arose in California. The early history of San Jose produced a new type of Spaniard, one who considered himself a Californian. Soon a new type of local nationalism developed and by the early 19th century a native political-economic consciousness was born.

The San Jose settlement was successful because de Neve skillfully planned each detail. The city was organized according to Spanish settlement patterns. A town plaza was designated with solares or house lots adjacent to it. Each settler was granted ten and a half acres of land to sow crops. Since the presidios were expensive and the military poorly disciplined, San Jose appeared to be the answer to Spain's permanent settlement problems. Organized in minute detail with a marketplace, a residential section, and an agriculture area, San Jose offered the first serious hope for settlement activity.

To induce colonists to populate the civil pueblos, the Spanish granted each settler a house lot, the use of a community pasture, a loan of livestock and agriculture implements, and, of course, a land subsidy. A grant of ten dollars a month for the first two years and five dollars a month for the next three years was created to induce permanent settlement. All new residents were exempt from taxation for the first five years. After five years each settler was given a deed to the land which they had settled.

The early years of San Jose were harried ones. A flood destroyed the first years corn crop while dams built to aid newly developing agriculture were lost in the winter of 1777–1778. However, a survey in 1782 indicated that San Jose was a resounding success. Over two thousand bushels of corn a year were raised in San Jose, livestock production was enormous, and the town prospered from trade with the Monterey and San Francisco presidios.

In 1781 Los Angeles became the second lay city in California. The original settlers were a mixture of poor Indians and Blacks who desired to escape New Spain. The total population of Los Angeles in 1781 was forty-six persons, and twenty-six were classified as Black. Thus, the initial founders of Los Angeles were primarily Black as they constituted 56.5% of the cities population. By 1790 population shifts in Los Angeles made it predominately a Spanish settlement.

The Franciscans immediately criticized Los Angeles and San Jose as gambling centers for the lazy and unfortunate. This criticism was unfair and ill-advised, because Los Angeles quickly developed agriculture and cattle industries. What was particularly impressive about Los Angeles was that its strength was due to neither ecclesiastical nor military influences. It thrived as an agricultural and livestock center in the midst of conflict between the Spanish military and the Franciscan friars.

Felipe de Neve and the Reglamento: Civil Rights on the Frontier

The most significant contribution during de Neve's years as California's governor was his revised reglamento. The reglamento was a code of law which defined each individual's place in Spanish society and specified the church's role. The original Reglamento of 1773 granted the Franciscans full control over the mission Indians. In addition, the missionaries were granted free mailing privileges and empowered to reject any soldier assigned to a mission. De Neve was concerned about Father Serra's excessive power, and he used a request to update the Reglamento to cut into the Church's power.

The revised Reglamento dealt with three problems. First, it set up administrative procedures to prevent a drain on the King's purse. Procedures were set up to quickly pay the troops and to check for fiscal corruption in the military. Second, lay settlement was encouraged in California. San Jose and Los Angeles were founded as the first towns, and de Neve continued to push for new settlers. Third, de Neve attempted to reduce the missions dependence upon Indian labor by suggesting secularization of the missions. When the mission system was created, the Indians were to be freed once they became Christians. This process was to have taken ten years, and at this point the missions were to become lay institutions.

The provisions dealing with the missions caused immediate controversy. De Neve's obvious attempt to weaken the missions prompted Father Serra to denounce the Reglamento. Governor de Neve was determined to maintain the government's authority by reducing the number of Franciscans from two to one at each mission. Before he left California in 1782, de Neve forbade the Franciscans from using free postage at Spanish government expense. Thus, at the conclusion of Felipe de Neve's gubernatorial tenure California was a permanent Spanish settlement with an uncertain future.

Bibliographical Essay

An excellent starting point for Spanish influences in North America is C.S. Sauer, *Sixteenth Century North America* (1971). Charles E. Chapman's, *History of California: The Spanish Period* (1921) is still a useful study, but Maurice G. Holmes, *From New Spain by Sea to the Californias, 1519–1688* (1963) provides an excellent supplement to the road to California.

For the discovery and initial exploration of California see, Henry R. Wagner, *Juan Rodriguez Cabrillo, Discoverer of the Coast of California* (1941); H.H. Bancroft, *History of California,* volume I (1886); Robert R. Miller, Cortés and the "First Attempt to Colonize California," *California Historical Quarterly,* LIII (Spring, 1974), 5–16; Jack D. Forbes, "Melchor Diaz and the Discovery of Alta California," *Pacific Historical Review,* XXVII (November, 1958), 351–58; and Philip W. Powell, *Soldiers, Indians and Silver: The Northward Advance of New Spain, 1550–1600* (Berkeley, 1952).

There is a great deal of controversy over the origins of the term California. To understand the debate see Herbert D. Austin, "New Light on the Name California," Historical Society of Southern California, *Publications,* XII (Los Angeles, 1923); Edward Everett Hale, *The Queen of California: The Origin of the Name of California* (1864); Donald C. Cutter, "Sources of the Name 'California'," *Arizona and the West,* III (Autumn, 1961), 233–43; and Irving B. Richman, *California Under Spain and Mexico, 1535–1847* (1911).

By examining early Spanish explorers it is possible to understand the basic thrust of Spanish exploration, see, for example, W. Michael Mathes, *Vizcaíno and Spanish Exploration in the Pacific Ocean, 1580–1630* (1968); Herbert I. Priestley, *José de Galvez, Visitor-General of New Spain* (1916); and Janet Fireman and Manuel P. Servín, "Miguel Costansó, California's Forgotten Founder," *California Historical Society Quarterly,* 49 (March, 1970), 3–19.

The economic and strategic importance of the Manila galleon trade is examined in William L. Schurz, *The Manila Galleon* (1939). Since the Manila galleons brought Sir Francis Drake into California see, Marilyn Ziebarth, editor, "The Francis Drake Controversy," *California Historical Quarterly,* LII (Fall, 1974); Adolph S. Oko, "Francis Drake and Nova Albion," *California Historical Society Quarterly,* XLIII (June, 1964), 135–58; Frank M. Stanger and Alan K. Brown, *Who Discovered the Golden State?* (1969); Robert F. Heizer, *Francis Drake and the California Indians, 1579* (1947).

There are a number of important interpretive works on the Mission system, see, for example, Herbert Eugene Bolton, *Rim of Christendom* (1936); and *The Padre on Horseback* (1932). Bolton's work is a magnificent piece of scholarship on the Jesuit influence and Father Kino's role in opening the land route to California. The best work on Father Serra is Maynard J. Geiger, *The Life and Times of Fray Junípero Serra* (1959), but, also see, Abigail H. Fitch, *Junípero Serra* (1914) and Agnes Repplier, *Junípero Serra: Pioneer Colonist of California* (1933). For an excellent analysis of early Mission success see, Maynard J. Geiger, "Fray Junípero Serra: Organizer and Administrator of the Upper California Missions, 1769–1784," *California Historical Society Quarterly* XLII (September, 1963), 195–220.

The early history of San Francisco is described in Theodore E. Treutlein, *San Francisco Bay: Discovery and Colonization, 1769–1776* (1968).

The success of early Spanish military government is described in a superb biography of Felipe de Neve, see, Edwin A. Beilharz, Felipe de Neve, *First Governor of California* (1972). An excellent study of an early Viceroy is Bernard E. Bobb, *The Viceregency of Antonio Maria Bucareli in New Spain, 1771–1779* (1962). For the development of early Spanish government see, Francis F. Guest, "Municipal Government in Spanish California," *California Historical Society Quarterly*, XLVI (December, 1967), 307–35.

For an excellent study of the relationship of the Franciscan's to the Spanish governmental establishment see, Daniel J. Garr, "Power and Priorities: Church-State Boundary Disputes in Spanish California," *California History*, LVII (Winter, 1978–1979), 364–75. Another version of Franciscan-Spanish government problems can be seen when Governor Felipe de Neve attempted to introduce limited political rights for the Mission Indians. Father Serra cleverly dodged Governor de Neve's mandate for Indian rights. A good discussion of the de Neve-Serra controversy is Daniel J. Garr, "Planning, Politics and Plunder: The Missions and Indian Pueblos of Hispanic California," *Southern California Quarterly*, LIV (Winter, 1972).

There is a strong feeling among Latin American historians that the Spanish were guided by a strong sense of justice for the Indian of the Western Hemisphere. Although many California historians chide the Spanish and Mexican governors and religious leaders for callous attitudes towards the Indian, there was a sense of Christian duty toward the native peoples. The best statement of this viewpoint is Lewis Hanke, *The Spanish Struggle for Justice in the Conquest of America* (1965).

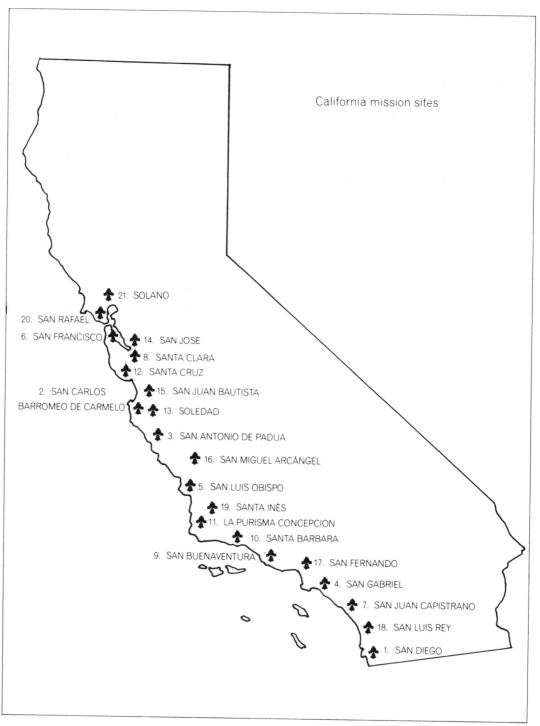

California mission sites

21. SOLANO

20. SAN RAFAEL

6. SAN FRANCISCO

14. SAN JOSE

8. SANTA CLARA

12. SANTA CRUZ

2. SAN CARLOS
BARROMEO DE CARMELO

15. SAN JUAN BAUTISTA

13. SOLEDAD

3. SAN ANTONIO DE PADUA

16. SAN MIGUEL ARCÁNGEL

5. SAN LUIS OBISPO

19. SANTA INÉS

11. LA PURISMA CONCEPCION

10. SANTA BARBARA

9. SAN BUENAVENTURA

17. SAN FERNANDO

4. SAN GABRIEL

7. SAN JUAN CAPISTRANO

18. SAN LUIS REY

1. SAN DIEGO

Map, courtesy Tom Summy

3

SPANISH CALIFORNIA: BOOM TO BUST, 1781–1822

Isolation, Growth, and Foreign Intruders, 1780–1822

From 1780 to 1822 Spanish-California grew in size and strength, but the promising beginning of the young colony suffered from Spain's preoccupation with European politics, the American and French Revolutions, and the political fluctuations of Napoleonic Europe. Many of the positive contributions of Spanish government were rendered obsolete. The attempts of Govenor Felipe de Neve to provide greater freedom for Spanish citizens by revising the reglamento to expand civil liberties was lost in the shuffle of European power politics. King Carlos IV was unable to provide the administrative leadership necessary to develop the California colony. This resulted in repeated requests for military and commercial aid from Spanish-California, requests which an increasingly beleaguered Spanish government viewed warily and made little effort to address. This is the reason that historians label the period from 1780 to 1822 as a pastoral interlude in the development of California civilization. The land had a rich potential but required the permanence and stability of civilized institutions, if that potential was to be developed. To add to the difficulty of settling California, the Spaniards did not begin large scale agricultural production. It was not until the mission system prospered that bountiful crops were produced for California settlers. Spanish-California was characterized by slow and steady growth punctuated with controversies over mission economic influences, military and political indifference, and foreign intrigue. While Spain firmly established a colony in California, it was never more than a marginal settlement.

In many respects, California was an isolated oasis in Spain's dying empire. Government officials in New Spain made sporadic attempts to improve economic, administrative and military problems in California, but the Viceroy generally ignored most requests for change. The result was that California developed attitudes independent of Spanish political and economic thought. A Spanish business mentality arose as a new and vibrant force in local politics. An example of this business influence was the emergence of the secularization debate. Secularization was a demand to curtail the church's economic activity by selling church land and livestock to private enterprise capitalists. Although secularization did not become a major issue in California politics until the 1830s, the antecedents to rising local nationalism emerged early in Spanish California. Most historians have de-emphasized the business activity of Spanish Californians. This economic impulse was evident when the private rancho emerged to produce a new class of political and economic leaders. The rancho was a large-landed estate which depended upon the vigor and businesslike leadership of the ranchero who produced agricultural and livestock goods for export trade. The rancheros were the earliest and most effective critics of Spain's neglect of Alta California. They believed that the stagnant business impulse in Spanish-California was the direct result of the pastorial isolation implemented by the Viceroy in Mexico City.

The Yuma Massacre and California Isolation

The primary reason for minimal permanent land settlement during the last forty years of Spanish California was due to the Yuma massacre of 1781. The commander of the California-Sonora border, Teodoro de Croix failed to provide adequate military defenses against the Yuma Indians. Located at the Colorado River crossing leading into California, Native-Americans were a strategic military concern to overland settlers traveling through Sonora. They held the key to the Arizona-California crossing, and the Spanish military had unwisely lavished bribes upon the Yumas for many years. A brief attempt to Christianize the Indians failed, and in 1780 de Croix ended the practice of giving them gifts. In 1781 Fernando Rivera and his party of 45 married soldiers were killed in a raid by the Yuma Indians. This ended any semblence of Spanish control of the Colorado river, and it cut off the most accessible land route to California.

The Yuma massacre was one of the most embarrassing military disasters suffered by Spain in the New World. It demonstrated that Spain had not only underestimated the Yuma Indian's military capabilities, but indicated Spanish troops were inept in meeting the rigors of frontier military life. Once the mainland route to California was closed, hopes and speculation for permanent California settlement faded. Spain was never again able to reestablish an effective land route to California.

The origin of the Yuma massacre reveals an extremely sensitive problem plaguing Spanish California. The construction of a mission and presidio near the Colorado river was the main reason for the increased hostility of the Yuma Indians. Had local Indians been consulted on the mission site the incident might not have occurred. The Indians were protesting the general insensitivity of Spain on the California-Sonora frontier. The trail blazed by Juan Bautista de Anza in the 1770s closed, and Spanish settlers remained cut off from California until the 1820s. One positive sidelight to the Yuma massacre is that it cut off supplies from California. As a result, there was new emphasis directed toward agricultural production. Californians suddenly faced the necessity of becoming economically self-sufficient.

Pedro Fages and the Problems of Spanish Rule in the 1780s

As a result of the Yuma massacre Spain had no intention of expanding California settlement, and the Viceroy showed little concern for appointing a highly competent governor. In 1782 Pedro Fages, who had been involved in disputes with Father Serra in the early years of Spanish-California, was selected as the new governor. Although there was a semblance of self-government in the San Jose and Los Angeles pueblos, the governor continued to wield an enormous influence. The Spanish governor's power resulted from a number of built-in-powers. He was responsible for appointing local commissions to help govern San Jose and Los Angeles. These appointees served the governor and allowed him to control the civil pueblos. He was also entrusted with protecting the rights of mission Indians which allowed the governor to interfere in the Franciscan's Christianizing efforts. The governor, for example, might possibly harrass the clergy by ordering mission

Indians out of the fields, thereby delaying agricultural production. The governor also had the discretion to decide whether or not the Franciscans would receive a military escort on a journey in California. Although these powers were petty ones, they served to develop specific and well-defined powers for the California governor.

In September, 1782, Fages began his nine year tenure as California's governor. Nicknamed "The Bear" for his gruff manners and huge physical characteristics, Fages was a two-fisted drinker who brawled nightly on Monterey streets. Although Fages wife, Eulalia de Callis, a highly aristocratic Catalan, attempted to bring family life to Monterey, she found the local citizenry brazenly crude, and she continually complained about the naked Indians walking the streets. The general poverty that she described in Monterey may have reflected her aristocratic background, and it also suggested that a great deal of reform was needed to make living conditions tolerable.

Eulalia Fages caused the governor a number of problems. She insisted on giving the naked Indians her husband's clothes, and it was not uncommon to find the governor undressing an Indian to regain his own uniforms. Mrs. Fages demanded that her husband resign his post, and when he refused she locked him from her bedroom. Fages became the laughing stock of Monterey, and he callously began to treat his wife like a common subject. He humiliated her publicly, and she responded by demanding a greater role in helping the poor citizenry of Monterey. She believed that Christian charity had vanished and criticized the Franciscans for their excessive political behavior. In August, 1784, after the birth of a daughter, Eulalia paraded down Monterey streets telling anyone who would listen that her husband was sleeping in the servant's quarters with an attractive Indian. She demanded that the Franciscan friars annul her marriage. The Franciscans ordered her to return to her husband and suggested that emotional problems were the cause of the rift. The significance of Governor Fage's marital problems was that they strengthened the power of the Franciscan order. In wise and judicious fashion the Franciscans aided Fages and his wife in solving their problems. This reaped heavy dividends for the Franciscans politically and socially in Spanish-California.

When Governor Fages returned to New Spain in 1791, he looked back upon almost a decade of service. While his accomplishments were not particularly important ones, nonetheless, he had maintained order and fostered progress in California. Fages also granted new land settlements which became the basis of the rancho system. His lengthy conflicts with the clergy prompted Spanish authorities to grant Franciscan requests for the removal of Fages from California.

The Franciscan Missionaries in Spanish California: The Indian Question

Father Serra's legendary feats and the zealous activity of the Franciscan missionaries have been extolled by historians for generations. In the initial stages of the process of bringing civilization to California, historians believed that the primary reason for Spanish settlement success was due to mission agricultural production. Starvation was averted by the early successes of the Spanish mission system. The skilled leadership of Father Serra and the Franciscan order maintained a half-hearted and poorly supported Spanish colony for a half century. By 1810 the Franciscans controlled 20,000 Christian Indian converts and nineteen missions scattered from San Diego to Sonoma. Although often exaggerated by anti-clerical critics, the alleged misuse of church wealth was an important factor in prompting secularization. Foes of the Franciscans charged that large herds of cattle, millions of acres of land, and a thriving craft industry produced a degree of wealth which made the clergy economically and politically powerful. This is a strange argument considering that no more than thirty to forty Franciscan friars managed the mission system. Yet, the detractors of the mission system charged that the Franciscans used devious means to accumulate wealth.

Early critics of the Franciscans suggested that Indian enslavement was the primary reason for mission economic success. Much of this criticism was voiced by local businessmen who found it difficult to compete with church economic enterprise. Thus began the negative, anti-clerical tone which permeated Spanish-California. It was reinforced by the jealous Spanish military officers who constantly demanded that the Franciscans supply the presidios with food. In 1884 Helen Hunt Jackson's novel, *Ramona,* popularized the century old argument that the Franciscans abused the mission Indians. However, long before the publication of this critical novel there were many critics who charged that the mission system was totally a result of Indian slavery. This argument did not have even a faint ring of truth. It simply reflected the tensions between the Franciscans and Spanish government officials. A good example of this type of behavior was Government Felipe de Neve's order which prevented the Franciscans from using free postage stamps. In the 1780s Governor Pedro Fages continually complained that the church interfered with his private life and undermined his political power. The debate between Franciscan supporters and detractors is a long standing historical controversy. The tension which developed between the clergy and governmental officials caused heated political differences. There is little doubt that petty jealousy was responsible for Spanish-California's slow growth. When foreign intruders sailed into California they often found themselves courted by both sides. In 1786 a French visitor, the Comte Jean de La Pérouse, sailed into Monterey Bay, and he immediately befriended Eulalia Fages. He informed her that the Franciscans violated the "natural rights" of the Indians by forcing them to work on mission lands. La Pérouse's journal is considered the first significant foreign account of Spanish-California, and his liberal French viewpoint was read widely by people searching for information on Spain's settlement activity in California. Reflecting the natural rights idealism of the French Revolution, la Pérouse raised the question of corporal punishment administered to the Indians. This began a very detailed debate over Franciscan misuse of Indian labor.

There were other serious accusations made against the Franciscan missionaries. The most persistent charge was that the mission master plan called for Christianizing, educating, and freeing the Indians after an apprentice period of ten to twenty years. Another complaint of Spanish-Californians was that the Franciscans' vow of poverty did not seem to square with the furtive preoccupation with agriculture production and export trade. This led to the argument that the Franciscans failed to educate the Indians properly, and many Spanish government officials believed that they minimized education because the Indian was continually needed in the fields. A final argument posed by Franciscan detractors suggested that armed repression was a necessary method to keep the Indians on mission lands. The debate over whether or not the Franciscans were saviors or exploiters is an insoluable one; however both sides present interesting arguments to substantiate their view point.

Historians who believe the mission Indians were exploited present an interesting array of statistics and arguments. Critics of Franciscan achievements believe that the Indians never fully adapted to the mission system. The conversion to Christianity generally resulted from a superficial desire to please the Franciscans. The heavy emphasis upon whippings to punish wayward thinking or runaway Indians is one of the strongest arguments against the effective alteration of Indian thought and conscience by this new set of religious beliefs and practices. The abnormally high death rate among mission Indians and the significantly low birth rate is another indication that mission life was less than idyllic. These facts note that European diseases, a new life style, and a lack of freedom together contributed to the decline of the Indian in Spanish-California. The number of Indian uprisings is another indication in decrying the influence of the Franciscan. The most serious revolts were those of the Yuma Indians in 1781 and a series of disturbances near Santa Barbara in the 1820s. Yet, throughout Spanish-California there were many small Indian disturbances which, taken together, strongly suggest that discipline was a serious problem for the Franciscans.

In defending the work of the Franciscan there are a number of equally persuasive contentions. The conversion to Christianity was a slow and well planned process, and a few Indians were given full liberty to return to their villages and remain pagans. Christianity was not forced upon the Indian but it was willingly accepted as a new way of life. In addition, many mission Indians did not convert to Christianity, and many of these Indians voluntarily remained as agricultural laborers. They preferred to live on the mission rather than face life in their formerly primitive surroundings. Another indication of the power of the Christian message was illustrated by the number of Indians baptized outside of the missions. In fact, a number of Indians were allowed to baptize their dying brethren; for example, Francisco Jalauehu, a well-educated Indian, baptized 39 Indians in 1814 on Santa Cruz Island.

The prevalence of Christian weddings among Indians is cited as another example of Franciscan work. The marriage ceremony was an indication that Spanish culture was readily accepted by large numbers of California Indians. Another example of the triumph of Christian culture occurred when Indians opted for burial ceremonies within or near a mission. The Franciscans respected Indian dignity by recording both their Christian and pagan name on death records. Perhaps the most interesting statistic is that most Indians died of old age and rarely was a case of murder reported in conjunction with a mission Indian death.

Many historians argue that the Franciscan friars were aware of the cultural and economic shock resulting from the years of adjustment to mission life. Consequently, the mission system maintained a light work schedule to make the transition to mission labor an easier one. This is an example of the generally humane treatment accorded to mission Indians. The large number of mission industries is frequently cited as an example of the Indians willingness to engage in a variety of occupations. The economic diversity of the mission system would have been impossible if the level of Indian discontent remained high. It is plausible, therefore, to argue that it was voluntary Christianity which caused the mission system to prosper in Spanish California.

Another argument extolling the positive nature of mission life is one which suggests that well-developed recreation and a number of holiday celebrations created a satisfied labor force. Mission Indians were allowed recreation and leisure as a means of reinforcing Christian values. A pattern of holidays had emerged by 1780, and the Indians were urged to share their new cultural patterns with their native villages. The Franciscans believed it was necessary to have a certain degree of leisure time for the Indians which would make it easier for them to survive in the mission environment; and the Franciscans argued that it was more difficult for a settler in San Jose or Los Angeles to engage in recreation than it was for the mission Indians. The same argument was made concerning nutrition and the Franciscans argued that Indians were healthier than Spaniards in civil pueblos. Mission freedoms accorded the Indians were pictured as giving the neophytes a positive place in Spanish-California.

It is difficult to suggest whether the mission's defenders or their detractors were correct in analyzing the Indian situation. The best way to solve the historical discussion concerning mission Indians is to outline some of the problems created by the controversy. One conclusion is that the seeds of racism were planted unwittingly as a consequence of the zeal with which the Franciscan friars sought to establish a profitable mission system. Indian labor in parts of California was often abused. The question of human rights was seldom, if ever, an important consideration. During the later period of Mexican-California, the Indian plight was debated extensively by Californians. This suggests that the Franciscans found it difficult to understand Indian culture. In the final analysis, the Indian did not fit into the mainstream of early California civilization. The inescapable conclusion is that the nature of Spanish society in California prevented the assimilation of an alien culture. Although the debate continues, there is a positive conclusion to Hispanic minority treatment; if one compares Spanish attitudes to those of English and American travelers there is a wider acceptance of minorities and children of mixed marriages. Black pioneers, for example, played a more prominent role in early California and the fact that more than half of Los Angeles' founding fathers were Black suggests a liberal Spanish impulse. Many of the problems encountered in California, however, can be traced to early Spanish societal patterns.

Spanish society in California was a rigid hierarchy with power and status dependant upon military rank and Spanish ancestry. The aristocracy consisted of all commissioned officers and appointed Spanish officials. The Spanish-born considered themselves naturally superior, and those born in the Western Hemisphere were known as Creoles. Below the Creole class in the social structure of Spanish-California were the Mestizos, who were a mixture of white and Indian blood. Indians and Blacks were accorded the lowest status in the society of Spanish-California. In this setting it was not surprising that the Indian had difficulty adjusting to the social structures of the mission system. Although Indians were taught to read and write, the primary role of the mission was to encourage the development of a skill or trade. As a result, Indians tended to develop useful labor skills rather than language and religious education.

Many historians point to statistics which suggest that the Indians were not overworked. It was typical for the mission Indians to follow a five day work schedule. Colorful religious ceremonies, parades, and holiday celebrations further brightened the generally dull routine of mission life. Since the Indians were freed from the task of seeking out food, foreign visitors often commented on the richness of their diet.

Despite the positive arguments for mission life, the Indian often found it difficult to adjust to a captive life. Indians who fled from the missions were mature men who found it impossible to adjust to the disciplined mission life. They were older converts and could not readily accept the confining mission life style. But a study of Indian runaways suggests that less than 10 percent of the Indians attempted to escape. White mission records are incomplete on runaway Indians. One mission, San Gabriel, reported that nine percent of the Indians successfully escaped. Yet, this statistic is a misleading one, because it fails to point out four common Indian attitudes. First, the Indian often emotionally resisted conversion to Christianity. Second, there were numerous flights to the native village as a result of being homesick. Third, Indians complained of crowded living conditions. Fourth, the separation of the sexes heightened resistance to confinement. These arguments tend to support the idea that mission life was far from an idyllic experience.

Perhaps the best way to analyze the success or failure of Indians on the mission is to point out that only 12 percent of the California Indian population lived on the missions. It is obvious that the mission system did not equip the Indians to take their place in California society. Spanish treatment of the Indians was neither better nor worse than that of other European colonies. In the final analysis, the Indians emerged as a second-class citizen in an alien society.

The most sensible way to view the Indian in Spanish-California is to suggest that they were the first ethnic minority in the Golden State. The general treatment accorded the Indians was better in civil pueblos like San Jose and Los Angeles where large numbers of Spanish settlers were of mixed blood. While tolerance and liberalism prevailed, this does not mean that minorities were considered the social and economic equals of Spanish military officials. Yet, the opportunity and impulse for greater social mobility attracted a hearty settler to Spanish-California.

Father Serra's Death and Changes in Franciscan Leadership

On August 28, 1784, Father Serra died. As he lay on his small bed at the Mission San Carlos Borroméo, the Franciscan order was uncertain about its future direction. An interim mission president, Father Palou, was named until a permanent successor could be selected to direct the Franciscan's work. Although he completed nine missions, Father Serra left most of his planned work unfinished and the Franciscans were aware that a major turning point had been reached in Alta California. The new president of the mission system would be responsible for completing Serra's fabled El Camino Real, and it would be necessary to implement a public relations policy to appease Spanish military authorities in California.

The search for Serra's successor was a careful one. After almost a year, Father Fermín Francisco de Lasuén was chosen as Father-President of the Alta California mission system. Lasuén had aided Father Serra in Baja California, and he had been active in California mission work since September, 1773, when he drew an assignment at San Gabriel mission. For the next eighteen years Lasuén provided capable, energetic leadership for the church in California. An intelligent, highly cultured man with a persuasive personality, Lasuén was the first Franciscan to attempt to work with Spanish military authorities. In his late forties when he took over the California mission system, Lasuén possessed a degree of personal energy and administrative skill unequalled in the history of Franciscan activity in California.

Perhaps the most significant new policy was Lasuén's idea to reshape attitudes and concepts for administering Spanish culture to the Indians. He believed that a well-fed, amply clothed Indian population would be an economic and social asset to the mission system. Prior to assuming the presidency of the mission system, Lasuén's policies made the San Gabriel mission the single most prosperous California mission. From 1785 until his death in 1803 he systematically expanded the mission system. Under Father Lasuén's leadership nine missions were constructed, and he recognized the inequities of Southern California civilization and attempted to bring this area closer to the church by building three missions in the Santa Barbara area. Santa Barbara's beauty impressed Lasuén and he believed that the majestic architectural structure at Santa Barbara would indicate to Southern California that they occupied an equal place in the Franciscan mission system.

The only mission to reflect negatively on Father Lasuén's leadership was the Soledad settlement. In August, 1791, Soledad mission was dedicated but by 1797 the buildings were disintegrating and the economy stagnant. Most of the problems at the Soledad mission were due to the mischievous nature of two missionaries, Mariano Rubi and Bartolomé Gili. In Mexico City the

The chapel of the mission San José de Guadalupe founded as the 14th mission by Father Lasuen

pair were noted for stealing chocolate from San Fernando College and rolling bowling balls through the dormitary halls. They often scaled the college walls to spend a festive night in town. At Soledad, Rubi and Gili ignored their duties and engaged in pleasureable pursuits. The result was that the 115 Soledad Indians were not seriously trained in the basic tenets of Christianity. Equally significant was the low level of craft and agricultural production at Soledad. It was a mission whose glaring failures were seized upon by mission critics to attack Franciscan advances in Alta California.

The Soledad mission was not typical of the Franciscans' accomplishments under Father Lasuén. His record was an amazing one as he doubled the number of Indian converts, rebuilt the original adobe structures at Serra's nine missions, and placed the mission economic system on sound footing. In addition, the mission economy was diversified with the introduction of saddle manufacturing, expanded carpentry activity and new agricultural crops. To promote a sound

The chapel of the mission San Jose de Guadalupe founded as the 14th mission by Father Lasuen

economy artisans and craftsmen were imported from New Spain, and the Indians were taught carpentry and other trades.

Father Lasuén's persuasive political personality was an early asset for the Franciscans. Using diplomatic skill and flexible administrative policies, Lasuén revived Franciscan power in Spanish California. Although Spain's disinterest in California helped to increase Franciscan power, he never experienced serious problems with local governors. In addition, he argued persuasively that two Franciscans were needed at each mission to insure the good conduct of the Indians, and this suggestion helped to revive Franciscan power. The leadership provided by Father Lasuén created a new political-economic prosperity for the Franciscan missions. This new strength was shown by the 20,000 Indians converted to Christianity and the new church wealth saw modern architecture dominate mission building. Yet, in the final analysis, Father Lasuén's monumental achievements were overshadowed by Father Serra's path breaking historical reputation. The Serra mystique was one that could not be matched in Alta California.

The Decade of Transition: California in the 1790s

Spain lost interest in California during the 1790s. A pastoral interlude emerged which cut into the governor's power and provided a strong native localism which promoted the first signs of a separate California nationalism. As a result, the governors appointed to supervise California found themselves lacking the military and financial resources to govern effectively, encouraging local nationalism to grow and prosper. From 1794 to 1800 Diego de Borica helped to foster this feeling of local nationalism. He attempted to encourage the migration of new, permanent settlers and actively sought trade with foreign nations.

However, less than a thousand permanent settlers occupied the California coast by 1790. Although Governor Borica continued to encourage new settlers, in 1800 only 1,200 settlers were in California. In an attempt to draw new colonists, the third civil pueblo, Branciforte, was founded in July, 1797, under Governor Borica. It was a strange city. With nine soldier-colonists and a total population of 17, Branciforte was little more than a nuisance settlement. Located near the Santa Cruz mission, Branciforte quickly developed a reputation as a settlement for idle, mischievous, retired Spanish military personnel. The Franciscans continually complained of the rowdiness and drunkenness at the nearby Branciforte settlement. The initial reason for the Branciforte settlement was to set up a civil pueblo that would provide protection for California. However, it soon became apparent that Branciforte was little more than a play station for retired military men. In addition, a number of convicts were released from Mexico City prisons to bolster the population, and this was one reason for Branciforte's reputation for deviltry.

Another interesting settlement development in the 1790s was the rise of the private rancho. In 1790 there were about 19 ranchos. The large ranchos were invariably granted to someone the Spanish crown owed a favor, and the Spanish King did not favor granting land to settlers already in California. The grants could not infringe upon mission land, and the maximum land grant allowed was 12 square miles. The ranchero ruled like a king over his land. With no more than twenty-five land grants during the Spanish era, the mission-dominated California settlement did not experience much influence from the rancho system. But an important precedent for settling land grants was established when Governor Pedro Fages granted three soldiers small land grants. The grants in the Los Angeles area whetted the appetite of local Spaniards desiring to settle upon permanent farms. The Viceroy in Mexico City agreed to allow small land grants if a stone house was built and at least two thousand head of livestock were tended. Following the emergence of Mexican-California in the 1820s, the rancho became the dominant force in creating strong local nationalism. The roots of California nationalism began in the Spanish rancho. But it was not until after Mexican rule liberalized land grants that native-born Spanish speaking Californians became a potent political force. The ranch concepts were responsible for the first independent political-economic thinkers in Alta California. In the Mexican period the native-born Californio defended the rancho as an instrument of land settlement which all Californians should have been allowed to experience. This argument brought the birth of egalitarian politics in nineteenth century California.

Spanish Governmental Problems in the Late 19th Century

The catalyst to rising California nationalism during the 1790s was Spain's inability to provide military and economic aid. As foreign nations encroached upon California, Spain naturally developed fears of losing her new found settlement; but the absence of military strength made it impossible to guarantee California's defense. Soon foreign visitors began to note the weak military control exerted over Spanish-California. Military weakness was mentioned in the voyage of the Comte de la Pérouse who was the first foreigner to visit California. The French ordered la Pérouse to investigate the possibilities of developing a fur trade in the coastal areas surrounding Alta California. The French hoped to compete with the Russians who were hunting the California sea otter and the British who had established trading areas in the Pacific Northwest.

In 1789 as a result of growing fears of foreign intruders, Spain instructed Estevan José Martínez to journey to Nootka Sound and build a presidio. In 1774, Nootka Sound, a harbor on Vancouver Island had been claimed for Spain by Juan Pérez. To fully establish the legitimacy of Spain's claims in the Pacific Northwest, Martínez was instructed to begin permanent settlement. But when he arrived in Nootka Sound, Martínez found several English ships anchored on Spanish land. In a pompous show of power the Spanish commander seized the crews for trespassing upon Spanish imperial soil. It was not realistic for Martínez to aggressively suggest that the Pacific Northwest was Spanish territory. The reality was that Spain had failed to occupy the area and the British trading interests were in complete control of the area. Since English and American fur trading interests dominated the area, Martínez' voyage appeared to be an exercise in folly. The dubious decision to establish a Spanish colony in Nootka Sound further intensified friction between English and Spanish colonial activity in North America. To complicate matters, Martínez was an ambitious colonizer who believed that he could drive the English from the Pacific Northwest. He dreamed of securing an otter-trade monopoly and acquiring great wealth. Martínez' scheming produced an international incident between Spain and England and the Spanish Viceroy eventually stripped Martínez of his command.

In 1790, three Spanish ships sailed into Nootka Sound to establish a presidio and a small permanent agricultural settlement. After hastily constructing a small colony at Neah Bay, in present day Washington state, the Spaniards encountered opposition to their plans. The motives of the Spanish were a mystery to all concerned observers, and the result was to force Britain to threaten Spain with war over the Nootka Sound Spanish settlement. In October, 1790, Spain concluded the Nootka Convention agreement with England. In this treaty, Spain yielded its sovereignty over the Pacific and recognized England's right to fish and trade near Spanish settlements. But it was not until February, 1793, that the question of damages was negotiated. The Nootka Claims Convention of 1793 awarded English sea captain John Meares more than a hundred thousand dollars for the seizure of his ship. Meares, a ship owner, persuaded the English government to pursue the claims and the result was international humiliation for Spain in the Western Hemisphere.

The impact of the Nootka Sound controversy had a profound influence upon California. Local California citizens believed that Spain would neither provide military protection nor trade and supplies to foster local growth. As a result, the mild form of local nationalism which had been evident for some time began to grow in the 1790s. Soon large numbers of Spaniards openly identified themselves as Californians. The international humiliation Spain suffered in the lengthy Nootka Sound controversy did little to foster positive feelings in California. In addition the Nootka Sound controversy demonstrated the possibility of successful encroachment upon Spanish-California by emphasizing the area's military weakness. Captain George Vancouver, who displayed blatantly anti-Spanish attitudes, helped to publicize the idea that California was ripe for foreign conquest. In a series of expeditions to California in the early 1790s, Vancouver scorned the level of Spanish settlement activity and labeled Spanish presidios as "mud huts" unsuitable for military purposes.

From 1794 to 1800 Governor Diego de Borica faced a great deal of local political pressure to increase California's military defenses. In an effort to calm local citizens, Governor Borica initiated programs to develop new industries and artisan crafts. The increased emphasis upon the production of new goods solidified California's shaky economic base. In addition, large scale irrigation projects were launched to increase agricultural efficiency. In his mania for reform activity Borica went so far as to implement a moral code for San Jose and Los Angeles settlers. His energetic activity, however, caused local Californians to forget the lessons of the Nootka Sound controversy, and by 1800 a strong, vibrant local California nationalism was at work.

Foreign Intruders and California in Transition

From 1790 to the 1820s, foreign explorers exerted an influence which began to alter the attitudes and concepts which had nurtured Spanish settlers from the earliest days of Alta California settlement. An important change occurred when foreign visitors transmitted an increasingly secular tone into the mainstream of California thought. The church no longer dominated social-economic thought, and the slow influx of foreign trade reinforced independent business attitudes which had been developing in California. A private business impulse was an important transition in California thought, because it was a prelude to the secularization of mission wealth in the 1830s. For more than forty years California's embryo business class was critical of church wealth, and this hastened the drive for the secularization of church land. Private enterprise capitalism was also an important factor in continuing the growth of local California nationalism. By the early nineteenth century a number of Spaniards began to describe themselves as Californios. This term was used to describe them as native born, Spanish speaking Californians, as individuals who generally identified with local California interests. The rise of local nationalism was the main reason for California's vibrant growth in the early nineteenth century.

The first Americans to explore California were marine frontiersmen who sailed to the Pacific Coast to fish for the sea otter. In 1796, the first American vessel to sail into Monterey Bay was the *Otter,* commanded by Ebenzer Dorr. This Boston based ship helped to launch a profitable trade between the East Coast and California. But Dorr also created some hard feelings among local citizens when the *Otter* sailed away after stranding ten men and a woman at Monterey. Governor Borica learned that the eleven were prisoners from Botany Bay in New Zealand who had stowed away on Dorr's vessel. Borica considered the incident a nasty American trick but he was surprised to discover that the stowaways were skilled workers. Their carpentry talents were put to immediate use and they began to construct a number of new buildings in Monterey. Despite the good fortune of finding skilled workmen, Governor Borica believed that Yankee businessmen could not be trusted, and he warned Californians to deal with foreigners cautiously. Although Spanish officials worried about foreign colonization schemes, Americans showed no inclination to settle California. The significance of early American interest in California is that Yankee traders developed strong commercial relations with local Californios. When the Mexican revolution began in 1810, trade between New Spain and California ceased. By the time Mexican independence was achieved in the early 1820s Boston traders had established a strong economic position in California.

Russian Interest and Settlement in California

During the latter years of Spanish-California the Russians came to explore the American West in search of furs. Since Russian settlements in Alaska needed supplies, California appeared to be a logical point to hunt, fish and grow small amounts of fruits and vegetables for the colonies. Russians were interested in establishing a permanent outpost in America, and California was the beachhead for this enterprise. The Russian-American Company, a private corporation, approached the czarist government for permission to trade in America. This was not surprising since a large number of government officials held stock in the Russian-American Company. Czar Alexander I believed that the government must direct private enterprise capitalism, and this created a strong desire to conclude a trading agreement with Spanish-California. It was difficult for Russian business interests to reach an agreement with Spanish officials to fish and trade off the California coast. As a result the Russian-American Company concluded an agreement with an American fisherman, Joseph O'Cain, to fish for the sea otter off the California coast. This joint business venture brought Russians and Americans to the western marine frontier. At this stage the profit from the California fishing industry was quite good, the sea otter brought prices ranging from $50 to $150 a pelt in China. In addition, New England and Chinese goods were quickly sold to Monterey merchants at handsome profits. Early American and Russian trading success was a strong factor in resurgent foreign interest in California.

In 1806, a representative of the Russian-American Company, Nikolai Rezanov, journeyed to San Francisco to purchase supplies to support Russian fishing ventures off the North American coast. The Russians were cordially received, but the Spanish refused to sell Rezanov supplies. California governmental officials were suspicious of Russian intentions. A curious incident helped to endear Rezanov to local citizens. Rezanov, a widower, fell in love with the San Francisco Presidio Commandant's sixteen year old daughter, and after they were engaged Governor José de Arrillaga began to sell the Russians supplies. The marriage never took place as Rezanov died on his return trip home to arrange for the wedding. The incident did serve, however, to lessen tensions between Spanish-Californians and the Russians. After some years of exploring the California coast the Russian-American Company built Fort Ross in 1812 several miles north of Bodega Bay. Fort Ross was a well-built, amply fortified stockade eighty miles north of San Francisco. What economic success it enjoyed was due partially to the Russians' ability to cultivate the friendship of local Indians.

The construction of Fort Ross was a major turning point in California history. It ended years of Spanish isolation and brought new social-political values into California. Also, the modest economic success of Fort Ross was assured by the 175 permanent settlers who were well suited to the rigors of frontier life. In the area of labor management, the Russians skillfully hired Indians as laborers to augment the work force. A Russian camp was set up on the Farallone Islands off San Francisco's coast to catch fish to feed the residents at Fort Ross. Soon fruit orchards and other crops dotted the countryside surrounding Fort Ross, and the Russians garnered a great deal of attention in California because of their successful colonization scheme.

From 1812 to 1840 Fort Ross fishermen and trappers helped the colony to survive. But after the first few years fur pelts ran out, and it became increasingly difficult to supply the Alaskan settlements. The sea otter diminished and Fort Ross quickly became an agricultural settlement. By the early 1820s grain, fruit and vegetable production made Fort Ross a leading California agricultural community. The Russians also invested much effort into a ship building venture.

Reconstructed chapel, Fort Ross

Although the vessels were well constructed they were made of poor wood and sun-rotted after a few years at sea. By the mid-1830s agricultural production became uneven and there was no longer a profit from wheat harvesting, vegetable gardening, and beef raising. The increased cattle trade between Mexico and California, and the rise of Californio ranchers was another factor in the economic decline of Fort Ross.

The Russian experience illustrated the difficulty of wandering from one economic enterprise to another. Yet, there was also a political problem. Neither Spain nor Mexico could afford to legally recognize the Russian settlement. In the mid-1820s the Mexican governor, José Echeandía, ordered the Russians to leave Fort Ross or to recognize Mexican sovereignty. Consequently, one of the by-products of early Russian settlement was strained foreign relations. This was an inevitable consequence of Russian settlement. During the Mexican-California era foreign commercial activity continued to increase and the result was to widen private enterprise business attitudes. The

Californios believed that foreign business interests often deprived native-sons of investment opportunities. As a result Californios called for restrictions on foreign investors.

In the 1830s local Californios displayed serious signs of resentment toward Fort Ross. When Mariano Vallejo, the best known and most powerful Californio ranchero, attempted to purchase Fort Ross, the Russians, while polite to Don Mariano, refused to sell to Californio business and political leaders. The lack of business success, however, convinced the Russians to sell Fort Ross in the late 1830s. As more and more Mexican, American, and local Californio settlers moved into the vicinity of Fort Ross, the decision was made to sell it. Had there been even a minimal level of economic success the Russian-American Company would have attempted to build a small empire in America, but time was running out on the Russians and bankruptcy was imminent.

John A. Sutter approached the Russians with an offer to purchase Fort Ross. In December, 1841, Sutter took possession of the Russian settlement in one of the slickest real estate ventures in California history. For $2000 down and a total purchase price of about $30,000, Sutter bought Fort Ross and the Farollone Islands. Sutter never made payments to the Russian-American Company for the land, and he complained of crop failures and poor business conditions. The last signs of Russian influence vanished with the sale of Fort Ross.

The Last Days of Spanish California, 1800–1822

The Mexican Revolution began in 1810 and by 1822 Mexico celebrated the achievement of its final independence. As Spain and Mexico engaged in a struggle for survival, a policy of benign neglect developed in California as neither Spain nor Mexico could risk money or troops on the northern frontier. The result was to bring drastic change to California society.

From 1800 to 1814 Governor José de Arrillaga faced the delicate task of appeasing local citizens, dealing diplomatically with foreign intruders and continuing to represent Spanish interests. Hostility to the Spanish government reached new heights in the early 19th century due to the limited number of land grants, and the general sluggishness of governmental institutions. The mania for land settlement gripped local citizens, and many Californians demanded an extension of the rancho system. This impulse destroys the notion that local Californians were not business-minded, although Spain was reluctant to create large ranchos. The result of this debate caused Californios to begin to speak of a declining Spanish loyalty. A mild touch of local revolutionary fervor filled Monterey and the California country side. Another innovation in Spanish-California during the early 19th century was the founding of a number of lay schools. Governors Arrillaga and Borica believed that public education was an essential ingredient in achieving harmony among Californians. Problems with social harmony, the increased intensity of secularization attitudes and general complaints over Spanish government inefficiency characterized the last days of Spanish-California.

Despite these problems José de Arrillaga was an excellent governor. From 1800 to 1814 he promoted local nationalism by encouraging local businessmen to expand their activity and invigorate the economy. He was the first Spanish governor to explore the interior of California. Arrillaga often stated it was ironic that Spanish settlement was no more than thirty miles inland. As a diplomat, Arrillaga was a master manipulator, and he used his ability to conduct foreign relations to increase trade with American ships. As a result of his leadership the population of the civil

Restored commandant's house. The walls date from the 1830s, Fort Ross

pueblos and ranchos nearly doubled. For the first time in Alta California history there was a noticeable increase in children born to permanent settlers. The pastoral desolated California coast produced a small but thriving permanent settlement under Governor Arrillaga's leadership.

Another notable achievement during Arrillaga's tenure was a reconciliation between military and religious authorities. In an effort to alleviate California's food problems Arrillaga persuaded the missions to supply any area in danger of running low on the necessities of life. In return the church was given more freedom and allowed some influence in governmental matters. It was an arrangement which allowed Governor Arrillaga to maintain a semblance of power while placing Franciscan influence under tighter controls than at any time in Spanish California. Moreover, since the missions were using surplus agricultural goods to honor the governor's request, they were not weakening themselves. Thus, in the last days of Spanish California the fractious divisions which kept unification ideas from dominating began to disappear. California was on the verge of growth and expansion, but the Mexican Revolution prevented Arrillaga's policies from reaching their full fruition.

On July 24, 1814, Governor Arrillaga died and an era of tranquility ended in California. A year later the testy and ambitious Pablo Vicente Solá was named Spain's last governor. The primary drawback to Solá's rule was that threats and cajolry were common in the last days of Spanish-California. A group of Russian traders, for example, were arrested in Monterey and sent to Mexico City. When a small party of Russian hunters brazenly invaded San Francisco, they were killed by Governor Solá's men. While these actions were not major concerns to most Californians, nonetheless, they suggested that the mellow and tranquil leadership of Governor Borica and Arrillaga, no longer dominated local politics.

Governor Solá was an opportunist who took advantage of Spain's weak controls. In February, 1816 Solá allowed the missions to engage in trade with Spain's enemies. In direct violation of Spanish law the California missions aided insurgent revolutionary forces. This was an important transition in attitudes for Spanish Californians, and the Mexican Revolution caused living conditions to worsen and commerce to stagnate. Suddenly, California was no longer a bustling colony. Much of the blame for this sorry state of affairs rests with Governor Solá. His continual adherence to pomp and ceremony, the sword rattling military threats, and the general corruption in government helped to bring an immediate decline in Spanish civilization.

As a result of the Spanish-American Wars of Independence outside attack was a possibility. In 1818 the Argentina pirate, Hippolyte de Bouchard, sailed into Monterey Bay. Bouchard, a Frenchman, commanded a fleet for the Buenos Aires republic. His crack crew of 266 was little more than a legal pirate brigade who took advantage of military weakness emanating from the revolutionary era. California was suddenly a vulnerable link in the Spanish empire and Bouchard prepared to seize the opportunity. One reason for California's weakened condition was that supply ships no longer sailed into California from San Blas. Since 1810 lack of supply ships hampered the economy and forced Californians to depend too heavily upon local agriculture. It also created ambivalent feelings toward the Mexican Revolution, because the lengthy revolution cut off much needed military and economic aid from California. Although Governor Solá attempted to maintain a neutral appearance, California public opinion grew increasingly loyal to an emerging Californio viewpoint. Local citizens became momentarily suspicious of both Spain and Mexico and the Californio demanded local rule.

Thus, an important catalyst to the drive for home rule was the invasion of Monterey by the Argentina pirate, Hippolyte de Bouchard. After being commissioned as an Argentina privateer, a form of legalized pirating, Bouchard sailed around the world plundering foreign ships. On his voyage Bouchard continually engaged in fierce battles with Spanish ships, and he was not overly successful in plundering Spanish treasure. As a result, Bouchard, a nasty man with a fierce temper, grew to hate Spain. His California invasion was due to years of bitter resentment and a well developed racial hatred for the Spanish. Once his ship entered Monterey Bay he envisioned getting even with his long time enemies. Despite the hopelessness of the situation, Governor Solá prepared to defend Monterey with an army of 40 men and 8 guns. It seemed ludicrous for Governor Solá's men to attempt to repel Bouchard, but a hidden gun embankment fired upon the Argentina ships, caught them by surprise and halted the initial invasion attempt. A number of new Spanish soldiers arrived and suddenly Governor Solá had 80 men to defend Monterey. Although Governor Solá's men were outnumbered and forced to flee up to the Rancho del Rey, the present day site of Salinas, they created strong local nationalism with their spirited defense of Monterey.

But this failed to stop Bouchard, and in November 1818 the Argentine flag was hoisted over Monterey. Bouchard's men immediately ransacked the town and eventually burnt it to the ground. This was a significant event because it prompted many Californians with pro-Spanish sympathies to ponder the question of whether or not Spain intended to protect California. A vibrant local nationalism was on the rise in Monterey. This new radicalism became increasingly evident when a number of Californians emerged as activist-minded radicals to criticize Spanish policy. Many Californians were also upset by the fact that Monterey was not rebuilt until April 1819. Only due to the efforts of the Carmel Mission Indians was the city rebuilt so quickly. The Bouchard incident provided the first serious political issue allowing local radicals to appeal to the emerging California nationalism.

In the aftermath of the Bouchard incident a cautious attitude was displayed toward the Mexican independence movement. The first triumph of Mexican Independence began in 1821 when Agustín Iturbide, a colonel in the Spanish Army, defected to the rebel side. However, Iturbide was not a democratic thinker, and he immediately took advantage of the fractious divisions in Mexican politics. The years of revolutionary activity in Mexico produced a conservative reaction, and Iturbide pandered to the feeling for law and order by declaring himself the ruler of Mexico. After brief negotiations the Spanish Viceroy signed a treaty recognizing Iturbide's rule. California was isolated from this revolutionary activity and did not learn of Mexican independence until January 1822. The Californians found it difficult to believe that Spain had lost control of Mexico. In March, 1822 Mexican officials informed Californians that they would be required to swear allegiance the new Mexican government. A few weeks later Governor Solá wisely selected a group of trusted Franciscans, local soldiers and lay citizens to meet as a quasi-legal legislative body to debate the question of Mexican independence. This junta recognized Mexican suzerainty and elected Governor Solá as the first territorial representative to the Mexican congress. On April 11, 1822, Solá's junta in a well publicized gesture formally swore an oath of allegiance to the Mexican government. It had been 280 years since Juan Rodríguez Cabrillo sailed into San Diego, and Spanish-California was now a thriving settlement in a formerly barren setting.

While Governor Solá's seven year rule was not a high spot in Spanish California, nonetheless, he made a number of positive contributions. Land grants were given freely to military veterans in order to maintain some semblance of permanent settlement. Under Solá's leadership trade with foreign nations expanded and created a positive business impulse. Perhaps the most important contribution was the birth of the Peralta land grant. This grant settled the Berkeley-Oakland-Alameda area and provided the east bay region with a magnificent rancho. In sum, Solá did everything within his power to insure the growth of local California nationalism. This policy was reflected in the increased demand of native-born Californians desiring home rule. Thus, in the last years of Spanish-California the seeds of a vibrant local nationalism blossomed to create a new political consciousness.

Spanish California: A Summary

Although Spain conceived California settlement as a logical extension of her imperial design, Alta California was little more than a marginal colony. The initial objective of developing California as a defense post and as a revenue producing trade and agricultural settlement quickly faded into obscurity. After more than a half century, California settlement failed to develop either wealth or loyalty from local citizens. A heavy investment of men, money and supplies produced little that was concrete for the Spanish Crown. Moreover, the Crown's neglect in the last two decades of Spanish-California dissipated any temporary loyalties which had developed in the remote colony.

The authoritarian nature of California society obviously did little to instill positive attitudes toward Spanish institutions. In addition, a feudal tone permeated social, economic and political thought. This led to a rejection of many traditional Spanish values and produced a new form of thought identified with the Californio. Local nationalism, then, predominated during the early 19th century and began to create the unique individual labeled a Californian. But in the final analysis it was military authorities and the Franciscans who were responsible for the failure of Spanish nationalism to take hold permanently in California. Although well-intentioned they both displayed authoritarian tendencies, and they violated the precept of helping to develop native rule and a free enterprise economy. Consequently, the rise of the Californio led to open conflict and a direct rejection of much of Spanish political and economic thought. The policies of the Spanish rulers made it difficult to reform California. Still Spain made an important contribution to the development of California institutions. The Spanish traditions surrounding customs and law, the large land grants, the early policy toward the Indians, and the trading impulse combined to create a Hispanic heritage which dominates California to the present day.

Bibliographical Essay

The Spanish developed specific techniques to justify their California settlement. For a series of articles examining the creation of Spanish governmental controls see, Manuel P. Servín, "The Instructions of Viceroy Bucareli to Ensign Juan Pérez," *California Historical Society Quarterly,* XL (September, 1961), 243–46; Manuel Servín, "Symbolic Acts of Sovereignty in Spanish California," *Southern California Quarterly,* XLV (June, 1963), 109–21; and Henry R. Wagner, "Creation of Rights of Sovereignty Through Symbolic Acts, *Pacific Historical Review,* VII (December, 1938), 297–326. Another important book to understanding Spanish government is Douglas S. Watson, *The Spanish Occupation of California* (1934).

A number of significant studies suggest the continued importance of the Church and the Franciscans, see, for example, Theodore Maynard, *The Long Road of Father Serra* (1954); Omer Engelbert, *The Last of the Conquistadores: Junípero Serra, 1713–1784* (1956); Francis F. Guest, *Fermén Francisco de Lasuén, a biography* (1973). An excellent study of the Spanish Royal Corps of Engineers and the significance of these officers in map making, military preparedness, and economic matters is Janet Fireman, *The Spanish Royal Corps of Engineers in the Western Borderlands, 1764–1815* (1977). Fireman's study is particularly useful in understanding early plans to defend Alta California.

The best study of Spanish governors is Donald A. Nuttall, "The Gobernantes of Spanish Upper California," *California Historical Society Quarterly,* LI (Fall, 1972), 253–80. On the significance of the Yuma Massacre see, Douglas D. Martin, *Yuma Crossing* (1954).

There were a number of early foreign visitors who provided perceptive comments on California see, George Vancouver, *A Voyage of Discovery to the North Pacific* (1798); and Jean Francois

Galaup, Comte de La Pérouse, *Voyage Round the World* (1798–99); and see the following interpretations, Francis J. Weber, "The California Missions and Their Visitors," *The Americas,* XXIV (1968), 319–36; and Donald C. Cutter, *Malaspina in California* (1960).

There is a great deal of historical debate over the Spanish influence in California. For a summary of this conflict see, Manuel P. Servín, "California's Hispanic Heritage: A View of the Spanish Myth," *San Diego History,* XVIII (Winter, 1973), 1–9. A dated but still useful look at the Mission system is the best way to summarize reading on Spanish California see, Hebert E. Bolton, "The Mission as a Frontier Institution in the Spanish American Colonies," in Bolton, *Wider Horizons in American History* (1939). The Servín and Bolton articles are an excellent comparison of the Spanish influence in California.

The earliest sign of foreign influences occurred when Fort Ross was constructed in Northern California in 1812. There is a great deal of highly useful material on this subject, see, for example, James R. Gibson, *Imperial Russia in Frontier America: The Changing Geography of Supply of Russian America, 1784–1867* (1976), esp. Chapters 7 and 10; Harvey Schwartz, *"Fort Ross, California: A Historical Synopsis* (1977); C. Bickford O'Brien, Dianne Spencer-Hancock and Michael S. Tucker, *Fort Ross: Indians-Russians-Americans* (1978); Hector Chevigny, *Lost Empire: The Life and Adventures of Nicolai Petrovich Rezanov* (1937); and S.B. Okun, *The Russian-American Company* (1951).

In order to understand some of the problems of overland travel to California see, Harlan Hague, *The Road to California: the Search for a Southern Overland Route, 1540–1848* (1978).

4

MEXICAN CALIFORNIA: THE TRIUMPH OF PERMANENT SETTLEMENT AND THE RISE OF FOREIGN INFLUENCES

Early Characteristics

In many respects, Mexican California differed very little from Spanish California. This was primarily due to the lack of change under Mexican rule. In addition, local Californios were a strong economical-political force, and they prevented Mexico from establishing military and economic controls. Internal political problems produced sporadic Mexican disinterest in California and accelerated the growth of local nationalism. From 1822 to 1846 Mexican California was plagued with liberal-conservative governmental problems, and the ideological tensions resulting from these debates created instability. As liberal-conservative forces tore California apart, there was a necessity to preserve order. The device developed to combat the fractious divisions was the pronunciamento. This was a proclamation which allowed parties engaged in a political dispute to solve their problems within the framework of government institutions. The pronunciamento allowed both sides to state the political problem and to suggest solutions to it. This avoided unnecessary bloodshed and enabled local forces to solve thorny problems. In Mexico the pronunciamento was used when an army faction seized the government. It stated the reasons for the change in government and the future direction of Mexican government. This was quite different from the California pronunciamento. In California, the pronunciamento was used to settle military-political disputes and it was the reason why a minimal amount of violence took place during the hectic quarter century of Mexican California.

In Mexico, the pronunciamento was used to justify every change in government by military force, but in California its importance was an instrument to settle any and all governmental problems. Without the pronunciamento California would have been torn apart by internal dissension. These were three problems which plagued Mexican-California and created chaos, instability, and a feeling of uncertainty. First, there was constant conflict between Monterey and Los Angeles politicians over the location of the capital. Los Angeles leaders, notably Pio Pico, complained that Southern California had never been treated as an equal by either Spain or Mexico. Since the early days of Spanish California, Pico charged, Los Angeles had never exerted any degree of political influence. This created a political system which excluded Los Angeles from the major decisions involving the growth and settlement of California. It also created meager economic and military support from Spain and Mexico. As a result, Pico talked of forming an independent state in Southern California. Much of Pio Pico's program was sheer rhetoric, but his antagonism illustrates the high degree of sectional misunderstanding early in California history. The debate over the location of the capital was merely the means used to disguise sectional antipathy. A second problem stemmed from the intensified debate over the Church's role under the new Mexican government. In reality, this argument was simply an indication of the popularity of secularization. The wealth of the church was a constant source of irritation to the Californios. Consequently, they used their rapidly growing political-economic power to demand that the Church devote its energy solely to saving souls. Lastly, Mexican-California was characterized by petty political clashes between local Californios, Mexican governors, and the Franciscans. As foreign influences grew increasingly stronger, another element of confusion entered California's chaotic civilization. As one historian has suggested, California was "a marginal province of a troubled Republic." Consequently, the divisions in California society made it impossible for Mexico to exert any concrete control over the area. The local California rancheros were to become the prime beneficiaries of Mexican California's chaotic condition, and Californios dominated the political scheme by 1836.

The Establishment of Mexican Government in California—The 1820s

One of the subtle changes in California during the 1820s was the increase of European settlers. Almost unnoticed, the European population increased by 33 percent in the 1820s. This helped to create diverse social and economic influences, and it was an important catalyst in attracting foreign merchants. Economic and social change occurred from the influx of new settlers. This coincided with the decline of mission influences and the Indian's flight from the missions. In the 1820s approximately 2,500 Indians left the Church. The number of people living on ranchos and in civil pueblos doubled during the first decade of Mexican rule. A number of contemporary observers noted that the Spanish heritage was undergoing a quiet revolution. Spanish institutions were being reshaped with local Californios and foreigners modifying institutions. These forces made Mexican-California a much more vigorous civilization than it had been during the Spanish era. The main political force was the slowly developing liberalism ignited by the Californio's. In fact, during the transition period in the early 1820s, local citizens of Mexican-California increasingly demanded that a native son be appointed as the interim governor. In 1822 Mexico responded favorably to this suggestion in order to secure a representative to Monterey to allow California's military districts—San Diego, Santa Barbara, Monterey and San Francisco, and the Los Angeles pueblo to select a new governor. Mexico was concerned about establishing loyalty to the new constitutional government. In a move designed to publicize the democratic structure of the new Mexican government, California was instructed to elect its own legislature. The diputación was an advisory body to the governor, and in reality had no power. It convened at the governor's discretion. Luis Argüello, the popular commander of the San Francisco presidio, was selected as the governor. The ayuntamientos, the city councils in Los Angeles and San José, were instructed to strengthen and expand their self-government roles. In essence, a republican form of government developed during the early years of Mexican-California. There was an outward display of democracy, but the governor was entrusted with the only significant political and economic powers.

Governor Argüello displayed an amazing amount of personal energy by implementing a great deal of change and innovation during his three years in office. He rarely abused his power and he pushed for local political rule. But Mexico cautiously approached democratic government for

Californians. Mexican governors lectured that the tools of democracy could be mastered only by constant practice. This is one reason for the turbulence of Mexican-California politics. No one could agree precisely what constituted democratic procedures. In light of the problems Governor Argüello's accomplishments were significant ones. The remainder of the mission system was completed under his leadership. The final two missions, San Rafael Arcángel and San Francisco de Solano, were completed in the 1820s despite opposition to the project. In addition to finishing Father Serra's legendary El Camino Real, Argüello exerted strong controls upon the Franciscans. This was necessary because of the forceful, increasingly aggressive behavior of the Franciscan order. An example of this meddlesome nature occurred when the San Francisco mission petitioned the diputación to remove itself to Sonoma. Argüello refused the request, and lectured the clergy to remember their place in the structure of Mexican-California society. They were no longer to engage in petty politics. He suggested that the highpoint of Franciscan influence in California was a thing of the past. Argüello's rhetoric and the increased public support for the governor's statements suggests that secularization was a popular notion.

Among Argüello's more constructive accomplishments was the cultivation of more agricultural land. He also implemented a government policy which encouraged the growth of local business in liaison with foreign economic interests. Argüello believed that outside economic influences would be useful in developing California's economy. These attitudes paved the way for Mexican governmental officials to work with foreign economic interests. As a result foreign economic activity escalated in California during the 1820s. Although Argüello did not believe that Russia's Fort Ross experiment was a positive factor, this did not prevent Argüello from making an agreement with the Russians to hunt the California sea otter. The arrangment to cooperate with Russia was due to Argüello's belief that the Russian-American Company was draining California's fishing wealth. Argüello's concern for local business development prompted him to argue that by cooperating with the Russians there would be an increase in local fishery activity. There were also attempts to encourage American and English traders to expand their activity to California.

In June, 1822, Hugh McCullough and William Hartnell began to negotiate with Governor Argüello to establish a branch of the English merchantile firm John Begg and Company in Monterey. Begg and Company offered to send one ship a year to California and purchase all hides available in the major ports. The Franciscans applauded this idea believing it would revitalize the mission economy; and Governor Argüello pointed out that British mercantile interests would benefit local Californios. It would allow local merchants to become independent of the Mexican trade. Los Angeles, San José, and the large ranchos would reap increased profits from English trade. Hides were sold for one dollar regardless of the size, and the English were given exclusive rights to the California's hide trade. The hide and tallow trade brought a young Harvard student, Richard Henry Dana, to California, and in his book, *Two Years Before the Mast,* Dana presented the first serious American account of Mexican-California.

Foreign traders, however, did not prove to be an immediate blessing. The English monopoly occurred before there was any competition for California hides, and this temporarily hurt the burgeoning economy of Mexican-California. Generally, Mexico pursued economic goals designed to open trade to foreign nations to California. This would produce revenue through import taxes and encourage the growth of a diversified economy. In anticipation of this expanded trade, Monterey and San Diego were designated as ports suitable for entry to foreign nations trading in

California. Mexico was determined to collect duties from foreign traders to finance California's government. Sensing Mexico's attitude, William Hartnell became the first notable foreign trader to become a Mexican citizen, embrace Catholicism, and to swear fealty to the Mexican government. Hartnell's exaggerated public support for the Mexican government earned him a special position in California's business climate.

The Indian in Mexican California: The 1820s

The instability of Mexican politics during the 1820s created tensions among California's mission Indians. Many Californians harbored negative feelings toward Mexican President Augustin Iturbide's decision to crown himself emperor. Liberal thinking Californio's believed that the promises of the Mexican Revolution were hollow ones. The Constitution of 1824 was no longer a part of Mexican government. Tyranny and cajolery replaced democratic political notions. Suddenly cries of freedom and liberalism occupied the thoughts and deeds of Californians. It was not surprising that the California mission Indians caught the spirit of liberty and drank in the democratic resistance to Mexican control. Many Indians were lectured by Californios to fight for their freedom from the tyranny of the Franciscans. As Iturbide fell from power in 1823, the Californios reassessed their political attitudes and began to actively support the reconstituted Mexican government. This change of attitude among Californios was due to the belief that Mexico would exert no more control over local affairs than Spain. The liberal-minded Californios hoped that the old Indian policy would change under Mexican rule. The question of civil rights for the Indians dominated the political rhetoric of Mexican-California. There were constant charges that the mission system created an institutionalized form of racism.

An important catalyst to the increasingly strong demand for a new Indian policy occurred in 1824 when the Indians settled in the area near Santa Barbara and expressed hopes for increased civil rights and eventually freedom. In this atmosphere, a soldier at the Mission Santa Ines flogged an Indian unmercifully and the local neophytes turned upon the guards and burned several buildings. The Indians then journeyed to the home mission of the beaten Indian, Las Purisma Concepcion, and they seized the mission as a protest against years of inhumane treatment. By February, 1824, Santa Ines, Purisma Concepcion, and Santa Barbara experienced Indian revolts. Invariably, the soldiers and their families were allowed to leave, and the Indians symbolically held the bastion of their former masters. Suddenly there was a problem with lawless Indians. Many neophytes left the Santa Barbara region and outlaw Indian communities sprung up around Bakersfield. A series of battles at La Purisma Concepcion led to the deaths of seven Indians and four soldiers. The Indians, although not trained for battle, refused to surrender to the Mexican army and they succeeded in holding the mission for a month. Under the Indian leadership the mission grounds were reinforced with new stockades, a large supply of guns were obtained, and they mounted the old cannons in the church walls. Military preparedness was a surprise to the Mexican army and they were baffled by the Indians' resistance. The Santa Barbara Indians staged their revolt after hearing about the success of the other Indian movements. But the Santa Barbara Indians were routed and they fled into the San Joaquin Valley. In retaliation the soldiers looted and burned the Indian dwellings.

Governor Argüello moved to squash the Indian revolt. He sent Lieutenant José Mariano Estrada with one hundred men to put down the uprising. The Indians were easily routed under the experienced leadership of Lt. Estrada. The leaders of the revolt were quickly brought to trial and the seven were condemned to death with 18 given prison terms. Once the Indian revolt of 1824 subsided, questions began to be asked concerning the origins of the uprising.

The Franciscan priests found it difficult to accept the fact that mission working and living conditions had contributed to the uprising. They preferred to blame the liberal-radical tone of politics created by the Mexican Revolution. Governor Argüello believed that the proposed Mexican Constitution must face the question of Indian slavery squarely. Slavery was a thorn in the side of the body politic, and the political problems which would result from it created dangerous tensions in California. Argüello believed that years of abusing the mission Indians created the potential for racial disturbances. He suggested that the seeds of racism were planted during the embryo development of the mission system. Prior to leaving office Argüello strongly urged Mexico to eliminate Indian slavery. While Argüello's motives were commendable ones, he was also hostile to the Franciscans because he believed that Indian slavery guaranteed mission prosperity. Argüello argued that secularization of mission land would enable the prosperity and influence of independent Californio businessmen to rise to a level where Mexico would have to recognize the political-economic influence of native-born Californians. Argüello was representative of the "new elite," a group of native sons who believed that a free enterprise business impulse, a decline in church influences and a liberal republican government would create a more prosperous Mexican-California. It would also result in a liberal political climate, and this would place the California Indian in the mainstream of local civilization. The significance of the Indian Revolt of 1824, was that it destroyed the stereotype of contented, well treated mission Indians. It indicated that there was dissatisfaction with the economic organization of the missions and legitimate concern by the Indians with their own freedoms. Many Californians envisioned a coalition of local citizens and Indians forming an integrated society, but the dream soon ended.

Mexico Takes Command: The Shaky Years of José Echeandía, 1825–1831

In 1825 the Mexican Constitution went into effect and California was organized as a territory under the control of the Congress. As a distant Mexican territory, California was ruled at the whim and discretion of the appointed governor. Mexican governors have been pictured historically as uniformly incompetent, personally abusive, and generally unconcerned with California's problems. While these conclusions adequately describe a few Mexican governors, there were others who were extremely competent administrators. In fact, a recent study indicated that Mexican governors were able to foster economic growth much better that their Spanish predecessors. A number of Mexican governors worked closely with the Californios to build local prosperity. The primary reason for the negative historical description of Mexican governors is due to the reign of José Echeandía. From 1825 to 1831 Echeandía exemplified the stereotypical tyrant image of the Mexican-California governor. Echeandía was a unique man; he was a tall, thin, blue-eyed Latin who spoke with a lisp and worried excessively about his health. A noted hypochondriac, Echeandía's personal idiosyncrasies provided ample evidence for his opponents to argue that he was unfit to govern California.

The main problem with Echeandía's approach to California government was that he was totally inflexible. An engineer by vocation, Echeandía was just as inexperienced in making policy as well as carrying out decisions for the general welfare of the people. His inexperience has prompted historians to view Echeandía as a tyrant in governing California. In reality, he was no better or no worse than most Spanish or Mexican governors. California was a difficult post for Mexican governors, and Echeandía was not given the economic support necessary for success. His reputation was partially due to his hostility toward Franciscans, and the leadership Echeandía displayed in setting the secularization process in motion. The primary reason for Echeandía's open hostility to the missions was Mexico's inability or unwillingness to pay, supply and reinforce his troops. He believed that the missions were wealthier than the military in California. Echeandía continually pleaded with his superiors for a transfer to Mexico City, and he displayed open disdain for the Californios. Echeandía believed the Franciscans and local Californios were not loyal to Mexico, and he argued that they should be punished for their independent attitude.

Another reason for the low opinion of Echeandía's years as California's governor was his continual attempt to move the capital from Monterey to San Diego. The only reason for Echeandía's desire to administer California from San Diego was that his health dictated a warmer climate. To the historically minded Californians this was a ludicrous reason for moving the capital. Consequently, the growing jealously between northern and southern Californians intensified as a result of Echeandía's decision to remain in San Diego. Sectional rivalry was a strong factor in California politics by the 1830s due to the capital debate.

It was not surprising that Governor Echeandía's own men rebelled against him because he found it difficult to make popular political decisions. In 1828 the Monterey presidio revolted due to the inability of the Mexican government to pay the army. The notoriously poor working conditions made it next to impossible to find good soldiers. Thus, the army strike reflected poor discipline, rising discontent, and growing sympathy for the Californio cause. But after lengthy negotiations the army returned to work. In November, 1829, another serious revolt occurred when the cholo troops seized their officers in a violent mutiny. Cholo troops were ex-convicts and it was not surprising that their leader, Joaquín Solís, an ex-convict, persuaded soldiers as far away as Santa Barbara to join the revolt. There were many Californians who encouraged those comic opera revolutions. Foreign business interests in Monterey paid lip service to the uprisings in hopes of weakening Mexico's control over California commerce. In December, 1829, Solís' army and Governor Echeandía's forces met in a showdown at Santa Barbara. The anticipated battle never materialized as a pronunciamento quickly settled the differences between Solís and Echeandía. As a gesture of reconciliation, Echeandía promised amnesty to the rebels, but he advanced quickly to Monterey to restore order. With equal rapidity Echeandía's gracious promise of amnesty was rescinded and, Solís and his followers were arrested and shipped to a Mexican prison. This incident highlighted the shaky nature of Governor Echeandía's political decision making. The most significant lesson drawn from the Solís led uprising was that California governors had little control over the Mexican army. This lack of discipline, combined with local intrigue, created problems for future governors.

By 1830 Echeandía's position was so weak that he was forced to seek support from the diputación in order to secularize the missions. Only the power of local Californias would enable Echeandía to sell mission lands, thereby creating some funds to pay the discontent troops. But since 1825 Echeandía had refused to allow the diputación to meet in regular sessions. This was a mistake since this quasi-legislative body possessed no more than advisory powers. By not allowing the diputación to hold regular meetings, Echeandía reinforced the argument that the Mexican governor was instructed to control local nationalism. This added fuel to the Californios who demanded home rule. But there was no other choice than to support Echeandía's request for assistance. Consequently, in 1830 when the diputación agreed to push hard in support of Echeandía's secularization plans they did so with demands of their own. Among these requests were increased land grants, the creation of a native cavalry, and establishment of town councils at Monterey and Santa Barbara. The town councils would allow local citizens to implement civil government and replace the unconcerned military. The Californios were no longer a minority and they were in control in every section of California. The obvious conclusion is that Echeandía's years as governor strengthened local nationalism and increased home rule fever.

Governmental Instability and Mission Secularization

One of the natural byproducts of Governor Echeandía's tenure was an increase of governmental instability. This uneasiness over the direction of Mexican government was aided by the appointment of a series of incompetent governors who displayed perpetual poor judgment. The result was to force the Californios to organize a drive to implement immediate home rule. In response to Mexico's disinterest in California affairs the demand for a native-born governor gained ground among a wide range of Californios. The presence of Americans and other foreign intruders was another important aspect contributing to the uncertain nature of California's frontier government. But it was delay in secularization which made it virtually impossible to govern California. The debate over church wealth was an old one and most Californios believed the church was too wealthy and well established. In 1830, the oldest mission was sixty-one years old, and the average age of an individual mission was forty-five years old. Initially, Spain decreed that any mission more than ten years old must be converted into a civil pueblo. The theory was that a decade would bring civilization to the Indians. An increasingly large number of Californios began to demand immediate secularization of the missions to bolster the sagging economy and free the Indians from mission slavery. Liberal Californios argued that the use of Indian labor violated Mexican law. In 1829 the Mexican Congress abolished slavery, and this placed the mission system in a precarious position. Since the Indians were predominantly forced labor, the Mexican government could not defend a proposal to continue the economic side of California missions. The dilemma of Mexican-California politics in the early 1830s was to secularize the missions while maintaining a sense of law and order.

The introduction of a proposal to abolish slavery led to a lengthy moral debate over secularization methods. The Franciscans immediately disputed the allegations that Indian labor was abused and the church defended the training of mission Indians. Christianity allowed the Indians to learn to read and write, the Franciscans argued, and the Indians mastered trades which made them productive members of Mexican-California society. Indian artists were often the most productive local mission artists and musicians, and the neophyte choirs and orchestras were considered the most musically accomplished groups in California. The artistic and musical skills mastered by California's mission Indians destroyed the old stereotype that the Indians lacked an appreciation of Spanish culture. In many respects, art and music would not have survived the mission period had it not been for the cultural contribution of California Indians.

The opponents of the mission system disputed the Franciscan argument that California Indians were being prepared to enter the mainstream of Spanish life. Perhaps the most persuasive argument used to highlight the evils of the mission system was the accusation that the Franciscans frequently whipped the Indians. One early example of Franciscan cruelty occurred when an American explorer, Jedediah Smith, was commissioned by a priest at the San Gabriel mission to build a bear trap to catch Indians stealing oranges. Although this incident was atypical of Franciscan behavior, it reflected negatively on the mission system. Liberal Californians believed that secularization was necessary because of the paternalistic nature of Indian slavery. Effective citizenship could result only from the Indians living in their own homes, experiencing equal protection under the law, and being integrated into local communities.

Without consulting Mexico, Governor Echeandía proposed a secularization scheme, and his original plan to secularize the missions was published on December 11, 1828. Under Echeandía's blueprint each Indian family was to receive two land plots. One would serve as the homesite, and the other was for agricultural purposes. In addition, a town composed of four square leagues of grazing land would be established to aid the newly created Indian ranchos. To ensure the permanence of the settlements, Indians would be given equipment, tools, and livestock to make the transition to an independent agricultural life. In theory, Governor Echeandía believed that California mission Indians would be rapidly integrated into the main stream of Spanish life.

This extralegal secularization plan failed to materialize, and the result was to cause further unrest among local Californios. As the Indians grew increasingly restive, there was a great deal of concern over the future of California. In January, 1831, Mexico wisely recalled Governor Echeandía and appointed Manuel Victoria as governor, and he faced the delicate task of directing the secularization process. Governor Victoria was a highly conservative appointee who believed that secularization was a mistake. Due to Victoria's pro-clerical position, a local revolution began to form prior to his arrival in California. In addition, local citizens were strongly opposed to Mexico's attempt to re-impose his authority. One of the problems faced by Victoria was that Mexico had recently experienced a governmental revolution; and a radical Mexican governmental appointee, José María Padrés, was replaced before he could take control of California affairs. Extremely unhappy over being suddenly replaced as governor, Padrés remained in California and united with the outgoing Governor Echeandía to form a revolutionary movement. Local citizens encouraged this organized opposition to Mexican military leadership, because they felt it would add credence to the growing power of local nationalism. This was a direct challenge to Governor Victoria's power.

In an attempt to show his military strength and establish his authority, Victoria imposed a number of tyrannical measures upon local citizens. Perhaps his most spectacular act was to decree the death penalty for anyone caught stealing bread. This glaring example of inept leadership helped the rebels to gain support from local Californios. The military conservatism of Governor Victoria frightened everyone, and this helped to promote a revolutionary atmosphere. After imprisoning a number of his critics, Victoria marched to Cahuenga Pass, near Los Angeles, and in early December 1831 met a rebel Los Angeles and San Diego army. Rather than declaring a truce and settling political differences with local citizens, Victoria's army attacked the rebels. This violated a sacrosanct rule that actual fighting would not occur in California. The Mexican government immediately recalled Victoria, and a scramble for power among a number of Mexican governmental figures occurred. This led to chaos and confusion in California government.

The result of Manuel Victoria's brief rule was to divide California into two separate and often competing sections. In Northern California, Augustin Zamorano, Victoria's territorial secretary, declared himself the governor and formed an army. José Echeandía established control over Southern California and Mexico faced the delicate problem of split loyalties among its California population. Local nationalism had grown precipitously by the early 1830s and Mexico recognized a desire for home rule. Another problem facing Mexico in the 1830s was the continued demand for secularization of the missions. Most historians believe that Victoria created new pressures for secularization because he was such a staunch defender of the mission system. Californians looked with suspicion upon most Mexican governors, and the strong defense of the church by Governor Victoria caused strong support for two governors. Californios believed that each section of Mexico's territory should control its own affairs.

As Echeandía and Zamorano vied with one another for political power, however, local citizens soon began to demand that some semblance of order be restored to California. Eventually the two rivals signed a pronunciamento in which they agreed to govern California jointly until Mexico appointed a new governor. Secretly, however, each man believed that he would be the new governor. Echeandía's belief was due to support from the local legislative assembly, the diputación, which was dominated by Southern California. Zamorano's claim to the governorship resulted from the support which Monterey businessmen had accorded him as acting governor. The end result of the differences between Echeandía and Zamorano was to create a demand for a governor who could bring order to Mexican California.

José Figueroa, Secularization and Governmental Stability.

After nearly a decade of instability and chaos in Mexican California, a governor was appointed who was able to secularize the missions and restore governmental order. General José Figueroa, who had spent six years governing the turbulent state of Sonora, was selected to re-establish order and a sense of direction in California civilization. Figueroa, a stocky, swarthy individual with Aztec blood, drank heavily, deserted his wife, and raised a second family with his mistress. Politically, however, Figueroa was moderate and intelligent in his dealings with local Californians. Although in poor health, Figueroa gained the respect and confidence of local citizens. He was a talented administrator, he treated the Indians fairly, and he was extremely democratic with local citizens. These qualities won Figueroa the admiration and respect of all Californians. Unlike previous Mexican governors, Figueroa was without prejudice. His first act was to issue a general amnesty to all Californians who had taken part in the revolutions of 1831–1832. This was a shrewd move, because it ended opposition to Figueroa's leadership.

In an attempt to revive Mexican power, Figueroa moved to take firm control of Northern California. At this juncture only San Rafael and San Francisco de Solano (Sonoma) were settled in the area north of San Francisco. Figueroa dispatched a local Californio, Mariano Guadalupe Vallejo, to select a site for a new presidio. Settlements were established at Petaluma and Santa Rosa as a result of Vallejo's explorations.

The primary political question which concerned Californians was secularization. This issue outweighed all others in Mexican California. As Figueroa suggested, the mission system was originally set up with the expectation of granting the Indians freedom to settle in pueblos. This had not occurred because the padres believed that the Indians were not ready to experience freedom. The missionaries argued persuasively that the Indians were wards of the church. These opinions depressed Figueroa, but he believed that the secularization process should be a carefully planned procedure. But Mexico did not heed Figueroa's warnings and the secularization scheme was a difficult experience for Mexican California. The thrust of democracy forced Mexico to support immediate secularization plans. The missions would become parish churches, and the economic activity of the Franciscan order would be reduced to virtually nothing.

The Secularization Process and Its Final Stages: Chaos and Confusion in California

The turmoil and argument generated over secularizing the missions prompted the Mexican Congress in August, 1833, to adopt a general secularization law. It was impossible for a democratic Mexican nation to continue to support the use of the mission Indians by the Franciscans. In addition, local Californios demanded an end to church economic activity because it hurt the growth of private enterprise capitalism. The intense debate over secularization occupied much of the energy of Governor Figueroa. It also provided a number of virtually insoluable problems. The secularization law was a vague and haphazard policy, and it was not designed to carry out immediate secularization. Figueroa's warnings concerning the degree of chaos and confusion which would result from immediate secularization went virtually unnoticed, and this made Figueroa a reluctant figure in the secularization process. He attempted to distribute half of the land and livestock from the missions to the Indian neophytes. But Figueroa was surprised to find that the Indians often remained on the mission. As a result, many citizens believed that secularization was a mistake.

Another problem with secularization occurred when a group of Mexican colonists attempted to settle upon California mission land. An influential Mexican politician, José María Padrés, convinced the Mexican government in 1834 to sponsor a settlement party of two hundred under the leadership of José María Híjar. The purpose of the Híjar-Padrés settlement party was to seize mission lands and livestock which had not yet been sold to private business interests. To compound their problems the Híjar-Padrés party brought in twenty-one Mexicans to administer missions lands. This increased local Californio resentment, and Governor Figueroa ordered Híjar and Padrés arrested. Some colonists were allowed to remain behind, but Governor Figueroa had established his control over California. Local citizens were extremely critical of Mexico and a number demanded a native born governor and some semblence of home rule. By the mid-1830s secularization had created a number of political problems and local tensions reached a new high.

Had it not been for Governor Figueroa's exemplary political leadership a local revolution might have ensued. On August 9, 1834, Governor Figueroa issued a proclamation ordering the immediate secularization of ten missions. He decreed that six more would be secularized in 1835 and the remainder in 1836. This timetable was excellent because it settled the question of when mission lands would be sold to private business. Unfortunately, tragedy struck when Governor Figueroa died two months after issuing the secularization edict. Without his strong leadership rival factions began to vie for power. Under Mexican law half of the land was to be divided among the Indians, and a number of Indians attempted to farm small plots near the mission. In general, however, these experiments faded quickly and the Indians found it difficult to fit into Mexican California society.

One of the tragedies of secularization was the plight of the unskilled and untrained Indian. They simply continued to live around the mission without visible means of support. The Indians trained as cowboys or farmers were able to secure employment on private ranchos. Strong pressure was brought to bear by the church against the secularization process, but it failed to slow the decline of church power. In the early 1840s, as Mexican-California faced the dangers of foreign invasion, a number of politicians attempted to revive the mission system. In fact, on March 29, 1843, Governor Manuel Micheltorena ordered the missions restored to the padres, but this was a symbolic gesture which came too late to save the missions. Church wealth was broken up and a new economic order began to slowly evolve in the last days of Mexican-California. But it was to be a decade before prosperity returned to California history. In the years after Governor Figueroa's death political instability increased throughout California. A series of incompetent governors were appointed to administer affairs in California. To compound matters, Los Angeles was declared the temporary capital of California and Mexico announced this was to punish revolutionary-minded Californians. This succeeded in re-establishing the north-south rivalry which had characterized California during the early years of Mexican rule. Local Californios reacted by demanding that a native son be appointed governor. If secularization was to become a final reality, the Californios argued, it must be completed by local citizens who understood the requirements of mission land dispersal.

Juan Bautista Alvarado and the Triumph of Home Rule, 1836–1842

The arguments for a native-born governor increased when Mariano Chico arrived to govern California. A hot tempered individual, Chico was a tyrant who believed that military discipline would solve California's problems. After three unsuccessful months of governing California, Chico was recalled to Mexico City. The local legislative assembly, the diputación, declared that Mexican governors were no longer welcome in California. The notion of independence was a political idea which appealed to many Californians, but Mexico recognized the problem and agreed to appoint a Californio governor. This action could not be taken without the assent and advise of the diputación.

As a result of the growth of the home rule movement, the California diputación began to play a more active role in local politics. From 1825–1836 there had been constant demands for home rule from a small, radical group. This soon became the dominant political mood, and in the fall of 1836 the diputación noisily issued a Plan of Independence. This plan was designed to allow the diputación president, Juan Bautista Alvarado, to exert enough political pressure upon the Mexican government to secure the governor's office. This was an inevitable result of the carefully designed problem which Alvarado had been working on for a decade.

In 1826, Alvarado, Mariano Vallejo, and José Castro formed a secret society in Monterey to study liberalism and revolutionary Latin American and European political thought. For the next decade this trio challenged many of the conventional beliefs of Mexican governmental and religious officials. Eventually Vallejo was excommunicated from the Catholic church for importing forbidden books from Mexico City. Vallejo's youthful idealism made him a rebel who advocated the growth of a completely democratic California.

The liberal political thought of the youthful Monterey Californio trio was a reflection of the advanced democratic nature of local politicians. The first casualty of this newly developed California liberalism was the Catholic church. Anti-clerical sentiment had simmered for some time in California and it now burst suddenly upon Monterey. A prime example of the changing mood in local political circles occurred when Mariano Vallejo refused to tithe to the church. This prompted the Bishop of California, Garcia Diego, to complain that anti-clerical sentiment had

Mariano Vallejo at home in Sonoma

reduced church services to the point that attendance was limited to women, children, and the elderly. This change in attitude was an important catalyst to the secularization movement, and the Mexican government began to face the question of how it would diffuse California dissent.

The triumph of Juan Bautista Alvarado's home rule program began in November, 1836, when California was declared a free and independent state from Mexican rule. Using his skillfully developed public image as a local patriot, Alvarado announced a three point home rule program. First, he stated that Alta California was declaring its independence until Mexico returned to the democratic principles of the Constitution of 1824. Second, Alvarado announced the formation of a Native Cavalry, under the leadership of Mariano Vallejo, to police and protect California. Lastly, Monterey was named the permanent capital of California. Alvarado publicly chided Mexico for making Los Angeles the capital as an act of punishment, and he indicated that home rule was the result of blundering governmental policies. In reality, the home rule program was far from a real revolution. It was more the culmination of a decade of grievances against Mexican governmental policy.

While Alvarado's statements were often excessive ones, Mexico recognized that some segments of public opinion supported the home rule idea. Southern Californians were not strongly in favor of Alvarado's programs, but this was due to the lack of governmental impact. The diputación was controlled by Alvarado, and they consequently demanded recognition of Alvarado's program. Pio Pico noted that Los Angeles had almost no influence in California's politics. This opinion was in line with Mexico's belief that Alvarado was not sufficiently loyal to warrant appointment as California's governor. As Mexico debated Alvarado's home rule request, he took a calculated political gamble by declaring his support for the newly created conservative constitution of 1836. Soon Alvarado's influence prompted Mariano Vallejo to swear his fealty to the new Mexican Constitution. Due to his well publicized decrees of loyalty to Mexico, Alvarado was eventually appointed governor of California. In addition, Vallejo was confirmed as the military commander, and the concept of a native cavalry was recognized. California secured control of its local affairs and a six year rule dominated by native sons went into effect.

The significance of Alvarado's half-dozen years as California's governor was that he established governmental institutions which created a base for Anglo California annexation. One of Alvarado's first important acts was to separate the civil and military powers of the governor. He was the first governor to set up a court system which adequately handled criminal cases. By pushing mission secularization to its final stages, Alvarado created a pluralistic society. This was a society based upon economic and political goals rather than upon religious influences. The rise of a pluralistic society brought a quiet revolution to California politics, and this energy resulted in immediate political and economic change which altered the power of the military and clergy. By the mid-1830s California was a new type of society; and this created a decade of confusion and controversy from 1836–1846 in developing local institutions. California was weakened by the controversy over home rule and an economic vacuum resulted from Mexico's reluctance to involve itself in California's affairs. But governmental institutions did become more protective of local citizens during the last days of Mexican California.

In essence, Alvarado established the diputación, the governor's office and the courts as three independent functioning agencies of Mexican government serving local Californians. Implicit in his theory was a separation of powers and the development of policies to protect and encourage the growth of local nationalism. He was highly democratic and many Californians complained that Governor Alvarado did not fully exploit the powers available to him. In 1839, Alvarado's quest for public approval caused him to engage in a drive for morality in government; he married his mistress, Marina Castro, to create an aura of respectability around Mexican governmental institutions.

After an idyllic period of local rule, trouble occurred in 1840. Alvarado and his uncle, Mariano Vallejo, parted as friends when the governor refused to appoint Vallejo as inspector for the California mission system. Then trouble developed in the Branciforte civic pueblo when American intruders began to challenge Governor Alvarado's leadership. A breed of mountain men had descended upon Branciforte and they were notoriously hostile to Catholicism, Mexican governmental officials, and local citizens. The Kentucky and Tennessee mountainmen's quarrelsome nature prompted the Santa Cruz Franciscans to complain about drunken attacks upon their missions.

The leader of the Branciforte community was the buckskin clad, bearded Isaac Graham, who was the proprietor of the first brandy distillery in California. Graham's combination cabin-tavern was a gathering place for sailors who deserted from foreign ships, for smelly trappers from the Rocky Mountains, and for schemers who envisioned immediate wealth in California. Without passports and any visible means of support, the Branciforte denizens worried Governor Alvarado and his home rule supporters.

In April, 1840, Tom the Trapper, an obscure frontiersman, believed that he was dying. He summoned a priest to Branciforte and babbled a death-bed tale of an American uprising. The priest promptly reported this story to Governor Alvarado, and he arrested 120 passportless foreigners. Eventually forty-six were shipped to Mexico, and the British counsel petitioned the Mexican government for clemency for the displaced California prisoners. In an obvious attempt to embarass Alvarado, the Mexican government ordered twenty foreigners, including Isaac Graham, to be released and returned immediately to California. Thus, to Alvarado's great surprise, in July, 1841, Graham and a motley group of prisoners returned to Monterey. The importance of the "Graham Affair" was that it caused Governor Alvarado to lose face and consequently cut into his political power.

Contemporary observers in the early 1840s described Alvarado as prematurely grey, paunchy, and showing visible scars of middle-aged physical and mental decline. Whatever the causes, Alvarado resigned as governor shortly after the Graham incident. He had developed an ulcer and for health reasons he announced that he would surrender the governor's office on January 1, 1842. But home rule was already a success in many respects. It provided the first workable separation of California governmental institutions and it enabled local Californios to dominate political and economic institutions. A new economy began to develop and the thorny question of mission secularization was finally settled. Many critics have suggested that Alvarado's personal friends took advantage of the situation by disposing of mission property to benefit local business interests and they often exploited the Franciscans and the Indians. However, the final result was to stimulate the continued growth of private enterprise capitalism. Alvarado generously bestowed land grants upon native and naturalized foreigners, and he sought to stimulate trade and create a diversified economy. It was now apparent that foreigners were acquiring large shares of California's wealth. Alvarado retired convinced that he had set California upon solid economic and political ground.

The Abortive Return to Mexican Rule Under Manuel Micheltorena

In August, 1842, Manuel Micheltorena, a former soldier under Santa Anna, arrived in California to assume his duties as governor. From the beginning Micheltorena's attempt to re-impose military discipline was doomed. His army of three hundred cholos or half-breed ex-convicts landed in San Diego naked with blankets draped over each soldier. Without proper clothing or the rudimentary necessities to survive on the frontier, Micheltorena's army soon turned to looting the countryside. It was an amazing sight to local citizens to see the Mexican army stealing chickens, commandering clothing, and robbing local citizens. The reaction to Micheltorena's motley army was one of immediate hostility, and the feeling among Californios was that Mexico was no longer interested in local political problems.

To compound Micheltorena's problems, rumors of war between the United States and Mexico circulated throughout California. In September, 1842, Commodore Thomas Jones, Commander of the American Pacific squadron, landed in Peru, and he was easily persuaded by local officials that war had broken out between the United States and Mexico. On October 20, 1842, Commodore

Jones hurriedly sailed into Monterey Bay, and seized the capital of Mexican California in the name of the United States. After a few hours, Jones realized that he had committed a grievous error, and he meekly lowered the American flag as curious local citizens looked on. This bizarre incident illustrated that War Department interest in California was a driving force behind Jones' escapade.

Foreign observers often remarked about Mexico's shaky control over California, and this made it difficult for Governor Micheltorena to function with any appreciable degree of political power. There were also a large number of foreign visitors who kept journals and diaries explaining California's development. One such early observer was Lieutenant Charles Wilkes who surveyed the Pacific Coast in 1841–1842. In general, Wilkes was not impressed with the Far West, but he was extremely enthusiastic about the commercial potential of San Francisco's port. He also reported on Mexico's weak military and political hold upon California, and his descriptions on the general tensions between the Californios and Mexicans indicated that local revolution was a distinct possibility.

These problems eventually brought an end to Governor Micheltorena's reign, because his policies encouraged local revolution. In November, 1844, Juan Bautista Alvarado and José Castro reorganized a Californio army to impose home rule and oust Micheltorena. Mariano Vallejo, who supported American annexation, attempted to intercede as a peacemaker, by urging Micheltorena to dispatch his troops to Mexico City. The spectre of revolution prompted Governor Micheltorena to march against the rebels. A brief skirmish appeared imminent near San José, but Alvarado's Californio army of two hundred and twenty easily outnumbered Micheltorena's one hundred and fifty Mexican soldiers. Rather than engage in a pitched battle, a series of elaborate negotiations took place which resulted in the Treaty of Santa Teresa. This strange document avoided violence because Governor Micheltorena agreed to leave California with his cholo army. But this was merely a ploy as Micheltorena had no intention of abiding by the treaty. The governor soon formed a coalition with foreign settlers and business interests to punish local Californios. The German-Swiss immigrant, John Sutter, took the field for Micheltorena; Isaac Graham organized a group of Branciforte sharpshooters to fight for the Mexican cause; a number of English businessmen quietly provided financial support. With this type of support Micheltorena announced eagerly he would punish the rebels.

Immediately Micheltorena's opponents organized in Los Angeles, and California took on the appearance of an armed camp divided between the North and South. Then the diputación took a calculated risk by announcing that Micheltorena was no longer the governor and that Pio Pico had been selected to replace him. On February 20, 1845, at Cahuenga Pass, a Californio army met Micheltorena's forces. The result was a comic opera battle; a mule was the only casualty from the gunfire. The following day a large number of Americans who had joined Micheltorena decided the fight was not theirs and they watched from the sidelines. This forced Micheltorena to capitulate to the rebel forces. By March, 1845 Pio Pico was appointed the last governor of Mexican California. José Castro was named as the military commander and Mariano Vallejo was selected to negotiate any differences between Californios and foreign interests. But political instability reigned, and it continued to plague California. Neither Northern nor Southern Californians were content with the state of political affairs under Mexican rule. Foreign interests were growing in power and influence, particularly the Americans, and the first signs of internal problems were apparent from the influx of new settlers.

Mariano Vallejo and his daughters

Courtesy, The Bancroft Library

Mexican California: A Summary of Influences

One of the most important developments during the years of Mexican-California was the rise of the rancho. The large ranchos made it possible to develop the economic base, and this created a new political aristocracy. For years the vast economic potential in California had remained largely undeveloped due to the problems of completing secularization. It was secularization which acted as a catalyst to the growth of private enterprise capitalism. Once secularization was completed, a number of large cattle ranches began to dominate California's economic growth. The main significance of the rancho is that it developed a local economic aristocracy. The large ranchos were a curious economic institution, because they operated solely by exporting hides and tallow. It was a simple but prosperous business and the profits provided wealth for a large ranchero. Yet, industry did not begin to develop permanently in California. Leather products for Californios, for example, were manufactured in New England. The relatively easy task of making soap and candles was completed in Chile and Peru. Consequently, foreign merchants began to occupy an important place in the California economy. It was this tenuous alliance between local rancheros and foreign business interests which helped to spark worldwide interest and eventual foreign immigration into California. Had it not been for the governmental chaos during the years of Mexican California, the Pacific Coast might have remained a remote and sleepy settlement.

But there were other influences which aided the growth of California civilization. The rise of local Californio businessmen led to the growth of public education. Only the reform-minded Mexican Governor José Figueroa had established a school system, and by the 1840s citizens complained about the problems of literacy. For years the missionaries had discouraged educating the Indians. Often the padres burned books which purported to impart the wrong type of knowledge to the Indians. Mariano Vallejo was typical of local Californios who continually complained that incompetent and disinterested teachers had almost destroyed the embryo educational system. Vallejo and Alvarado were lucky enough to have been schooled under Governor Solá, and they represented local Californio opinion which attempted to upgrade the general educational level in Mexican California. The only formal education in Mexican California came from the vocational skills and music training the Franciscans provided to the Indians in the missions. In the 1840s this began to change as the Californios demanded schools to match the growing economy.

In 1845 California remained an isolated Mexican province. Its settlement was permanent, but, excluding Indians, only seven thousand people resided in California. Some historians believe that California suffered from an excess of hospitality. That is Mexican society was too friendly to foreign visitors. Despite Spanish and Mexican laws restricting immigrants, foreigners found it quite easy to fit into the mainstream of California society. In order to understand the annexation of California by the United States during the Mexican War it is necessary to examine the role of foreign intruders.

Bibliographical Essay

The best starting point for the political history of Mexican-California is Woodrow J. Hansen, *The Search for Authority in California* (1960). The early chapters of Leonard Pitt, *The Decline of the Californios: A Social History of the Spanish-Speaking Californians, 1846–1890* (1966) are the models for much of what I have attempted to do in reconstructing Spanish and Mexican influences in early California. Pitt's pioneer work is responsible for the recent surge of ethnic history, and he was the single most important historiographical influence upon this study.

For the secularization crisis and the role of the Californios, see, for example, Gerald J. Geary, *The Secularization of the California Missions* (1934); John B. McGloin, "The California Catholic Church in Transition," *California Historical Society Quarterly,* XLII (March, 1963), 39–48; Madie B. Emparan, *The Vallejos of California* (1968); Myrtle M. McKittrick, *Vallejo: Son of California* (1944); and George L. Harding, *Don Agustin V. Zamorano* (1934). An extremely useful article on Mexican government and the Indians is C. Alan Hutchison, "The Mexican Government and the Mission Indians of Upper California, 1821–1835," *The Americas,* XXI (1965), 335–62.

There were a number of foreign visitors who demonstrated a great deal of insight in observing the American West and California, see, Marguerite Eyer Wilbur, *Vancouver in California, 1792–1794* (1953) for an edited version of Vancouver's California adventures. Vancouver is important in understanding the last days of Spanish California and the transition to Mexican rule.

The best study of Mexican-California by a literary figure is Richard Henry Dana's *Two Years Before the Mast* (1840). An excellent study examining the shift from Mexican to American-California from a cultural standpoint is James D. Hart, *American Images of Spanish California* (1960).

There are some interesting biographies on foreign settlers in California which shed a great deal of light upon the changing economic climate and its impact upon secularization, see, Susanna Bryant Dakin, *A Scotch Paisano: Hugo Reid's Life In California, 1832–1853* (1939). A useful account of Mexican intrigue in California is C. Alan Hutchinson, *Frontier Settlement in Mexican California: The Híjar-Padrés Colony and Its Origins, 1769–1835* (1960). Hutchinson believes that the colonization scheme would have benefited California. For early American economic interest prior to the secularization controversy see, Magdalen Coughlin, "Boston Smugglers on the Coast: an Insight into the American Acquisition of California," *California Historical Society Quarterly,* XLVI (June, 1967), 99–120. For an excellent case study of early American attitudes in Mexican-California see, John A. Hawgood, "The Pattern of Yankee Infiltration in Mexican Alta California, 1821–1846," *Pacific Historical Review,* XXVII (February, 1958), 27–38.

There are a number of very useful early travel accounts of Mexican-California see, Thomas J. Farnham, *Travels in the Californias, and Scenes in the Pacific Ocean* (1844); Henry A. Wise, *Los Gringos: or an Inside View of Mexico and California* (1849); Doyce B. Nunis, editor, *Josiah Belden, 1841 California Pioneer* (1962); John Bidwell, *A Journey to California in 1841* (1842); Alfred Robinson, *Life in California* (1846); and Doyce B. Nunis, editor, *The California Diary of Faxon Dean Atherton, 1836–1839* (1964).

There is an extensive body of literature on the California ranchos, but the best single work in this subject is Sheldon G. Jackson, *A British Ranchero in Old California: The Life and Times of Henry Dalton and the Rancho Azusa* (1977). This is a detailed biography of Dalton as well as an economic history of Southern California. For an interesting study of a Northern California ranchero see, Albert Shumate, *Francisco Pacheco of Pacheco Pass* (1977). For a somewhat dated but interesting view of the rancho see, W.W. Robinson, *Ranchos Become Cities* (1939).

5

THE EARLY DAYS OF AMERICAN-CALIFORNIA

Early Ideas on the Golden State

American infiltration into California resulted primarily from a desire to profit from trade with China. New England merchants dreamed of exploiting the vast Chinese markets, and this brought ships representing Boston commercial interests into California in the late 18th century. The diaries of Boston sea captains indicate that they were struck immediately by the cosmopolitan nature of Spanish-California. They often remarked that Spain's ideas about commerce were similar to those of Yankee traders. This observation indicates that while American commercial interests hoped to participate in the lucrative California trade, there was no early commitment to permanent settlement. This is an important remark, because it indicates that American commercial interests had the same desire to reap the economic and trade wealth of California while foresaking a commitment to permanent settlement.

One of the unique characteristics of American penetration into California is that it was carried out in a haphazard, largely unplanned manner. Unlike the carefully organized and mapped-out plans of the Spanish and Mexican governments, early American intruders settled in unpredictable, often chaotic groups. This haphazard settlement was the first real challenge to established institutions. Coming by land and by sea, American invaders searched for new forms of wealth in a spontaneous, carefree manner which reflected both a vibrant American frontier spirit, and a vigorous entrepreneurial drive. It proved to be an important precedent to permanent American settlement, because it challenged the strict governmental controls of Spanish and Mexican settlement and by doing so altered the tone of California civilization. No longer did the average settler follow the dictates of governmental officials. This new freedom was reflected in the lifestyles and economic exploits of American settlers. By examining the stages of American immigration into California, it is easier to understand the eventual process of annexation.

Early Frontiersmen: The Challenge of Mexican-California

The first Americans to display an interest in California were marine frontiersmen. Since New England merchants found a ready market in China for the California sea otter, the popularity of the black fur riveted business attention upon Monterey. In 1821 maritime traders persuaded Mexico to open the Monterey and San Diego ports to foreign ships. The result was an influx of foreign economic interests. In 1822 William Hartnell, an Englishman, established himself as the agent for the British firm of John Begg and Company, buying pelts from the missions for one dollar each. Hartnell negotiated an agreement to sell all the hides that the missions could produce for three years. This was an important step in establishing foreign trade in California. But the first important American trader, William A. Gale, arrived a few weeks later and was able to take over the hide and tallow trade by offering two dollars a pelt. He then opened an office for the Bryant and Sturgis Company of Boston. In fact, 80 percent of all California hides were sent to Boston and they were called "banknotes," because they were now the main form of legal California tender. The hide and tallow trade thus brought an American business impulse into California.

American Beaver Trappers: Early Overland Contact

The American beaver trapper became the advance agent of permanent settlement. The trapper was an adventurous individual who travelled unexplored desert areas to reach California. The desolate, remote geographical terrain between Salt Lake City and California seemed an impenetrable barrier to all but the mountain men. As the advanced agent of American settlement, the beaver trappers created overland routes for future settlers. The first American frontiersman to explore California was Jedediah Smith. He deserves the nickname, "The Great Pathfinder," because of his miraculous feats of exploration. After purchasing the Rocky Mountain Fur Company, Smith and seventeen men explored the region between the Great Salt Lake and California. He hoped to open a profitable beaver trading business in the American West.

In 1826, Smith arrived at the entrance to the San Gabriel mission in Southern California. He was not candid about his reasons for exploring California when he met with Father José Bernardo Sanchez. Despite a festive welcome, Smith remained evasive. This was due to Smith's belief that a river flowed from the Rocky Mountains into California. If it could be found, furs trapped in the interior could be more easily marketed. When Governor Echeandía confronted Smith, the American explained that he had entered California to purchase food and other supplies. Governor Echeandía suspected that Smith's explanation was less than candid, and because he was determined to maintain Mexico's military hold upon California, he reacted swiftly. The result was the first Anglo-Mexican confrontation in which ethnic and political differences indicated that a cultural clash was probable in the future. Echeandía arrested Smith, but the pleas of American merchants and Franciscan friars resulted in his release. Smith was instructed to leave California, but he ignored Echeandía's orders. As a result of his travels, Smith mapped a great deal of California. His journey suggested some of the problems of travelling through the Sierra, and he hinted at the vast economic potential in California. Jedediah Smith became a legend due to his California travels, epic journeys which encouraged American traders and trappers to migrate to the Far West. Smith charted two of the three overland routes to California, and contributed to geographical knowledge with his precise descriptions.

Another reason for Jedediah Smith's importance is that he offered an alternative to the mountainman stereotype. For years historians described early overland explorers as a drunken breed who murdered, raped, and plundered anything and anyone who stood in their way. While there was an element of truth to this argument, in fact many young explorers were serious businessmen. Smith was a Christian who refused tobacco, drank moderately, and hoped to find fame and fortune in the American West. His description of the San Joaquin Valley as a trapper's paradise was an important catalyst to attract permanent agricultural settlers.

One of the most important contributions of the mountain men was the creation of a body of literature on the American West. Many early explorers maintained careful diaries and composed thoughtful reminiscences of their travels. This provided a body of literature describing the opportunities and dangers of life in California. Perhaps the most exciting early account on California is *The Personal Narrative of James O. Pattie*. This remarkable book was published in 1831 and it stimulated new interest in California. It recounted the legendary feats of James Ohio Pattie, a well-known fur trapper, who was a contemporary of Jedediah Smith. The young, hot-headed Pattie first entered California in the late 1820s, and he encountered problems with Governor Echeandía. After spending a period of time in jail, Pattie was released when a smallpox epidemic broke out. He travelled throughout California and claimed to have immunized more than 20,000 Indians. When he died, Pattie's journal was edited by Timothy Flint, a missionary, and it is impossible to tell fact from fiction. The effect of Pattie's narrative was to romanticize California and encourage permanent American settlement. But Americans only trickled into California, as the time was not yet ripe for conquest. To this day Pattie's volume stands as a blend of fact and fiction, an original "Western" with a gunsmoke syndrome, replete with good and bad guys.

In the 1830s, a large number of fur traders followed Smith and Pattie into California. Thus, trade between Southern California and Santa Fe opened on a regular basis. Soon Southern mountain men began to trek through the Southwest into California as a consequence of this burgeoning trade. The most famous was Ewing Young, a Tennessee trapper, who brought young Kit Carson with him as a guide. Because of Smith and Pattie's difficulties, Young cautiously avoided local authorities. But Kit Carson became a folk hero to many Mexicans and to the padres at the Mission San José, when he retrieved a herd of horses stolen by Indians. As the Young party journeyed to Los Angeles, Mexican authorities decided to arrest them for travelling without a passport. But this plan was abandoned when Mexican soldiers witnessed two members of the American party engaging in a fight in which one man shot another to death. The importance of Young's journey was to bring in large numbers of mountain men from Santa Fe during the 1830s, and thus American infiltration into California began.

The role of American trappers and traders was a peculiar one. They were welcomed by the Franciscans and treated with contempt by many of the Mexican civil authorities. While American traders talked of the mutual advantages of commerce, they were not able to establish strong working relationships with local citizens. This was early evidence of cultural conflict in California. But the Santa Fe trade opened California up to American settlers.

The Influx of Early American Settlers in Mexican-California

American merchants began to take an active interest in California during the Mexican period, and this led to the first permanent settlers. The most significant early American merchant was Thomas Oliver Larkin, a Massachusetts businessman, who came to Monterey in 1832 to engage in the import-export trade. Building a two-story wooden house in Monterey, Larkin transplanted a bit of New England architecture and culture. Without giving offense, Larkin rejected repeated overtures to become a Mexican citizen. As he journeyed to Monterey, Larkin met Mrs. Rachel Hobson Holmes, and he immediately proposed marriage to the young widow. She accepted the offer and became the first American woman to live in Monterey. Larkin opened a mercantile store in Monterey, and he became the first important American businessman in California. Because he

Thomas Oliver Larkin, first American consul

Courtesy, The Bancroft Library

spoke Spanish and lived quietly within the prevailing Mexican culture, Larkin's store profited from its trade with Mexican ranchers. Most Monterey citizens came to respect Larkin, and this general acceptance would work to the advantage of later American arrivals. Larkin was quick to capitalize on this feeling. The result was to revitalize Monterey's stagnant consumer economy. He introduced charge accounts, and in a few years the most important Mexican government officials were in debt to Larkin. The significance of Thomas Oliver Larkin is that he became the most vocal proponent of American annexation, and Californians listened carefully to the arguments of a respected local businessman.

In addition to American settlers who resided in Monterey, a number of important new inland ranchers and merchants migrated into California. The first American settler in the inland regions of California was Dr. John Marsh. A Harvard graduate who intended to pursue a medical career, Marsh fell in love with a young woman of French-Canadian and Sioux blood. After living together for a time Marsh and his common-law wife had a child. This prompted Marsh's parents to disown him, and he appeared to be unemployable. However, Marsh was named a subagent to the Sioux nation, where he sold the Indians guns in direct violation of federal law. Forced to flee from his post as an Indian agent, Marsh journeyed to Los Angeles in February, 1836. He convinced the town council that his Harvard diploma was a medical certificate and that the Latin inscriptions on his Harvard degree qualified him as a medical doctor. Thus Marsh became the first licensed doctor in Southern California.

Soon after Marsh's arrival in California, he became an important land owner and merchant. He purchased 11 square leagues of land for $500 and raised livestock while practicing medicine. Marsh was able to maintain the goodwill of the Indians by treating malaria with quinine. Soon the Indians were working as casual labor, planting figs, grapes and pears on Marsh's ranch. In addition, Marsh sent letters with glowing reports on California to his close friends. While his attempt to encourage immigration failed, Marsh persuaded trappers and traders to journey into California. Because he believed that his land would rise in value only if the United States annexed California, Marsh was an early advocate of American expansion into the Far West.

Due to Marsh's letters, a party of fifty set out from Missouri in May, 1841, to explore California. Led by John Bidwell and John Bartleson, this party of mid-western farmers offered the first hope for American settlement in California. As the party travelled to California, a large number became apprehensive about the unknown route that they were exploring, and they suddenly decided to follow the known route to Oregon. But thirty-one men and a woman with a year old baby elected to continue on to California. The woman, Nancy Kelsey, was nineteen years old, and she became the first woman to follow what became known as the California Trail. After a torturous journey the remainder of the Bidwell-Bartleson party reached the San Joaquin Valley, where they killed some deer to satisfy their appetites. Encountering a number of John Marsh's Vaqueros, they shortly were introduced to Marsh, who to their amazement, turned out to be greedy and inhospitable. He indicated that they would have to buy his good will. At Marsh's request General Mariano Vallejo arrested half the settlement party near San José, but he issued temporary passes allowing the American visitors to freely move about in California.

The Bidwell-Bartleson party popularized the overland route known as the California Trail. They were also the first permanent American settlers to attempt to inhabit California, and this served as a significant catalyst to subsequent settlement ventures. In December, 1842, the Mexican government noted that a number of settlement parties had entered California, and the Mexican minister to Washington warned recent emigrants that Mexico did not desire permanent foreign settlers. Minister Juan Almonte declared that special permission was required to settle in Mexican-California. This statement characterized Mexico's feelings, and it began to illuminate the hostile feelings that would culminate in the Mexican War. It is probable that Mexico's hostility diverted large numbers of settlers to Texas or Oregon.

Foreign Schemers and the Rise of American-Mexican Hostility

In the early 1840s Sutter's Fort became the principal locale of foreign schemers. Perhaps the most notorious was Lansford Hastings. In league with John Sutter, Hastings began to call for a Pacific Republic, an independent American settlement to be established in Mexican-California. Hasting's grandiose scheme to rule California angered Mexico, increased official American interest in California, and produced talk of revolution. In 1842 Hastings arrived from Oregon where he led a party of 160 settlers. When in the following year he arrived in California with a party of forty settlers, no one was alarmed; but, the Mexican government soon became suspicious when John Sutter sent a number of letters to Governor Manuel Micheltorena complaining of Hasting's ambitions. Sutter's attempts to play both sides of the political fence hurt his credibility and added to the growing confusion in California politics. Governor Micheltorena made Sutter a member of the California militia in 1844, and by the following spring rumors were floating throughout

California about the possibility of war with the United States. Mexican officials were suspicious of any American who visited Sutter's Fort, and the general feeling was that Yankee intruders had gone too far in California. Both sides appeared to desire war.

John C. Frémont and the Rise of Official American Interest in California

The first important official American visitor to California was John C. Frémont, a lieutenant in the elite United States Army Corps of Topographical Engineers. Frémont, a brilliant mathematician and surveyor, was married to Jessie Benton, the daughter of one of the most distinguished members of the United States Senate. Frémont, the advance agent of American imperialism in California, had substantial political connections. In 1843 the army sent Frémont to explore the Oregon Trail, and he immediately disobeyed his orders by heading for Sutter's Fort. Using the excuse that he needed fresh horses, Frémont along with his young guide Kit Carson pushed a large number of horses through the Sierra. The party lost thirty-three horses and a pet dog. The latter was consumed by the freezing soldiers in a savory stew. Out of this exploratory venture came the discovery of Lake Tahoe.

Frémont's presence in California angered Mexican officials. Governor Micheltorena sent word to Sutter's Fort demanding an explanation for Frémont's venture into California. By this time Frémont had departed Sutter's Fort and was travelling through the San Joaquin Valley bound for Utah. The second Frémont expedition into the American West in 1843–1844 was a controversial trip. He aroused the ire of Mexican officials, produced skeptical comments from foreigners and Americans at Sutter's Fort, and maintained a journal which became a best seller. Combining his wife's sparkling literary style with his own penchant for exaggeration, Frémont established himself as a national hero.

One of the most persistent rumors about Frémont's travels into the American West was that he was preparing California for eventual annexation. These rumors were given credence when Frémont quietly checked out a howitzer for his supposedly scientific expedition into California. Moreover, the publication of Frémont's journals from his first and second expeditions into the American West provided fascinating descriptions of California's economic potential.

In 1845 Frémont's third expedition into California brought a small American military force in the West. Accompanied by sixty Kentucky longrifles, Frémont arrived in California in December, 1845. A number of Mexican and Californio officials charged that Frémont's sharpshooting brigade was the advance agent of American imperalism. While there is no evidence that President James K. Polk authorized Frémont to engage in covert military operations, the fact remains that the Great Pathfinder did everything in his power to encourage war between the United States and Mexico.

After consulting with William Leidesdorff, the Black Vice-Consul of Yerba Buena (San Francisco), Frémont visited Monterey in February, 1846. After conferring with José Castro, the military commander, Frémont sought permission to winter in the Central Valley. The Mexican government granted Frémont permission to winter in California provided that he keep away from all permanent settlements. Frémont immediately moved within 13 miles of San José. He then became involved in a dispute over the purchase of some horses, and this was followed by a slow, arrogant march toward Monterey. It was obvious to most contemporary observers that Frémont was abusing Castro's hospitality. Finally, while enjoying the hospitality of William Hartnell's ranch near Salinas, Frémont received a mandate from Castro to leave California.

John C. Frémont

In an effort to challenge Castro's military authority, Frémont withdrew his men to the Gavilan mountains overlooking the Salinas Valley. A makeshift barricade was hastily constructed, and it was christened Fort Gavilan. With 68 well-trained American frontiersmen, Frémont posed a psychological threat, if not a military one, to Mexican military authority. After raising the American flag, Frémont defiantly began to prepare for a military confrontation. Castro called for volunteers and raised a force of two hundred angry Californians. The American Consul in Monterey, Thomas Oliver Larkin, immediately became apprehensive over the possibility of war. The American navy was not in sight and Frémont's 68 frontiersmen would not be much of a match for over 200 Californians. Larkin did not share Frémont's self-serving motives, and he believed that violence would create irreparable damage between Americans and Californios. Moreover, there were persistent rumors that Great Britian was poised to seize California. Since Frémont and Castro were both demonstrating a macho military posture, it was relatively easy to bring peace and tranquility back into California. Yet, the problems between Frémont and Castro were indications that American-Californio differences existed concerning California's future.

As Frémont journeyed north to Oregon in the spring of 1846, events were moving in the direction of war. For many years the United States had coveted Texas and California, and the outbreak of the Mexican War in 1846 provided the reason for annexing these areas. Shortly after Frémont's departure from California a secret agent representing the United States Marine Corps arrived in Monterey. The young hot-tempered Archibald Gillespie crossed into California from Mexico disguised as an invalid in search of a health spa. Gillespie carried written dispatches for Larkin, but he was so frightened by anti-American sentiment that he burned the dispatches after committing them to memory. Larkin was informed that he was to foment a Texas-style revolution in California, and at the appropriate time would encourage the people of California to request American annexation.

The reason for such overt hostility towards the United States was the Slidell mission. President James K. Polk had sent John Slidell to Mexico to negotiate the purchase of California. It was finally agreed that Slidell would offer up to $30 million ($5 million for New Mexico, and $25 million for California). The reaction in California to the Slidell mission was one of total disapproval, and a number of demonstrations were held to protest annexation by the United States. But war was imminent so the attempt to purchase California was quickly forgotten. It does, however, destroy the myth which a number of historians have fostered about Californians desiring annexation by the United States.

A number of historians have speculated that Gillespie carried secret instructions from the War Department for Frémont. There is no reasonable documentation to back up this idea. However, Frémont's actions demonstrated an intent to foment war with Mexico. Armed with excessive ambition and a lack of personal restraint, Frémont returned to California during the summer of 1846 to help annex Mexico's former territory.

The Bear Flag Revolution: A Prelude to American Annexation

One of the by-products of rumors circulating about the possibility of war between the United States and Mexico was the intensification of hostile relations between Americans and Californios. As the influx of American pioneers increased, the Sacramento and Napa Valley regions were deluged with rumors of impending conflict. These stories were spread by John C. Frémont as he fled to Oregon. To make matters worse, Colonel Castro issued a proclamation warning foreigners that they were no longer welcome to settle in Mexican-California. Soon rumors spread that a Mexican army was being shuttled to California to force Americans off Mexican land. This prompted American leaders to talk of an armed massacre at the hands of Castro's cavalry. This rumor created an intense hostility among Mexican-Californians and Americans. Many of the settlers around Sutter's Fort were rankled by Castro's expulsion of Frémont from California, and this led a number of prominent Americans to argue that military protection was needed to protect foreigners from Castro's native Californio cavalry. American frontiersmen were extremely nervous and they began to talk of forming a republic which would petition for immediate American annexation. In order to support the idea of an American republic a rumor was spread that Castro had instructed his soldiers to encourage local Indians to set fire to crops raised by Americans. The paranoia of American settlers forced them to develop a carefully concocted plan for self-defense. Since the majority of Americans were rough frontiersmen, they reasoned that they had to strike before the local Californios could act. A group of thirty armed settlers organized for the purpose of seizing a herd of horses intended for use by Castro's native cavalry. Castro had instructed a small portion of his men to pick up 170 horses from Vallejo's Sonoma ranch. Americans believed that the horses were intended as part of a military excursion against foreign settlers. This raised the fears of American settlers to new heights. Goaded by the extreme statements of John C. Frémont, who had just returned from his Oregon exile, Americans prepared for an attack upon Castro's troops.

American actions took a new twist in the early morning hours of June 14, 1846, when Mariano Vallejo's Sonoma ranch was seized as a symbolic protest of local Californio injustice. Vallejo, a strong advocate of American annexation, immediately offered his captors a glass of home-made wine, and he urged them to explain their actions. The thirty armed Americans who seized Vallejo's ranch stated that they were establishing a new American republic. The American frontiersmen dubbed their new government the Bear Flag Republic. Most of the Americans got roaring drunk on Vallejo's brandy, therefore the only remaining sober frontiersmen, William Ide, prepared the proclamation stating the grievances and future governmental plans of local foreign settlers. William Todd, a nephew of Mrs. Abraham Lincoln, produced a flag with a grizzly bear in the middle and the words printed "California Republic" on it. As the flag slowly ascended the Sonoma plaza flagpole, a number of observers caustically remarked that it looked more like a pig than a bear. The Bear Flag Republic was not popular among local Mexican-Californians.

By seizing Vallejo's ranch, Americans were holding hostage the most respected Californian. By spiriting Vallejo to Sutter's Fort, the Bear Flaggers outraged Mexican-California. For two months Vallejo was kept in a dark, dingy cell. He was denied proper food, exercise, and forced to endure constant racial taunts. The opportunistic John C. Frémont moved back into the forefront of local politics by placing Sutter's Fort under his command. Many contemporary observers charged that Frémont plotted the Bear Flag revolution, but he remained largely in the background since he believed that local Californios would charge that he had helped to establish an independent American Republic in California as a precedent for immediate annexation. In subsequent years, Frémont and Ide both claimed that they had provided the opportunity for the United States to seize California during the Mexican war.

In the aftermath of the Bear Flag revolution, a number of ugly incidents occurred which intensified the budding hostility among local Californios and Americans. Local hatred reached new heights when José Castro sent a small, inadequately equipped force to liberate Vallejo's ranch. On June 24, 1846, Castro's men, under the leadership of Joaquin de la Torre, tried to recapture Sonoma only to be beaten at the battle north of San Rafael, which historians have labeled the Battle of Olompali. During the entire course of the Bear Flag revolution, many Americans and Californians were unaware of the Bear Flag Republic. In fact, only two Americans and six Californians were killed during the uprising. But stories of cruelty and barbarism were spread by Frémont. The result was to create a bitter racial climate and to encourage American frontiersmen to seek revenge. This led to a number of indiscriminate killings. In addition, a comic opera touch was added when Frémont quietly led a commando raid into Yerba Buena (San Francisco) and dismantled the firing mechanism on the presidio's ten strategically placed cannons. It was a ridiculous act because the presidio had been abandoned for some time, and the cannons had not been in firing condition for at least forty years. This was the kind of grandiose behavior that Californios had come to expect of Frémont. His daring exploit was typical of Frémont's romantic, often nonsensical leadership. The only positive result of Frémont's commando raid was that he named the entrance to San Francisco Bay the Golden Gate.

On July 4, 1846, after a celebration at Sonoma, Frémont announced that he was organizing the California battalion of volunteers to protect Americans in California. In reality, Frémont hoped to reap the glory of maintaining control of Mexican-California prior to official American annexation. This created a quasi-legal American army at precisely the time that the American navy seized Monterey in the early stages of the Mexican War. It was not coincidental that Frémont had organized a capable military force prior to formal annexation of California. While little concrete evidence existed to support a War Department conspiracy to seize California, the convenient appearance of Frémont's battalion of volunteers and the seizure of Monterey would appear to be more than mere opportunism. Frémont's previous exploring expeditions and his constant meddling have prompted a number of historians to imply that Frémont instigated the Bear Flag Republic to set the precedent for American annexation. The inevitable result of Frémont's activity, however, was to further strain relations between Americans and Californios. In fact, the first open signs of ethnic hostility grew out of Frémont's leadership. The cries of greaser, directed toward local Californios, resulted from the activities of the Bear Flaggers. Since Frémont was in the forefront of the Bear Flag Republic, he established the dubious legacy of helping to conquer California. The importance of the short-lived, three-week Bear Flag Republic is that it created the illusion of a Texas-style republic, and this was an important precedent for American annexation. Many historians describe the Bear Flaggers as a confused, motley group filled with open racial hostility toward Mexicans and Californios. While there is an element of truth to this idea, this conclusion fails to recognize that the Bear Flaggers did create a semblance of control over at least part of Mexican-California.

The Mexican War and the Annexation of California

On May 13, 1846, President James K. Polk asked Congress for a declaration of war against Mexico. Congress agreed and the United States launched the Mexican War which resulted in the annexation of California. The causes of the Mexican War are complex, but it was due primarily to problems resulting from westward expansion. Americans who came to California dreamed of establishing a Texas-style revolution. Thus, the Texas experience was a significant one. In 1836 the Republic of Texas was established, but Mexico refused to recognize this predominantly American nation. President Andrew Jackson attempted to purchase it, and in 1845 the United States Congress invited Texas into the Union. Shortly after President Polk was inaugurated Mexico charged that American intentions were to illegally annex Texas. Mexico pointed out that Polk had campaigned for the Presidency on the promise of annexing Texas and California. But President Herrera of Mexico realized that his nation was too weak to prevent the United States from annexing Texas and California. John Slidell was quickly dispatched to Mexico City to work out the details of California's purchase. But Herrera changed his mind and Slidell failed to bring home a common agreement on the purchase of Texas. This made war inevitable between the United States and Mexico. The stage was set for the American navy to seize the port of Monterey.

In the early stages of the Mexican War the commander of the Pacific fleet, John D. Sloat, was instructed to occupy the key California port of Monterey, which would establish American hegemony in the Mexican territory. On June 17, 1846, Commodore Sloat, cruising off the coast of Mexico, was informed that Zachary Taylor's forces had clashed with Mexican troops. The stage was set for Sloat to raise the American flag over Monterey. On July 2, 1846, Sloat occupied

Monterey Bay. But Sloat, a sixty-six-year-old military man slated for retirement, wondered whether or not he should seize California. After five days of indecision Sloat finally decided to occupy Monterey. He promised local citizens greater political freedom and guaranteed the lands and civil rights of Mexican-Californians.

When Sloat arrived in the Monterey harbor, there was no armed resistance to American occupation. In fact, many local citizens found it a peculiar situation to see a shipload of foreign sailors proclaim the establishment of a new government. The only casualty in American annexation of California was a woman who broke her leg running from a church to watch Sloat's men land. Following Sloat's arrival political intrigue and confusion began to dominate California. Thomas Oliver Larkin, the well-known American merchant, hoped that Sloat could curb Frémont's excessive personal political ambition. As the American flag was raised on Monterey on July 7, 1846, Larkin and Sloat met to discuss the future of Frémont's Battalion of Volunteers. Both agreed that Frémont's power had to be curbed, but this was not to be the case. But Sloat announced his retirement and Robert Field Stockton assumed command. Sloat's power had lasted less than two weeks, and on July 15, 1846, Commodore Stockton, known as Gassy Bob for his bragging, announced that Frémont's battalion would be officially sworn into the United States Army. Stockton's action alienated most Californios. Frémont's reputation caused him to be hated by most segments of California's diverse population. The most obvious result of this atmosphere was to create bands of Californios and Mexicans who resisted American military controls in California. Organized opposition to American annexation surfaced when Stockton's and Frémont's excessive personal ambitions were recognized by local Californios.

José Castro fled with a hundred man army to Los Angeles to establish a base to resist the conquest of Southern California. The last Mexican governor, Pio Pico, was aware that most Americans desired land. Consequently, he issued more than 800 last-minute land grants in an attempt to forestall the wholesale destruction of Mexican land settlement. But Pico made a strategic blunder by awarding so many Mexican land grants, because it appeared that Governor Pico was acting fraudulently. He went so far as to back date many of the land deeds, and this became the basis for subsequent invalidation of many of the larger land grants. At the conclusion of Pico's hasty land grant binge, it was estimated that between 12 and 13 million acres had been granted to local Mexicans and Californios. Californios were particularly adamant about the necessity to respect Pico's grants, and Sloat and Stockton had issued public proclamations promising that the United States would respect legitimate title to Mexican-Californian lands. The debate over land title was a smoldering issue which broke wide open in the 1850s, but its roots were in the conflict surrounding the Mexican War.

The American occupation of California forced Pico and Castro to flee into Mexico. They vowed to return with an army of liberation, and this stiffened local Californio resistance to annexation in Southern California. In August, 1846, the former marine spy, Archibald Gillespie was left in charge of Southern California. Gillespie's troops, stationed in Los Angeles, acted in a manner which immediately alienated Los Angeles citizens. Arbitrary rules and oppressive acts failed to win friends among Southern California's diverse population.

In addition, Frémont's California battalion of volunteers acted in an inappropriate manner and displayed a type of behavior that was ethnically insensitive and even menacing. It was clear to the Californios that the Bear Flaggers who staffed Frémont's army were little more than a group of revenge-seeking frontiersmen. This created a tension-filled, almost revolutionary atmosphere and forced a showdown in Southern California.

In the fall of 1846, Frémont's army and Commodore Stockton began to organize a military expedition designed to defeat Californio and Mexican sympathizers in Southern California. The result was to stiffen already formidable opposition to American annexation. The stage was set for the first important military test of American control of California. When California was seized, it was divided into two military districts for administrative purposes. Although the Mexican alcaldes were asked to remain in charge, they generally refused to serve their conquerors. The statements of Mexican alcaldes on civil rights and land ownership failed to warn the American military that seeds of dissatisfaction might lead to open rebellion. Aiding this growing discontent was the decision made by American military authorities to impose a strict curfew upon Los Angeles. This use of force and coercion prompted Angelenos to protest American annexation. Armed rebellion was in the making and tensions grew daily in Los Angeles. Gillespie responded by threating those who complained, and this prompted the rebels to organize a native cavalry. The surprising effectiveness of José Flores' combined army of Mexicans and Californios became apparent in a revolt in Southern California against American leadership. On September 24, 1846, Gillespie was forced to withdraw from Los Angeles. One of Gillespie's men, Lean John Brown, rode immediately to San Francisco to inform Stockton of the rebellion. Reinforcements were dispatched immediately to the San Pedro area south of Los Angeles, and American military officials began a military drive against the South.

Southern Californians allowed Gillespie and his men to journey to San Pedro to hail a boat for the trip to Monterey. They were surprised to meet the contingent American military forces who arrived to march upon Los Angeles. On October 8, 1846, the American force met a small army led by José Antonio Carrillo, who surprised the Americans with a hidden cannon and won a psychological victory against the newly arrived occupation forces. The cannon had been buried during the early days of American occupation, and the weapon suddenly provided both a military and psychological edge to the insurgent Californio-Mexican forces. The sixty Californios under Carrillo's leadership dazzled a larger American force with rapier like military thrusts. After five Americans were killed, Gillespie's force withdrew to ships waiting in San Pedro harbor. Because the gun was buried in the garden of Señora Inocencia Reyes, the Californio victory was dubbed the "Battle of the Old Woman's Gun." It was an important boost to the morale of Mexicans and Californios who dreamed of preventing American annexation.

For three months Los Angeles remained the bastion of rebel resistance to American annexation. But American forces were slowly converging upon Southern California. Frémont marched from Monterey with the California Battalion and Commodore Stockton regrouped in San Diego. General Stephen W. Kearny led a detachment of American troops crossing the New Mexico desert, and they converged on California to bring an end to organized and armed resistance to American occupation of California. In essence, American military forces were faced with the perplexing dilemma of reconquering Southern California. From October 20 to November 17, 1846, American military units strengthened their forces for the final assault upon Southern California. As Kearny rode west with a hundred men it boosted the morale of the troops under Frémont, Gillespie, and Stockton in California.

On December 6, 1846, Kearny's force was resting some thirty-five miles north of San Diego when news came that a rebel Californio force was nearby. Kit Carson boisterously suggested that the Californios would not fight and this convinced Kearny to attempt to seize the rebel horses. But the damp weather acted as a deterrent by preventing Kearny's men from using their weapons effectively, and this resulted in twenty-two Americans being killed in the Battle of San Pascal. The rebel victory did not long prevent the systematic conquest of Southern California, however.

A combined force, led by Stockton and Kearny, finally reached Los Angeles in January, 1847. This prompted Governor Flores, who had recently been elected by Southern Californians, to flee to Mexico. Recognizing the precarious nature of the Californio's military situation Andrés Pico surrendered to Frémont's forces. On January 13, 1847, John C. Frémont received the final surrender of California and in a document labeled the Treaty of Cahuenga, Frémont recognized Mexican land ownership, promised full civil rights, and allowed the rebel insurgents to keep their guns and horses. A full pardon was extended to all the rebels and California became a pastoral military district under American army control. Californios believed that they would have the same political self-determination and economic opportunities that they had enjoyed under Mexican rule.

The American Military Legacy and the Mexican War

The Treaty of Cahuenga brought a cessation of hostilities between the Californio military and American troops. When Frémont negotiated the Cahuenga agreement he promised to recognize civil and land rights for local Californios. This seemingly statesmanlike action was the reason a calm set in over Southern California. While some mild opposition continued over American annexation, nevertheless, the general hostility to United States control over California ceased to be an important issue. As local politics calmed, Californians turned to the economic problems of a frontier state. But once the Americans and Californios ceased fighting there suddenly developed a three-way struggle among American military commanders for control of California. For years America's naval and military officers had found it difficult to compromise with one another. A conflict in orders from the nation's capital led to a serious dispute between Frémont and General Kearny over who was actually in command of American-California. During the struggle to subdue Southern California, Frémont had sided with Commodore Robert Field Stockton, and this prompted Stockton to appoint Frémont as a temporary governor of California. Following a period of confusion, orders from Washington clearly established Kearny as California's governor. However, Frémont continued to use the title despite warnings from his superiors. With sagging morale and a number of serious complaints about Frémont's high-handed tactics, there was no choice but to recommend a court martial. General Kearny arrested Frémont and prepared to transport him overland to Washington D.C. for the court martial proceedings. Before leaving for the East, Kearny appointed Colonel Richard Mason as the military governor of California.

On November 2, 1847, Frémont was brought to trial on three charges of insubordination and on failures to obey orders. The nation's press covered the trial with a flair for exposing the conflict inherent in American military matters. After three months of charges and denials, Frémont was found guilty of all charges. The sentence was dismissal from the service. President James K. Polk reviewed the case and announced that he would alter Frémont's punishment. In a shrewd political manner, President Polk agreed with the verdict while announcing that other circumstances allowed for Frémont's sentence to be lightened. In a fit of the rage Frémont resigned from the service, and he scoffed at Polk's offer of executive clemency. Frémont returned to California politics and became a United States Senator. Prior to leaving California Frémont had purchased a 45,000 acre tract—the Rancho Mariposa. Located on the east side of the San Joaquin Valley, it was

San Francisco, 1846–1847

Courtesy, The Bancroft Library

uninhabitable due to hostile Indians. The land was purchased by Thomas Oliver Larkin at Frémont's request for $3000. The question of the legality of the Rancho Mariposa deed brought Frémont actively back into California politics in 1849.

As California was formally passing into the hands of the United States, a number of changes became obvious in Monterey. One was the appearance of an aggressive American press. In 1846 Walter Colton set up an old printing press and introduced California's first English language newspaper, the *Californian.* The influence of the newly created newspaper was obvious when Colton was elected Monterey's alcalde. Americanization also brought political change. By 1848 large numbers of Americans were demanding a state government and equal rights with other parts of the Union. As a military district, California was awkward to govern. Many Californios and Mexicans were strong supporters of state government. Mariano Vallejo believed that the differences between the newly arrived Anglos and local citizens would ease with state government. But Vallejo also demanded that steps be taken to guarantee the civil and land ownership rights of all foreigners in California.

The dawning of American California altered the nature of established institutions. A quiet revolution was in the making in politics. The Gold Rush would alter the local economy to such a degree that Eastern business interests would demand state government. Changes in California society were about to come which would transform the sleepy San Francisco settlement of 800 people into a bustling metropolis of more than 100,000 in less than two years. The lure of gold was about to create a new California.

Bibliographical Essay

The fur trade and the general economic development of the Golden State was one of the earliest attractions for American immigrants. For the Mountain Men see Robert G. Cleland, *This*

Reckless Breed of Men: The Trappers and Fur Traders of the Southwest (1952); Dale L. Morgan, *Jedediah Smith and the Opening of the West* (1953); Rosemary K. Valle, "James Ohio Pattie and the Alta California Measles Epidemic," *California Historical Society Quarterly,* LII (Spring, 1973), 28–36; Iris Wilson, *William Wolfskill: 1798–1866 Frontier Trapper to California Ranchero* (Glendale, 1965); and LeRoy Hafen, editor, *The Mountain Men and the Fur Trade of the Far West* (6 vols., 1965–68).

There is a substantial literature on early foreign schemers in Mexican-California and during the early days of Anglo occupation. For John Sutter see, James P. Zollinger, *Sutter: The Man and His Empire* (1939); John A. Hawgood, "John Augustus Sutter: A Reappraisal," *Arizona and the West,* IV (Winter, 1962), 345–356; Richard Dillon, *The Decline and Fall of Captain John Sutter of California* (1967); and a biography told orally to Hubert Howe Bancroft, *Sutter's Own Story,* edited by Erwin G. Gudde (1936).

The literature on the overland migration to California is voluminous see, George R. Stewart, *The California Trail* (1962); Irving Stone, *Men to Match My Mountains: The Opening of the Far West* (1956); and Rockwell D. Hunt, *John Bidwell: Prince of California Pioneers* (1942). An interesting revision of an old myth about travel to the American West is Thomas F. Andrews, "The Controversial Hastings Overland Guide: A Reassessment," *Pacific Historical Review,* XXXVII (February, 1968), 21–34. This revisionist article credits Hasting's book, *The Emigrants's Guide,* with much more significance than historians have recently attached to it.

The literature on the acquisition of California is large and uneven, see, Norman A. Graebner, *Empire on the Pacific* (1955) for an argument emphasizing the importance of California seaports; Frederick Merk, *Manifest Destiny and Mission in American History* (1963) places the annexation of California in the broader context of American history; Earl Pomeroy, *The Pacific Slope: A History of California, Oregon, Washington, Idaho, Utah and Nevada* is the best interpretive study of California annexation in respect to the Pacific Coast and American history; Frederick Merk, *The Monroe Doctrine and American Expansionism, 1843–1849* (1966) is an important interpretation of Manifest Destiny in light of the Monroe Doctrine; and Charles G. Sellers, *James K. Polk: Continentalist* (1966) is important for the American President's motives.

In order to understand the controversial role of John C. Frémont, see, Ferol Egan, *Frémont, Explorer for a Restless Nation* (1975); Allan Nevins, *Frémont: Pathmarker of the West* (1939); Richard R. Stenberg, "Polk and Frémont, 1845–1846," *Pacific Historical Review,* VII (September, 1938), 211–227; and John C. Frémont, *Memoirs of My Life* (1887) which was not completed but one volume was published. The best castigation of historians and romantics who viewed Frémont as a hero is Bernard DeVoto, *The Year of Decision, 1846* (1942). An interesting account of Frémont's court martial is Kenneth M. Johnson, The Frémont Court Martial (1968).

There are a number of biographies of significant early Americans, see, John A. Hawgood, editor, *First and Last Consul: Thomas Oliver Larkin and the Americanization of California* (1970) for a collection of important Larkin letters and notes on his life; Fred B. Rogers, *William Brown Ide: Bear Flagger* (1962) is interesting on the Bear Flag leader; John A. Hawgood, "John C. Frémont and the Bear Flag Revolution: A Reappraisal," *Southern California Quarterly,* XLIX (June, 1962), 67–96; Doyce Nunis, *The Trials of Isaac Graham* (1967); on Archibald Gillespie's role see Werner H. Marti, *Messenger of Destiny: The California Adventures of Archibald Gillespie, 1846–1847* (1960); and Dwight L. Clarke, *Stephen Watts Kearny, Soldier of the West* (1961).

Amongst the most creative scholarship on foreign interest in California is Sheldon G. Jackson, "Two Pro-British Plots in Alta California," *Southern California Quarterly,* LV (Summer, 1973), 105–40; Sheldon G. Jackson, "The British and the California Dream," *Southern California Quarterly,* LVII (Fall, 1975), 251–70; John A. Hawgood, "A Projected Prussian Colonization of Upper California," *Southern California Quarterly,* XLVIII (December, 1966), 353–68; Russell M. Posner, "A British Consular Agent in California: *The Reports of John A. Forbes, 1843–1846, Southern California Quarterly,* LIII (June, 1971), 101–12.

The early military occupation of California is traced in Theodore Grivas, *Military Governments in California* (1963); and Fred B. Rogers, *Montgomery and the Portsmouth* (1959). An important study for placing California's acquisition into the broader context of the Mexican War is Glenn W. Price, *Origins of the War with Mexico: The Polk-Stockton Intrigue* (1967).

A pioneer attempt to interpret early California is the work of a noted philosopher and well-respected historian see, Josiah Royce, *California, from the Conquest in 1846 to the Second Vigilance Committee in San Francisco; a Study of American Character* (1886, reprinted with a pathbreaking historiographical introduction by Earl Pomeroy, 1971).

The development of Anglo-California is ably covered in Bradford Luckingham, "Libraries and Museums in Emergent San Francisco: A Note on the Pursuit of Culture in the Urban Far West," *The Pacific Historian,* XVII (Fall, 1973), 4–11. Professor Luckingham's extensive work on the urban nature of California is one of the major themes of this textbook. His pioneer interpretive work on San Francisco and the culture of the Golden State is a monumental contribution to California historiography.

6

THE GOLD RUSH AND CALIFORNIA STATEHOOD

Economic and Political Revolution

From the discovery of gold in January, 1848, until California was admitted to the Union in September, 1850, a political and economic revolution occurred which produced the population and business base essential for statehood. The degree of change in California changed every phase of life in the sleepy settlement. San Francisco, for example, grew from a small village of about 800 to a city of 100,000. This rapid rush of settlers brought the institutions necessary for an American-California. Yet, during the gold rush the economic-political revolution was confined primarily to Northern California and the mining regions of the Sierra Nevada. Southern California remained a relatively undeveloped area with a predominent Spanish-speaking population, and this intensified the north-south political rivalry which had carried over from the days of Mexican-California. Since gold was discovered only nine days before the signing of the Treaty of Guadalupe Hidalgo, it was only natural that many discharged veterans from the Mexican War wandered into California. This helped to create a macho frontier society and a local spirit which challenged governmental rules and institutions. Consequently, a turbulent political and economic atmosphere developed in California.

The Gold Rush and the Revolution in California's Economy

It is ironic that Spain and Mexico settled California largely as a result of a thirst for precious metals. The lure of gold and silver had brought the combined resources of Spanish and Mexican military-governmental power into Alta California. Spain had failed to discover gold largely due to the absence of exploration parties searching California's interior. The Franciscan missionaries also added to this failure by concentrating upon Christianizing the Indians. Mexico failed to find gold because they had a number of internal governmental problems which prevented exploration for gold. But there were stories of gold discoveries and a minor Mexican gold rush occurred in the early 1840s.

Francisco López and the Mexican Gold Rush

There were signs of gold in California during the Mexican era. In 1842 Francisco López, a rancher, discovered a small gold deposit in the San Feliciano Canyon in the mountains behind the San Fernando mission. While pulling up some wild onions one day, López noticed gold particles on the roots. Suddenly a minor gold boom began in the area near present day Newhall. For almost

John Sutter, early foreign schemer and founder of Sacramento

Courtesy, The Bancroft Library

two years forty to sixty miners were employed to extract gold. A portion of this gold was sold to the United States mint in Philadelphia, but the sales failed to spark any official interest in California. There were also occasional reports of gold being discovered by Indians or Franciscan missionaries, and the Mexican government displayed some interest in the economic potential in California. A local Los Angeles businessman, Antonio Coronel, invested in mining parties searching for gold and silver deposits. This entreprenurial impulse is in marked contrast to the myth that business values did not predominate in Mexican California. On the contrary, Coronel was an active businessman investing in mining ventures that he believed would bring a substantial return. But the Newhall gold find was an insignificant one and it drew little serious attention. It was important, however, in suggesting the skill of Mexican miners and the business acumen of Californio entrepreneurs.

The Early Gold Rush: The Role of John Sutter

Johann August Sutter had developed an eleven square league ranch known as New Helvetia from two Mexican land grants. Commonly known as Sutter's Fort in present day Sacramento, the settlement was a gathering place for foreign intriguers. Initially, Sutter had hoped to develop a lumber business. He imported a large number of workers and soon mills and shops surrounded Sutter's Fort. One of the characteristics of Sutter's Fort was a multi-ethnic population which included Mexicans, Indians, Hawaiians, Germans and French workers. It also attracted American explorers with schemes for quick wealth. As a result, the reputation surrounding Sutter's Fort was questionable among local Californians. This is an important point, because most people did not believe that gold discovery would be a significant catalyst to the economy.

In January, 1848, James W. Marshall, a thirty-five-year old construction foreman, was dispatched to Coloma Indian land on the American River to construct a sawmill. During the final stages of construction it was discovered that the portion of the creek which turned the main waterwheel was too shallow. After some digging and blasting, particles of gold began to appear at the bottom of the creekbed. On January 28, 1848, Marshall entered Sutter's Sacramento office and quietly showed him some gold nuggets the size of a dime. Every known test was applied to the gold to determine its content, and they were soon convinced it was gold. It was no longer possible to obtain a Mexican land grant so Sutter negotiated an agreement with the Coloma Indians to lease a twelve-mile-square track of land for three years. For $150 worth of hats, shirts,

James W. Marshall, the discoverer of
California gold

Courtesy, The Bancroft Library

flour and other miscellaneous goods Sutter was granted the right to mine the Indian lands. It is interesting that while Sutter bragged to everyone about the gold discovery, he would then ask them to keep the gold discovery a secret. This peculiar brand of behavior did little to authenticate the gold rush. Also, Sutter's reputation as a liar caused many to discount the stories of mineral wealth.

To Sutter the discovery of gold offered the possibility of immense wealth. He had constructed New Helvetia along the lines of a medieval feudal society with himself as the local baron. It was an entirely self-sufficient settlement which included a fort, farm, trading post, and a livestock ranch replete with cattle, horses, sheep and hogs. Only the difficulty in obtaining labor prevented Sutter from setting up an independent republic in the Sacramento Valley. The grandiose nature of Sutter's thinking was shown when he dispatched one of his employees to request that the American military governor, Colonel Richard B. Mason, grant Sutter the right to all California gold deposits. Sutter supported his request by sending six ounces of gold samples to the military government. Colonel Mason refused Sutter's request, but he began to speculate upon the wealth possible in the new gold discovery. It appears that Sutter's gold find was taken seriously by American military officials, and they began to express enthusiasm to military and government officials. During 1848 President James Knox Polk began to quietly promote migration to California. This was a prelude to Polk's exhortation to search out any economic and settlement potential in California and to reap the profits of the gold fields.

Although the news of a gold discovery at Sutter's saw mill circulated throughout California, few local citizens were excited about the possibility of immediate wealth. Rumors of gold had been frequent in Spanish and Mexican California, and the general feeling was that it was just a good story. In fact, it was not until March 15, 1848, that the San Francisco weekly newspaper, the *Californian,* mentioned the gold discovery. In a small story on the last page the gold discovery was noted, but the lack of conviction in the story made it appear to be an unimportant event. Ten days later, another San Francisco based weekly, the *California Star,* printed a short notice which further contributed to the general skepticism surrounding Sutter's gold find. The difficulty in convincing Californians about the gold find was a blessing in disguise. The first gold rush was a small, localized phenomena which built permanent mining towns and established the institutions necessary for the frenetic 1849 gold rush.

The Season of '48: A Quiet Revolution in the Sierra

On May 12, 1848, a mild form of gold fever struck Californians when Sam Brannan, a Mormon merchant, arrived in San Francisco with gold samples. Brannan, a mercantile store owner in Sacramento, stood to profit from a rush to the gold fields. He told a story of possible wealth for anyone who was able to scoop gold from the ground. Brannan's tales of simple diggings were not necessarily false ones. However, he had no idea of the magnitude of the gold discovery. Brannan's only interest was to create a business impluse in the Sierra. Soon San Francisco emptied as gold fever hit California.

Brannan's tale of gold exerted a hypnotic hold on San Francisco. Merchants closed their shops, skilled and unskilled working men left their jobs, and most itinerant travelers headed for the Sierra Nevada foothills. Brannan's general store at Sutter's Fort was well stocked to meet the gold rush. Prior to lobbying in San Francisco, Brannan had purchased every piece of equipment

Mining life in the Sierra Nevada

and type of supply necessary for miners. This created a price revolution as shovels jumped from $1 to $10, and the cost of most other goods reached epidemic proportions.

The gold craze spread to every corner of California and even the most skeptical acknowledged the importance of the gold nuggets coming out of the motherlode country. Almost every town in California lost young men to the gold fields. The frenzy for gold became so prevalent that the San Jóse jailer transported ten Indian convicts to the gold fields to work his claim. The Military Governor reported it was impossible to keep his troops from deserting. At one point only the Military Governor and his cook remained to provide protection for Californians. In July, 1848, Governor Mason toured the gold fields to see firsthand the mystic hold that the gold rush had upon Californians. He came away convinced that California's population and wealth would soon be sufficient enough to make it a state. As a result, Colonel Mason began to encourage local citizens to press for immediate statehood.

The season of '48 was a crude gold rush. Most of the miners worked surface diggings. Much of the early gold rush centered around surface diggings and shallow streams, and operated at a low technological level. The gold was gathered in a pan full of sand and gravel and washed out with water leaving the heavier gold in the bottom of the pan. This crude method was soon replaced by the cradle. Isaac Humphrey, an experienced Georgia miner, introduced the cradle. This device was a simple oblong box mounted on a set of rockers with a mesh wire bottom. Water was run through the dirt and sand while the device was rocked and the process left only gold flakes at the bottom of the wire meshed rocker. It was a simple technique and indicated the low level of mining technology in the California gold fields.

Many times miners were forced to create technological innovations. Problems with water demanded that dams be constructed, and this brought the earliest scientific impulse to gold country. Soon canals and ditches were built to bring water to the most obscure mining claims. In the early 1850s river mining required extensive planning and a heavy financial outlay before a substantial monetary return was realized.

The major change in California mining occurred in the early 1850s when hydraulic mining was introduced in the Sierra Nevada foothills. This process involved bringing a stream of heavy water pressure down upon a hillside to wash away the dirt. While an ecologically disastrous method, hydraulic mining introduced the elements of big business to the California gold fields. One mining company spent more than a half million dollars to develop hydraulic mining and soon ditches as long as fifty miles could be seen in Northern California. The importance of hydraulic mining is that it was a large scale industrial development which brought big business into California. It changed the nature of the mining economy by transforming a treasure hunt atmosphere into one resembling a modern capitalistic venture. However, prior to the "scientific revolution" in the mines, California experienced difficulties due to the lack of established law and order.

One of the earliest problems concerned the regulation of mining claims. Mining communities were often founded before established legal institutions began to function. A hurried form of mining camp law developed to fill this legal void. It ignored the rights of Indians and most foreign mining claims during the gold rush. But it was also difficult to decide which mining claims were legal, because there was no Federal mining law in the California military district. In the transition from Mexican to American-California there seemed to be little legal protection or precedent for mining claims. Consequently, the mining camps developed their own laws. Ad hoc organizations of miners formed instant courts to judge the validity of a claim. Each mining community organized a mining district and elected representatives to draw up a set of laws. Institutional growth was rapid as more than 500 mining camps established the first viable political and legal foundations in California. They were important in that they reflected the tendency for American frontiersmen to engage in a highly formalized, almost legalistic, type of local self-government. Moreover, early American miners repeatedly mentioned the past tradition of frontier self-government dating back to the Mayflower Compact. This indicates a degree of historical awareness which helped to establish American hegemony. Soon energetic Americans set up a type of local mining law which defined the size of each land claim and imposed rules for working it. The mentality of early American miners was one influenced by the Protestant work ethnic. If you didn't work a mine or a piece of land someone else could pre-empt it under mining camp law. In California land title was more a permit to use the land than outright ownership.

A boom town atmosphere permeated California's mining camps. Towns sprang up within weeks in the foothills of the Sierra. The prospect of quick wealth was the element which created the psychological drive necessary for gold miners to continue the search for precious metals. California miners generally failed to recognize the uncertainty of gold veins and the hard work required for quick wealth. Many newcomers realized that business was the quickest means to a respectable income. Charles Crocker, Collis P. Huntington, and Mark Hopkins were merchants during the gold rush days, and they used their business skills to form the Central Pacific railroad. By providing the miners with tools, food, and clothing many of California's subsequent economic and political leaders began their careers.

The economic advantages of California's gold rush made San Francisco the fourth most productive port in the United States. More than $322 million was produced during the gold rush, and the economic base was laid for modern California. There were also a number of political changes during the gold rush.

One of the most significant political innovations in California mining communities was the development of the office of the alcalde. This office was a transformation of the old Mexican alcalde who governed in lay cities. Each mining district elected a person to record deeds, thus an alcalde's primary duties were to register claims and settle disputes over mining and land deeds. The alcalde also acted as a judge and jury, but many times he selected a panel of local citizens who acted as arbiters to aid in deciding mining claims. The alcalde system was an example of Spanish and Mexican influences permeating the American mining community. In mining communities the alcalde was a combination mayor, court system, and city government. While an alcalde system worked very well as a means of deciding American land claims, Spanish and Mexican mining claims were generally ignored, and this led to the first ethnic tensions in the gold fields. Despite these crude attempts at justice, however, lynchings and vigilantism continued to predominate. The hostile racial oppression toward Mexcians, Californios, and Indians created a vexing problem for early American settlers. Often extralegal means were used to punish individuals, and this created a law and order problem in gold country. Consequently, one of the side effects of the gold rush was to create a disregard for the law and a lack of respect for established institutions. It was difficult to fully develop Californian civilization because of ethnic conflict and law and order problems.

Racial conflict was inevitable in California's gold fields. The earliest mining impulse was an individualistic one, as the lone miner operated without assistance from the outside world. Initially, mining techniques were so simple that no equipment was required and little investment was needed to begin a mining operation. This type of placer mining gave way to the more sophisticated cradle or rocker methods of mining, and eventually technological types of mining emerged. When the United States acquired California, Mexican and Chilean miners were already very successful in gold country. Soon Americans were forcibly evicting Mexican miners from prosperous claims. But Mexican miners on the American River fought back and soon Americans were talking of legislation to prevent foreign miners from operating in California.

The increased violence in California's mining communities was an indication that cultural differences were creating racial tensions. Soon large numbers of Mexicans moved into the San Joaquin Valley. In effect, racial differences forced Latins out of the mines and into ranching areas. In 1849 Chile dispatched a war ship to look after his nationals after riots took place in San Francisco's neighborhood dubbed Little Chile. These first signs of ethnic strife were an ominous indication of future racial problems. But by 1848–1849 gold fever was on everyone's mind.

The excitement surrounding the gold rush was not limited to the United States. In 1848 Hawaii was hit by gold fever, because of supplied labor and services to San Francisco. News of the gold rush passed quickly among the Hawaiians, and soon they were immigrating to California in search of quick wealth. Oregonians talked about the potential for fortune hunting, and within a year almost two-thirds of the territories 10,000 people migrated to California. In northern Mexico, in the state of Sonora, miners began to answer the call of the gold rush. Then the eastern press discovered that gold sold newspapers. By the winter of 1848–1849 there were well-circulated stories of the California gold rush, and the stage was set for a population boom unprecedented in American history.

The 49ers: The Gold Rush as the Catalyst to Permanent Settlement

In December, 1848, President James Knox Polk's annual State of the Union message explored the changes in the United States due to the recent gold discovery. President Polk used statements from Governor Mason to urge Americans to explore and exploit California's new-found mineral wealth. Unwittingly, Polk was encouraging the migration of thousands of permanent American settlers to California. The end result was a well-organized settlement in Northern California, and the transformation of a raucous new American society. Two days after Polk's address, a tea caddy filled with 230 ounces of gold was delivered to the President by Governor Mason, and it was promptly displayed at the War Department to illustrate the vast potential for sudden wealth in California. Suddenly a mania for gold swept the United States. The influx of American settlers created a rush to California, and historians point out that the season of '49 created an economically sound and socially active settlement.

One obvious change in California was the growth of cooperative societies and clubs. Cultural and social activity was transmitted from Boston and New York. Every piece of information concerning California suddenly appeared valuable to Easterners, while Californians emulated Eastern culture. It is not surprising that the publication of guidebooks to the American West became an important reflection of this mania for material about California. The most successful guidebook was Lansford Hastings, *The Emigrant's Guide to the Gold Mines*. The Hastings' book was an instant best seller when it was published in New York in December, 1845. Although it contained only thirty pages, there was a fascinating do-it-yourself guide for traveling to the land in California. Maps of the gold mining regions were included in later editions, but they proved to be virtually worthless. *The Emigrant's Guide* was a book of dubious value as the Donner party discovered when it followed its geographical shortcuts to doom and disaster. The popularity of Hastings' guide book was an indicaton that Americans were interested in permanent settlement in California.

The three routes to California were via the Isthmus of Panama, traveling around Cape Horn, or the Overland Trail. Perhaps the most romantic route was the Overland Trail, and its scenic beauty conjured up images of adventure.

In 1846 the Donner party was trapped in the Sierra and they engaged in cannibalism in order to survive their confinement in the mountains. The tragic fate of the Donner party indicated that experience was necessary for settlement. Most migrants traveling to California were frontier farmers who were escaping the confining atmosphere of the east or middle west. Mariano Vallejo casually remarked that many Yankees were hostile to Spanish speaking Californians, and he believed this showed the low level of education among Americans. Since Vallejo was fluent in Latin and spoke several languages, he found it amusing that the Californios and Mexicans were often stereotyped as less than civilized. Vallejo confided to a friend that deteriorating relations between Americans and Spanish-speaking Californians would continue to plague California.

In 1849 a stampede of gold prospectors, businessmen, and farmers began to alter the shape and structure of California civilization. Cities were bursting with recently arrived settlers and goods, and the major California cities like Monterey, San Francisco, and San Diego did not have the facilities to accommodate the newcomers. An Asiatic cholera epidemic struck and killed more than 5,000 people in the summer of 1849. In addition to disease, geographical obstacles, a shortage of supplies, and a lack of grass for grazing animals hindered permanent settlement. From the available records, it was very difficult to accurately record the number of Americans who traveled

The Hopkins and Crocker mansions, San Francisco: wealth in the aftermath of the gold discovery

into California. The best estimate is that more than 150,000 Americans migrated to California to find a new home in 1849–1850.

The California Gold Rush: A Social Perspective

One of the byproducts of the California gold rush was the creation of a cosmopolitan society. All nationalities were attracted to the gold fields and this helped to create a diverse cultural strain. By 1850 small ethnic communities sprang up in the mining camps and in the major cities like San Francisco. The multi-ethnic tone of early San Francisco prompted many visitors to comment on the variety of fine food, and the presence of numerous European opera productions astounded many travelers. But it was still a quiet social life which developed in San Francisco. During the heyday of the gold rush only 2 percent of the city's population was female, and by 1850 it had increased to only 8 percent. It was not uncommon for photographs of that era to show one finely dressed woman standing among eight or ten men in the gold fields. One remarkable woman, Louise Amelia Knapp Smith Clapp, wrote a series of observations known as the *Dame Shirley Letters*. This small book described the life of the only woman in a typical mining camp in 1851 and 1852. The 23 letters illustrated the problems created by frontier civilization, and Mrs. Clapp admirably chronicled the fear and violence which resulted from declining gold deposits. The *Dame Shirley Letters* provide one of the first documentary sources to examine Anglo-Mexican differences. The problems of women and minorities were very similar in nature within California's mining communities. All ethnic minorities and women faced hostile attitudes when they stepped out of the bounds of established conformity.

The mode of conformity in the mines was the result of a change in dress and attitudes brought about by Levi Strauss. The young Jewish merchant migrated from the east, and helped to set clothing standards when he began making heavy trousers from tent material that he had brought to California. Originally, Strauss came to California to repair and manufacture tents. It was ironic that he failed in this venture, because he used the remainder of his material to found the Levi Strauss Company which popularized jeans in the mines. A number of historians have commented on the lack of individuality in dress and suggested that this indicated a general conservatism in the mining regions. This is an erroneous assumption, because jeans were heavy trousers with a belt which could hold knives and guns. Thus, Levi Strauss' jeans were more of a necessity than a sign of total conformity. But it is a strange twist of history that Strauss was forced to use the tent fabric to make his jeans, thereby creating what became a multi-million dollar clothing industry. Jeans became accepted for social purposes, and this created a revolution in western dress.

The social highlight of the mining camps was the presence of female entertainers. Many women came to California's gold fields to find a husband, but the general reason for migrating west was to find instant wealth in the gold fields. While many women found husbands and a simple life in California, others came for business opportunities. The dance halls were dominated by Latin and Australian women, and French girls ran many of the gambling clubs which sprang up in the Sierra Nevada. Women also had a stablizing influence upon most mining communities. Many times churches were built in a mining settlement to bury a woman. The church at Gold Run, for example, was built to bury a young school teacher who died suddenly. Rather than bury her in a saloon, a church was hastily constructed. This illustrates the concern for traditional institutions.

The theater brought a form of advanced culture to the miners. The most popular plays were performed in the various mining communities, but equally popular was a morality play, "The Reformed Drunkard." It spoke of the evils of alcohol while fifty drunken miners roared their approval. In San Francisco in the years after statehood, more than 900 different plays were performed, 48 operas were sung in five languages, and 66 separate minstrel shows entertained local citizens. The best known performers were Lola Montez and Lotta Crabtree. Lola Montez' reputation was similar to that of recent Hollywood sex symbols. She posed intermittently as the daughter of a Spanish gypsy, the daughter of a Turkish Sultan or the daughter of the famous English Lord Byron. In reality, Montez was born in Ireland in 1818, and she was married to an English officer for a short time. After her divorce Montez toured Europe as a dancer. After an affair with the composer Franz Liszt, she married a young man ten years her junior. In desperate need of money, she came to San Francisco in the early 1850s. She became an instant success with her spider dance, in which she slithered around the stage warding off imaginery spiders. The legendary performances of the spider dance created a very profitable reputation and career for Lola Montez. Her career was always a turbulent one, and a few weeks after arriving in San Francisco she married a third husband. After moving to Grass Valley, Miss Montez discovered a young performer, Lotta Crabtree. The young Lotta was taught to act, sing, and dance, and she was a perfect performing companion for Lola Montez. Many contemporary accounts suggest that

Lola Montez, the famous spider dancer

the spider dance was an early day form of exotic dancing which excited the miners and produced an economic windfall for Lotta and Lola.

The social history of California during the gold rush is a blend of sophisticated Shakespearean plays combined with low-level dance hall entertainment. In many respects this duality mirrored the upper and lower extremes of California's newly created gold country society. There was something for everyone in the newly created gold rush society.

The California Gold Rush: A Summary

The California gold rush brought a new economy and a vibrant social settlement to the Golden State. Commercial growth, urban expansion, and cultural diversity were the hallmarks of the gold rush. The sleepy province of Mexican-California was transformed into a booming civilization. By the 1850s, 91 newspapers and magazines were published in California, including seven in foreign languages. Almost half a million people a year came to California to hunt for gold, and this strained governmental, social, and economic institutions. Much of the confusion surrounding California in the 1850s can be traced to the rapid growth during the gold rush. In summary, the importance of the gold mania was in its creation of an Americanized California.

Courtesy, The Bancroft Library

Lotta Crabtree, post goldrush entertainer

California and State Making: The First Constitution

The struggle among American military personnel prevented the implementation of any workable form of civil government. In effect, the military governor acted in civil matters, and this angered a number of citizens. In February, 1847, the San Francisco newspaper, the *California Star,* called for a constitutional convention to write a state constitution which would lead to statehood. As a military district, California was poorly governed, but President Polk did not have the power to create territorial government. Only Congress could allow Governor Mason to implement territorial policy. But Congress was slow to act on the question of creating a California territory, because there were a number of problems with the national debate over slavery. Many congressmen believed that California was important in an eventual compromise over slavery.

One of the strongest voices for statehood was Walter Colton. Prior to leaving California, Robert Field Stockton had appointed Colton as Monterey's alcalde. A graduate of Yale University,

Colton had also studied at the Andover Theological Seminary, and he came to California in 1845 to seek his fortune. After his appointment to office, Colton's intellectual abilities and his willingness to deal fairly with people prompted the voters of Monterey to continue to reelect him. Colton urged Californians to think of immediate statehood and to drop any thoughts of territorial government.

The discord between the North and the South over slavery was a significant influence upon Congress' indecision in setting up territorial government in California. In the end this worked to California's favor as statehood was used as a political compromise to help avoid the Civil War. Thus, as California was governed in a virtual vacuum, local public opinion demanded immediate statehood. The only major administrative official in California was the alcalde, and this was one of the main reasons for demanding a more stable form of government.

There were signs of local government developing in California. In San Francisco in August, 1847, a town council of six men was elected to assist the alcalde. Governor Mason stipulated that local government be financed with customs duties, and he rigorously collected taxes to insure adequate government funds. As local government grew stronger and California's mining wealth encouraged the growth of the population, a general restiveness developed over military government. It was generally agreed that California was too populous and too wealthy to remain a military district.

When General Bennett Riley arrived in California in April, 1849, to assume the Military governorship, public opinion pressured him to call a state constitutional convention for the fall of 1849. The drive for statehood intensified when the United State's Congress adjourned in May, 1849, without providing territorial government for California. One of Riley's prime considerations in calling for a state constitution was his fear of Mexican institutions continuing to dominate California. The transformation to an American-dominated society was the reason these fears of Mexican influences were aired publicly in Northern California. There was no better example of the transformation brought by the gold rush than the increase in San Francisco's population from 800 in 1848 to 6,000 the following year and to over 100,000 by 1850. Lots in the center of San Francisco sold for $10,000, and a local police force, the Regulators, emerged to give a semblance of order to San Francisco. The Regulators were a volunteer police force who attempted to control the mounting crime rate. It was the continued increase in murders, robberies, and other forms of violence which led to the demand for state government.

The delegates to the Monterey Constitutional Convention were selected by a vote in which all male citizens of California twenty-one years old or older who claimed California as their place of residence established eligibility. The elections resulted in 48 delegates, ten from Southern California and 38 from Northern California, who were instructed to convene in Monterey in September, 1849, to write a state constitution. The Constitutional Convention was dominated by representatives of the Sierra mining regions. For this reason, the final document prevented banking from developing and excluded the assessment of gold from the tax structure. The final result was a weak constitution that would have to be rewritten in 1878, but the delegates meeting at Colton Hall in Monterey produced a framework of government which secured admission to the Union the following year.

The Minority Impulse in the Constitutional Convention

The Monterey Constitutional Convention of 1849 is the only major event in California history which has been strongly influenced by Mexican-Americans. The Spanish-speaking representatives made up more than 16% of the delegates and were unusually vocal in defending minority rights. The "native delegation" as it was dubbed sat at one table dressed in traditional garb. Many of the Californios had been in the middle of political battles with the American invaders for a number of years. Jóse A. Carrillo, for example, was one of the signatories of the Treaty of Cahuenga, and he had been instrumental in delaying Southern California's annexation. Mariano Vallejo and Pablo de la Guerra were the leaders of the Californio delegation. Vallejo was a moderate, compromising voice, and this split the Californios. His nephew, Pablo de la Guerra, had been an important voice in Santa Barbara politics since 1838, and he was instrumental in challenging the delegates who were intent upon restricting the rights of Mexicans, Californios, and Indians. Another significant voice was Jóse M. Covarrubias who was born in France, but as secretary to Governor Pio Pico had become an important political voice supporting Californio land ownership. The Californios were very skillful in parliamentary debate, and threatened to bolt the convention if they were not heard on key issues. This confrontation tactic was very successful and it allowed the Californios to mold key provisions on voter qualifications, taxation, state boundaries, and civil liberties.

The Californios' influence would have been greater had they voted as a bloc on key constitutional questions. However, on 35 roll-call votes they split on 17 issues. It was this division between northern Californios like Vallejo and southern Californios like de la Guerra which doomed the Mexican-American political influence. Yet, the Californios did unite in the face of arguments on the question of limiting civil rights. Pablo de la Guerra, for example, opposed a suggestion to limit voting to white males, and he argued that many Californios were dark-skinned and to disenfranchise them would be a travesty. De la Guerra pointed out that the Treaty of Guadalupe Hidalgo guaranteed citizenship. The Californios were particularly incensed with provisions to ban the Indians from voting.

Another key contribution of the Californio delegation was to protest the heavy taxes upon land and the general lack of taxation upon gold. The Californios demanded the election of local tax assessors to insure equitable taxation of ranch land. Jóse Carrillo argued that since the ranchers paid a heavier tax they should have more representation in the state legislature. This was easily voted down as was Carrillo's suggestion that Santa Barbara become the capital. But Pablo de la Guerra was successful in securing a provision providing that all laws be printed in Spanish. When the Constitutional Convention broke up the Californios were generally satisfied with their efforts, and they provided most of the liberal provisions written into the new California constitution.

The Monterey Constitutional Convention: The Main Debates

After electing Dr. Robert Semple, a well-known newspaperman, as the permanent chairman of the Constitutional Convention, the delegates began the arduous task of writing a state constitution. The delegates ranged in age from 25 to 53 years old, and the median age was 36. In terms of occupation, 16 were farmers, 14 were lawyers, 9 were merchants, and one delegate listed his profession as "elegant leisure." In general, the members of the Monterey Constitutional Convention were white, middle-class, and Protestant.

The first important issue evolved around the question of whether or not California should apply for immediate statehood. Many Americans believed that territorial government was preferable to statehood, because federal money could be used to develop California. However, the majority of delegates pointed to California's wealth and its burgeoning population as an indication that statehood was the appropriate course. The Californios supported territorial government, because they believed that large landowners would otherwise bear an unusually heavy share of taxation.

On the question of whether or not California should be a free or slave state, there was a lengthy debate which resulted in a decision to apply for statehood as a free state. Although fifteen members of the Constitutional Convention had migrated from the South, most of the delegates either opposed slavery or realized that it would be a potential block to admission to the Union.

Equally important to the delegates was the status of big business. A number of delegates had experienced a variety of problems in business including bankruptcy. Thomas Oliver Larkin argued that banks were necessary to ensure the credit and lending potential which could create a healthy business climate. Delegates who opposed banking argued that hard money transactions did not require banking institutions. They also pointed out that banks led to small numbers of investors amassing huge sums of money. William Gwin of Mississippi argued that he had gone bankrupt in the Panic of 1837 due to a lack of governmental controls over banking. This opinion reflected that of the majority of the delegates and banks were severely restricted in the Constitution of 1849.

The banking issue touched off a fierce debate over how California government was to be financed. The delegates established a $300,000 limit on spending by the state legislature, but inserted a provision for increased spending if state voters approved it. On the question of taxation, the delegates decided that all property should be taxed on its value. Local tax assessors would establish this value and the tax rate. Since tax collectors would be elected in local elections, this quieted fears of ranchers who believed that they would pay a disproportionately high tax.

Establishing a state boundary was a vexing issue at the Monterey Constitutional Convention. The debate was both heated and long, and it revealed a great deal about the delegates. The primary question was over the eastern boundary. Oregon and Mexico provided the northern and southern boundaries, but the question of an eastern boundary evolved into large state and small state factions. The large staters argued that Colorado or Utah should be the boundary. But such an extreme boundary created problems, because the thousands of Mormons settled around Salt Lake were not represented at the Constitutional Convention. Dr. Robert Semple argued that the Sierra should be the natural boundary, and he exhibited a strong anti-Mormon tone in his rhetoric. When the President and Congress indicated that statehood might be threatened should the large state proposal carry, the delegates swiftly voted for the Sierra boundary.

There was a number of enlightened features in the California Constitution. A liberal strain was apparent in the provision for public schools and a university. The free public school system was instructed to meet for at least three months each year. Married women were allowed to own property, a concession designed to encourage female migration to California. Dueling was forbidden, and this was another example of democratic liberalism. These advances were among the most forward looking political concessions in western American history and stamped California as a leading liberal state.

There was also a strong strain of conservatism in the Monterey Constitutional Convention. The restrictions upon banking are the best example of this philosophy. Bank notes were illegal, thus reflecting a fear of paper money. While banks were restricted, provisions were made for associations to hold gold and silver deposits for business interests. The delegates, uncertain how to promote, feared that a capitalistic economy would develop which might exclude the vast majority of Californians from business ventures. The end result was to create a stagnant economic picture and to set the stage for the revision of key economic portions of the state's original constitution.

The Monterey Constitutional Convention of 1849: A Summary

The liberal-conservative differences among convention delegates made compromise a necessity, and these compromises led to a highly conventional state government. A bill of rights was included with the typical guarantees of assembly, religion, and speech, but it also guaranteed foreign residents of the state the same rights of citizenship and of property. Qualifications for voting were relatively simple. All white males over the age of 21 who had been residents for 30 days were granted the franchise. This applied not only to Americans, but to every Mexican who decided to claim citizenship under the terms of the Treaty of Guadalupe-Hidalgo.

The distribution of governmental powers was a common one. A governor, a judicial system, and a bicameral legislature were created to provide adequate government. A two-house legislature with a senate and an assembly was structured so that members were elected to two-year terms, as was the executive branch. This provision reflected a suspicion of government officials who remained too long in power. There was general agreement that lengthy stays in office led to political corruption. Most of the institutions and provisions in the California Constitution were copied from the Iowa and New York constitutions. The founding fathers of California state government were political pragmatists who while representing the interests of their local constituency, fully intended to produce a workable government. In general, sectional and partisan political issues were set aside to ensure that government functioned smoothly in the Golden State.

Once the document was completed it was distributed to local citizens in both English and Spanish translations. All citizens were included in the ratification process and more than $10,000 was spent in publicizing the new California Constitution. In October and November, 1849, the Constitution was debated in the midst of election campaigns for the new state offices. All the candidates supported the new Constitution and this was reflected in a vote of more than 12,000 for approval, and only a little more than 800 who disapproved the document. The governor was Peter Burnett of Sacramento, an Independent Democrat, whose campaign benefited from the presence of his two beautiful daughters. Burnett was born in Nashville, Tennessee, in 1807 and as a young man he went into politics in the Oregon Territory and was elected to the legislature. He made a local name by opposing the sale of alcholic beverages and arguing for legislation to exclude Blacks from migrating to the American West. In 1848 Burnett migrated to California to open a law business and to advise John Sutter on fiscal matters. His successful gubernatorial campaign owed as much to the large numbers of transplanted Oregonians as it did to his alluring daughters. On December 20, 1849, Bennett Riley, the Military governor, turned over the reins of government to Burnett. Although Riley had no constitutional authority to make such a decision, he did it because he believed it was in the best interests of California government.

In sum, California had framed a new Constitution and implemented a new government without authorization from the United States Congress. It was now up to Congress to decide whether or not California had acted legally. Much to California's benefit the controversy over slavery in national politics caused Congress to overlook the independent attitude taken by the Golden State. The United States Congress approved California statehood as part of a compromise to avoid Civil War. The two United States Senators from California, William Gwin and John C. Frémont, were popular and influential figures in the nation's capital and they were extremely helpful in gaining the passage of the Compromise of 1850, which granted California statehood. On September 9, 1850, California entered the Union.

Bibliographical Essay

The literature on the Gold Rush is voluminous and very entertaining. For the best general studies see, John W. Caughey, *Gold Is the Cornerstone* (1948), republished as *The California Gold Rush* (1975). Caughey's study is the finest overall treatment of the Gold Rush and it is excellent reading. An equally impressive book is Rodman Paul's, *California Gold* (1947) because it places a great deal of emphasis upon technology and legal aspects of the mining industry. Charles H. Shinn's. *Mining Camps: A Study of American Frontier Government* (1885) is an excellent study of how not to write mining history. For years it has been erroneously described as a "classic study" of American mining, but this critical acclaim ignores its bias toward foreign miners and its preaching of American virtues. For an important and highly interpretive work on ethnic mining, see Richard H. Peterson, *Manifest Destiny in the Mines: A Cultural Interpretation of Anti-Mexican Nativisn in California, 1848–1853* (1975) and Leonard Pitt, "The Beginnings of Nativism in California," *Pacific Historical Review,* XXX (February, 1961), 23–38.

Some interesting biographical material is Theressa Gay, *James Marshall, Discoverer of California Gold* (1967); Paul Bailey, *Sam Brannan and the California Mormons* (1953); and the account of an army lt., Bernarr Cresap, "Early California as Described by Edward O. C. Ord," *Pacific Historical Review,* XXI (November, 1952), 329–40.

Recent scholarship which places the gold phenomena in a broad perspective is Ralph J. Roske, "The World Impact of the California Gold Rush, 1849–1857," *Arizona and the West,* V (Autumn, 1963), 187–232; Ralph P. Bieber, "California Gold Mania," *Mississippi Valley Historical Review,* XXXV (June, 1948), 3–28; and Charles Bateson, *Gold Fleet to California: Forty-Niners from Australia and New Zealand* (1964).

There is an excellent body of contemporary letters and diaries of the gold rush see, Gary F. Kurutz, "California is quite a different place now: The Gold Rush letters and sketches of William Hubert Burgees," *California History,* LVI (Fall, 1977), 211–229 for the observations of an artist, jeweler, miner and teacher in California's gold rush. For the season of 1848 see, James Carson, *Early Recollections of the Mines* (1852) and E. Gould Buffum, *Six Months in the Mines* (1850). The classic study of letters from the mines by a knowledgable articulate woman was written by Louise Amelia Knapp Smith Clappe, and published under the psuedonym Dame Shirley, *The Shirley Letters from the California Mines* (1949 edition). A series of letters which interpret the gold rush from contemporary standards is William D. Wyman, *California Emigrant Letters* (1952). Another useful contemporary account is Robert Wienpahl, editor, *A Gold Rush Voyage on the Bark Orion* (1978).

A pioneering historiographical work on mining two decades after the gold rush is Richard H. Peterson, *The Bonanza Kings: The Social Origins and Business Behavior of Western Mining Entrepreneurs, 1870–1900* (1977). Peterson's sophisticated study is a study of the social origins of western mining magnates, and it is only peripheral to California. However, *The Bonanza Kings* is an important piece of scholarship in reminding California historians how much work remains to be done on individual mining barons. For an excellent attempt to test the ideas of Frederick Jackson Turner in mining territory see, Richard H. Peterson, "The Frontier Thesis and Social Mobility on the Mining Frontier," *Pacific Historical Review,* XLIII (February, 1975), 52–67.

The United States Department of the Army, Sacramento District Corps of Engineers has commissioned some excellent studies which examine mining see, W. Turrentine Jackson, Stephen D. Mikesell and Harvey Schwartz, *Historical Survey of the New Melones Project Area* (1976) for a study of the parts of Calaveras and Tuolumne counties covered by New Melones. It is a pathbreaking look at local history with an emphasis on the growth and development of mining, water power, transportation, and ranching from Spanish discovery to the 1970s.

The road to statehood and the early Constitution is sketched in William H. Ellison, *A Self-Governing Dominion: 1849–1860* (1950); Earl Pomeroy, "California, 1846–1860: Politics of a Representative Frontier State," *California Historical Society Quarterly,* XXXII (December, 1953), 291–302; and William E. Franklin, "Peter H. Burnett and the Provisional Government Movement," *California Historical Society Quarterly,* XL (June, 1961), 123–36.

For the role of Mexican-Americans during the Monterey Constitutional Convention of 1849 see, Leonard Pitt, *The Decline of the Californios: A Social History of Spanish-Speaking Californians, 1846–1890* (1966) for a pioneer interpretation of Californio ideas and attitudes during the Constitutional Convention.

7

CALIFORNIA: THE FIRST DECADE OF STATEHOOD

Statehood

In the first decade of statehood California grew from a frontier settlement with precarious social, economic and political institutions into a thriving civilization. Most Californians found it difficult to adjust to the violence, the vigilante mentality, and the instability of government which characterized the 1850s. As greedy politicians established well-organized political machines excessive patronage and open bribery made the honest politico an extinct species. There was a general public apathy as most Californians realized that political reform was not a popular idea. It was not until the secret or Australian ballot was introduced in 1891 that elections began to take on a semblance of honesty. Yet, this was a colorful time in which the most obscure and ordinary citizen could become a power broker in the political or business arena. The general trend in California politics and business activity was to encourage open corruption and a free wheeling attitude which ignored the law.

The Age of the Common Man descended upon California during the 1850s, and the idea was reinforced that anyone could serve as governor or make a million dollars. Once a political party gained control of the state, anyone who received an appointive political office was expected to donate a portion of their salary to the party. The Democratic party informed all current office-holders that ten percent of their salary must be donated to party coffers. The result was to provide large sums of money for political campaigning, and the free flowing champagne during election week was financed from this money.

The degree of patronage or appointive political offices was massive in mid-nineteenth century California. In the major cities offices like the city attorney, positions on the fire department, and jobs as policemen were ones which a small number of politicians appointed loyal party members to fill. Federal patronage was distributed by United States Senators and included positions as judges, law enforcement personnel, tax collector, customs collector and sitting on special boards dealing with land or mining claims. The governor and key members of the California legislature were able to appoint state tax collectors, some law enforcement personnel, and a number of administrative individuals to oversee state spending. The drive for these appointive offices led to the development of political party bosses in state politics.

This type of political system was highly unstable as voters continually switched political parties. In the first decade of statehood eleven political organizations entered state elections, and this prompted most citizens to take a dim view of the political process. Professional politicians manipulated elections and it was not uncommon for votes to be purchased at a dollar per vote during local elections. In this atmosphere of self-interest and political manipulation California developed a system of politics centered around personality.

Democratic Politics in the 1850s

The turbulent political atmosphere in California politics during the 1850s was largely the result of two competing and highly divergent Democratic party bosses. While the Democrats controlled almost every significant election in the decade prior to the Civil War, Democratic loyalties were divided between two quite different politicians.

One faction of the Democratic party was led by David Broderick, a New York Irish-Catholic, who organized a system of neighborhood or ward political machines. Initially organized in San Francisco, Broderick's political machine was an Irish-Catholic workingmen's organization. It was a carryover from the "Young Ireland" movement of the 1840s and it represented the first sign of blue collar, working class interest in local politics. There was also a strong feeling against slavery and a general revulsion against the pompous Southerner who attempted to transplant the genteel Virginia tradition to the streets of San Francisco. In essence, Broderick's political machine was a liberal, almost radical, organization supporting the growing demand for increased rights for the working man.

There is a great deal in Broderick's background which made him well suited to lead a liberal political machine. After growing up in the slum-infested Five Points district of New York City, Broderick migrated to California where he was a member of the Monterey Constitutional Convention. In his first year in California the twenty-nine year old Broderick made a fortune minting a special currency used for business prior to statehood. This scheme coupled with key real estate investments made Broderick a wealthy man. In his free time Broderick organized fire clubs or volunteer fire fighting units to serve local neighborhoods. In reality, these clubs were political organizations geared to turning out the Democratic vote. The fire clubs became a vehicle to further Broderick's political career. Should a citizen vote the wrong way in an election the fire club might elect not to respond to a fire alarm at his house or business establishment. Another important aspect of Broderick's political strength was that he recognized the necessity of serving local neighborhood interests.

As a result of this carefully organized political machine Broderick became the most important figure in San Francisco politics. During the first sixty years of statehood San Francisco controlled much of the destiny of state government. As a member of the California Senate, Broderick quickly rose to a position of leadership, and he was President of the Senate from 1851 to 1856. This provided him with the power necessary to promote an anti-slavery, liberal Democratic political program.

Although personally sloppy and often insulting to people, Broderick was a major foe of slavery, and he chastised the Gwin Democrats for supporting outdated ideas. On more than one occasion Broderick accused the Chivalry Democrats of outright racism. Yet, Broderick's political voice was not an effective one. He refused to develop an image or to use even the most fundamental manners in dealing with people. The result was that many important political allies either ignored Broderick or openly opposed him.

The pro-slavery faction of the Democratic party was led by William Gwin, a Southerner who had been a protege of President Andrew Jackson. A former Congressman from Mississippi, Gwin

David Broderick

migrated to California seeking political fame. He was dispatched by the national Democratic party to oversee the writing of the California Constitution. From his earliest days in California, Gwin's suave speaking tones and his strong ties with national Democrats made his political voice a powerful one. Gwin was a physician and lawyer who was often very rational in defending the maintenance of slavery in California. In many respects Gwin reasoned that slaves were a property investment which needed protection for investors. This argument did not appeal to the majority of Californians, but the Gwin political machine did control one segment of state politics until the Civil War.

As a United States Senator Gwin controlled the federal patronage. The large number of appointive jobs Gwin doled out helped to create a strong pro-slavery Democratic machine. The Chivalry Democrats were also active supporters of economic growth. Gwin introduced a bill for a transcontinental railroad, and he was generally a strong advocate of federal spending in California. Although the transcontinental railroad idea was defeated in the 1850s, Gwin was able to persuade Congress to build a naval yard at Mare Island and a branch of the federal mint in San Francisco.

The Gwin-Broderick rivalry broke into open hostility in the mid-1850s. Since both men were extremely successful in different spheres of government, it was only a matter of time until an open clash took place. Their differences on the slavery question, national issues and the direction of state politics made a clash inevitable. In 1854–1855 Broderick used his power in the California Senate to attempt to elect a successor to Gwin a year before the election was to take place. The result was an open feud between Gwin and Broderick which destroyed the Democratic party in California. From 1855 to 1857 only one United States Senator represented the Golden State, and Broderick was manipulating local politics to retire Gwin from office. The end result of this confusion was to create an atmosphere of political uncertainty. In 1857 the California legislature ended the fight by sending both Gwin and Broderick to the United States Senate. The problem created for the average Californian was to differentiate between Gwin and Broderick and support one or the other. As Californians debated the pro and anti-slave viewpoint a new political party emerged with an alternative message.

Nativism and the Know Nothing Movement

In the mid-1850s strong feelings developed against foreigners in California. This was a natural impulse emanating from the mines and farming regions of northern and central California. The dominance of American institutions and the growth of private enterprise capitalism was an important reason for the strong reaction against foreign influences. Because much of the population believed in a white, anglo-saxon, protestant based America, a political organization formed to exploit these feelings. In May, 1854, a secret society calling itself the American Party organized to build the anti-Catholic and anti-immigrant vote into a political machine. The tactic used to attract membership was to employ secrecy, and the stock answer of an American Party member was that he knew nothing about the political system. By employing an elaborate system of secret handshakes, passwords and other symbols of secret organization the American Party attracted a following which was in favor of Asian exclusion, hostile to the sale of alcoholic beverages, anti-Catholic, and prone to Bible quoting statistics.

The Know-Nothing platform appealed to the nativist instincts in California. The key element in its political appeal was the proposition that free immigration be curtailed because the wrong type of Europeans were immigrating to America. It turned out that this was a ploy to hide anti-Catholic prejudice. The Know-Nothings attacked Catholic influences in the public schools and suggested a Popish conspiracy to control California politics. Members of the American Party also displayed a strong bias against the Spanish-speaking Californian, and they went as far as to recommend that tax money not be used for ethnically integrated schools. During the course of campaigning in the mid-1850s the American Party drew a sordid picture of Andrés Pico's recently formed California lancers, and Know-Nothing orators charged that this "Mexican-American" Cavalry posed a danger to law and order. This ludicrous argument suggests the degree of political chaos in the 1850s, but it also points up the resentment against Latin surnamed Californians.

Many Californians believed that the Know-Nothing party offered an alternate solution to state political problems. By promising to unite Californians against foreign influences the Know-Nothing movement departed from the slavery debate. This gave the American Party the illusion of presenting fresh political ideas to the voters. In reality, the appeal of this new political party was that of a group which harked back to the old notion of a simplistic, rural America.

In 1855, J. Neely Johnson, a twenty-eight year old political novice, carried the banner of the American party into the gubernatorial election. After an election campaign highlighted by secret meetings, mild threats against most ethnic groups and a promise to stop Catholic influences, Johnson was elected governor. The reason for his election was the growing dissatisfaction with the Democratic party. The Gwin-Broderick dispute caused large numbers of Californians to vote for

Johnson as a protest against the dreary state of local politics. At this point in California history governors were elected for two year terms. This proved to be a blessing as Johnson was one of the most inept individuals ever to hold public office. His tenure in office resulted in the San Francisco Vigilante Committee of 1856 openly defying his request for dispersal of this law and order mob. Had Governor Johnson spoke out against urban crime and exercised responsible leadership the San Francisco Vigilante Committee might not have taken action. It was this type of leadership which made the American party a temporary experiment in California politics. Its significance was that it represented a strong feeling against Catholics, European immigrants and the Spanish-speaking population of California.

Slavery and the Democratic Party

The major issue in California politics during the 1850s was the continued debate over slavery. Although a free state, California was inundated by Southerners with a pro-slavery philosophy. As William Gwin's Chivalry Democrats clashed with David Broderick's anti-slave Democrats the major issues and feelings about state politics came into focus. This debate also served as a useful tool for Broderick's blue-collar, Irish-Catholic political machine to persuade working class Californians to resist the ways of Southern Democratic aristocrats. The language of the day was the type which led to demagoguery in politics and Broderick and Gwin were equally skillful in appealing to the emotions rather than to the mind. An example of this type of rhetoric occurred in the State Senate in 1850 when Broderick labeled slavery as "unholy, unpatriotic and partisan" in its political tone. As President of the California Senate Broderick was in a position to influence the rise of anti-slavery sentiment. In fact, the feeling against slavery which dominated the state by 1860 was largely the result of Broderick's political influence.

Yet, the power of the pro-slavery faction was strong in California. Thomas Jefferson Green, a Texan who represented Sacramento in the Senate, introduced a State Fugitive Slave law which would allow slavecatchers to pursue Blacks into California. In 1852 the California passed this law which was designed to discourage Black migration to the Golden State. There were many reasons for a Fugitive Slave law. The most significant was the strong feeling among the Chivalry Democrats against free Blacks. The Broderick Democrats displayed an equally impressive anti-slavery sentiment in the California courts. In 1850 Judge Thomas, a Sacramento justice, ruled in favor of a Black man accused of being a runaway slave, and he used the court to lecture Californians on the evils of slavery. In 1851 Judge Morrison of San Francisco ruled that once a Black slave was brought to California that person immediately was freed from the peculiar institution. Judge Morrison reasoned that slavery was illegal and this meant that freedom was the only recourse for Black Californians. The strong hand of California Courts helped to create a fear that the Golden State would become a haven for runaway slaves. There was no evidence to back up this feeling, but the notion spread throughout California.

There was an immediate challenge to the Fugitive Slave Act. The case involved the freedom granted to three Black men, Robert and Carter Perkins and Sandy Jones. The three Black slaves had worked for their owner, C. S. Perkins, in the California gold fields. In 1851 they were placed under the supervision of Dr. John Hill who freed them in November, 1851. This outraged pro-slavery zealots, and in retaliation the three men were seized on May 31, 1852 by the sheriff of Placer County and charged with being fugitive slaves. They were quickly brought to Sacramento where local justices were sympathetic to slaveowners. This aroused the ire and indignation of the Black and white community in Sacramento and San Francisco. After a number of fund raising meetings, Cornelius Cole, a prominent civil rights attorney, was hired to defend the three Blacks. The object of this court test was to have the Fugitive Slave Act of 1852 declared unconstitutional.

The Perkins case became the focus of a civil rights controversy when the three Blacks were kidnapped and placed aboard a ship headed for the South. Although the Fugitive Slave Law had been on the books for only a month there was strong public interest in it. Blacks organized political pressure groups and raised money to aid the three defendants. On July 1, 1852, the Perkins case came before the state supreme court, and the court ruled that the Constitution protected slave property. The Perkins decision appeared to be a victory for proslavery forces. As the three Blacks headed for Mississippi a number of their white supporters, particularly attorney Cole, complained that physical threats made it impossible to defend free Blacks.

Although the law expired in April, 1855, the Fugitive Slave Law was an important catalyst to the rise of early Black politics. The same year an organization known as the Colored Convention of California met to discuss means of implementing civil rights. The changing climate of opinion led to another important court case involving slavery.

In 1857 an eighteen year old Black Mississippi slave, Archy Lee, was brought to Sacramento. Lee worked as a casual laborer earning small sums of money for his master Charles Stovall. After a brief period of time Lee began to hang out at the Hotel Hackett, a business owned by free Blacks, and he talked of freedom in California. Stovall responded to this attitude by attempting to send Archy back to Mississippi. He took refuge in the free Black community in Sacramento and Stovall had him arrested. This led to a series of important court room battles. On January 7, 1858, with well known antislavery lawyers representing Archy Lee, the case of whether or not a Black slave could be declared a free person was heard in a California court. Archy Lee was declared free only to be arrested and spirited to a friendly, proslavery supreme court justice.

This type of political behavior aroused the hostility of antislavery forces. In the San Francisco area the Black community continued to raise money and to demonstrate their dissatisfaction with the debate over slavery. California Blacks were determined to free Archy Lee. Stovall attempted to smuggle his slave out of California, and Lee was arrested and placed in protective custody. After near race riots over the case Archy Lee was granted his freedom in April, 1858. Black and white Californians who had worked for Lee's freedom celebrated the victory. But the tense situation took its personal toll on Lee, and he moved to British Columbia.

The significance of the Archy Lee case is that it demonstrated that a Black civil rights movement was visible in California politics. The presence of large numbers of antislavery attorneys made it possible to challenge discriminatory laws. While the Lee case was the last important civil rights dispute during the first decade of statehood, it did suggest the possibility that civil rights was a major issue in California civilization.

There is little doubt that a large number of white Californians protested the restrictions placed on the movements and employment of free Blacks. The agitation for Black civil rights increased during the 1850s, and public opinion grew increasingly hostile toward slavery. This changing attitude was due to migrational patterns that brought in large numbers of non-slave owning northerners. The several hundred slaves in California were freed by either purchasing their freedom or escaping from servitude. Yet, California's legal code forbade Black testimony in court. If a Black was robbed and a white witness was not present there could be no court action. Finally, in 1863 with the American Civil War raging, Black Californians were granted the right to testify in local courts.

Neither Gwin nor Broderick were in the forefront of the drive to outlaw slavery and protect basic human rights. While Broderick was an anti-slavery advocate, he never really battled for Black rights. This hurt the Democratic party and drove Blacks into the Republican organization. The slavery controversy also indicated that Black Californians would fight in a militant manner for their civil rights.

The Divisionist Movement and Sectionalism

Another early sign of internal political conflict in California occurred in 1850 when Southern Californians began to complain about a lack of political and economic power. Southern California requested the right to secede because of high taxes and too little representation in the state legislature. In April 1852, Governor John McDougal delivered a speech to the California legislature which pointed out that the six counties in Southern California paid more than twice the tax that twelve mining counties paid in Northern California. This statement touched off a bitter sectional dispute which prompted Southern Californians to charge that they were being unfairly treated by the north. To counter this unfair treatment Los Angeles Assemblyman Andrés Pico proposed that the Territory of Colorado be created in Southern California. This touched off almost a decade of political fighting which highlighted the highly divisive sectional nature of California politics.

The significance of the divisionist movement is that it highlighted the differences between northern and southern California. It also was an indication that the Democratic party failed to provide either leadership or constructive solutions to tax and representation problems. This reinforced the notion that Democratic politicians were motivated by little more than self-interest. Although legitimate economic grievances led to the divisionist movement there were also racial overtones to it. The proslavery supporters of Senator Gwin and a small group who followed State Senator's Thomas Jefferson Green and Henry Crabb believed that the Territory of Colorado scheme would rid California of much of its Spanish-speaking population. There was a great deal of hostility to Mexican-American businessmen, and Andrés Pico was criticized frequently for wielding too much economic and political power. In the final analysis, a sense of hostility to Spanish-speaking Californians made the divisionist movement a negative one.

Filibustering and California's Frontier Spirit

One of the fundamental characteristics of California in the 1850s was a general disdain or lack of respect for established institutions. There was a dim view of and little compliance with the law, local courts, and the general law enforcement community. Most Californians considered established institutions as another means of allowing manipulative politicians access to prized politicial plums. The large number of appointive jobs created scandals and favoritism which angered most citizens. It was not considered important to follow prescribed rules. The end result of this controversy was to make law and order important issues in the first decade of statehood and to create an important public debate concentrating on the causes of this disorder.

Californians often complained that few of the state's institutions, whether political or economic, worked very well in the 1850s. Much of the blame for this instability was placed upon the filibustering craze. The restless adventuring spirit of the 1840s contributed to the rise of filibustering. It was a form of latent Manifest Destiny and served to highlight the lack of law and order in the Golden State. Individuals who engaged in filibustering were private citizens who organized an army to conquer another nation. The majority of filibustering expeditions were directed against Latin American nations. While the announced objectives of most filibustering expeditions were to introduce Yankee capitalism, the Protestant faith and democratic government, a more realistic assessment of filibustering indicated that it was a movement to extract mineral wealth from Latin American nations. Filibustering leaders compared themselves to Davy Crockett and Sam Houston, and they talked of establishing new power from the United States in Latin America. In California early filibustering expeditions displayed outright racism toward Latin nations.

There was no general concern over the rise of filibustering. This was due to the comic opera nature of the early expeditions. Sam Brannan, the Mormon merchant who gained notoriety by publicizing the gold rush, organized a filibustering expedition to conquer Hawaii. The island nation seemed an easy target with its antiquated government and tribal mentality. Brannan's ship, the *Gamecock,* sailed from San Francisco in 1851 only to find the Hawaiians fierce and nonconquerable. The California press was intrigued by Brannan's voyage and public opinion followed his escapade. The result was to create a filibustering fad in the 1850s which further strained relations between Spanish-speaking Californians and the Anglo population.

There was a great deal of evidence that state governments and leading politicians supported filibustering activity. It was common for Mexico to charge that United States Senators, key business figures and state politicians used their financial resources to support filibustering expeditions. An example of this type of activity occurred in the spring of 1851 when Joseph Morehead, the quartermaster of California, used state funds to outfit an expedition intent upon invading Sonora, a state in Northern Mexico, and Baja California. Although Morehead's action was taken at the request of discontent Mexican politicians, the Mexican government charged that it was an example of Yankee imperialism. Morehead defended his actions by stating that lawless Indians were ruining the fabric of Mexican life and his expedition would restore law and order. In reality, Morehead was a fortune seeker who barely escaped from Mexico with his life. The hostility of the Mexican government was reflected in statements comparing Morehead to the Texas revolutionaries.

The result of Morehead's action was to create hostile relations between Mexico and California. The Mexican government immediately strengthened its borders, and a plan was introduced to establish a French buffer colony in Northern Mexico. In the early 1850s more than three thousand French goldseekers swarmed into California, and they were quite unpopular with local citizens. A French Marquis, Charles de Pindray, led a force of one hundred and fifty Frenchmen to establish a colony near Guaymas. Although the Mexican government was instrumental in setting up the colony, they failed to provide financial aid to the French settlers. The hostility of local Apache Indians led to Pindray's murder and his motley crew fled for California. The survivors of this expedition charged that the Mexican government murdered Pindray after promising him land. These charges created bitter resentment and they provided the means for justifying future filibustering expeditions.

There were a number of French filibustering expeditions into Mexico. The most famous filibustering expedition was led by Count Gaston de Raousset-Boulbon, known as the "Little Wolf." After arriving in California in 1850, he failed to gain fame or fortune in California's mining regions. In an attempt to exploit Sonora's wealth, de Raousset-Boulbon convinced key Mexican officials to collaborate with local French diplomatic officers to support a new colony. Once he moved into Mexico, de Raousset-Boulbon failed to comply with the instructions provided by the Mexican government, and he became an armed enemy operating within Mexico. After capturing Hermosillo, he recognized the superiority of the Mexican army and fled to San Francisco. What is significant about de Raousset-Boulbon is that his expedition caught the fancy and imagination of a large number of Californians. His dashing personal style combined with intriguing stories of adventure whetted the appetite of local thrill-seekers.

It was impossible for de Raousset-Boulbon to control his own desire for exploration, and he began to plan new expeditions into Mexico. After organizing five hundred men and landing in Guaymas on the ship, the *Challenge,* he was captured by local authorities. A trial on the charge of conspiracy resulted in a verdict of guilty and de Raousset-Boulbon was executed in August, 1854. The significance of his trial and execution is that it reaffirmed the Mexican government's desire to end all American filibustering expeditions. However, the vast majority of adventurers in San Francisco ignored this serious warning and from 1854 to 1857 a season of filibustering emerged in California.

Probably the best known filibustering figure was William Walker. A medical doctor trained in France, Walker was a traveler in search of adventure. After briefly practicing medicine he arrived in San Francisco and worked as a journalist for a short time. Walker then moved to Marysville and practiced law. In his travels he began to dream of his own empire. He followed the deeds of the French colonizers with careful attention to their failures. Walker reasoned that he could successfully carve out a small nation in Mexico. Although Walker talked of annexing Baja California and the state of Sonora to the United States, his real passion was to become a ruling monarch in these regions. In talking with contemporaries he showed an almost unbalanced obsession with conquest.

In 1853 Walker led a crew of 48 men for Baja California. With the aid of Mexican rebels, Walker seized La Paz in January, 1854, and proclaimed the Republic of Lower California. But his army soon rebelled against Walker's leadership. As his force dwindled to thirty-five men, he made the hasty decision to conquer the Mexican state of Sonora. This scheme was never enacted and Walker returned to the United States. He was arrested for violating neutrality laws, but he was acquitted by a sympathetic jury. He then returned to his law practice a hero.

The final bizarre chapter in Walker's life was written in 1855 when he sailed to Nicaragua to assume the presidency of its government. The old filibustering insanity had never left Walker and he was finally executed in Latin America in 1860. Walker's life was typical of the glory-seeking, greedy American who embraced the filibustering craze.

The last significant filibustering expedition was led by Henry A. Crabb. As a schoolmate of Walker's, Crabb was interested in the exploits of his fellow adventurer and this curiosity resulted in a filibustering scheme. In 1849 Crabb moved to Stockton where he practiced law and served in the California legislature. A close follower of William Gwin and a pro-slavery Democrat, Crabb was aided in his dreams by a wife who possessed a Mexican land grant. In 1857 Crabb organized the Arizona and Gadsden Colonization Company to settle a portion of the mineral-rich state of Sonora.

As a result of the previous experiences with filibustering expeditions the Mexican government was determined to make an example of Crabb's party. The Mexican government also believed that it was time to teach local revolutionaries a lesson, and they were intent upon punishing Ignacio Pesquiera. He was a local politico who encouraged Crabb to settle in Sonora. But Pesquiera deserted Crabb and the Mexican army seized him. Crabb's execution by the Mexican army ended the filibustering craze.

The reaction to filibustering varied in California, and there was strong feeling among many individuals that the movement was an unnecessary one. The Los Angeles Spanish-printing newspaper, *El Clamor Público* editorialized that Crabb was merely the advanced agent of American imperialism in Latin America. His hatred of Spanish-speaking Californians was a well documented fact while he served in the California legislature. This view of Crabb caused many Mexican-Americans to demand a new generation of Spanish-speaking politicians. In San Francisco *El Eco del Pacífico* described Crabb as a revolutionary and a thief and urged a resurgence of Spanish-speaking political activity. One result of the filibustering phenomena, then, was to create a renewed demand for political activity from the Mexican-American community.

In sum, the significance of filibustering was that it carried on the strained ethnic relations which plagued California in the 1850s. The conflict between Spanish-speaking and American interests received only peripheral attention at the time, but it did point out the vacuum in second generation Californio leadership. Lacking political leaders like Mariano Vallejo, businessmen like José Castro, Pablo de la Guerra and Pío Pico, and social symbols like the Berryesa and Peralta families, the second-generation Californio seemed doomed to perpetual second-class citizenship.

The San Francisco Vigilante Committee of 1851

As California political institutions found it impossible to cope with economic and social change, violence increased to the point where citizens formed private law enforcement groups. In 1850 less than ten per cent of California's one hundred thousand settlers were natives, and the Golden State was a natural migration point for restless elements. In the American West it was fairly common for "popular tribunals" to settle questions of law and order. Due to the absence of a legal system that was workable, Californians devised their own forms of law enforcement. The failure of law enforcement resulted in a vindictive brand of justice which reflected the instability of California institutions.

Once gold was discovered San Francisco became the natural migration point for young men seeking fame and fortune. In 1849 groups of young men known as the Hounds or Regulators organized to enforce the law. In reality, these bands were young Mexican War veterans who drove Spanish-speaking Californians out of San Francisco. In a part of the city where residents of the British prison colony in Australia lived, a group of thugs known as the "Sydney Ducks" organized, and they led an attack in July, 1849, against Chilean families living in tents. Sam Brannan led a group of citizens who dispersed the Sydney Ducks, and Californians began to debate the problems of law and order. The problem was that the Hounds claimed to be a police force, but San Francisco merchants often remarked that the individuals who enforced the law were more dangerous than the common criminal.

Although the illegal activity of the Hounds ended in 1849, nevertheless, there was a strong feeling that theft, extortion and other minor criminal acts could not be controlled. In Marysville,

The 1851 Vigilante Committee in action

Sacramento, Stockton and Sonora vigilante organizations had cleaned up local criminal elements, and this caused San Franciscans to believe that all known criminal elements were descending upon the city.

The catalyst to the formation of the San Francisco Vigilante Committee of 1851 was the beating and robbery of C.J. Jansen. In February, 1851, Jansen's business was robbed in broad daylight; this resulted in a mob forming to establish law and order. Two innocent Australians were seized, but after some argument the people's court failed to convict the pair. They were turned over to regular law enforcement authorities, and the vigilante experiment appeared to have died out.

The Hounds and the Sydney Ducks were believed to have set a number of fires in retaliation against the harrassment they experienced from the vigilante committee. On May 4, 1851, a fifth major fire broke out, and this led to the reorganization of the San Francisco Vigilante Committee. By June, 1851, a citizens court was set up to handle cases that local law enforcement officials did not properly adjudicate. The main reason for this court being established was that the Hounds and Sydney Ducks were continuing to set fires and commit minor crimes. Sam Brannan acted as President of the Vigilance Committee and members were known only by a number identity. A fee of five dollars a member was used to build a jail and investigate criminal activity. The executive committee handled all trials and reported the results to the membership.

There was a bloodthirsty atmosphere and the vigilante committee was determined to find a criminal who would serve as an example to other lawless elements. John Jenkins was caught stealing a small safe and after a brief trial he was hanged by the light of a summer moon. To many citizens it seemed dangerous to hang a man so suddenly, but the California legislature had adopted the death penalty in 1851. It was not surprising that it was repealed in 1856 due to the excesses of law and order mobs.

To the casual observer the San Francisco Vigilante Committee of 1851 imposed some strange sentences. In addition to four hangings there was one whipping, fourteen deportations to other countries and a banishment. In many respects the vigilante experiment was a reaction to corrupt law enforcement personnel, disinterested courts and conniving local politicians. The business community resented the prevalent system of special privileges for individuals with political connections. It is interesting that not a single lawyer belonged to the vigilante committee. The legal profession spoke out against the abuses of civil rights and openly criticized the terrorism and intimidation flaunted in the name of law and order.

In Los Angeles vigilante activity was an excuse for wholesale lynchings. The mayor of Los Angeles and the city council approved of the organization of a vigilante committee in 1851, and they applauded the wholesale murder of anyone considered to be a criminal. One of the best examples of Los Angeles lawlessness came when Mayor Stephen Foster persuaded vigilantes to turn a gambler over to the police; the mayor promised that if the gambler wasn't convicted that he would join the vigilantes in a hanging. When the gambler's attorney secured him a stay of execution after his conviction, Mayor Foster led the vigilantes in breaking the gambler out of jail and hanging him publicly. The first stage of vigilante activity ended with a rash of hangings and personal abuses in northern and southern California.

The San Francisco Vigilante Committee of 1856

In the mid-1850s a depression occurred in California. As miners, farmers and the generally unemployed migrated to San Francisco, local business activity was minimal. Banks and small businesses failed daily, the corruption in city government became even more blatant, and the stuffing of ballot boxes was accomplished with contempt for the system. The conditions in San Francisco were ripe in 1856 for the reemergence of vigilante activity. Since 1851 leading San Francisco merchants had periodically praised vigilante action. They believed that it was a tool to be used to cleanse the city of the criminal element.

The restructuring of the vigilante organization in 1856 was due to the shooting of James King, the editor of the *San Francisco Daily Evening Bulletin*. The *Bulletin's* editor was a journalistic muckraker who frequently attacked corrupt local politicians. For almost a year the *Bulletin* challenged the honesty and credentials of a San Francisco supervisor, James P. Casey. King alleged that Casey was little more than a common crook. In New York Casey had been involved in a ballot stuffing scheme while working for the Tammany Hall machine, but he was no more or no less crooked than the average California politician.

When the *Bulletin* charged that Casey had served a brief sentence in New York's famed Sing Sing prison, the New Yorker demanded an apology for Editor King. This demand for an apology was ignored and one day Casey burst into King's office. After a vicious argument in front of a number of witnesses, Casey stormed from the building threatening to kill King. An hour later

The San Francisco Vigilante Committee of 1856

Casey and King met in the street; the final end to this argument came when a gunshot killed *San Francisco Bulletin* editor James King. The general conclusion was that Supervisor Casey had murdered his political foe.

Local officials spirited Casey to jail for safekeeping. In the same jail was an Italian gambler Charles Cora who was accused of killing the Federal Marshall for Northern California. It took only three days for the vigilante committee to organize and seize Casey and Cora. In Sacramento, Stockton and Fresno meetings were held to support the San Francisco vigilantes. Most public officials were afraid to speak out against the vigilante group. The vigilantes chose thirty-two year old William T. Coleman as their leader for the second time. A local businessman who operated a prosperous mercantile firm, Coleman was a respected figure. But Coleman continued to demand absolute secrecy and he threatened the local sheriff to the point where the vigilantes could direct an acquittal or a conviction. Coleman believed that law and order could be established only through vigilante action. The large majority of San Franciscans agreed with this conclusion and helped to support this idea.

The San Francisco Vigilante Committee of 1856 represented the downtown business community. Its direction and purpose was to create business controls over city government. The numerical strength fluctuated between six and ten thousand, but they were able to raise almost $100,000 in the first weeks of organization. In a few weeks patrols of one hundred men roamed the streets armed with the latest weapons.

There were a small number of courageous citizens who spoke out against the excesses of the mob mentality. One was San Francisco Mayor James Van Ness who called the mob an example of miscarried justice. The *San Francisco Herald* was the only newspaper to criticize the vigilantes

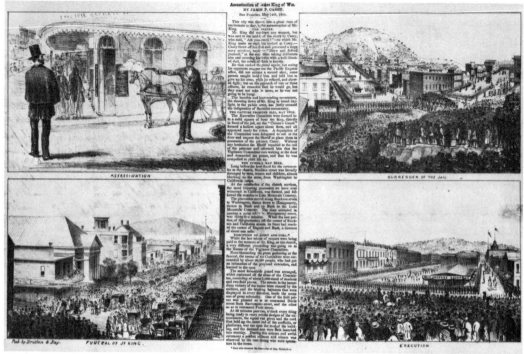

The execution of Casey and Cora

and local businessmen almost caused it to go bankrupt by withdrawing advertising. The Reverend W. A. Scott of the Calvary Presbyterian Church charged that vigilante activity was un-American, and he was hanged in effigy for expressing his opinion. As a result of these criticisms a Law and Order party formed to end vigilante terrorism.

The Law and Order party began to publicize the illegal activities and the self-fulfilling intentions of the vigilantes. These critics urged Governor J. Neely Johnson to call out the militia to prevent further intimidation and chaos in San Francisco. Governor Johnson's backbone stiffened with this encouragement from law and order-minded citizens. He drew up careful plans with the newly appointed general of the state militia, William Tecumseh Sherman. The commander of the United States Army arsenal at Benicia, John E. Wool, promised a loan of firearms if the state militia was called out to protect San Franciscans. When Governor Johnson declared San Francisco to be in a state of insurrection due to illegal vigilante activity, he imagined that the state militia would disband the law and order mob. Much to everyones surprise General Wool refused to deliver arms to the militia without a direct order from the President of the United States. Preparing for the attack the San Francisco Vigilante Committee organized six thousand armed men in a fortress known as Fort Gunnybags. Then General Sherman turned political by announcing that he recognized the general popularity of the vigilante committee and he refused to march on Fort Gunnybags.

David Terry, a justice of the California Supreme Court, acted as legal adviser to the Law and Order party, and he discovered a statute which required the federal government to lend the state weapons in the event of a declaration of martial law. But the San Francisco viligantes seized the 113 guns sent to the state militia. In the aftermath of this escapade Justice Terry stabbed a member of the vigilante committee during a violent confrontation. Forced to flee from a mob of vigilantes, Terry was arrested and tried for attempted murder. After brilliantly conducting his own defense, Terry was released by the vigilantes.

The day after the Justice Terry trial the vigilante committee disbanded. Despite public statements that the committee would continue to function, its leaders privately agreed it should cease to enforce the law. Yet, there was a strong feeling that local citizens must be reminded of the potential power of the vigilantes. On August 18, 1856, a parade of six thousand hickory ax handled vigilantes signaled the end of the San Francisco Vigilante Committee of 1856. The vigilante headquarters, Fort Gunnybags, was kept open for a few months as a tourist attraction.

In many respects the vigilante activity was a signal that San Francisco businessmen were beginning to influence political affairs. One historian has alleged that the San Francisco Vigilante Committee of 1856 was an indication that business interests could readily administer justice. This ignores the harsh treatment accorded anyone who disagreed with the committee. In the aftermath of the vigilante movement a new political party, the People's Party, was formed by the vigilantes and they swept the city elections in 1856. For the next decade the People's Party controlled San Francisco politics. This led to tax cuts which closed schools and cut funds for fire and police services. The vigilante committee was an early expression of popular distrust of government's abilities to provide for the common citizen.

The Demise of Democratic Politics

The legacy of slavery, the divisionist movement, the filibustering expeditions and the vigilante experiences highlighted the unworkable nature of California institutions. Since the early days of the Gwin-Broderick feud it had been obvious to many Californians that political institutions were too weak to function with any skill. But the tumultuous activity in 1856 brought Gwin and Broderick together in a peace mission to save the Democratic party. They failed to realize that almost a decade of strife had torn the Democratic machine into fractious divisions.

According to contemporary sources Gwin and Broderick agreed to share the two United States Senate seats. They would also control the activity of the Democratic state legislature. But Broderick held the balance of power in the California Senate, and he agreed to Gwin's reelection on the condition that all federal patronage be dispensed by the Broderick Democrats. By squeezing Gwin out of his federal patronage, Broderick had triumphed in California Democratic politics. This moment of success created bitter resentment and led to open rebellion against Broderick's leadership.

As Senator Broderick arrived in Washington D. C. New York Democrats fired a one hundred gun salute to her native son. It was to be Broderick's last triumph as President James Buchanan announced his opposition to Broderick. President Buchanan made it very clear that he considered Broderick unethical, and he would not award much federal patronage to the Golden State. This was an obvious attempt to undermine Broderick's political strength. It was also recognition that Broderick had manipulated the California Senate to name him to the six year Senate term while selecting Gwin for a four year term. For the next two years Gwin and Broderick battled each other in the United States Senate and in California politics. The result was to create even wider differences within the strife torn Democratic party.

In speeches in the United States Senate and in campaign appearances for Democratic candidates throughout California, Broderick personally denounced Gwin and his followers. The attacks upon the Secesh Democrats were virulent ones, and a large number of Californians began to complain about Broderick's libelous charges. In the state elections of 1859 Gwin's machine campaigned in support of President Buchanan's plan to admit Kansas to the Union under a proslavery constitution. The resurgence of the slavery question baffled most Californians and they ignored the issue.

The elections of 1859 in California had a peculiar effect on Justice David Terry. When he discovered that the Democratic party was not going to renominate him for election to the California Supreme Court, he delivered an emotional tirade against Senator Broderick. He accused Broderick of being a dupe for anti-slavery forces, and Terry suggested that Broderick lacked even an ounce of political skill. What was ironic about the Terry attack was that Broderick had defended Terry when the San Francisco Vigilante Committee of 1856 attempted to convict him. Broderick spent more than a thousand dollars of his own money to defend Terry, and he was livid about the attack on his leadership.

In a crowded restaurant Broderick exploded with a number of vindictive tirades against Justice Terry, and this led to a challenge for a duel. On a misty dawn morning on September 13, 1859, in an open field in San Mateo County, Broderick and Terry met in an ill-fated duel. Although dueling was outlawed by the California Constitution, there were almost a hundred people on hand to witness the spectacle. Broderick had never fired a weapon and his seconds were unfamiliar with dueling regulations. As a result Broderick's gun was jimmied and it fired prematurely. Justice Terry turned slowly, aimed with precision and killed David Broderick. The bullet ended the Democratic party as a serious factor in state politics for the next century. In ten years in California Broderick had given birth to liberal Democratic reform politics. His presence made California a strong supporter of civil liberties and led to the first multi-ethnic political coalition in the American West. When Broderick set up his Ward machines in San Francisco he brought most ethnic groups into the mainstream of Democratic politics. This was a lesson many politicians learned from in establishing their own political strength.

The next governor of California was a Republican, Leland Stanford, and this ended an era of Democratic party rivalry and extravagance. The future of California was assured, however, as the Republican party began to concentrate on developing the economy. Although the Democratic party had failed in its quest to build a permanent political machine, they did lay the firm foundations for a modern state.

Bibliographical Essay

The literature surrounding the first decade of California history is a varied and uneven mix. The best examples of recent work on the 1850s are: David A. Williams, *David C. Broderick: A Political Portrait* (1969) which is an excellent biographical revision of the most important Democratic politician of the 1850s; an equally impressive piece of scholarship is Gerald Stanley,

"Racism and the Early Republican Party: The 1856 Presidential Election in California," *Pacific Historical Review,* XLIII (May, 1974), 171–187; useful is William E. Franklin, "Peter H. Burnett and the Provisional Government Movement," *California Historical Society Quarterly,* XL (June, 1961), 123–136; A. Russell Buchanan, *David S. Terry, Dueling Judge* (1956); Peyton Hurt, "The Rise and Fall of the Know-Nothings in California," *California Historical Society Quarterly,* IX (March and June, 1930), 16–49, 99–128; and Cardinal L. Goodwin, *The Establishment of State Government in California, 1846–1850* (1914).

For an understanding of slavery and the Democratic party see, Rudolph M. Lapp, Blacks in Gold Rush California (1977); William E. Franklin, "The Archy Case," *Pacific Historical Review,* XXXII (June, 1963), 137–154; and J.A. Fisher, "The Struggle for Negro Testimony," *Southern California Quarterly,* LI (Fall, 1969), 313–324. The relationship of slavery to the development of the Republican party is brilliantly covered in Gerald Stanley, "Slavery and the Origins of the Republican Party in California," *Southern California Quarterly,* LX (Spring, 1978), 1–16.

In order to understand the strained feeling in Southern California and the sense of regionalism see, Michael Weiss, "Education, Literacy and the Community of Los Angeles in 1850," *Southern California Quarterly,* LX (Summer, 1978), 117–142. This article is extremely important in examining the relationship of ethnicity to literacy. Only community leaders and those with wealth and occupational status were normally literate. This helps to explain some of the tensions in California due to social class differences and ethnic background.

There is not an adequate biography of William Gwin, but there are a number of useful pieces see, James O'Meara, *Broderick and Gwin, A Brief History of Early Politics in California* (1881) for a dated view of Gwin's role. For a study of the period painted in lavender prose see, Lately Thomas, *Between Two Empires: William McKendree Gwin* (1969).

On the divisionist movement see, William H. Ellison, "The Movement for State Division in California: 1849–1860," *Southwestern Historical Quarterly,* XIX (1914), 101–139 and Joseph Ellison, *California and the Nation* (1927).

The best historiographical works on Filibustering are: Rufus K. Wyllys, *The French in Sonora, 1850–1854* (1932); Diana Lindsay, "Henry A. Crabb, Filibuster, and the *San Diego Herald, San Diego History* XIX (Winter, 1973), 34–42; Andrew F. Rolle, "California Filibustering and the Hawaiian Kingdom," *Pacific Historical Review,* XIX (August, 1950), 251–263 and Laurence Greene, The Filibuster (1937) for an analysis of William Walker.

The best study of the SF Vigilante mentality is John W. Caughey, *Their Majesties, the Mob* (1960). Another valuable look at San Francisco is Roger W. Lotchin, *San Francisco, 1846–1856: From Hamlet to Modern City* (1974). Lotchin is extremely critical of the vigilante experience is as Ted R. Gurr and Richard Maxwell Brown, Pivot of American Vigilantism: The San Francisco Vigilance Committee of 1856," in John A. Carroll and James R. Kluger, *Reflections of Western Historians* (1969). For generally sympathetic accounts of the vigilante experience see, George R. Stewart, *Committee of Vigilance, Revolution in San Francisco, 1851* (1964); Roger Olsted, "San Francisco and the Vigilante Style," *The American West,* VII (January and March, 1970) and James A.B. Scherer, *The Lion of the Vigilantes: William T. Coleman and the Life of Old San Francisco* (1939).

For the demise of the Democratic party see, L.E. Fredman, "Broderick: A Reassessment," *Pacific Historical Review,* XXX (February, 1961), 39–46; and Earl Pomeroy, "California,

1846–1860: Politics of a Represenative Frontier State," *California Historical Society Quarterly,* XXXII (December, 1953), 291–302.

An extremely important study of early government bureaus and the manner in which they stimulated the economy of the Golden State is Gerald D. Nash, *State Government and Economic Development A History of Administrative Policies in California, 1849–1933* (1964).

The response of the California courts to social change is examined in an excellent article by Gordon M. Bakken, "The Development of the Law of Tort in Frontier California, 1850–1890," *Southern California Quarterly,* LX (Winter, 1978), 405–419.

8

MINING, LAND AND RACIAL ATTITUDES IN 19TH CENTURY CALIFORNIA

Stereotyping in the 1850s

One of the primary reasons for the lack of law and order in California and the rise of a vigilante mentality was the unanswered question of who would acquire rights to mining and land claims in American-California. As title to key land and mining wealth was debated the local economy failed to develop, and this led to a bitter atmosphere in political and economic circles. An enduring legacy of this conflict was the rise of strong feelings among the Latin, Asian and Black population over the racial bias of state and federal officials. It was not uncommon for ethnic minorities to charge that legislation was written and enforced for a predominantly Anglo-California. The smooth transition to statehood was marred by a feeling that many land claims and mining properties were being usurped by a new legal system. In the spring of 1850 the California legislature enacted the Foreign Miners' Tax Law which taxed non-American miners, and the result was to displace thousands of successful Mexican, Chilean, Peruvian and Californio miners. In Sonora more than four thousand Mexican miners protested the law before leaving California's Sierra mountains. The following year the United States Senate enacted the Land Law of 1851 to settle disputed land claims, and this further intensified conflict between foreign land owners and Americans. The debate which followed over these laws resulted in the first serious signs of ethnic conflict in American occupied California.

The Foreign Miners' Tax Law of 1850

In 1849 and 1850 California's mining frontier underwent an ethnic revolution as Mexicans and Californios suddenly found themselves outnumbered by Americans. Large numbers of Mexican miners from the state of Sonora in northern Mexico refused to accept the hostile racial slurs of white Southerners. When a Mexican miner would not leave Sonora the local sheriff often killed him with a bowie knife. Many merchants were instructed not to sell supplies to foreign miners, and one hundred and fifty members of discharged American army units marched into Sonora prepared for battle. A few days later after eating and drinking to epidemic proportions more than four hundred angry Americans marched toward Columbia Camp to persuade all foreign miners to leave California. In a comic opera escapade two Frenchmen were seized and fined five dollars for treason, and this brought 500 angry German and French miners into Sonora. After some serious drinking the so-called French Revolution ended in Sonora, but the incident reflected the lack of law and order in the mines. The rash of robberies and unexplained murders were generally blamed upon Mexican and Californio miners.

From May to August, 1850, approximately fifteen thousand foreign-born miners fled the mines. This was due to the fact that the Mexican and Chilean miners developed the more prosperous claims, and the hostility to their skills was masked in public acceptance of a twenty dollar a month tax on foreign miners. There was also a great deal of interest from large mining companies. A number of important eastern firms hired gangs of Chilean laborers to work their claims, and this created the argument that foreign miners were depriving Americans of jobs. When the Chinese and Indians began to work on labor gangs the racial taunts increased and the Sierras appeared headed for open racial warfare.

The defenders of the Foreign Miners' Tax Law of 1850 claimed that it would reduce ethnic conflict by forcing non-American miners to pay the twenty dollar a month fee. Senator Thomas Jefferson Green, the Texas Democrat who introduced the bill, defended it as a piece of legislation designed to raise revenue for state government. Green, a slave owner and one of Senator William Gwin's proteges, privately boasted that his bill would prevent large numbers of Latin surnamed miners from continuing to operate in California. Publicly, Green stated that the law would create more than two million dollars in state revenues, but only thirty thousand dollars was raised for state government. In Stockton a number of important citizens decried the law for its arbitrary taxation of Mexican and Californio miners.

The hostility to the mining tax spread to French miners who complained of problems with aggressive tax collectors, and in 1851 French miners threatened to riot near Mokelumne Hill. In San Francisco the Peruvian consul complained of the Yankee vigilante mentality and offered sixty dollars for any Peruvian who desired to return home. Racial hostility continued to grow in the mines. One of Dame Shirley's letters from Rich Bar on the North Fork of the Feather River described how a "Spaniard" stabbed a white miner in protest of sexual and racial remarks, and this led to the formation of a vigilante committee to hang the offending foreign miner. As Dame Shirley remarked all Latin surnamed miners were lumped together as "Spaniards" regardless of nationality. In this instance the miner escaped and five Mexicans were arrested and publicly humiliated with floggings. In essence, there was a law and order problem in the mining counties of northern California.

In 1852 the Foreign Miners' Law was directed toward Chinese miners. The new tax was from three to five dollars a month, and local tax collectors frequently spoke of the Chinese as a highly visible minority. Although only twenty thousand Asian miners immigrated to California, there were fears that cheap labor would inundate the Sierra. This proved to be a false rumor, and the small assessment on Chinese miners was designed to control them rather than to force a wholesale exodus from the mines. The Chinese were useful as they would pay the mining tax and high prices for local goods. They did not mix with local citizens, like the Mexicans, and the Chinese appeared to accept segregated schools, poor housing and high prices. It seemed to many ethnics that the Foreign Miners' Tax Law of 1850 was designed to promote an anglo gold country. It was not coincidental that by 1860 ethnic minorities were moving into the farming regions of the San Joaquin Valley and into Fresno, Sacramento and San Francisco.

Racial Stereotyping on the Mining Frontier

In the aftermath of the Foreign Miners' Tax Law of 1850, the California mining frontier underwent an ethnic revolution. When Chinese miners replaced Mexicans and Californios at the

Chinese miners in the Sierra Nevada

bottom of the social structure, there was little doubt that a rigid social-economic class system governed the mining communities. It was typical for local judges to speak of the "Greaser's criminal conduct" in reference to the arrest of Latin surnamed men and women. Generally, the courts stereotyped Latin surnamed men as bandits and the women as prostitutes. The fact that the vast majority of Latins arrested were charged with banditry and prostitution is statistically improbable, and the obvious reason for this approach was to use the legal system to control any possible political or economic dissent.

The result of ethnic stereotyping was to create a brand of justice which reflected stratified economic, social and political conditions, and one critic has suggested that Mexicans and Californios were caught between two cultures. Local citizens preferred to believe that Mexican morals were lower than those of the Yankee. A steady stream of propaganda emanated from local magistrates who constantly pointed out that prostitutes were imported from Northern Mexico, and the larger gambling halls were owned and operated by wealthy Mexican families. The highly vocal stand of local judges in combination with their prestigious position in the community created strong racial tensions.

The most explosive situations resulted from a social atmosphere which often brought inter-marriage. The union between a Latin woman and an American man was not common in the Sierra. As a result when John S. Barclay married Martha Carlos in Columbia he was subject to numerous racial taunts. As the local newspaper pointed out Barclay was marrying a woman who owned a house of prostitution and this lessened his prestige amongst local citizens. After a great deal of pressure, Barclay shot a man to protect his wife's honor. A vigilante mob seized Barclay and twelve leading citizens condemned him to an immediate hanging. The sheriff's attempts to rescue Barclay led to a fierce beating from local citizens. What is interesting about Barclay's hanging is that Columbia Camp was seven years old in 1855 when the incident occurred and the presence of established courts should have prevented a vigilante trial. The significance is that this was a clear warning to anyone who considered the possibility of crossing class and ethnic lines to marry.

Perhaps the most spectacular incident involving moral values was the hanging of the first woman in Downieville in 1851. During a wild July 4th celebration a miner named Cannon came to the home of a local prostitute, Juanita, but after he crashed through her door he staggered home in a drunken stupor. The next day Cannon returned to apologize and was attacked by Juanita's boyfriend, a Mexican gambler named José, and during the ensuing fight Juanita stabbed Cannon to death. Amidst cries of "Hang them" Juanita and José were seized by a fiery mob. On July 5th a vigilante court spent a great deal of time lecturing local citizens on the evils of alcohol, prostitution and mixing with wrong kind of people. After this self-righteous orgy of local law enforcement, José was exiled and Juanita was condemned to death. Many Downieville citizens protested against a type of local justice that would hang a woman, but these cries were not important ones as the five month pregnant Juanita was executed by a vigilante mentality. A number of historians have suggested that Juanita's hanging brought about five years of lawlessness in the mines. These comments ignore the fact that Juanita's hanging was a powerful device in controlling Mexican dissent about the quality of American justice.

Another popular stereotype examined the deeds and actions of the Latin men who roamed the Sierra Nevada—the bandidos. There are a number of reasons for the rise of bandits. This was a means of protesting the loss of California to American invaders. It was also a means to protest the Foreign Miners' Tax Law. Another theory is that crime among a particular group of people is related to the decline of family life and suppression of a particular race or class of people. There was a striking similarity between California bandits and the banditlike chieftains who roamed Mexico. Bandits lived outside of society and were a law unto themselves. They were symbols of a new culture and they turned their back upon old ways. In sum, the bandit became a folk hero for oppressed Mexicans and Californios. It was not surprising that the first fears of bandits arose about the time the Foreign Miners' Tax Law of 1850 began to alter the freedoms of Mexican miners. In the San Joaquin Valley large numbers of Mexican cowboys were arrested and hanged for cattle rustling. Well-known Spanish surnames began appearing in newspaper reports linked with crime.

While bandits often did exist, there is little doubt that crime was becoming an alternative career to many Latin surnamed Californians. The reason was that many Spanish surnamed families experienced the problems of the Pacheco rancho. On a cold, winter day in 1851 about twenty Americans sought shelter at the Pacheco rancho. After receiving food and the promise of shelter for the night the Americans robbed Pacheco at gunpoint. A few days later a local tax collector presented a bill for four thousand dollars. This befuddled Pacheco who was unfamiliar with local tax policy. Then Pacheco's son was caught with a band of petty thieves, and he was whipped one hundred times by an angry vigilante mob. Such harsh treatment for petty theft was not a common practice and local Mexicans and Californios organized to burn Martinez. The law and order controversy surrounding the Pacheco family was a good example of the changes occur-

An advertisement for German miners

ring in California during the first decade of statehood. Law and order was a definite problem in the Golden State.

The bandit stereotype resulted in one of the most interesting legends in California history. This was the story of the mysterious "Joaquin" who terrorized Calaveras County in the winter of 1852–1853. In a sense he was a mythological horseman who was known as the "Napoleon of Banditry." Although there is not a great deal of historical agreement on Joaquin Murieta's life, the following story is the most accurate one. Murieta was born in Sonora, Mexico and was one of many young Mexicans immigrating to California looking for wealth. For a brief period of time he worked in Stockton herding wild horses, but he was arrested in 1850 on suspicion of robbery. Although he was released, Murieta was unhappy and moved to Sonora to live among Mexican miners. He became increasingly bitter as he heard the Foreign Miners' Tax Law being labelled the "Greaser Act." After moving to Sonora, he built a cabin and staked a small mining claim at Saw Mill Flat. It was rumored that Yankee miners raped his wife and drove Murieta from his mining claim. Caleb Dorsey, the Harvard educated district attorney of Tuolumne County, described Murieta as a quiet gentleman who was forced into becoming a reluctant revolutionary.

As a bandit, Murieta's early robberies were comic opera ones, but he quickly attracted a following of discontented Mexican miners. In fact, early in his escapades the American press praised him for looting and killing the Chinese. After a brief period of organizing a small band of followers, he began to attack American miners. The rumor was that he was avenging a raped wife and beaten relatives. Whatever the reason, Murieta became a folk hero to Spanish-speaking Californians.

An interesting aspect of the Murieta legend was that four other bandits calling themselves Joaquin roamed the Sierras and the San Joaquin Valley. As a result of the Joaquin scare a number of crimes were credited to Joaquin Murieta that he had nothing to do with, but his image was enhanced by the stories of a bandit who robbed from the rich to aid the poor. In sum, Murieta was a symbol of hope and pride for dispossessed Mexican-Americans.

The Joaquin scare prompted the California legislature to hire a Texas Ranger, Captain Harry S. Love, to bring law and order to the Sierra. Arriving in California with twenty other ex-Texas Rangers, Love searched the San Joaquin Valley for some time. As the fears increased over Joaquin's exploits the California legislature increased the reward to a record five thousand dollars. During the summer of 1853 Joaquin Murieta's band of horsemen raided the entire San Joaquin Valley, and it was rumored that many of the oldest and wealthiest California dons were hiding Murieta's band. As Mexican and Californio rancheros aided him they quietly proclaimed their distaste for the new American system.

In late July, 1853, it was rumored that Captain Love found Murieta at Ponoche Pass near Tulare Lake. Love claims to have shot and beheaded Murieta. The evidence used to substantiate Love's claim was the body of a three-fingered lieutenant in Murieta's band. This body together with his head were presented to the California legislature in Sacramento in a triumphal procession proclaiming a new law and order. In fact, the California Highway Patrol dates its inception from the work of Captain Love. After a great deal of public fanfare, state officials rewarded Love and his men, and Murieta's head was sent on a two year world tour. The interest in the legend of Joaquin Murieta did not dissipate, and the pickled head was on display in a San Francisco bar until it was destroyed in the Earthquake and Fire of 1906.

There is good evidence which indicates that he escaped to Mexico, and his staunchest supporters maintained that he had made a mockery of Anglo justice. For many years after his escapades Murieta was warmly called the "rebel chief" of early California. His supporters pointed out that he highlighted the inequities in the legal system. American justice, Murieta's followers argued, was a double edged sword-one side dealt fairly with Yankees and the other side discriminated against Mexicans and Californios. In the California barrios Murieta is still referred to as El Patrio-The Patriot.

The significance of the bandit and prostitute stereotypes is that they reflected a double standard of law enforcement. This created a double standard in housing, education and employment opportunities. The result was to institutionalize Mexican-Americans into a position of second-class citizenship. Without political radicals like Mariano Vallejo, José Castro and Juan Bautista Alvarado, the Mexican-American community found it difficult to raise its voice in protest against the inequities of the new governmental, social and economic system.

Californios in the Second Generation

In the 1860s a noticeable change occurred in the Mexican-American community. This was due to two Civil Wars, the American Civil War, 1861–1865 and the Mexican Civil War, 1860–1864. In the American Civil War large numbers of Californios symbolically protested their strong feelings against American annexation by refusing to fight in the American Civil War. A large number of Californios and Mexicans renewed their allegiance to Mexico by siding with the Mexican revolutionary Benito Juárez in his attempt to drive France's Ferdinand Maximilian and his wife Carlotta from the throne. As a result of the two Civil Wars Californios and Mexicans questioned their place in California society. There were a number of Latin surnamed politicians and business leaders who recognized that racial and ethnic differences had crept into schools, jobs and government attitudes. In 1880 Mexican holidays were celebrated throughout California, and this is one indication of the search for a useable Hispanic heritage in the Golden State.

There were a number of Californios and Mexicans who were extremely loyal to the Union and California during the American Civil War. They organized the Native Cavalry of California to aid the North during the Civil War. In Los Angeles, San Jose, San Francisco, and San Juan Bautista units of the Native Cavalry proclaimed their loyalty to the Union. The Yankee press called the Native Cavalry California's true patriots, and the Southern California newspapers constantly pointed out that fifteen percent of all American soldiers in the California military were Spanish-speaking. A close check of enlistment rolls, however, indicates a much different story. Most of the so-called "Native Sons" who fought in the American Civil War were Mexicans or South Americans. In fact, one volunteer was from the Island of Sardinia. The truth was that most Californios and Mexicans did not prefer to fight in the American Civil War. The strong feeling against annexation remained among many Latin surnamed Californians.

In Los Angeles and Santa Barbara the Civil War was a highly unpopular cause. As late as July 4, 1865, the Confederate flag flew over the city of Los Angeles, and this was ample proof that local sentiments on the Civil War favored the South. A well-known Californio, Servulio Varela, fought as an officer in the Confederate army, because he believed that the treatment of Mexicans, Californios and foreigners in general had created second-class citizenship for the majority of Latin surnamed Californians.

The general hostility of Californios and Mexicans toward the American Civil War received President Abraham Lincoln's careful attention. In an attempt to appease the Spanish-speaking citizens of California, Lincoln invited Mariano Vallejo to the nation's capital to persuade Spanish-speaking Californians to support the Union cause. Vallejo's son, Platon, an army surgeon, arranged the visit with Lincoln, and Don Mariano confided his belief that the Foreign Miners' Tax Law of 1850 and the Land Law of 1851 had disenfranchised Mexicans and Californios. In fact, Vallejo suggested that a mild form of racism was shown in these laws. President Lincoln ignored Vallejo's remarks and was only concerned with publicizing his symbolic appeasement of Spanish-speaking Californians. Had Lincoln heeded Vallejo's main argument that Mexicans and Californios were placed in a position of second-class citizenship the ethnic problems of modern California might well have been altered.

President Lincoln announced that Vallejo's arguments had persuaded him to do something for disadvantaged Spanish-speaking Californians. Lincoln then recommended that Congress pass a relief bill granting Vallejo $1.25 an acre as compensation for Americans who had settled on his vast land holdings. This form of appeasement was insulting to Vallejo as well as to most of the Mexicans and Californios who believed that they had been treated unfairly. Vallejo demanded that the federal government guarantee that squatters would not seize his land or those of his people, but this argument was one that Lincoln ignored. The Vallejo family urged their father to press litigation before the United States Supreme Court to recover lost land. Vallejo refused and spoke of himself as an "old fool" who realized too late in life his political mistakes. By supporting American annexation, Vallejo mused, he had brought misfortune upon himself and his people.

In summarizing the two Civil Wars in California, there are a number of important changes reflected in the period. It brought a resurgence of Californio and Mexican interest in politics. The old political radicals of the Mexican-California era were no longer significant figures in local politics. In Southern California new Spanish-speaking political leaders emerged to take the place of the Vallejos, Castros and Alvarados. A large number of Californios immigrated to Mexico and many Mexicans returned home to protest economic, social and political inequities. This defection of Spanish-speaking ranchers and businessmen resulted in declining land ownership and business activity. There is a strong correlation between this economic and political decline, and the type of second-class citizenship which the Spanish-speaking experienced in California.

As a new generation of Californios emerged from 1865 to 1890 they tended to be urban, underemployed and sympathetic to the problems of Mexico. There was a rejection of much that was American, and this was a means of protesting a half a century of hostile relations with the Yankee population. Although a number of influential Californio and Mexican businessmen continued to dominate the ranchos, these successful Spanish-speaking enterprises were exclusively located in Southern California. During the latter half of the nineteenth century these ranchos were systematically destroyed by land laws, opportunistic lawyers, and an economic system which worked against the non-capitalist minded Mexican and Californio. Rather than thinking in terms of a yearly profit and planning for the future, the ranchero was concerned with the quality of his families life.

The best example of how the new American institutions destroyed Spanish-speaking influences in California can be seen in the breakup of the Southern California ranchos. In the Los Angeles area Mexicans and Californios dominated local business activity, but the power and prestige of local rancheros quickly declined with the influx of Americans. An excellent example of this change occurred when Ygnacio del Valle's Rancho Camulos was destroyed by an economic system that its owner failed to understand. Located north of the San Fernando mission, the Rancho Camulos was a highly profitable 48,500 acre ranch. Each year its owner borrowed money to cover his losses and a charitable neighbor never bothered to collect the debt. Eventually land was sold to pay important debts and only 1,500 acres remained from the original grant. When del Valle died in 1880 he still owed his creditors. This depressing situation was repeated time and time again throughout California. Another example of economic problems was highlighted when Don Julio Verdugo's Rancho San Rafael experienced financial problems after borrowing money to fix up his rancho. In 1861 Don Julio borrowed three thousand dollars at 35% yearly interest, and by 1870 he owed almost sixty thousand dollars to the bank. At a public auction Verdugo's lawyers purchased his property. Although a sympathetic Yankee donated 200 acres to the Verdugo family, there was little doubt that this was one of the worst real estate frauds in California history. These examples are typical of the manner in which vast Californio land holdings were decimated from 1865 to 1890.

There were other significant changes among Spanish-speaking Californians. In the job market, for example, by 1867 the largest group of miners were Spanish-speaking, but they received low wages and worked for large corporations under trying circumstances. In many industries Spanish-speaking workers were replaced or often isolated from permanent employment. The newly emerging oil industry did not employ Mexican or Californio workers. It was ironic that the first oil refinery was at Newhall the site of Francisco Lopez' Mexican gold rush in the 1840s. As the fruit industry emerged in the valley and fields of California's lush agricultural areas Chinese workers replaced Mexicans and Californios as field hands. The obvious conclusion is that Spanish-speaking workers were placed in a disadvantaged position in the labor market. There were often racist assumptions used to employ Mexican labor. The railroads, for example, believed that Mexican and Californio workers had a natural advantage when working in the hot desert regions. In sum, employment conditions for the Spanish-speaking were marginal and wages extremely low.

The Mexican-American Political Impulse

One of the byproducts of second-class citizenship for the Spanish-speaking was to create political unrest. It was only natural for Spanish-speaking politicians to emerge in the late-nineteenth century. Unfortunately, the vast majority of politicians representing Mexican and Californio interests were tied to the Republican or Democratic political machines. They were politicians who lacked independence and power.

Perhaps the best example of a token Mexican-American politico was Romualdo Pacheco. In 1854 the twenty-two year old Pacheco was elected a California judge in San Luis Obispo County, and he served in a distinguished manner for a four year term. His performance and his mature outward image attracted both major parties. In 1857, Pacheco was elected to the California Senate as a Democrat from a district in Santa Barbara and San Luis Obispo Counties. During the American Civil War Pacheco displayed his loyalty for the Union by switching his allegiance to the Republican party. In 1863, Pacheco was elected state treasurer. He was defeated for reelection to this position, but Pacheco returned to the state senate in 1869. In 1871 the Republican party staged a comeback in California politics by campaigning strongly against the Chinese and actively seeking the Spanish-speaking vote. In the previous election an unknown Democrat was elected governor because of strong feeling against Chinese immigrants, and the Republican party learned from their past experience of not appealing to a broad spectrum of California political interests. As an attempt to appeal to the Spanish-speaking vote the Republican party selected Pacheco as its lieutenant-governor candidate, and in the election Pacheco and gubernatorial nominee, Newton Booth, were an excellent campaign team. In 1875 Governor Booth was selected by the California legislature to fill a vacant United States Senate seat, and Pacheco became California's first Spanish-surnamed governor.

During his nine months as California's governor Pacheco was not confronted with any momentous decisions. One of the intriguing aspects of his gubernatorial reign is that he granted 79 pardons to individuals of all ethnic groups. Pacheco talked of the problems that crime created in the Golden State, and he urged legislators to consider the possibility of prison reform. In addition to displaying a special empathy for prison conditions, Pacheco was a shrewd economic analyst. In his annual message to the state legislature, he warned that uneven taxes would cause California fiscal problems. Pacheco urged state legislators not to consider quick and unwise tax reforms. The most surprising portion of Pacheco's annual message was the recommendation that prisoners be put to work as an economy measure, and he cited the rehabilitation possibilities in such a program. In his brief term as governor, Pacheco supported additional buildings and library space for the University of California, and he generally attempted to upgrade the quality of education. As an interim governor, Pacheco was an unqualified success, and he hoped to garner the Republican gubernatorial nomination.

The Republican party considered Pacheco a token and nominated another candidate to succeed him. Pacheco was not even considered for the lieutenant governor's position. As a result of this treatment he angrily quit the Republican party, but he reconsidered his hasty decision and ran for the United States House of Representatives in 1876. As a candidate in the fourth Congressional District, Pacheco won a strange election victory by one vote. There were rumors of Republican fraud and ballot stuffing. Pacheco countered these charges by suggesting that a successful Spanish-speaking politician was not welcome in the Santa Clara area. Pacheco pointed to the large numbers of attacks upon local Mexican and Californio ranchos as an example of the racist mentality. After a lengthy court battle, Pacheco was sworn in as a Congressman, and he served three terms before retiring to private business. In 1890, President Benjamin Harrison appointed him as an Envoy Extraordinary and Minister Plenipotentiary to Central America. This recognition came too late to satisfy Pacheco, and he moved to northern Mexico to operate a prosperous cattle ranch.

Romualdo Pacheco's career in California politics was an important one. He contradicted the myth that Mexican or Californio politicians could not govern the state effectively. The far-sighted leadership he displayed in prison reform and the state economy was a reflection of a new Mexican-American political impulse. Pacheco was a strong voice for the small person in California politics, and the reticence of the Republican party to recognize his abilities was testimony to the lingering ethnic stereotypes and racial biases in California politics.

Although Pacheco was the best known Mexican-American politician, he was only one of a large number of Spanish-speaking politicos. In many respects Pacheco's success paved the way for José G. Estudillo to serve as state treasurer from 1875 to 1880. Andrés Castillero was a successful candidate for Congress in 1880, and Martin Aguirre was elected Los Angeles sheriff in 1885. All of these politicians came from old line, established families, and they represented a second-generation political impulse designed to end housing, job and educational discrimination. But the land boom of the 1880s in Southern California brought an end to Mexican-American political influences and by 1885 the "Americanization" of all of the Golden State was successful.

The Schizoid Heritage: A Summary

By the 1880s pioneer Californios like Mariano Vallejo looked upon themselves not merely as victims of annexation but of deliberate betrayal and bone-crushing repression. Many Californios complained that the agents who represented the famed California historian, Hubert Howe Bancroft, would only purchase material which reflected violence and hatred. Perhaps the best example of changing attitudes in California was shown when Friar Osuna was arrested in San Diego on the charge of lunacy. The reason was that the itinerant friar was dressed in the Franciscan robe and sandals that had not been popular in San Diego since the secularization of the missions. After Osuna was released from jail someone remarked that the old Spanish-Mexican heritage was virtually forgotten by the new flood of Yankee settlers. If the local police believed Osuna to be insane they had certainly no knowledge of California history. This bizarre incident is an excellent example of why many Mexican-Americans believed that they were caught between two cultures. Many were unsure of whether to embrace Yankee values or to cast their loyalties with Mexican cultural institutions. It was this conflict over which heritage was the dominant one which produced the so-called "Schizoid Heritage."

Historians during the late nineteenth century helped to perpetuate racial stereotypes and encouraged the growth of the Schizoid Heritage. In 1885, for example, Charles Shinn's *Mining Camps: A Study in American Frontier Government* discussed Anglo-Saxon virtues and Latin vices in the mines. Spaniards were pictured as cruel, indolent and fanatical. Bancroft's multivolume history of California argued that the Spaniards were troublemakers who deserved to be displaced in the mines. The Harvard philosopher, Josiah Royce, suggested that Spanish-American were amoral people and this was the reason for many of their problems. After growing up in Grass Valley, Royce graduated from the University of California, Berkeley, and he eventually became one of America's best known philosophers. California history was Royce's hobby, and his book *California from the Conquest in 1846 to the Second Vigilance Committee in San Francisco,* published in 1887, was the most influential study of California. Royce subtitled his book, "A Study of American Character," which allowed him to make sweeping generalizations about the human condition. Most of these conclusions were slurs on the slow moving, indolent Spaniard. It was this view of Mexican-Americans by historians which reinforced racial stereotyping and produced a "Schizoid Heritage."

The Land Law of 1851

Land ownership was the most complex question facing California in the early years of statehood. The lack of law and order and the propensity toward violence encouraged squatters to ignore Spanish and Mexican land grants. The controversy which resulted over land ownership was intensified by the introduction of an American legal system which seemed to differ with Spanish and Mexican law. The Yankee approach to land claims was one which emphasized that a land claim must be worked to be a valid one. Under American law land claims were highly legalistic and sharply defined; this differed a great deal from the Spanish and Mexican concept of land ownership.

The Treaty of Guadalupe-Hidalgo contained a phrase which suggested that all foreign residents in California would enjoy the "rights of the United States according to the principles of the

Constitution." This phrase seemed to guarantee Spanish and Mexican land grants. In fact, an earlier version of the treaty had included a guarantee of local land claims. It was the vague nature of the Treaty of Guadalupe-Hidalgo which allowed those who opposed Spanish and Mexican land settlement to argue for a new means of deciding disputed claims.

Many Spanish and Mexican land grants were imprecisely drawn and often improperly settled, and this provided an open invitation for American squatters to challenge most foreign land grants. It was relatively easy to challenge Spanish land grants as all newly discovered land belonged to the crown. In Spanish law, California was the King's backyard, and he could dispose of the land in any manner he saw fit. As a result Spanish land grants were often uncertain ones. In Union City and San Leandro in the Bay Area more than 1,500 American squatters descended upon the Peralta and Estudillo claims. Most squatters organized formal leagues or associations to attempt to persuade governmental authorities that they should occupy the land. Often crops were stolen and cattle sold which belonged to the large ranchos to support squatter's associations. Mexican law was very broad in interpreting land grants, but the general respect for these grants was diminished when the last Mexican governor, Pio Pico, awarded more than 800 last minute land claims. Pico then fled to Mexico, and the cry of land fraud was heard throughout California. This created an issue of false land grants which proved very useful to American squatters.

For some time the United States government had attempted to deal with the land controversy, but the land question was an insoluable problem for a variety of reasons. The lack of professional maps to provide a key to legitimate land claims was a serious problem. Since federal law demanded that the burden of proof be placed upon the grant holders this was an open invitation to unscrupulous land developers. In Mexican-California there was a great deal of imprecision in drawing up land grants, and this resulted in a request for clarification of many land settlements. The pressure upon federal officials to clear up land disputes led to a number of surveys in California.

In an attempt to clarify disputed land claims Governor Richard B. Mason ordered Captain Henry W. Halleck to draw up an official study of California land titles. In 1849 Halleck dutifully complied with Governor Mason's request in a scathing report which concluded that most Mexican claims were imprecise ones. He also believed that a number of Spanish and Mexican land settlements were the product of outright fraud. In addition to the improper settlements, most rancheros did not meet the requirement to build dwellings and introduce livestock. The California diputación had to formally approve each rancho, and this recognition often was ignored.

Governor Mason predicted that there would be many challenges to local land settlements. The most obvious sign of the influence of Halleck's report was the squatters uprising in Sacramento in the summer of 1850. During the miserable winter of 1849–1850 Sacramento was inundated by miners, the unemployed and ruffians looking for fun. A large number of miners were washed out of the Sierra during a period of severe storms, and they filled every vacant corner of Sacramento. When the miners tried to purchase land they found that a small number of local citizens held title to land obtained from John Sutter's Mexican land grant of 1839. The Mormon merchant, Sam Brannan, had fraudulently obtained two hundred prime lots from Sutter, and this type of real estate speculation angered the discontent miners. In March, 1850, more than ten thousand people occupied Sacramento, and as city government organized the most pressing issue was land settlement. The newly elected Mayor, Harden Bigelow, announced that squatters must leave the lands that they occupied. When local squatters refused to vacate the land, the sheriff was brought in to tear down the shacks which were built by dispossessed miners. This led to a lengthy riot in which Sheriff Joseph Mc Kinney was shot to death, and the violence in Sacramento led to a demand for a federal land law.

The federal government appointed a young attorney, William Carey Jones, to investigate California land claims. Jones, the son-in-law of Thomas Hart Benton and the brother-in-law of John C. Frémont, delivered a report which most Californians ignored because of its findings. Although Jones attempted to conduct an impartial survey of California land settlement, his findings were curious ones. He recommended that the majority of Mexican land grants be recognized by the federal government. In addition, Jones stated this his fluent use of Spanish had enabled him to feret out the illegal land grants. His critics pointed to his own land holdings as well as those of John C. Frémont as ample proof that he was serving his own interests. Another problem with Jones' report was that it was delivered in March, 1850, and this was a time of massive hostility to Mexican land grants. In the final analysis, Jones recommended a liberal land grant policy which would guarantee the rights of Spanish, Mexican and early American settlers. It was now up to President Millard Fillmore and the United States Congress to decide the future of California land policy.

Senator William Gwin prepared a legalistic attack upon the disputed land claims. Gwin recognized that the Treaty of Guadalupe-Hidalgo recognized foreign land grants, but he believed that only an impartial panel could decide which grants should be allowed and which should not be rescinded. The idea of an impartial land commission did not appeal to Senator Thomas Hart Benton of Missouri who argued that such a law would prove costly, it could cause a land owner great expense to prove title, and, finally, it would provide a means for legal confiscation of old land grants. In an impassioned speech, Benton spoke of first hand experience in Louisiana with a land commission, and his conclusions were that it led to violence and fraud. These arguments were ignored and Congress passed the Land Law of 1851.

The three-man Land Commission began to hear disputed titles in San Francisco in January, 1852. For the next four years a large number of land cases were presented to the federal commissioners. Since either the claimant or the United States government could appeal a decision to a federal district court or the United States Supreme Court, it was not surprising that the average case with appeals spanned a seventeen year period. The expense for this litigation was usually high enough to force a land owner to liquidate most of his assets. This resulted in a large number of land owners losing their holdings by complying with the law. This was one of the reasons for the general popularity of violence and vigilante action.

It is to the credit of the commissioners that they attempted to impartially decide all disputed land claims. From a strictly statistical standpoint the vast majority of land settlements remained with the original owner. About three of four cases resulted in a victory for the owner. Yet, these claims were generally 640 acres or less, and the commission made it clear that larger, undeveloped claims did not deserve the same protection. In addition, a large number of Spanish and Mexican land grants were decimated by the commissioners. The rancheros formed a Mexican-American social and economic aristocracy which left a vacuum in California society.

There were also a number of cases of slick claimant's fooling the commissioners. Often a claimant who persisted in filing false land claims would be awarded property. The most successful practitioner of this type of deception was José Yves Limantour, a Frenchman who lived in Mexico. Arriving in California in the early 1840s, Limantour attempted one con game after another with little success. His smooth speech, courtly manners and elegant dress fooled many Californians, and this air of elegance helped him to swindle the land commission. He presented a series of forged documents which purported that he owned much of San Francisco. Limantour claimed to have been an agent for a Mexican governor who had granted him large amounts of land surrounding San Francisco. The documents appeared authentic and the land commission awarded Limantour more than 600,000 acres of land in the city and county of San Francisco. It was soon discovered that he had stolen eighty blank petitions presigned by the governor, and Limantour used these documents to support his fraudulent land claims. Finally, Limantour's grants were disallowed, but he was able to escape prosecution by fleeing the country. While Limantour's adventures were not typical of land claims, nevertheless, it does demonstrate that fraud was a continuing danger.

Los Angeles and San Francisco land claims were the most difficult for the land commissioners to decide. There were a number of reasons which made these land decisions impossible ones. As an original Spanish pueblo, leading Los Angeles citizens inflated the amount of land that encompassed the city limits. Once statehood was achieved the federal government argued that the boundaries of the City of the Angels were illegal, and it was not until 1858 that this sticky question was settled. The predominantly Mexican and Californio population of Los Angeles screamed that this was another example of Yankee racism. The more recent Los Angeles citizen argued that Spanish-speaking dominance was retarding the economic and social growth of Southern California. It was obvious to even casual observers that there were serious questions about Southern California land ownership. The federal government also questioned the San Francisco boundary. When city government asked for a standard presidio grant of four square leagues, the federal government denied this request. Federal officials stated that they were suspicious of the earlier Mexican settlement patterns. In 1835 San Francisco was founded as the port village of Yerba Buena, and the reason for the emergence of this small city was to take advantage of the secularization of Mission Delores. In 1847 Yerba Buena was renamed San Francisco and the first dock was built to receive ships. Thus, the federal government did not envision the potential greatness of the city by the bay and there was a general feeling that its boundaries should be restricted. This led to a lengthy boundary dispute which was not resolved until 1866.

One of the byproducts of the San Francisco and Los Angeles land disputes was the rise of squatters. Taking advantage of the legal confusion squatters settled upon disputed lands. Professional real estate developers were drawn to both cities, and they used federal preemption laws in the early 1850s to file small land claims. By filing 40 to 160 acre claims speculators believed that they would eventually be awarded some of the land. A large number of speculators built fences around their land and employed armed guards. In 1855 and 1856 three ordinances were passed by the San Francisco Board of Supervisors to compromise local land claims with the squatters. In specific areas of the city squatters were allowed to settle. Noe Valley, for example, was settled by a series of squatters ordinances. Eventually more than two hundred settlers received title to San Francisco land through squatter's rights.

The chaos surrounding California land settlement was a reflection of the lack of law and order and the weak nature of California governmental institutions. In addition to the problems caused by squatters, lawyers created a number of headaches by charging outrageous fees and performing sloppy court work. In addition opportunistic lawyers often appealed to juries and judges sympathetic to squatters. Often squatters resorted to violence when the courts would not confirm their land settlement. At public meetings squatters often spoke of "shotgun titles" and this was an indication of the mob mentality of the day. The significance of squatters rights is that it broke up large land areas for new settlers. As a result settlement patterns and economic power was reshaped in California.

Many of the early decisions on land grants were liberal ones. The recognition of John C. Frémont's Rancho Mariposa, the only Mexican grant in the Mother Lode, was more the result of Frémont's place in California history than of judicial judgment on the legality of the land. To contemporary observers the recognition of Frémont's grant was an example of outright fraud. Frémont had never met any of the requirements to occupy or develop the land, and the presence of wild Indians on much of the settlement made it a dangerous proposition. The grant was purchased from Governor Juan Bautista Alvarado who had never seen the land. Thus, the Rancho Mariposa was typical of floating land grants that were sold from one speculator to another with little regard for boundaries, proper ownership or eventual settlement. It was not coincidental that Frémont's land claim was approved a few months before he began to campaign as the first Republican candidate for the Presidency.

Large land grants owned by Californios were not afforded the same protection. A good example of this double standard was shown in the case of the Rancho San Antonio. This land grant was awarded to the Peralta family for lengthy service to the Spanish crown. Vicente Peralta stubbornly refused to allow settlers on his grant which spanned the present day cities of Oakland, Berkeley and Alameda. In 1850 a band of squatters laid out plans for the city of Oakland. But local courts recognized the legality of the Peralta grant, and it appeared that the East Bay might escape permanent settlement.

After a period of time a smooth-talking lawyer, Horace Carpentier, worked his way into Peralta's confidence. The three million dollar Peralta estate was Carpentier's goal, and he approached the family with a get rich scheme. After signing the papers, Peralta discovered that he had signed a mortgage on his property. In a bizarre fashion Carpentier could be seen daily on the Rancho San Antonio cutting down trees, slaughtering cattle and selling plots of land. In a short period of time the 19,000 acre Peralta estate was confiscated by Carpentier. In reality, Carpentier had tricked Peralta in signing legal papers that he did not understand. When Peralta refused to pay the fraudulent mortgage the sheriff sold the Rancho San Antonio to Carpentier. He immediately founded Oakland, and as its first mayor he was responsible for its rapid growth.

The Carpentier-Peralta incident suggests that clever, unscrupulous lawyers were often able to fraudulently obtain large land grants. It is also an interesting exercise in cultural contrasts as Peralta admired the articulate lawyer, but he failed to understand the implications of the American legal system. It did not help matters that Peralta was going insane while this controversy developed over the Rancho San Antonio. Many Mexican and Californio rancheros simply left California rather than attempt to compete in a system they did not understand, and the result was to decimate the Mexican-American economic aristocracy.

California Land Settlement: A Summary

Between 1865 and 1890 the entire basis of California land settlement was profoundly altered as more than four million acres of public lands were sold to private citizens. California governmental officials defended these sales as an attempt to equitably disperse state lands to private citizens. There was a serious attempt by state government officials to create the illusion that public land sales were being dominated by small farmers. This was totally untrue as large corporations and individual entrepreneurs bought up the best land. In 1871, 122 farms covered more acreage than the total of the remaining 23,000 small farms. Monopoly in land ownership was the obvious result of the new land policies, whatever the intent of the legislators who framed them.

There were a number of changing attitudes resulting from the redistribution of land. Large numbers of middle-class and poor farmers supported politicians and pressure groups that attacked land monopoly. The demand for secret elections or the Australian ballot increased due to the land monopoly debate. Finally, the role of big business in controlling wages, prices and the direction of the California economy created a labor union mentality.

The cataclysmic changes in late 19th and early 20th century California can be partially traced to the fears and hatreds that the land question brought out in state politics. There is also good evidence to indicate that many of California's current racial problems and housing controversies have roots in this earlier period.

Bibliographical Essay

The best description of the Foreign Miners' Tax of 1850 is Leonard Pitt, *The Decline of the Californios* (1966). For Mexican migration to the California mines see, M. Colette Standart, "The Sonoran Migration to California, 1848–1856," *Southern California Quarterly,* LVIII (Fall, 1976), 333–358; and R. H. Morefield, "Mexicans in the California Mines, 1848–1853," *California Historical Society Quarterly* XXXV (March, 1956), 37–46.

The work of Paul W. Gates on California land policies is a staggering contribution to the historiography of California land development see, Paul W. Gates, "Carpertbaggers Join the Rush for California Land," *California Historical Quarterly,* LVI (Summer, 1977), 98–127; Adjudication of Spanish-Mexican Land Claims in California," *The Huntington Library Quarterly,* XXI (May, 1958),213–236; "California's Embattled Settlers," *California Historical Society Quarterly,* XLI (June, 1962), 99–130; *California Ranchos and Farms, 1846–1862* (1967); "The Suscol Principle, Pre-emption and California Latifundia," *Pacific Historical Review,* XXXIX (November, 1970), 453–471; "The California Land Act of 1851," *California Historical Quarterly,* L (December, 1971), 395–430; and "Public Land Disposal in California," *Agricultural History,* XLIX (January, 1975), 158–178.

The best history of Mexican and Californio bandits is Pedro Castillo and Alberto Camarillo, *Furia y Muerte: Chicano Social Banditry* (1973). For a dated view of California outlaws see, Joseph Henry Jackson, *Bad Company* (1949) and Walter Noble Burns, *The Robin Hood of El Dorado* (1932).

There is a good deal of excellent material on Southern California lands see, W.W. Robinson, *Land in California* (1948); Robert G. Cleland, *The Cattle on a Thousand Hills* (1941); and John W. Caughey, "Don Benito Wilson," *Huntington Library Quarterly,* II (April, 1939), 285–300.

An excellent study of governmental attitudes toward ethnic minorities is R.F. Heizer and A.F. Almquist, *The Other Californians: Prejudice and Discrimination Under Spain, Mexico, and the United States to 1920* (1971). A doctoral dissertation which deserves publication for its sensitive portrayal of 19th century California Indians is James J. Rawls, "Images of the California Indians: American Attitudes toward the Indians of California, 1808–1873," (University of California, Berkeley, 1975). Also see Part III of Sherbourne F. Cook, *The Conflict Between the*

California Indian and White Civilization (1943), which deals with the period of the American invasion, 1848–1870.

For an excellent recent article on the role of the press in prompting use of the Foreign Miners' Tax Law see, Cheryl L. Cole, "Chinese Exclusion: The Capitalist Perspective of the *Sacramento Union, 1850–1882," California History,* LVII (Spring, 1978), 8–31. There is need for research on the ethnic side of the mining and land policies of the United States. Professor Pedro Castillo of the University of California, Santa Cruz has presented a series of papers on the need to reassess the Chicano experience see, "The Re-Emergence of Hispanic Culture in America," Paper presented to the International Conference on Current Trends in the Study of America," Sevilla, Spain, 1977 and "Continuity and Change in California Chicano Society: From the Mexican War to the Great Depression," National Association of Chicano Social Scientists, 1977.

There are two excellent studies examining the shift from Spanish to American attitudes in Santa Barbara and the resulting levels of ethnic tension see, Albert M. Camarillo, "The Making of a Chicano Community: A History of the Chicanos in Santa Barbara, 1850–1930," (Unpublished doctoral dissertation, University of California, Los Angeles, 1975); and James C. Williams, "Cultural Tension: The Origins of American Santa Barbara," *Southern California Quarterly,* LX (Winter, 1978), 349–377.

A major article on the influence of rivers upon the state's capital city is Marvin Brienes, "Sacramento Defies the Rivers, 1850–1878," *California History,* LVIII (Spring, 1979), 3–19. Brienes' article is a brilliant interpretation of the geographical influence upon history.

Collis P. Huntington

Leland Stanford

Mark Hopkins

Courtesy, The Bancroft Library

9

THE CIVIL WAR, THE TRANSPORTATION REVOLUTION AND A NEW ECONOMY

The Civil War

In 1860 the influence of Southern-minded politicians began to decline in California. The new governor was an Alabama native, Milton Latham, who had been educated in the North, but he served only five days before the California legislature selected him for a position in the United States Senate. The lieutenant-governor, John Downey, ascended to the top position in the state with a general lack of concern for slavery amd most other political issues of the 1850s. It was obvious that most Californians were loyal to the Union as the American Civil War approached, and the four electoral votes cast for President Abraham Lincoln attested to California's new political attitude.

Despite the changes in California politics there was still evidence that many favored a Pacific Republic. This scheme was one which promoted the creation of a separate nation, and it reflected the continuation of southern political thinking. In 1861 the California Senate and Assembly debated the Pacific Republic scheme and the Assembly voted four to one against the proposal. To establish loyalty for the Union a mass demonstration was held in San Francisco. Yet, many Americans continued to bear pro-Confederate sentiment in California. This is the reason that Californians were unable to fight with any degree of success in the Civil War.

Californians with Confederate sympathies were a colorful and vocal group. They founded secret societies like the Knights of the Golden Circle or the Knights of the Columbian Star and spread vicious rumors about seizing federal property in the Golden State. A group of Confederate supporters purchased a small ship, the *Chapman,* with the romantic idea of capturing a larger ship which would be used in the Confederate navy. Federal officials quickly squashed this scheme, but the publicity resulting from it made Californians appear as Southern sympathizers.

The pro-Confederate fears were destroyed in the state elections of 1861 when the Republicans and Union Democrats swept into office. Most successful state politicians spoke out strongly against secession and supported President Lincoln's Unionist policies. A Republican governor, Leland Stanford, was elected due to his strong campaign on the dangers of secession. In fact, from 1863 to 1867 the Republican party called itself the Union party and built a great deal of its future strength upon ties with the federal government. An important factor in pro-Union sentiment was the Rev. Thomas Starr King. A Unitarian minister, King arrived in San Francisco in 1860 from Boston and promptly became a major political figure. He was a spellbinding speaker who lectured Californians on the merits of charitable works. During the Civil War, King used his influence and prestige to raise large sums of money for the Sanitary Commission, the Red Cross of the American Civil War, and Californians donated one of every four dollars provided for war charity.

There was no significant military participation by Californians during the Civil War. The cost of transportation for small numbers of California soldiers and the laxness of enforcing draft regulations made it impossible to include forces from the Golden State. Andrés Pico hoped to demonstrate his loyalty and that of most Californios by fighting in the Civil War. Pico persisted and the state of Massachusetts paid the cost of transporting the Native Cavalry to the east. Pico's group, known as the "California Battalion," fought with the 2nd Massachusetts Cavalry in more than fifty campaigns in and around Virginia. Less than 20,000 Californians served in the Union army and most were sentries or guards to protect overland mail routes or to control hostile Indians.

The change in California life was apparent to everyone during the Civil War. There was now a concern with developing local industry and creating a business climate. This could not be completed without substantial construction of new roads and the completion of a railroad. It was the Civil War which brought the first important ties with eastern business interests, and this helped to create ideas and attitudes necessary to a transportation revolution.

The Transportation Revolution: The Early Years

While the Gold Rush created a demand for improved transportation facilities, there was only slow growth in the development of new roads and routes into California prior to the Civil War. As early as 1847 private transportation companies brought mail and passengers into San Francisco, but the routes were often hazardous ones, the cost was extremely high, and traveling conditions were abysmal. The Gold Rush created a need to link small mining towns with Sacramento and San Francisco, and this prompted early transportation pioneers to descend upon California. By February, 1848, the Panama Mail Line inaugurated monthly deliveries to California, but this proved to be less than satisfactory to local citizens. The desire for information from the outside world led to 34 post offices by 1857, but the slow mail deliveries prompted local citizens to petition the federal government for daily mail service. It was citizen interest which created the transportation explosion in California.

In 1857 Congress passed the Overland California Mail Act which made it possible for private business interests to bid on an overland stagecoach mail route between St. Louis and San Francisco. John Butterfield who headed the Overland Mail Company was the successful bidder for mail and passenger service. A brilliant theoretical planner, Butterfield was able to guarantee 24 day service between the middle west and San Francisco for passengers. What was unique about Butterfield's route is that it ran through the Southwest bringing Americans into contact with Southern California. Although the Butterfield passenger line brought people into Southern California, there was no rush to settle that area. In fact, there was much more permanent settlement in the San Joaquin Valley as a result of the stage line. But the 2,800 mile stage line was too expensive to effectively provide transportation. The Butterfield line spent a million dollars on the route from Tipton, Missouri, to San Francisco, and the twenty-five passengers traveled only five miles an hour; this resulted in numerous complaints about the slowness and the cost of overland travel. The significance of the Butterfield line was that it provided the first regular service to California as well as a commuter route between San Francisco and Los Angeles. This led to increased commercial intercourse between Northern and Southern California. The slowness of the stage line caused large numbers of complaints, and the ensuing debate led to a demand for a transcontinental railroad.

Although the Butterfield line provided quick, efficient mail service, there was little to attract the common traveler. It was an uncomfortable ride to California with little chance to sleep and only cold food provided at short rest stops. To complicate the harsh conditions meals were highly priced, jerked beef, fried pork, corncakes and coffee cost forty cents to a dollar at the local rest stops. Fist fights and an occasional duel broke the monotony surrounding the Butterfield Stage line. Often disturbances were a protest against the high priced fare of $200 from St. Louis to San Francisco. In addition to these problems, extravagant spending by John Butterfield kept the company from making the necessary profits to continue expanding into the American West.

The American Civil War disrupted the southern route of the Butterfield line and cost the company a great deal of revenue. When the southern route was closed Butterfield was fired as president of the line, and the business was reorganized to minimize costs and maximize efficiency. The end result was to lessen transportation in California and force public opinion to demand federal transportation subsidies. Eventually the federal government began to investigate the Butterfield line, and this resulted in the Wells Fargo Company taking over the Butterfield controlled Overland Mail Company. Wells Fargo was reticent to use its name in the western transportation industry, and it organized a number of subsidiary companies. This sophisticated approach to western business revolutionized the economy of California. By 1860 Wells Fargo had established 147 offices throughout California's mining districts, and this created a business monopoly in the California-Nevada area. In addition to the express business Wells Fargo operated banking services which extracted heavy profits in gold dust.

By 1866 Wells Fargo had bought out all of its competitors, and the result was to make the company a mammoth corporation in the transportation and banking field. In 1869 the completion of the transcontinental railroad ended mail deliveries by stage lines, and the Wells Fargo Company reorganized to provide stagecoaches as a connecting link with railroad travel. This skilled business approach made the Wells Fargo Company the most successful transportation corporation prior to the Central Pacific railroad.

In many respects the overland mail service created more myth and legend about California than it actually contributed to permanent settlement. The majority of new settlers continued to arrive by steamers sailing into San Francisco. Yet, public attention was focused upon short lived transportation experiments like the Pony Express. On April 3, 1860, this transportation route began mail service between St. Joseph, Missouri, and Sacramento. The Pony Express received a federal government contract to deliver mail, but the firm of Russell, Majors and Waddell, a well-known freighting company, also formed the Central Overland California and Pike's Peak Express Company to engage in passenger service. For five dollars an ounce a letter was delivered in ten days which was half the normal amount of time. Using young men who weighed less than a hundred pounds the Pony Express carried 40 to 90 letters, but this arrangement was not a particularly profitable business enterprise. As a private business venture the Pony Express did not receive the degree of federal subsidies that many other transportation companies garnered in the 1860s, but the average citizen preferred to do business with the Pony Express rather than the Post Office. In less than a year the Pony Express declared bankruptcy, but the federal government stepped in with a six month subsidy to keep the Pony Express operating.

In the final analysis new forms of technology made the Pony Express an antiquated transportation system. On October 20, 1861, the transcontinental telegraph was completed between New York and San Francisco, and this ended the demand for prompt delivery of business materials.

Soon Los Angeles and San Francisco were linked by the telegraph and the Pony Express faded from the transportation scene. The demand for a transcontinental railroad can be traced to the early controversy over the Pony Express and overland passenger travel.

The advances of the transportation industry prior to the birth of the railroad were important ones to California's economic development. In addition to stage lines and the Pony Express, California was invaded by wagon traders. As enormous sized wagons carried 5 to 16 thousand pounds of goods into California there was a demand for the construction of new roads through the Sierras. In Placerville a fledging wagon industry developed and merchants like John Studebaker and Mark Hopkins established successful business interests. There were other important manufacturing industries due to the Gold Rush. Large numbers of sawmills sprang up to produce the lumber necessary for placer and hydraulic mining. The new towns were built with lumber and this created a boom in the early lumber industry. Flour and woolen mills were hastily constructed and iron manufacturing began in a crude way in San Francisco.

These early transportation and manufacturing interests were not particularly successful ones. The lack of coal and iron deposits, a minimal labor supply and the lack of available investment capital doomed early industrial growth. In addition the California Constitution of 1849 restricted business and banking development. Eastern business interests were reticent to enter the California market due to a general lack of demand for many consumer goods. California's population was so tightly settled in the Sierra and San Francisco areas that most eastern business concerns shied away from the Golden State.

Early Dreams of a Transcontinental Railroad

The sense of geographical isolation Californians experienced was one of the strongest influences upon developing a transcontinental railroad. In the United States Senate Southerners predicted that a railroad network spanning the nation would create new free states, and they opposed any northern route. For almost twenty years Congress debated where a transcontinental railroad should be built and five separate routes were proposed in a 13 volume government survey published in 1855. The only common area of agreement among railroad buffs was that federal money was necessary to finance a transcontinental transportation system. The actual construction of the railroad was delayed until the American Civil War stilled the voice of southern dissenters.

Most California transportation pioneers were oblivious to national politics. The most important early California railroad promoter was a transplanted New Yorker, Theodore Judah. Known as Crazy Judah because of his fanatical devotion to railroading, the young New Yorker established the first California railroad. In 1854, Judah built the Sacramento Valley line from Sacramento to Folsom. There was a great deal of opposition to railroad builders and the California legislature passed a law requiring a deposit of one thousand dollars a mile for each railroad construction plan. California politicians believed that early transportation pioneers were akin to snake oil salesmen. The profits from Judah's railroad serving the mining regions of the Sierra Nevada attracted the interest of a large number of California business interests.

From 1854 to 1859 Judah preached the virtues of a central route for the transcontinental railroad, but the general consensus was that it would be impossible to build across the Sierra Nevada range. In an effort to promote his schemes Judah organized the Pacific Railroad Convention of 1859. Although supported by the California legislature, the San Francisco meeting of

Theodore Judah, early railroad pioneer

Courtesy, The Bancroft Library

railroad buffs failed to attract the financial support necessary for a large scale venture. The Pacific Railroad Convention planned to build the first stage of a transcontinental railroad from Sacramento to Dutch Flat. The 115 mile route was the natural first stage toward Emigrant Gap and Donner Pass. A local druggist, Daniel W. Strong, personally guided Judah through the Dutch Flat area. On horseback Strong and Judah traveled to the mountains north of Lake Tahoe and found a long, timbered ridge that would provide access around the seven thousand feet Donner Summit. The dream of a transcontinental railroad was about to become a reality and it would change the course of California civilization dramatically.

The Birth of the Central Pacific

It was very difficult for Judah to find investors. He urged local businessmen to put up their money in a sense of public spirit, and the result was to create the view that the new railroad would be a charity venture. Faced with the prospect of losing large sums of money most California businessmen refused to invest in Judah's scheme. This changed when Judah began to emphasize the large sums of money that could be made from a transcontinental railroad, and he spoke of receiving large amounts of federal aid to build the railroad. Once Judah appealed to the greed of local investors he found a number of Sacramento businessmen who were interested in the railroad venture.

On a warm autumn evening in 1860 at the hardware store of Huntington and Hopkins, Judah met with the men destined to become the Big Four. Leland Stanford, Charles Crocker, Collis P. Huntington and Mark Hopkins listened to Judah's ideas. They agreed to invest in the Dutch Flat scheme and reasoned that a railroad into the Sierra Nevada region would reap large profits. They were men of limited vision who did not believe in the concept of a transcontinental railroad.

On June 28, 1861, the Central Pacific railroad was formally organized in Sacramento. The new corporation selected Stanford as President, Huntington as Vice-President and Hopkins as Treasurer. Judah was awarded a salary of $100 a month and instructed to ride into the mountains to survey a route and estimate costs. This survey almost destroyed the early interest in the Central Pacific railroad as Judah reported that 18 tunnels would have to be drilled, a great deal of land filled, and numerous trestles would have to be built. Judah estimated that $13 million, nearly $93,000 a mile, would have to be invested in the effort to reach the Sierra Nevada. In order to obtain the sums necessary to complete the venture federal subsidies must be secured. As Californians speculated about the wisdom of a transcontinental railroad, national events occurred which acted as a catalyst to the creation of a national transportation system.

The outbreak of the American Civil War placed President Abraham Lincoln in a difficult situation. He overestimated the degree of Confederate sympathy in California, and this prompted the Republican President to support massive federal aid for a transcontinental railroad. Sensing President Lincoln's predicament, the Big 4 began to squeeze Judah out of the corporation. In a series of shrewd corporate maneuvers they virtually ended Judah's influence over the Central Pacific railroad. With only 800 of 85,000 shares of stock and combined assets of about $100,000 Crocker, Hopkins, Huntington and Stanford were on the verge of instant wealth. By 1880 their total fortunes were in excess of 200 million dollars. It is ironic that in 1861 they began the formidable task of attempting to reach the Sierra Navada with only $10,000 in cash.

Government Subsidies and the Railroad

The capital to develop the Central Pacific railroad was provided by the federal government. As the Civil War raged the Big Four realized that it would be much easier to convince President Lincoln and a Republican Congress that a transcontinental railroad would bring loyalty and economic rewards to the Union. Theordore Judah was sent to Washington D.C. to lobby for federal aid. He had made a number of trips to the nation's capitol and was well connected with a number of Senators and Congressmen. Judah was given $66,000 worth of Central Pacific stock to distribute to sympathetic politicians.

On July 1, 1862, Congress passed the Pacific Railroad Bill which provided the necessary federal aid for a transcontinental railroad. The Central Pacific was granted the right to build from Sacramento until it met the Union Pacific which was building from Omaha, Nebraska. A great deal of financial support and land grants were guaranteed to the railroads. Government loans were set up as 6% interest thirty year bonds with $16,000 provided for each mile of flatland track. For

Charles Crocker

railroad construction in the foothills a sum of $32,000 a mile was awarded to the Central Pacific. In the Sierra Nevada a princely sum of $48,000 was provided for each mile of track. Land grants of 6,400 acres for each completed mile of track appeared to be generous subsidies, but as late as 1941 the Central Pacific offered to sell some of this Nevada land for as little as 91¢ an acre. In addition the federal government retained a first mortgage on the Central Pacific and this served to discourage many investors.

Under government regulations the Central Pacific had to construct at least 25 miles of track a year, and the first government funds would not be forthcoming until 40 miles of track were completed. With great public fanfare the Central Pacific laid its first mile of track from Sacramento in February, 1863. The earliest map of California which Congress consulted showed Sacramento in the middle of the Sierra Nevada, and this was the first indication that trickery and dishonesty would be the hallmark of the Central Pacific railroad. In order to build the first few miles of the railroad Charles Crocker organized a contruction company. On the surface the Charles Crocker Construction Company appeared to be a legitimate business device. Crocker resigned from the Central Pacific board of directors, and he bid a low figure to construct the first 18 miles of track. As a favor to the railroad Crocker agreed to accept Central Pacific stock as partial payment for construction. This led to a great deal of financial manipulation and outright fraud by the Big Four.

There were other problems for the Central Pacific. The engineering work of the 250 pound Crocker was sloppy and imprecise. One problem after another emerged to hamper early track construction. The financial picture was clouded by the fact that federal money was not available until the first 40 miles of track were completed. Governor Stanford came to the rescue by persuading the California legislature to allow counties to issue bonds which were used to purchase large amounts of Central Pacific stock. Sacramento, San Francisco and Placer counties exchanged $1.15 million in county bonds for railroad stock. To obtain a railroad terminal the city of San Francisco contributed almost half a million dollars to the Central Pacific. Governor Stanford personally strong armed city and county governments into investing millions of dollars in the transcontinental railroad.

The chicanery of the Big Four struck a sour note with Theodore Judah. His feeling was aided by an anonymous pamphlet, *The Great Dutch Flat Swindle,* which alleged that the Big Four were not concerned with a transcontinental railroad, but they hoped to collect heavy profits from Sierra Nevada trade and government subsidies. The charges appeared true and Judah confronted his partners demanding a reappraisal of business conditions. After a number of heated arguments Judah accepted $100,000 for his interest in the Central Pacific. In a strange business deal Judah was given the option of buying out the Big Four for $400,000. This arrangement indicates that Crocker, Hopkins, Huntington and Stanford did not fully realize the economic potential of the Central Pacific railroad. As he traveled to New York to secure funds to repurchase his railroad, Judah was striken with yellow fever and died a few days before he arrived in New York.

The Construction Controversy

Once the Civil War ended, the Central Pacific's economic problems began to ease. The influx of federal, county and state funds created a sizeable treasury. There were still serious construction problems to overcome as Charles Crocker had little knowledge about constructing a railroad through the desolate Sierra Nevada region. It was also difficult to find a reliable source of labor.

In 1865 Crocker brought in a skeleton crew of 50 Chinese workers, and they proved so adept that more than 10,000 were hired to construct the Central Pacific. Working long hours at low pay the Chinese speeded construction and in June, 1868, the railroad reached Reno. The construction of this phase was phenomenal as Chinese workers were fitted with ropes and lowered down the side of mountains to chisel out a route. In addition a tunnel had to be drilled and constructed through a quarter of a mile of solid granite. The completion of the so-called Summit Tunnel was due to the pioneering use of nitroglycerin. During the winter of 1866–1867, 44 separate blizzards killed large numbers of Chinese workers and caused many delays. Labor unions from San Francisco protested that the conditions were inhumane, and for a brief moment the Chinese agreed by engaging in a strike. In July, 1867, almost four thousand Chinese workers demanded a 12 hour day and an increase of ten dollars a month in wages. The striking Chinese workers argued that

Chinese workers near Truckee

Irish labor was paid $30 a month plus another $30 to be spent on food, clothing, medical supplies and housing. In effect the Chinese were working for half the wages of the less productive Irishmen. This logic failed to sway Crocker and the strike was quickly broken.

The lack of success of Charles Crocker's Construction Company was shown when only 20 miles of track were laid in 1865 compared to 30 in 1866 and 50 in 1867. As the years progressed the engineering skills of the Central Pacific rapidly accelerated and in 1867 one observer remarked that tracks were laid with great skill. Considering the weather conditions this was an amazing feat. To build through the Sierra Nevada 37 miles of snowsheds were constructed.

Once the Central Pacific reached Reno, Crocker made impossible demands upon his crews. Building his Chinese labor crews to 15,000 Crocker bellowed that heaven was around the corner, and he devised a scheme to lay ten miles of track in a single day. Once this task was completed public interest in the completion of the transcontinental railroad reached a point of zealous intensity. Crocker's detractors pointed out that it took a week to scatter all the equipment and supplies and embed all the ties prior to laying the track. Still these complaints failed to diminish the general interest in the Central Pacific's race to catch the Union Pacific.

As the railroad race reached its conclusion Promontory, Utah, was selected as the site to join the transcontinental railroad. On May 10, 1869, a large crowd gathered to watch a young lady with a radiant smile present a spike of gold, silver and iron to begin the elaborate ceremony of completing the transcontinental transportation system. A telegraph wire was placed around each spike and every barroom in America exploded with cheers as the last spike was driven into the ground. It was ironic that the transcontinental railroad was completed a century after the Spanish settled San Diego. This cataclysmic event marked a new phase of economic and urban growth in California civilization.

The Southern Pacific Railroad and California

Although the Big Four remained skeptical about the profits that they could garner from the railroad, they organized a new group of local railroad lines. After gaining control of the San Francisco bay and Oakland the railroad magnates began looking toward Southern California. In December, 1865, a new corporation, the Southern Pacific Railroad was organized to connect San Francisco and San Diego. The announced purpose of the SP was to encourage intrastate trade, but the real intent was to monopolize California's shipping and passenger traffic. From 1865 to 1900 Collis P. Huntington ruled the SP with an iron hand, and he used it to control the political and economic direction of the Golden State.

The Central Pacific controlled Contract and Finance Company was selected to construct the Southern Pacific railroad. There were immediately cries of fraud but it was impossible to unearth any corruption against the Big Four. In fact, on paper the Big Four were not associated with the SP, but they acquired control of it in the late 1860s. The general suspicion was that other investors were front men using Central Pacific funds. These allegations were never proven, but they attest to the financial genius of the Big Four. New federal and state subsidies were collected as the SP was built and the city of Los Angeles granted both land and money to the SP. With only six thousand people Los Angeles realized that the new railroad would be the catalyst to permanent settlement. Charles Crocker threatened Los Angeles leaders until they paid a subsidy in excess of a half a million dollars. This lack of concern for the general public created an intense hatred that led to the eventual downfall of the railroad empire.

The Big Four maintained that the Central Pacific, the Southern Pacific and a small number of feeder lines were under the control of a number of corporations. This fraud was discovered by investigative reporters who began to refer to the Big Four as the Octopus. The Depression of 1873 lessened competition and helped to create new public hostility to the railroad.

The Southern Pacific received over 11 million acres of land within California. Scores of new urban settlements emerged due to the SP, but the heavy handed threats to San Joaquin Valley farmers created a legacy of hatred and distrust. Among the new towns were Fresno, Merced, Modesto and Bakersfield, and the increase in agricultural productivity was noticeable as a result of this San Joaquin Valley urban boom. In order to monopolize river traffic the Big Four purchased the California Steam Navigation Company thereby effectively ending riverboat shipping competition. In a complicated business maneuver the Big Four gained control of the Pacific Mail Steamship Company, and this ended competition to the Far East. The significance of the Southern

The Union Pacific and Central Pacific Railroads meet, May 10, 1869

Pacific and the large number of smaller transportation lines is that they ended any form of transportation competition in California. The Big Four controlled every phase of transportation, and this led to higher freight and passenger charges. In addition there was an unbearable arrogance on the part of the captains of industry, and this led to a growing demand for reform of big business practices.

A New Economy and the Railroad

The California economy began to attract national attention from 1870 to 1900. Unlike many states that depended upon a single crop, the Golden State produced more than 200 marketable crops. The diversity of California agriculture is partially explained by geographical differences, but the Spanish missionaries had introduced European irrigation which made many infertile spots lush agricultural areas.

The life of Henry Miller is a perfect caricature of the successful California rancher. A German immigrant, Miller opened a butcher shop in San Francisco, but he found that by purchasing land and raising cattle his profits soared. His method was to acquire swamp lands and then to control water routes along the San Joaquin river. Miller formed a partnership with Charles Lux, a German immigrant with a flair for the English language, and they organized a company which controlled more than a million acres of land. In the San Joaquin Valley a herd of 100,000 cattle roamed on Miller and Lux lands. Recognizing the agricultural possibilities of the San Joaquin Valley the Miller and Lux enterprise built storage and irrigation systems and planted crops on about 500,000 acres of land. The smaller farmers charged that Miller and Lux controlled water rights so as to bankrupt any agricultural competition. There were many lawsuits against the company and feelings ran strong about their business tactics.

The most significant change in California's economy was the rise of the wheat industry. In 1860 six million bushels of wheat were harvested, but by 1890 more than forty million bushels were harvested each year. The Sacramento Valley was the initial site of Wheat prosperity in the Golden State. Dr. Hugh Glenn, a Missouri rancher, was known as the "Wheat King of America" in the 1860s and 1870s. His business tactics were ruthless ones, and he began the pattern of exploiting ethnic farm labor that still remains an integral part of California history. He used cheap Mexican and Chinese labor in his wheat operation and the French-Glenn Livestock Company dominated agricultural production in the Sacramento Valley.

Another well known wheat baron was Isaac Friedlander, a 300 pound, six foot-seven rancher, who made his fortune selling wheat to Europe. Friedlander developed a near monopoly in shipping California wheat to foreign markets by becoming a skilled middle man in arranging storage sacks, ships and marketing services in foreign ports. By monopolizing wheat shipments to Liverpool, England, Friedlander incurred the wrath of the Grange. For a brief period of time the Grange attempted to compete with Friedlander, but the financial support provided by the Bank of California made the wheat baron the undisputed leader in marketing crops. The importance of Friedlander's monopolistic tactics is that they stabilized a poorly organized and operated industry.

As California agriculture increased its economic potential the Central Pacific, Southern Pacific and smaller feeder lines reaped huge profits. The extension of the railroads into the San Joaquin Valley and Southern California created a population boom. In 1880 San Francisco's population accounted for two of every five Californians. This changed in the land boom of the 1880s as Los Angeles reached over 100,000 settlers by the turn of the century. In the California interior the first signs of permanent settlement were taking place. To promote an interest in California the railroad created *Sunset* magazine to praise the virtues of the Golden State. In the 1870s and 1880s health seekers helped to publicize the California climate and tourism became a legitimate industry. The railroads serving Southern California aided the settlement rush by engaging in passenger fare wars that temporarily lowered a ticket to a dollar to travel from the Southwest to Los Angeles. The boom collapsed in the late 1880s but it influenced the settlement of Southern California and the San Joaquin Valley.

Urban Growth and Economic Speculation

As San Francisco grew as a business and commercial center the increase in fraud and outlandish financial schemes brought an air of disillusionment to California investors. The earliest economic speculator was a portly, bearded San Franciscan, William C. Ralston. In 1864 a change in state banking laws allowed Ralston and a group of investors to incorporate the Bank of California. The purpose of this enterprise was to control the Comstock mining lode near Virginia City, Nevada. It was a strange venture because the best period of productivity had passed in the Comstock Lode. In essence, Ralston engaged in a speculative venture to revive interest in Nevada mining stocks. Poor management, inadequate equipment and a lack of scientific knowledge about mining were factors which aided shady speculators.

An agent of the Bank of California, William Sharon, was sent to Virginia City to entice near bankrupt mine owners to borrow from the San Francisco bank. At night Sharon sat in Virginia City saloons as old-timers mesmerized him with stories of fabulous mineral wealth. A nationally known Yale geologist, Benjamin Silliman, Jr., reported that the Comstock Lode was no longer a productive mineral producing region. Sharon chose to ignore this report and he persuaded Ralston to open a branch bank in Virginia City. By 1867 Sharon had finagled control of 17 mining ventures and this led to the founding of the Union Mill and Mining Company. This corporation dominated the Comstock Lode and most mining firms were required to ship with the company or face the possibility of no bank credit.

This led to a temporary revival of the Comstock Lode, and the Bank of California became the most prosperous financial institution in the American West. Soon Ralston expanded his business interests to include furniture manufacturing, custom watchmaking, woolen mills, sugar refineries and a vast network of property. In rural Belmont he built a sumptuous villa with a distinctly European flavor to its architecture and furnishings. In fact, Ralston's power was so vast that the Central Pacific attempted to name a town in the San Joaquin Valley after him, when Ralston refused the city was dubbed Modesto. The reason Ralston turned down the offer was due to his ego; he believed that San Francisco should be renamed Ralston City. This type of arrogance was no doubt useful in the financial jungle of late 19th century California.

By the early 1870s competing mining firms placed Ralston in a position of overextending himself to maintain the Bank of California's financial status. A number of unwise investments which included a salted diamond mine led to the loss of large sums of investment capital. When Ralston's competitors produced a $105 million in the early 1870s, his control over the Comstock Lode ended and competition reemerged. In 1872, despite these business problems, Ralston began construction of the Palace Hotel in San Francisco. It was to be the most spectacular inn in the world. The construction featured a beautiful-tiered central garden and at a cost of almost seven million dollars it was a sumptuous architectural feat. Yet, the degree of luxury offered by the Palace Hotel was too great for most San Franciscans. It was ironic that the nicest hotel in the American West usually was occupied by very few guests. This became an economic liability which further strained Ralston's financial empire.

In order to revive his fortunes Ralston gambled desperately by purchasing large numbers of mining ventures surrounding his competitors business interests. Ralston reasoned that the rich mineral veins must extend beyond the property lines of his competitors. The result of this tactic was to increase the purchase prices of smaller mining ventures. In January, 1875, public confidence was shaken in the Bank of California when it was announced that the newly acquired claims were not rich with mineral deposits. After months of public apprehension a run began on the Bank of California's funds. By August 26, 1875, Ralston's bank closed and the board of directors demanded his resignation. The result of Ralston's business practices was to deepen the depression in San

Interior court, Palace Hotel

Courtesy, The Bancroft Library

Francisco. While Comstock Lode profits benefited California, the resulting depression made it virtually impossible for local citizens to find jobs. Had the Bank of California invested its funds in solid business ventures in San Francisco the great depression of the mid-1870s would have been a mild recession. No one will ever know what Ralston believed he was doing when he went for a swim in the San Francisco bay one morning and drowned. Most contemporary observers charged it was a deliberate suicide to hide the financial misdeeds of the Bank of California.

The saga of William Ralston offers ample evidence that the Big Four were not the only dishonest entrepreneurs operating in California. What the Ralston story indicates is that the city was now the center of financial planning. It was only natural that people should begin to develop an urban ethos.

The first signs of the growth of urbanization were reflected in the rise of streetcars and interurban electric transportation. Once an electric railway system was built the rise of suburban settlements was rapidly developed. In the horse and buggy era it was not possible to live more than two miles from work, because the time necessary for commuting would be too great. The electric railway led to suburban settlement five to twelve miles from the center of San Francisco.

Perhaps the most colorful transportation device was the cable car. San Francisco's rugged hills were formidable obstacles, and Andrew S. Hallidie overcame this with a wire rope that hauled cable cars up the steep hills. Soon the cable car became the symbol of San Francisco tourism, and although it was an impractical transportation device it remained to attract visitors.

From 1890 to 1920 the trolley and the electric railway were the main modes of transportation in California. Many of the early transportation moguls used their influence to sell suburban real estate developments. The most successful street railway promoter was Henry Huntington. He was the nephew of Collis P. Huntington and appeared destined to take over the Southern Pacific railroad. This never materialized and young Huntington moved to San Marino on the outskirts of Los Angeles.

For a number of years Huntington developed San Francisco and Los Angeles, but his love affair with Southern California caused him to sell his Southern Pacific and San Francisco business

Suspension of the Bank of California,
1875

Courtesy, The Bancroft Library

In memory of William C. Ralston

interests. In 1902 Huntington formed the Pacific Electric Railway Company to serve the greater Los Angeles area. In a short time Huntington's Pacific Electric line spread out 35 miles from the center of Los Angeles and served 42 separate cities in a transportation network that was considered one of the finest in the United States. In San Marino, Huntington purchased a vast mansion with magnificent grounds, and he began to collect rare books and manuscript collections in the fields of English and American history. When he died in 1927 the fabled Huntington Library was opened to scholars and the general public. It was a fitting tribute to the wealth of the railroad barons, and the collection of paintings and art pieces created an aura of cultural activity previously unknown in Southern California.

The Politics of the Railroad Era

From 1870 to 1900 political corruption was so strong that an honest politician found it almost impossible to operate in California politics. It was not just railroad corruption that influenced the times. Most Californians preferred to emulate Leland Stanford than the President of the United

States. The tycoons of the Gilded Age were heroes to the common person. An English writer, James Bryce, remarked that the entire state was at the mercy of railroad interests. At the pinnacle of its power the Southern Pacific railroad began to experience difficulties with public opinion. In many respects the decline of railroad power was due to personal infighting among the Big Four.

In 1874 David C. Colton became a partner in the Southern Pacific railroad. Using the title, General Colton, he served as manager of the railroad's California properties. Much like Collis P. Huntington, Colton was adroit at manipulating politicians and garnering special favors. When Colton joined the Big Four he was given the opportunity to purchase a large amount of stock using credit. Displaying almost a manic desire for public recognition, Colton referred to himself as an intergral part of the Big Five. Local newspapers sarcastically called the Southern Pacific the Big Four and a half.

When General Colton died unexpectedly after falling from his horse while riding at his Marin ranch, the Big Four paid his wife Ellen a small settlement of about a half a million dollars. A short while after Colton's tragic death, Mark Hopkins died and Mrs. Colton realized that her settlement was much lower than it should have been. When the railroad paid her for Colton's stock they used an extremely low figure, and this pointed up the lack of moral values by the railroad leaders.

In 1883 Mrs. Colton sued Leland Stanford and his partners alleging that she had been cheated out of four million dollars. During the course of the trial some six hundred letters written between Colton and Huntington were introduced as evidence of railroad malfeasance. The correspondence highlighted the influence that Colton had upon California legislators. The letters also indicated that the railroad controlled the scope and direction of legislation. It was a frightening picture of big business corruption extending into every aspect of California civilization. Huntington's letters indicated that federal representatives and senators were easily bought off by the railroad. When the letters became public, newspapers throughout the nation eagerly excerpted segments to highlight the malevolent deeds of the Big Four.

The surrounding controversy almost overwhelmed the trial, and the California Supreme Court refused to award Mrs. Colton a larger settlement. The Court ruled that she had accepted the initial offer of the railroad and this prevented her from suing for increased damages. The public scandal created a strong demand for political reform. It was not surprising that politicians began to use images of railroad corruption to appeal to the new breed of voters who demanded honest government. It would not be until 1910 that state politics were no longer controlled by big business, but the Colton Letters were instrumental in creating a desire for political change.

It was surprising that the railroad magnates continued a public-be-damned attitude in the late nineteenth century. Huntington's letters were particularly venal in their attitudes toward the general public. A bitter man with an egomaniacal personality, Huntington resented Leland Stanford's favorable public image. This led to a bitter public feud in which Huntington and Stanford fought openly in California politics. But in 1885 Stanford was elected to the United States Senate by a friendly California legislature. This incensed Huntington who believed that Stanford was not well-suited to politics, and Huntington lost face because he had promised a close friend the Senate seat. By the mid-1880s both Huntington and Stanford were obsessed with economic and political power and this boded ill for the future of the railroad.

In 1890 Huntington gained revenge by replacing Starford as president of the Southern Pacific. The Great Persuader, as Huntington was known, dec led that it was time for the railroad to leave the political arena. This was a wise decision as public hostility had grown increasingly strong since the publication of the Colton Letters. For a brief period the odious smell of railroad corruption was missing from state politics. It was strange to see Huntington denounce his business partner, Leland Stanford, as a corrupt politician who had bought his United States Senate seat. Many of Stanford's close friends claim that his death in 1893 was hastened by the public controversy with Huntington. This sentimental conclusion ignores Stanford's poor health, and the worry brought about by the financial strain of founding Stanford University. When he died Stanford was millions of dollars in debt and this further exasperated hostile public opinion.

The Railroad Funding Controversy

Perhaps the most sensational issue involving the railroad during the late nineteenth century was the so-called funding controversy. This complicated debate evolved around the original loans made to the Central Pacific for railroad construction. Under the terms of the thirty year bonds the loans of almost 30 million dollars were not due until 1899. Since the 1870s the Big Four had dissipated much of their capital by voting themselves large dividends, and they failed to maintain a fund to repay government loans.

In 1878 the United States Senate pushed an act through Congress requiring the Central Pacific to set up a fund to retain twenty-five per cent of the net earnings to repay federal loans. This regulation was easily evaded by bookkeeping techniques that kept this fund at a low level. Then Collis P. Huntington proposed a fifty to hundred year grace period for repayment of federal loans. In addition, Huntington prevailed upon his friends in Congress to introduce a 2% interest fee for the remaining Central Pacific indebtedness. The public reaction to this charade was widespread protest. Most Californians believed that freight and passenger rates would be boosted to pay off railroad debts.

There were two important opponents of the railroad—Adolph Sutro and William Randolph Hearst. Sutro was a millionaire who had made his fortune building the Comstock tunnel which led to quicker access to Nevada's mineral wealth. He then shifted his operation to San Francisco where he brought land at depression-level prices. In a short period of time Sutro owned almost ten percent of San Francisco land. What set Sutro apart from other men of wealth was his public-spirited personality. His stately home as well as the Cliff House were opened to visitors, and he often remarked that wealth should make San Francisco an easier place to live for the poor and middle-class Californian. The test of Sutro's liberalism came when the Southern Pacific railroad monopolized streetcar transportation in San Francisco and raised passenger rates to a level of near extortion for the common man. With a dramatic flair, Sutro announced that he would build a "people's" railway to serve San Francisco citizens.

When the Depression of 1893 hit California, Sutro talked of a political reform movement that would make the Southern Pacific railroad pay for the economic chaos. In 1894 Sutro was elected mayor of San Francisco on a radical third party ticket, the Populist movement. In many respects Sutro's election was due to his bellicose promise to revoke the Southern Pacific business charter. As his chief campaign slogan Sutro attacked the railroad's funding plans, and citizens voted for the Populist candidate as a means of expressing their hostility to railroad control of San Francisco.

An anti-railroad cartoon

THE CURSE OF CALIFORNIA.

An equally significant foe of railroad funding was William Randolph Hearst, editor of the *San Francisco Examiner*. In 1894 the *Examiner* circulated anti-railroad petitions which netted almost a quarter of a million signatures opposing any concessions for railroad debts. Hearst charged that Huntington had embarked upon a campaign to persuade the federal government to forgive all of the railroad's debts. In an effort to end railroad control in California, Hearst sent a young correspondent, Ambrose Bierce to Washington D.C. Young Bierce sent detailed descriptions of Huntington's attempts to intimidate Congress. These stories, coupled with entertaining editorial cartoons, created a groundswell of public opinion hostile to the railroad funding program.

It was difficult for most Californians to believe that the Southern Pacific railroad was on the verge of bankruptcy as Huntington suggested to a Congressional investigating body. In 1896 the California Senate and Assembly urged the federal government to demand full payment of its debts from the railroad. When Congress voted to ignore the railroad's pleas for reconsideration of its debts California Democratic Governor James Budd declared a legal holiday. The significance of the railroad funding controversy was to highlight the changes in public attitudes and the demand for political reform. Although the Southern Pacific machine would continue as an important force in California politics, its days as a political leader were clearly numbered. A new political consciousness began to seep into California politics and this led to an increasingly strong anti-railroad bias.

Lawyers and the Railroad Machine

The key to Southern Pacific political and economic power was the use of talented and high-priced lawyers. The SP legal department was a highly respected arm of the railroad machine. Its head, William F. Herrin, was able to continue railroad power for many years because he understood the legal and political rules of California civilization. As an attorney for the mammoth Miller and Lux land interests Herrin was able to become intimate with California economic and political thought. From 1893 until a reorganization plan took effect in World War I, Herrin headed the Southern Pacific Political Bureau. This organization was a public relations device intent upon rebuilding the Southern Pacific's image with the public and reinstituting some of the old political power. It was ironic that the railroad should begin to consider public relations at a time when the force of popular opinion was destroying the Southern Pacific's octopus-like hold upon California.

When Collis P. Huntington died in 1900 William Herrin climbed the corporate ladder to a position as Vice-President, but he was unable to restore the old luster to the Southern Pacific machine. It was impossible to ignore merchant complaints that the SP owned 85% of all railroad mileage in California and used that power to arbitrarily charge high shipping and passenger rates. In addition land owners pointed out that 11 million acres of federal land was apportioned to the railroad in California, and this made traditional American farm land almost obsolete. The Southern Pacific countered these charges with virtually incomprehensible statistics on employment and per capita wealth in California and argued that the prosperity Californians knew was due to the railroad. Had the Southern Pacific Political Bureau been a bit more skilled in the arena of public relations much of the criticism of railroad economic manipulation might have subsided in late 19th century California.

California and the Transition to Modernity

The generation that spanned the 1880s and 1890s in California experienced the modernization of the Golden State's burgeoning urban-industrial complex. Corporate expansion, urban growth, sporadic economic depression, and large population shifts strained California's political and economic structure. In essence, the 1880s and 1890s witnessed the rise of a political boss who dominated a local political machine. Suddenly city politicians controlled state politics. The demands of running a modern city made the boss system virtually inevitable. It was impossible to efficiently operate a major city without a power broker to smooth the way for big business interests.

It was not surprising that San Francisco dominated late 19th and early 20th century California. In 1880 27% of the state's population resided in San Francisco and more than 40% of all Californians lived in the Bay Area. In 1880 San Francisco's 234,000 citizens ranked it as the number one city in the Golden State, and Oakland had only 34,555 people with a number two ranking. In many respects Bay Area politics dominated the direction of state government.

There were various attempts to reform the corrupt political atmosphere but nineteenth century reform movements were dismal failures. One significant change was the rise of the Australian or secret ballot in 1891. For many years Californians had picked up a ballot at a local bar. It was usually a bright colored and lengthy piece of paper. When a voter showed up at the polls it was very easy to see what party the voter had selected. It was also not uncommon for fires to break out in the homes of individuals who had voted contrary to local politics. The volunteer fire departments found it difficult to put out these fires. In addition to this type of voter intimidation, there often were reports that some districts in San Francisco cast 105% of its vote. This proved highly embarrassing to local politicians when they were asked to explain how more voters than lived in an electoral district could cast a ballot. It was obvious that the system needed a great deal of reform to put politics back onto an even keel.

In the 1890s Californians began to argue that direct popular democracy must be instituted in local politics. This idea was one which had been building since the Great Depression of the 1870s. The failure of party bosses to consider public opinion when selecting candidates for public office led to strong demands to end the system of caucus politics. This method allowed party bosses to select one candidate for each office without consulting local citizens. The reaction to boss politics created the first currents of political reform in the Golden State.

A cynicism combined with a popular dislike for the Republican and Democratic parties led to the growth of third party movements in the late 19th century. The Independent Taxpayers party suggested that curbs be placed upon state spending. The Temperance Reform party was interested in regulation of liquor, curbs on state taxes and a means of regulating prices and wages. The Nationalist party was a political organ that supported the creation of a Christian Socialist state that would modify wages and production while increasing government regulation of land and transportation monopolies. While most of these political movements were considered ideological rather than practical political organs, the issues raised by the third party movements dominated early twentieth century political thought.

Bibliographical Essay

The Civil War and California is a rather neglected phase in the history of the Golden State. For selected aspects of the Civil War see, Leo P. Kibby, "Some Aspects of California's Military Problems During the Civil War," *Civil War History,* V (September, 1959), 251–262; Helen B. Walter, "Confederates in Southern California," *Historical Society of Southern California, Quarterly,* XXXV (March, 1953), 41–55; and Oscar Lewis, *The War in the Far West* (1961).

For the transportation revolution see, W. Turrentine Jackson, *Wagon Roads West* (1952) and "Wells Fargo Staging over the Sierra," *California Historical Society Quarterly,* XLIX (June, 1970), 99–134. A pioneer interpretation of the relationship between stagecoaches and the pony express is W. Turrentine Jackson, "A New Look at Wells Fargo, Stagecoaches, and the Pony Express," *California Historical Society Quarterly,* XLV (December, 1966), 291–324. For popular works on transportation see, Samuel H. Adams, *The Pony Express* (1950); and Edward Hungerford, *Wells Fargo: Advancing the American Frontier* (1949).

The relationship of early California agriculture to the new economy can be examined in James M. Jensen, "Cattle Drives from the Ranchos to the Gold Fields of California," *Arizona and the West,* II (Winter, 1960), 341–352; Walton Bean, "James Warren and the Beginnings of Agricultural Institutions in California," *Pacific Historical Review,* XIII (December, 1944), 361–375; and Nelson Klose, "California's Experimentation in Sericulture," *Pacific Historical Review,* XXX (August, 1961), 213–228.

The literature on the building of the railroad is voluminous and highly uneven in quality. For the railroad see, John D. Galloway, *The First Transcontinental Railroad* (1950); Oscar Lewis, *The Big Four* (1938); Henel H. Jones, *Theodore D. Judah* (1969); Stuart Daggett, *Chapters on the History of the Southern Pacific* (1922); George T. Clark, *Leland Stanford* (1931); Norman E. Tutorow, *Leland Stanford: Man of Many Careers* (1970); David S. Lavender, *The Great Persuader* (1970); Wesley S. Griswold, *A Work of Giants: Building the First Transcontinental Railroad* (1963); and the Southern Pacific's official history, *Southern Pacific's First Century* (1955).

For changes in the California economy as a result of the railroad see the sophisticated study by Mansel G. Blackford, *The Politics of Business in California, 1890–1920* (1977). Also see, Richard Orsi, *"The Octopus* Reconsidered: The Southern Pacific and Agricultural Modernization in California, 1865–1915," *California Historical Quarterly,* LIV (Fall, 1975), 197–220; Gerald Nash, *State Government and Economic Development: A History of Administrative Policies in California, 1849–1933* (1964); and Rodman W. Paul, "The Great California Grain War: The Granger Challenges the Wheat King," *Pacific Historical Review,* XXVII (November, 1958), 331–350.

The rise of urbanization and the growth of the economy are traced in Robert M. Fogelson, *The Fragmented Metropolis: Los Angeles, 1850–1930* (1967).

A brilliant analysis of the Democratic party is R. Hal Williams, *The Democratic Party and California Politics, 1880–1896* (1973).

10

FORCES OF CHANGE, 1850–1900

The neglect of ethnic minorities, women, and blue-collar workers by historians has obscured the fact that they were important catalysts in changing attitudes and ideas concerning social, economic, and political problems in nineteenth century California. From 1850 to 1900, the bitter criticism of these groups reflected the political inequities, the class bias, and the cultural stereotyping which prevented the common person from enjoying the full benefits of the California dream. The end result of this social-economic intolerance prompted women, ethnic groups, and working class people to militantly oppose this brand of discrimination and forced Californians to reevaluate their attitudes and ideas on such sensitive questions as race, labor unionization, and women's suffrage. The end result of this revolution was to create a more liberal political and economic climate in twentieth century California.

California Indians

The California Indian faced an unusually hostile American attitude because most local citizens believed that the Indian should be removed from the Golden State. Since 1820, the federal government's Indian policy had continually shifted tribes westward in an attempt to create an Indian frontier. California Indians could not be sent any farther west, and this grated on the Anglo populace. In 1847, federal Indian agents began to drift into California to encourage the growth of agriculture and artisanship among local Indians.

Many early Indians agents were political appointees who used the positions to their own economic advantage. Important local politicans, like Mariano Vallejo and John Sutter, were appointed to the $750 a year positions, but they did little more than harrass and impede the progress of local Indians. In 1850, approximately 50,000 Indians remained in California—which was only one-third of the Indian population living in the Golden State when the Spanish arrived in 1769.

During the Gold Rush, a number of Indians mixed socially with the white miners; they mined in the gold fields with some degree of success, and for a time, achieved a degree of financial prosperity. There were a number of factors which led to the decline of the Indian population. Diseases, new social institutions, and forced Indian labor led to the decimation of Native Americans. The stage was set for Indians to move into remote areas of California and to prepare for a series of ill-fated Indian wars.

It is interesting that a number of California Indians were active miners in the gold rush. In fact, one State government source in 1848 suggested that almost half of California's mining population consisted of Indians. The majority of Indians worked as cheap labor for white Californians, but there were also Indians who were independent miners. An American miner, William G. Johnston, suggested that independent Indian miners possessed values close to and thoughts similar to the white man. The large number of whites who established trading posts and general merchandise stores suggests that there was a great deal of trade between whites and Indians.

One of the by-products of the white-Indian trade was the increase in commercial sophistication among California Indians. Indians soon demanded that their gold be weighed before trading, and they argued that special Indian prices were often discriminatory. The cheating of California Indians was so widespread that a British miner, William Kelly, wrote a book which delved into the subject. Kelly's *An Excursion to California,* published in 1851, charged that white merchants were mining a legacy of hatred and creating a revolutionary spirit among the Indians by unfair treatment.

As California mining turned to corporate production in the mid-1850s, the Indian was no longer a factor in the gold rush economy. The end result of this decline was to force Indians to remote parts of California or onto a federal government reservation. The increase in violence and differences of opinion between whites and Indians was due to the creation of the reservation system.

When the United States government created Indian reservations, they believed that this would lessen the tensions between whites and Indians; however, it was necessary to convince Californiᵃ Indians to move to the local reservations. In January, 1851, a three-man federal commiss. . tried to persuade California Indians to move out of the mountains into valley lands. When the Indians balked, California politicians called for war against the heathen invaders of the Golden State. In a tense racial atmosphere, politicians appealed to the emotions and ethnic hatreds of Californians. The result was to create strong tensions between the Indians and white settlers. Both state and federal politicians attempted to solve the so-called Indian problem. The by-product was 18 treaties negotiated with 130 tribes, or families. The intent was to remove Indians from the profitable mining regions in the Sierra Nevada. To induce the Indians to leave the mines, a reservation system totaling more than seven million acres was established in California. The reservation lands made up 7 ½% of the state's land, and this prompted many Californians to argue that local Indians were being provided with an economic windfall.

In 1853, Edward F. Beale, the Superintendent of Indian Affairs for California, suggested that the reservation system be modified, and this created a new system of reservations which was also used for military posts. In essence, this restructured reservation system was a recreation of the Spanish mission system. The major emphasis was placed upon teaching the Indians handcrafts and developing agricultural skills. After five reservations were established, Beale was suddenly removed from his position, and the dispensation of federal Indian funds became a political plum. For many years, only a small amount of the money designated to alleviate Indian problems reached the tribes. Graft and wholesale corruption were the cornerstones of federal Indian policy. A federal investigation revealed that Beale's brief tenure as Superintendent of Indian Affairs had cost the government almost a million dollars in unpaid debts. Shipments of supplies for the reservations were not delivered, and bills mounted for unreceived goods.

In the 1850's and 1860's, a number of Indian wars broke out to protest these conditions. The majority of Indian uprisings occurred in Northern California along the Humboldt, the Eel, and the Rogue rivers. As American military leaders attempted to drive the Indians into remote areas where they could be easily subdued, a new militancy crept into many Indian tribes.

The most important Indian uprising was the Modoc War. It was the last and possibly the most revealing look into white-Indian relations. In northern California, where the Modocs developed a reputation for independence and ferocity in battle, they were assigned to a reservation in Oregon where their enemies, the Klamath Indians, also lived. After a brief period in Oregon, the Modocs fled, only to be rounded up and returned to the reservation.

The leader of the Modocs, Captain Jack, persuaded his tribe to defy the federal government and return to northern California. During the winter of 1872, United States army troops moved into Modoc lands. One day, a young Modoc girl spotted the army forces. She quickly rode seventy-five miles to warn her people of the impending army intervention. To the Modocs, Wi-ne-ma was a heroine who risked her life to save her people from bloodshed, and the Modocs decided to heed her advice to retreat from the American army. In the process of attempting to surrender their weapons to the U.S. Army, an Indian called Scar-Faced Charley refused to give up his knife, and he was savagely beaten by army officers. In retaliation for the beating, eleven settlers were killed by marauding Modoc Indians. The Modoc leader, Captain Jack, then led his warriors into a series of lava beds; they were cut off from supplies, and subsisted on meals of mice and bats in the caves. The Modocs stated that they were not at war with the United States, and if they were left alone in the lava beds, there would be no further trouble. General E.R.S. Canby stated that the United States Army would drive the Modocs out of the lava beds and back into the reservation. The ensuing Modoc War was the most expensive military operation in American history. It cost in excess of one million dollars to defeat the Modoc Indians. The army lost almost one hundred men to one Indian casualty, and the legacy of hatred could not be measured in terms of dollars.

One of the by-products of the Modoc War was to create strong hostility towards California Indians. The reason for this hatred was an incident on April 11, 1873, when Captain Jack and General Canby met for a peace conference. After a brief discussion, the Indians brandished knives and pistols, and attacked the American troops. Canby was killed, and the Indians fled. But Captain Jack's Modocs could no longer hold out. Finally, in October, 1873, Captain Jack and three of his warriors were hanged after a brief military trial. There was a strong reaction from the American press over the excessive expenditure to hunt and capture a small band of Indians.

The Modoc War provided a case study of the slow, but steady, disintegration of California Indians. The decline of the Indian population was dramatic in late nineteenth century California. By 1900, approximately 15,000 Indians resided in California. The main cause of Indian casualties was disease, and almost two-thirds of Indian deaths were due to white diseases. Large numbers of Indians were forced onto welfare roles, many worked as tenant farmers, and a small number stole for survival. As the Indian problem became visible, a number of white reformers attempted to aid the distressed Indian minority. Helen Hunt Jackson, a novelist, wrote two important books: *A Century of Dishonor,* 1881, and *Ramona,* 1884. Both books studied the mistreatment of Indians in the American West. They were eagerly read by the general public and a large number of humanitarian-minded westerners worked to better Indian-white relations.

The federal government allotted various Indian tribes large grants of land from the 1880's to the 1950's, but the tribes often sold their lands to unsavory businessmen. Most of California's present-day Indian population has been assimilated into the general mainstream of California life, but the legacy of bitterness and hatred lingers in the Golden State. In the twentieth century, state and federal agencies have attempted to meet the problems of Indian education. It was long believed that Indians were disadvantaged because of educational, not cultural, differences. Therefore, in order to understand the role of the Indian in modern California, it is necessary to examine modern Indian education.

The Tragedy of Twentieth Century Indian Education

It was not until August, 1924, that the American Indians were admitted to California public schools. The story of early Indian education centers largely around young Alice Piper, who won a court battle to gain admittance to a school in the small Owens Valley community of Big Pine. The Piper versus Big Pine case was the first to publicize the fact that Indian children had been forced to attend inadequate and poorly staffed federal schools. It was not until 1866 that California schools agreed to admit Indian children who were living in white homes, but this produced only 63 Indian students in state public schools.

The early schools for Indian children were federally administered reservation institutions, but the attitude of local Indian agents made such schools a joke. George Hoffman, the Indian Agent at Tule River, stated that he believed the Indian could not be educated. In a racially inflammatory statement, Hoffman pointed to hereditary signs of mental incapacity to justify his opposition to Indian education. Hoffman concluded his racist diatribe by suggesting that the Indian was on the verge of extinction.

It soon became apparent that the Indian was not vanishing from the California countryside. By 1872, federal schools were operating at Hoopa Valley and Tule River. There were only 127 Indian students in these schools; however, the federal government attempted to remedy this situation by appropriating large sums of money for Indian education. Mismanagement, graft, and racial hostility prevented effective use of these funds. In the 1890's, 14 Indian schools flourished in California. By 1900, the Bureau of Indian Affairs expanded to 26 schools with more than 900 students. In spite of this increase, many Indians complained about the level of education and the inability, or unwillingness, of federal educators to understand Indian culture. The curriculum and structure of the federal Indian schools was aimed at assimilating the Indian into the white man's world. In effect, the schools systematically destroyed the tribal way of life.

A number of educators recognized the problems of Indian education and, in the early 1890's, a small number of children were placed in California public schools. The Bureau of Indian Affairs reluctantly agreed to pay the expenses of 51 students in three school districts in Shasta, San Diego, and Inyo Counties. The object of this experiment was to provide public education as a viable alternative for young Indian children. In 1893, the California legislature mandated that Indians attend separate, but equal, public schools. Thus, a form of Jim Crow education, similar to that faced by Blacks in the South, was established throughout California. The idea of segregating Indian children carried over into Black and Asian families, who found it impossible to enroll their offspring in white public schools. By 1902, Indians and most other minorities accepted the inevitability of segregated second-class schools for Indian, Asian, and Black students.

Many Indians refused to accept this racist attitude, and in 1907, the Northern California Indian Association demanded that Indian children be admitted to public schools. A strong argument for integration was that only half of all Indian children attended the reservation schools. By the early 1920's, more Indian children attended public schools than the federally financed Indian schools. C.E. Kelsey, a federal Indian agent, complained that only the small public schools enrolled

Indian students because they needed the state and federal aid. This criticism was correct, as federal subsidies persuaded many school districts to accept Indian students. In 1921, the California legislature amended Section 1662 of the School Law to force Indian students back into federal schools. This set the stage for Alice Piper's challenge to California law.

On June 1, 1924, a court order mandated Alice Piper's right to attend the Big Pine school. As a citizen of California, the Court ruled that Miss Piper was an American and not affiliated with any Indian tribe. In fact, the Court pointed out that she was barely visible in the Indian community. In addition, Judge Seawell noted that education is directly correlated to economic and social standing, and for this reason, he believed that all Indian children should be admitted to public schools. By 1931, almost three thousand Indian children attended public schools, but 70 segregated Indian schools remained in existence. In 1935, California law was amended to end the segregation of Indian children. In the present day, there is still a strong feeling that California government does not do enough to properly educate Indian children.

The Tragedy of Indian Education: A Summary

What is intriguing about Indian education in California is that the Piper decision did not change the educational, economic, or social conditions of local Indians. By 1960, 43.3% of the Indian population had not progressed beyond the eighth grade. Less than 2% of California Indians had four or more years of college, as compared to 11% of the white population. California Indians have the highest unemployment rate, and the lowest per capita income of any ethnic group in the Golden State.

In the 1960's, school administrators blamed the Indian for their educational problems because they were supposedly not interested in school. But this ignores the public school curriculum which offers little, if any, relevant education to modern Indians. Another problem is that Indians have moved into Los Angeles and San Francisco in large numbers, and school districts in these cities have shown great insensitivity to Indian education. One important factor was the increase in Indian population, which had tripled from 1900 to 1960.

The growth in urban Indians created new demands from California's original settlers. In 1967, Indian educators organized the California Indian Education Association and demanded Indian-controlled schools which met Indian needs. It was ironic that many progressive Indian educators fought for a return of federally funded schools. Soon federally funded poverty programs emerged in major California cities. In San Francisco, the American Indian Historical Society began to campaign against the unfavorable image of the Indian in public school tests and in courses dealing with Native Americans. By the 1970's, a change was noticeable as Indian history courses were more often taught by educated Indians than by whites.

Another aspect of recent Indian history has been the attempt to challenge the takeover of Indian lands. In the 1950's and 1960's, a series of proceedings were held before a federal Indian Claims Commission which determined that approximately 64 million acres of California land had been taken from the Indians and they were awarded 45.2 cents an acre. The 29 million dollar settlement did not satisfy many Indians, who believed that they had rights to compensation in excess of 100 million dollars from the federal government. These recent legal battles have only served to highlight the continued unhappiness of California Indians.

Black Californians

During the 1850's, the prolonged debate over slavery highlighted many of the problems faced by Black Californians. In the first decade of statehood, Blacks were active in seeking the right to testify in court, but the slow progress led to a mass exodus to Victoria, British Columbia, in the late 1850's. In 1863, Black testimony was admitted as part of the legal system. This was partially due to a Black press, in particular, the San Francisco-based Black newspaper, *Pacific Appeal,* which fought extensively for Black rights. In 1865, Blacks were granted the right to vote, but they still were forced to send their children to segregated schools.

The 14th Amendment to the United States Constitution was ratified in 1868, and this new constitutional change provided a weapon to attack segregated schools as being unequal and unfair. The 14th Amendment protected anyone who desired a public school education, and Blacks soon began to press for admission to white schools.

California Blacks were highly urban in the 1850's and 1860's, residing primarily in San Francisco, Sacramento, and Stockton. The migration of Blacks to California resulted in large numbers of free, New England families settling in Sacramento, San Francisco, and San Jose. Their New England backgrounds produced a higher level of education, and a stronger sense of economic and political knowledge than many white immigrants possessed in California. In terms of employment, California Blacks conducted successful businesses in service or laboring occupations. In 1870, census figures revealed that for every two white paupers per capita in California, there was only one Black pauper. The lesson demonstrated from this statistic is that Blacks were highly employable and not prone to welfare rolls. Black Californians tended not only to be employed, but they owned homes and had stable family units. As early as 1854, Black parents demanded that the San Francisco Board of Supervisors establish educational facilities, and on May 22, 1854, the San Francisco School Board complied. The St. Cyprian Church was established as an all-Black educational institution, and by 1860, more than 100 Black students attended the school.

Soon other California communities followed San Francisco's lead. In 1855, Sacramento established an all-Black school. By 1873, there were 21 Black schools in California. The growth of a Black school system produced a small body of influential Black educators. The best known was Jeremiah Sanderson, born of Scottish and Black parents in Bedford, Rhode Island. Sanderson was an avid abolitionist who charged in 1854 that segregated schools were discriminatory. As the principal of the Sacramento and San Francisco Black schools, he upgraded academic standards and pressured politicians to end school segregation. Andrew Jackson Moulder, Superintendent of Public Instruction, stated that it was too soon to integrate California schools; the California legislature agreed in the 1860's by refusing Black demands for school integration.

In 1863, the new Superintendent of Public Instruction, John Swett, stated that more money must be spent on Black schools. While not publicly supporting integrated schools, Swett did attempt to appropriate enough money to equalize educational opportunity. In a subtle manner, Swett attacked the principle of segregation. Another important force, in the drive for school integration, was an organization known as the Colored Citizens of California who continually pressed for equal educational goals. The major argument was that Blacks were taxed for education but failed to receive educational opportunity commensurate with taxes paid. When San Francisco Blacks petitioned the local school board to integrate public schools, the Black school was moved to a virtually inaccessible part of the city. By 1870, James Denman, San Francisco Superintendent of Schools, was so worried by Black parent protests, that he spoke favorably of integration.

It was during the 1870's that school integration became a hot political and social issue. When Oakland closed its Black school in 1871 because there were fewer than ten students, there was a sense of crisis. State law mandated that a community establish a Black school if ten or more students lived in the area. The *Pacific Appeal* urged Black parents to protest the closing of any Black schools. In January, 1872, State Senator Sheldon Finney, of San Mateo, introduced a bill designed to remove all mention of race from the school law and require open admission for all students. But the Finney bill was defeated, and the state legislature indicated that Indian, Black, and Asian students must be segregated.

In September, 1872, Mary Francis Ward sued Noah Flood, the principal of the all-white Broadway school in San Francisco. In pressing litigation, Miss Ward attacked the generally accepted notion of separate but equal educational facilities. John W. Dwinelle, a prominent San Francisco attorney, argued that the United States Constitution forbade school segregation practices due to race. San Francisco school board attorneys agreed but stated that attendance in integrated schools was a privilege granted only by the local board. In February, 1874, the California Supreme Court ruled that separate but equal schools were constitutional. Black parents renewed their court battles by suing for admission of their children to a number of white schools. Soon favorable court decisions resulted in Blacks being admitted to white schools. Other advances were made for Blacks as California courts legalized marriage between whites and Blacks, and delivered decisions reaffirming the basic civil liberties of Black Californians.

Despite these newly won rights, most Blacks lived in sections of the city referred to by race-conscious whites as "Nigger Towns." One of the most interesting phenomenon in the late nineteenth century was the growth of Black settlement in Los Angeles. By 1900, the Mudtown section of Los Angeles was a Black ghetto which drew many Southern Blacks, as well as those who were dissatisfied with San Francisco. By 1900, almost 20,000 Blacks lived in California, and this was an indication that the twentieth century would witness an explosion in this minority.

Asians in Early California

The rise of anti-Asian attitudes was the result of heavy Chinese immigration from the 1850's to the 1870's. By 1850, only 500 Chinese had immigrated to California. In fact, the Census of 1850 did not list the Chinese as a separate ethnic group. The Gold Rush brought the Chinese to California, but by the 1860's, they were farmers or laborers on the railroad. In the 1850's and 1860's, California's Chinese population was rural; as late as 1860, in fact, only eight percent of the Golden State's Chinese lived in San Francisco. It was not until the 1870's that a strong anti-Chinese movement began in California, but the two decades prior to the 1870's were important in focusing public attention on the Chinese question.

Despite the fact that only a few Chinese miners immigrated to California in July, 1849, there was an anti-Chinese riot in Tuolomne County against sixty Chinese who worked for a British mining firm. In 1852, the California legislature further inflamed anti-Chinese feeling when a bill was proposed to allow coolie contractors to bring in Chinese labor. The result was the organization of anti-coolie associations and the beginnings of a movement to ban Chinese immigration to the United States. In April, 1852, Governor John Bigler delivered a speech to the State legislature

A Chinese family in San Francisco

suggesting prohibition of future Chinese laborers. In 1854, a state law was introduced which prevented the Chinese from testifying in court against whites, but it failed to pass the state Assembly and Senate; however, in 1854, the California Supreme Court ruled that the Chinese could not testify in the courts. Judge Hugh C. Murray reasoned that California's original settlers, the Indians, had immigrated from Asia, and the fact that Indians could not testify meant that the Chinese were prohibited from testifying against whites in court. This equation of Indians with the Chinese defied the most elemental logic, but there were few voices raised in protest of this ridiculous decision.

The earliest signs of anti-Chinese sentiment occurred in 1854 when the San Francisco Board of Supervisors passed the Pig-Tail Ordinance which required any Chinese convicted of a minor crime to have his pigtail shaved as punishment. This was simple harrassment, since it was intended to humiliate the Chinese. In later years, queue ordinances were passed which aimed at taxing the length of the pigtail worn by the Chinese. It was also common for cities to pass cubic air ordinances which required a certain number of square feet for each person living in an area. When it was discovered that the San Francisco city jail was in violation of this ordinance, however, it was not generally enforced.

During the 1870's, the United States economy limped along and was bothered by declining productivity. A major depression from 1873 to 1876 raised new fears of having an overabundance of Chinese labor in a market glutted with unemployed Americans. The contract labor system under which the Chinese immigrated was antithetical to the American system of free wage labor. By the mid-1870's, more than 150,000 Chinese had been brought to California under the labor contract system.

Most Californians blamed the Burlingame Treaty of 1868, which allowed free immigration, and the Civil Rights Act of 1870, which protected foreigners from discrimination, for the large numbers of Chinese laborers. Although Chinese immigrants could not become naturalized citizens, fears persisted of the "Yellow Wave" inundating California. Since three out of every four Chinese immigrants settled in California, it was easy for politicians to exploit this fear.

From 1872 to 1875, a number of very subtle, yet important, changes took place in California. Unemployed workingmen escaping the depression of 1873 came into California along with jobless Civil War veterans. Wages were low, and the standard working day was ten hours. Many Americans were angered that the Chinese no longer worked for white employers but worked for Chinese business concerns. In 1859, a group of San Francisco merchants formed the People's Protective Union to protest the rise of Chinese cigar makers. Another condition which agitated white workers was the use of Chinese laborers during strikes. Although the Chinese were still cheap labor, it was no longer possible to exploit them as the mines and railroad interest had done in the 1850's and 1860's. There was also a strong psychological blame placed upon the Chinese for the depressed state of the California economy.

From 1873 to 1876, California felt the full impact of the depression. The immigration of more than 25,000 Chinese each year took place at a time when the economy declined into a critical state. The San Francisco Benevolent Association reported that there were more people on welfare in 1876–77 than in all the years combined since the Civil War. The California legislature enacted a law fining anyone from $1,000 to $5,000 for illegal Chinese immigration; but the requirement for immigration was simply to provide an affidavit of good character, and this was easily available for most immigrants. Soon county ordinances and state laws were passed prohibiting the use of Chinese or Japanese labor in public works.

In 1876, San Francisco's Mayor, Andrew Jackson Bryant, received an inordinate amount of publicity for his strong stand against Chinese immigration. At Bryant's urging, a joint committee of the United States Senate and House of Representatives met in San Francisco to scientifically study the Chinese question, and the result was a report predicting that California could become a "lesser China" by 1900. An organized lobbying effort was designed to convince federal authorities to restrict Chinese immigration because only the federal government had the power to ban Chinese immigrants. After close presidential elections in 1876 and 1880, neither the Republicans nor the Democrats could risk alienating Californians. In 1882, President Chester Arthur signed the Exclusionist Act banning Chinese immigration for ten years. In 1892, the Geary Act continued exclusion for another decade; and in 1902, the Chinese were permanently excluded from the United States. In order to understand Chinese exclusion, it is necessary to examine the rise and influence of the Workingmen's Party in San Francisco labor and politics.

The Workingmen's Party and the Modern City

In the 1870's America's major cities were crowded with "workingmen," or wage-earners, engaged in manual or industrial labor. In San Francisco, the rapid growth of the workingmen's population presented an opportunity for the organization of a political party to represent blue-collar workers. The large proportion of skilled and unskilled laborers were vocal about the necessity of guaranteeing labor a bill of rights. As working conditions deteriorated in San Francisco, there was increased agitation for new forms of labor organization. There was no one to represent the worker in negotiating with the employer for better wages and working conditions. It was common for wage cuts and longer hours to be invoked without warning. The workingmen's struggle was not just an economic one. Due to long hours and poor working conditions, the common laborer lived near his job. This created a small industrial housing center in the south of Market Street area. This district was the most crowded quarter in San Francisco, and the drab dwellings were hastily constructed for the laboring class. Many were poorly built and did not contain adequate plumbing.

Among San Francisco workingmen, the divorce rate was much higher than for other workers. The breakup of family life led to the proliferation of gangs and widespread problems with the police. In the local saloons and taverns, politicians and labor organizers found it very easy to convince the average workingman to support a political machine or a labor group which would better the blue-collar worker's life.

The crisis which caused San Francisco workingmen to revolt against the major business interests in California was the severe unemployment brought on by the drought during the 1876–77 winter. As unemployed workers flooded into San Francisco, there was a new concern over the glutted labor market and the stiff competition from Chinese labor. A movement among San Francisco employers to cut wages arose due to the abundance of cheap labor. The two dollars per day wage on the waterfront led to a move among local employers to cut wages. In July, 1877, the Southern Pacific Railroad announced that it was cutting wages, and this led to a series of anti-Chinese riots throughout San Francisco. "The Chinese must go!" was a cry used to publicize the arrival of more than 20,000 Chinese in 1876.

In order to quell the riotous conditions surrounding San Francisco, William T. Coleman, the head of the San Francisco Vigilante Committee of 1856, was persuaded to command a "merchants' militia" to defend the rights of the business community. Organizing an army of six thousand hickory pick- and ax-handled deputies, Coleman posed a threat to the demands of the working man. On July 25, 1872, the docks of the Pacific Mail Steamship Company, largest importer of Chinese labor, were burnt to protest Coleman's Committee of Safety, and its obvious intimidation of local workers. As blue-collar laborers cried, "Get the coolie out of California," there appeared to be a revolution in the making. As workers drunkenly searched the streets for Chinese labor, the clear impression was that the workingmen and the property classes were at war. It was an opportune time for a third party political movement. On October 21, 1877, a group of militant labor organizers formed the Workingmen's Party.

The leader of the Workingmen's Party was a young Irish-American by the name of Denis Kearney, a small businessman who believed that the Chinese were a menace to America. Born in Cork County, Ireland, Kearney was a spell-binding orator who harangued local mobs on the threat of the Chinese to the labor market. Kearney advocated violence as a means of securing rights for the workingman. In October, 1877, more than three thousand workers turned out at a sandlot adjacent to the San Francisco City Hall to hear Kearney demand new rights for the worker. Kearney was arrested for attempting to incite a riot. The membership rolls of the Workingmen's Party swelled as a protest against the tactics of local police. A Thanksgiving Day Parade was held by workers to demand Kearney's release, and he was eventually acquitted of all charges in a short jury trial.

The most significant influence of the Workingmen's Party occurred in January, 1878, when it held its first annual political convention to elect members to write a new State Constitution. Kearney was selected as the party chairman, and he urged that state laws exclude the Chinese from the labor market. In a short period of time, the Workingmen's Party became a major influence in state politics. The drive to exclude Chinese immigrants was fought intensely by the Kearneyites until its ultimate success in 1882. When the federal government banned the Chinese from California in the Exclusion Act of 1882, it was directly the result of the politics of the Workingmen's Party. The ban on Chinese immigration attests to the power of anti-Chinese forces in California, and the writing of a new State Constitution in 1878 was due to this new political force.

On September 5, 1877, California voters had approved a convention to revise the Constitution of 1849. This led to a six-month Constitutional Convention which modernized the basic structure of California government. When the Constitutional Convention convened in September, 1878, one out of three delegates was a member of the Workingmen's Party.

There had been a great deal of dissatisfaction with the Constitution of 1849 due to its restrictions on banking and the general failure to provide adequate revenue for state government. Although the Workingmen's Party was a new force in California politics, it was instrumental in convincing the 42% of California voters who lived in the Bay Area to approve the calling of a new Constitutional Convention. The public feeling was that California government was hampered by a weak and imprecisely drawn Constitutional document. In place of the short, concise Constitution of 1849, a lengthy and detailed document was written in 1879 which dealt with virtually every facet of California government.

It was unfortunate that much of the discussion evolved around John F. Miller's Committee on the Chinese. After a great deal of debate, a lengthy nine-section anti-Chinese statement was reported to the delegates. The result was a four-part anti-Chinese section which prevented the employment of Asians on any state or county project financed with tax money.

There were questions other than the Chinese one in the Constitutional Convention of 1878. One dealt with an adjustment of the tax system, whereby corporations and big business would be taxed adequately. The California Grange, which represented farm interests, demanded this change; the result was the creation of the State Board of Equalization. The old system of independent county tax assessors was replaced by a tax schedule set in Sacramento for both farmers and business.

Another important issue was railroad regulation. A California law in 1876 prohibited extortion and unjust discrimination by the railroads; however, there was only one state commissioner to handle complaints against the railroads. The new Constitution created a State Railroad Commission with three members elected for four year terms. This Commission had the power to establish railroad rates in matters of shipping, grain storage, and passenger rates. In addition, the Railroad Commission had the power to impose fines for flagrant violations. The railroads frequently controlled the commissioners who were elected to public office. When a commissioner was

Courtesy, The Bancroft Library

Denis Kearney crying "The Chinese must go"

elected, he often found himself able to make extraordinary private business deals with the railroad. Joseph Cone of Red Bluff purchased selected lots of land he sold back to the Southern Pacific for profits of more than $100,000. Had Cone not been elected to the Railroad Commission, this business opportunity would not have come his way.

On May 7, 1879, the new California Constitution was adopted by a small majority of voters in the lightest election of the decade. It was almost by default that the Constitution of 1879 became law. As a governmental document, it was an important turning point in California history. The tools of governmental reform were written into the new Constitution. The idea of regulating the railroad was written into state law, and the tax structure was re-evaluated. However, it was not until Governor Hiram Johnson came to office in 1911, that these constitutional changes were effectively transmitted into action.

One of the reasons for the failure of the 1879 Constitution was the rapid decline of the Workingmen's Party. In September, 1879, the Workingmen's Party appeared on the verge of controlling state politics. Party candidates were elected to the California Supreme Court, and 11 Senators and 16 Assemblymen were sent to Sacramento. The party was scandalized when the Reverend Isaac Kalloch was elected San Francisco's mayor. In a stormy campaign, Charles de

Chinatown in the 1880s

Young, newspaper publisher of the *San Francisco Chronicle,* accused Kalloch of chasing young girls in Boston and Kansas. The hints of scandal broke into an abusive campaign in which Kalloch used the pulpit to accuse de Young's mother of having been a prostitute. A few days later, de Young shot Kalloch. Many historians feel that Kalloch's election was due to the sympathy arising from the shooting. Eventually, Kalloch's son shot and killed de Young, but he was acquitted of murder. As the scandal increased, Denis Kearney left for New York, and the Workingmen's Party faded into oblivion.

This was an interesting interlude in California. It provided effective pressures to exclude the Chinese. Some important changes were made in the structure of California government. The Workingmen's Party was the first political organization that attempted to appeal to the public opinion of the blue-collar working class.

Women in Early California

The role of women in early California history is heavily influenced by literary myth. The early novels and short stories concerning California life emphasized the beauty, grace, kindness, and chaste behavior of Spanish and Mexican women. Early American explorers, like James O. Pattie, described California women as noble minded and kind hearted. He spoke of virtue, piety, and beauty, and this became the stereotype of early California women. It is interesting to note that most early books on California women were written by American men who married into wealthy Spanish or Mexican families. Thus, the early literature on women lionized the California female for possessing extraordinary beauty and intelligence. While in many cases this may have been true, it influenced attitudes which placed women into an extremely confining role.

In 1849, the California Constitution granted women the right to own land. This was considered one of the most liberal components of state government. During the 1850's, women became an integral part of California society. The census of 1850 revealed that only seven thousand women resided in California, but by 1860, the census showed that more than 100,000 women lived in the Golden State. This was an important turning point for a female population which had numbered eight women for every one hundred men.

The early women of California had similar reasons for migrating as the men: searching for fame and fortune in California's gold fields. Most women were not interested in the land but were imbued with a get-rich scheme. Yet, the small number of young women in California led to special treatment by San Francisco males. They placed women in a special status. The absence of large numbers of women led to a level of female acceptance which was not realistic. Sara Royce, mother of the well-known philosopher and historian, Josiah Royce, wrote a brief description of her life, *A Frontier Lady,* in which she noted that the plainest and homeliest woman was the belle of the ball in San Francisco society. Mrs. Royce suggested that there were few long-standing traditions concerning dress, manners, and morals in early San Francisco. Thus, early California women enjoyed an unusual degree of freedom and mobility. By 1900, fashions and changing thought limited women and forced them into a highly restricted lifestyle. By this time, more than half a million women lived in all parts of the Golden State.

The assimilation of women into California society was a slow, but steady, process. At the mining camp of Horse Shoe Bar, Abby Mansur wrote home that she felt fortunate to be able to choose from among thousands of men. Her enthusiasm did not attract large numbers of women West, however, and the single woman was still a rarity in California. Most women migrated to California with their husbands or as part of a family unit. For every five women who came to California, one was from a foreign country. Although Black, Asian, and Mexican women were the most numerous immigrants during the 1850's, they left very few historical reminiscences. The general conclusion is that women were included in California's lifestyle only in social terms, and there is little evidence that female opinions were sought in matters of politics or business.

In mining camps and in San Francisco, women wrote letters East complaining about the living conditions in California. They also complained of cultural isolation, and indicated that virtually all forms of entertainment were directed toward men. In many respects, women simply reflected the differences between life in a refined eastern city and the hustle and bustle lifestyle of undeveloped California cities. One important factor aiding in the development of the role of women in California was that the large male population established permanent institutions. Since many men had little more than get-rich schemes, there was little thought given to culture, family, and community values.

Many women were determined to remedy the instability of the California frontier. It was not uncommon for women's clubs and civic organizations to develop programs emphasizing morality, family life, religion, and the values necessary to create a stable society. The ideas of morality, hard work, and integrity permeate the writings and public statements of early California women. It was this commitment to establish sophisticated social institutions which led women into the political realm. The ease of divorce, combined with a community property law, gave women a freedom in California they had not possessed in the East. In 1854, Sarah Pellett, a physician, made the first serious speech demanding political rights for women. After weeks of newspaper ridicule, it became obvious to early suffragettes that it would be a long, tough fight for voting rights.

The history of early woman suffrage in California is one of failure, but a foundation was created for future success. In 1870, the first suffrage association for women was founded in an attempt to gain the vote. In the election of 1896, women were denied the vote by opposition from liquor interests, the strong reaction against the vote by the Catholic Church, and a "no" vote by rich and poor voters. It was a strange political mixture which denied California women the right to vote. The women who led the movement began to develop a new political consciousness.

Many early suffrage leaders had extraordinary careers. Clara Foltz, president of the first California suffrage association, was a Los Angeles bank executive and the second woman admitted to the California Bar. In 1884, Foltz was a candidate for presidential elector, and she was active for thirty years in Democratic party politics. Another significant Los Angeles woman was Katherine Phillips Edson, who pioneered a door-to-door campaign to pressure women to influence their husband's vote. Edson believed that women must be organized, but this was virtually impossible outside of the Los Angeles and San Francisco areas.

Alice Park, suffrage publicist and an officer of the California Equal Suffrage Association, advocated personal feminism. This was a means of re-educating men concerning their language and thought processes. Park complained that men used language to destroy a woman's identity. To remedy this injustice, she protested the use of the term "consent of the governed" during a Stanford University commencement address, and she stated that this meant the consent of men. When someone asked Park how she would advance the women's movement, she stated that violence on the part of suffragists was preferable to hundreds of years of political castration.

There were a large number of suffragists who were men, and most were Christian idealists who believed that attitudes concerning women were similar to those on slavery. Judge Waldo York believed that since women were a strong force for morality and decency, this was one reason to grant them suffrage. It is important to realize that many men supported the vote for women for intellectual reasons. Charles Edson stated that he believed that a woman's full freedom could only be developed with voting rights. Yet, men were not always welcome in the woman's suffrage movement because they rejected militant demonstrations and personal suffrage ideas.

Since there was never a great deal of unity among women, the suffrage movement was split between northern and southern California. The first effective woman's suffrage movement was the Los Angeles-based Political Equality League. Its success came from organizing two state central committees to pressure the major political parties and the California legislature. From 1906 to 1911, the Political Equality League was instrumental in helping women win the vote. The key to this organization's strength was the development of many political issues. In Los Angeles, middle-class women were warned of the problems associated with child labor, inequitable education, and the white slave trade. It was this well-organized attempt to educate women voters which led to massive public pressure for the vote. In fact, it is safe to argue that women formed a political machine similar to that of New York's Tammany Hall. An Oakland suffragette, Charlotte Anita Whitney, believed that the right of women to vote had to be sold like breakfast cereal. She was one of many women who used psychological propaganda to gain support for women's suffrage.

The most effective propaganda was addressed to blue-collar workers who were having trouble supporting their families. Many laboring men were informed that the industrial revolution had driven women out of the home and into the job market. Low wages, it was argued, resulted in large measure in the denial of the vote to women. Since blue-collar workers believed in better wages for women, a large number saw the vote as the means to female pay increases.

While most suffragists were very careful to point out that they did not want to disrupt the family, they did urge women to reexamine their home environment. A number of personal feminists suggested that to be as successful as a man, a woman had to analyze her own family situation. There were also numerous protests against clothing, household work, and the failure to provide women a serious political forum.

By the summer of 1911, women realized that forty years of political organization and activism were changing the attitudes concerning the vote. Men were no longer hostile to the idea, and there was a strong push from Governor Hiram W. Johnson to grant immediate suffrage. It was not by accident that the politically unknown Johnson benefited greatly from the support of women. Both major candidates for governor in the election of 1910 vowed to push the California legislature for immediate suffrage. On October 10, 1911, suffrage was formally granted to women.

There were many important changes in California politics and society as a result of women's suffrage. A minimum wage law was established due to pressure from women's organizations. A new educational system with increased rights for women evolved at the high school and college level. The laws were changed allowing women equal guardianship of children. A Red Light Abatement Act was passed in 1913 to control prostitution, dirty books, and race track gambling. In consumer areas, women demanded stringent state regulation of dairy and meat products. The decline of the mortality rate among children was a direct reflection of these successes.

In the final analysis, the most significant change resulting from the success of the suffrage movement was the new attitude among women. They realized that through organization, lobbying, and education, change could be instituted in California civilization. Yet, the women's movement lapsed into a low key phase. The drive for voting rights ended the first phase of the suffrage movement, and the changes in female roles in California would await the second state of the women's movement in the 1960's and 1970's.

Forces of Change: A Summary

In the last half of the nineteenth century, racism and sexism in California were combated in a much greater degree than historians have previously suggested. As World War I approached, Californians were aware of the need to resolve the Indian problem; there were many voices sympathetic to Asian people, and women were becoming a force in California life. It was the urban-industrial process in the first fifty years of the twentieth century which postponed the second period in which racism and sexism would be attacked in California. The slow process by which attitudes were reshaped was the most important contribution of the forces of change from 1850 to 1920.

Bibliographical Essay

For California Indians in the early American period see James J. Rawls, "Images of the California Indians: American Attitudes Toward the Indians of California, 1803–1873," (Unpublished doctoral dissertation, University of California, Berkeley, 1975). Also valuable on Southern California is George Phillips, *Chiefs and Challengers: Indian Resistance and Cooperation in Southern California* (1975), and for a dated version see Ross J. Ross Browne, *The Indians of California* (reprint 1944).

For an analysis of the role of Edward F. Beale see, Richard E. Crouter and Andrew F. Rolle, "Edward Fitzgerald Beale and the Indian Peace Commissioners in California, 1851–1854," *Southern California Quarterly,* XLII (June, 1960), 107–132, and John W. Caughey, editor, *The Indians of Southern California* (1952). The Modoc War is examined in Keith A. Murray, *The Modocs and Their War* (1959) and Richard Dillon, *Burnt-Out Fires: California's Modoc Indian War* (1973).

On the question of Indian rights see Kenneth Johnson, editor, *K-344, or the Indians of California vs. the United States* (1966). A useful article is David G. Shanahan, "Compensation for the Loss of the Aboriginal Lands of the California Indians," *Southern California Quarterly,* LVII (Fall, 1975), 297–320.

The story of Indian education and that of most other ethnic groups is told superbly in Charles Wollenberg, *All Deliberate Speed: Segregation and Exclusion in California Schools, 1855–1975* (1976). Another useful volume is Irving G. Hendrick, *The Education of Non-Whites in California, 1849–1970* (1975).

The Asian in the late 19th century is examined in Elmer C. Sandmeyer, *The Anti-Chinese Movement in California* (1939); Gunther Barth, *Bitter Strength: A History of the Chinese in the United States, 1850–1870* (1964); Stuart C. Miller, *The Unwelcomed Immigrant: The American Image of the Chinese, 1785–1882* (1970); Ping Chiu, *Chinese Labor in California, 1850–1880: An Economic Study* (1963); and the dated but still useful study by Mary Roberts Coolidge, *Chinese Immigration* (1909).

A brilliant article on anti-Asian stereotypes is Luther W. Spoehr, "Sambo and the Heathen Chinese: California's Racial Stereotypes in the Late 1870s," *Pacific Historical Review,* XLII (May, 1973), 185–204. H. Brett Melendy's, *The Oriental Americans* (1972) is the best survey on the subject.

On the Workingmen's Party see Neil L. Shumsky, "San Francisco's Workingmen Respond to the Modern City," *California Historical Quarterly,* LV (Spring, 1976), 46–57; Ralph Kauer, "The Workingmen's Party of California," *Pacific Historical Review,* XIII (September, 1944), 278–291.

The Mussel Slough controversy is examined in John A. Larimore, "Legal Questions Arising from the Mussel Slough Land Dispute," *Southern California Quarterly,* LVIII (Spring, 1976), 75–94; and Gordon W. Clarke, "A Significant Memorial to Mussel Slough," *Pacific Historical Review,* XVIII (November, 1949), 501–504.

On Blacks in California see Rudolph M. Lapp, *Blacks in Gold Rush California* (1978); Delilah Beasley, *Negro Trail Blazers of California* (1919); and Rudolph M. Lapp, *Archy Lee* (1969).

There has been a great deal of material on women in 19th century California see, Christiane Fischer, "Women in California in the Early 1850s," *Southern California Quarterly,* LX (Fall, 1978), 231–254; David J. Langum, "Californio Women and the Image of Virtue," *Southern California Quarterly,* LIX (Fall, 1977), 245–250; Ronald Schaffer, "The Problem of Consciousness in the Woman Suffrage Movement: A California Perspective," *Pacific Historical Review,* XLV (November, 1976), 469–494; Norris C. Hundley, Jr., "Katherine Philips Edson and the Fight for the California Minimum Wage, 1912–1913," *Pacific Historical Review,* XXIX (August, 1960), 271–286; and Donald W. Rodes, "The California Woman Suffrage Campaign of 1911," (Unpublished M.A. Thesis, California State University, Hayward, 1974).

A pioneering study which analyzes insanity in California and is a unique study of the forces of change as they relate to mental illness is Richard W. Fox, *So Far Disordered in Mind: Insanity in California, 1870–1930* (1979).

11

CALIFORNIA SOCIETY, 1850–1915

The first half century of cultural and intellectual growth in California was highly uneven. While the Gold Rush lured the businessman, banker and general fortune-seeker, it also attracted a wide variety of writers, artists and promoters of intellectual life. The legacy of the gold mania was to transform a California settlement of less than twenty thousand people into an urban, cosmopolitan civilization representing the likes of Boston or New York. The explosion in cultural activities was in part a reflection of California's general wealth. In the 1850s San Francisco's per capita income was the nation's highest, and the growth of literature, the arts and popular entertainment was encouraged by this vast wealth.

To many outsiders California culture appeared vulgar and second-rate compared to the arts in New York, London and Paris. This snobbery was an indication that the level of social democracy in California was largely unacceptable to easterners who promoted the arts in California. The leveling effect of the Gold Rush created a strong desire for all types of social and intellectual activity. The large number of fraternal societies which sprang up to represent a wide variety of ethnic, religious and occupational groups was the strongest indication of cultural diversity. Though immigrants were an important catalyst to cultural growth, California was predominantly American in the late nineteenth century and the interaction between recent immigrants and old line Yankees created a highly diverse culture. In particular, writers, artists and local theatre reflected the themes of Europe and America meshing on the California frontier.

The Gold Rush became a stabilizing theme to Californians. It was the beginning of the Yankee period in the Golden State. In *The Overland Monthly* magazine in the late 1860s and early 1870s, Francis Bret Harte described the Gold Rush as a part of the character of California which created individualism and self-reliance. This emphasis upon premature idealism explains why more cynical Californians looked to the Gold Rush as a time of freedom and opportunity. The energy generated from this period, the search for excitement, and the continual speculation in social-economic life became an engrained part of the California temperament.

Social and Educational Progress

In California social class was determined largely by wealth, and it was not uncommon for a relatively uneducated person to become the patron of the arts. The legends of railroad and banking barons serving beer in a champagne dinner setting is a significant example of social democracy in the Far West. No longer did breeding and aristocratic training serve as the primary qualification for social status. A new elite of landed and business wealth arose in California and they were responsible for the raucous social change in the late nineteenth century. San Franciscans proudly boasted that its population of eligible batchelors was the highest of any city in the United

The opulence of the Colton and Crocker mansions, San Francisco

States, and this contributed to a varied social life. There was little mention that San Francisco's divorce rate was the nation's highest and its birth rate the lowest of any major city. The macho nature of California society was demonstrated when the state legislature passed a law defining men as the head of the household and legally regulated women to an inferior status. It was not coincidental that the drive for women's suffrage began when this law was passed.

Perhaps the strongest aspect of California culture in the early years of statehood was the family. It was pressure from leading families in California which prompted the 1849 Constitutional Convention to provide for an elected state superintendent of public instruction, and the proceeds of public land sales were used to support elementary education and a state university. In 1851 the legislature authorized local communities to establish public high schools, but it was not until 1856 that San Francisco and Sacramento opened such institutions. Public education failed to grow at a rapid rate. In 1858 Superintendent of Public Instruction Andrew Jackson Moulder reported that California spent three dollars on prisons for every dollar it contributed to public education. In a scathing attack upon the reluctance of politicians to spend money on public education, Moulder called it a crime to appropriate only nine dollars per student for public education. It was pressure from the leading families in both large and small communities which led to the creation of elected local school boards to hire teachers and recommend the construction of new schools. By 1860 many judged public education a dismal failure in California as less than 25% of the eligible students attended school.

The slow growth of public education brought organized pressure for change, and state super-intendent John Swett responded with several important changes. In the 1860s Swett revolutionized education by persuading the state legislature to provide uniform educational opportunities. Jeremiah Sanderson, a Black educator, was a leading figure in demanding equitable educational opportunities for Black Californians. As a result the all-Black St. Cyprian's elementary school attracted one hundred students to a segregated public school. Reverend Sanderson, the principal instructor, was attacked by local citizens who believed that spending tax money on Black education was a wasteful project. Sanderson replied that only half of San Francisco's Black children were in school, and he demanded increased spending for minority education. Many Black parents enrolled their children in church schools and were reluctant to send their offspring to the basement classroom at St. Cyprian's school. The Black school lacked maps and blackboards and most of the necessary instruments of public education. Yet, the Reverend Sanderson was an important figure in breaking the prevalent stereotype that Black Californians did not seek a quality education.

In 1864 as the American Civil War raged, the humiliating conditions at St. Cyprian's Church ended when a new school opened at Broadway near Powell for Black children. Two years later

John Swett, Superintendent of Public Instruction

Courtesy, The Bancroft Library

Sacramento Blacks established a grade school. The gains in Black education caused a strong white backlash and in 1869 the California legislature refused to grant Black Californians equal rights by failing to ratify the Fourteenth Amendment to the United States Constitution; this amendment guaranteed citizenship rights and due process for Blacks. The early gains of Black education were virtually forgotten in the post-Civil War rush to build a transcontinental railroad, but a small coterie of Black educators and concerned citizens continued to push for public education for all Californians. It would not be until the 1950s that all ethnic groups would be guaranteed equal educational opportunities.

One of the most intriguing attempts to establish Black education took place in the remote Tulare County town of Visalia. An educated Black man from Massachusetts, Daniel Scott, migrated to Visalia in the early 1870s. Scott became friendly with a well to do Black farmer, Tom Hinds, and they set up a school for local Black children. In the fall of 1873 the Visalia Colored School opened with both Black and Mexican children attending an educational operation funded by the Tulare County Superintendent of Schools. For two years the school was a model of educational opportunity for minorities, but in 1875 Scott left California. The Visalia school was then moved to a one acre site out of town and for twelve years Black and Mexican children went to school in a highly segregated setting. There was one plus factor in that large numbers of Black students were sent from other parts of the San Joaquin Valley to attend the Visalia school. The result was that the opportunities for Black and Mexican education appeared for the first time outside of a major California city.

As young Blacks were afforded educational privileges their parents began to complain about the segregated nature of local education. When Arthur Wysinger applied to attend a Visalia public school the principal S.A. Cruikshank refused the young Black students request. After lengthy legal proceedings Black school children were admitted to local schools by a decision of the California Supreme Court. This caused the Visalia Colored School to close its doors in 1890, but the controversy helped to highlight the problems of public education for Black and Mexican students. This educational problem would continue into the twentieth century.

In contrast to the sluggish growth of public education, California's colleges and universities vigorously pursued top flight educational objectives. Largely due to the first Archbishop of California, Joseph S. Alemany, Catholic educators dominated the early years of higher education. The University of Santa Clara (1851), the University of San Francisco (1855), and St. Mary's College (1863) became the training ground for a large number of business, educational and political leaders in nineteenth century California.

In 1868 the University of California, Berkeley, was chartered as the state of California's main educational institution. A state university was not a popular decision in the mid-nineteenth century, and it was only after a lengthy and bitter fifteen year debate that the state legislature approved the money for the University of California. In 1869 UC opened its doors to a select number of students, and in time an agricultural branch flourished at Davis and a medical and law faculty in San Francisco. The birth of the UC system was the result of continuous efforts by public spirited citizens who believed that the quality of public education would determine the level of political, economic and social democracy for future Californians.

During the depression-ridden decade of the 1870s private liberal-arts schools flourished throughout California. Loyola in Los Angeles and Mills College in Oakland were two fine examples of this early desire for fine educational opportunities. Then in October, 1880, the University of Southern California opened its doors with an emphasis upon liberal arts. In the 1890s the California Institute of Technology began to attract worldwide attention as a scientific and engineering school. Perhaps the finest private university in the American West was Stanford in Palo Alto. In 1891 Leland Stanford founded the beautiful, tree-lined campus to commemorate the death of his young son. Due to Stanford's generous financial base large numbers of scholars were attracted to this model university. One American President, Herbert C. Hoover, graduated with a degree in engineering. Today the prestigious Hoover Library of War, Peace, and Revolution stands as a living monument to the fine progress of California education. In Northern and Southern California educational opportunity was very strong by the early twentieth century, and this attests to the far-sighted mentality of pioneer Californians.

The Frontier Literary Tradition

The development of California literature was highly influenced by the frontier society of the mid-nineteenth century. It was the rapid pace of urban life in San Francisco which contributed to a merging of western frontier ideas with older eastern cultural patterns to produce a new and distinct California thought. But this instant cultural explosion was one which many criticized for its vulgarity and lack of sophistication. This charge seemed an accurate one, because the California theatre catered to notorious performers like Lola Montez and Lotta Crabtree. In May, 1853, Montez arrived in San Francisco to display her dancing and acting talents. In England and on the European continent she had received mixed reviews as an entertainer and she was laughed out of New York due to a general lack of talent. The secret to Ms. Montez' success was the public acclaim accorded her famous Spider Dance. Wearing almost no clothing she would pretend to dance away from the grasp of a large spider. The sexual implications of the Spider Dance left little to the imagination and the female starved Gold Rush population went crazy over this obscure dancer. It did not take long for other performers to copy the Spider Dance and this forced Montez to move on to new territory. In Sacramento rotten fruits and vegetables greeted her act, and she moved to Grass Valley to settle into a peaceful life with her third husband. While living in this area Lotta Crabtree was discovered by Ms. Montez, and they began to perform a series of highly suggestive and entertaining dances. While touring the mining camps around Grass Valley, Montez' husband was shot by an admirer. Her popularity was so great that a one hundred dollar a head admission fee did not discourage her fans. Appearing on stage with a whip dressed in a small, seethrough negligee Ms. Montez created a sensation. It was ironic that many Californians described her as the Golden State's most precious cultural asset. In fact there was a booming entertainment industry.

The wide range of cultural interest resulted in more than 1,100 separate plays and novellas being performed on the San Francisco stage in the 1850s. This prompted snobbish eastern critics to label California culture as immature and lacking direction. This criticism failed to note that most plays attracted a male population which averaged 25 years in age and had a sizeable amount of money to spend on entertainment. With money and time young San Franciscans stated that they desired a wide range of the best theatre. As a result Shakespeare's work enjoyed a great deal of popularity and twenty-two of the English bard's plays were presented in the first decade after statehood. There was also a vogue for simplistic melodramas like The Reformed Drunkard. This vignette of frontier life was one play local citizens loved, because it carried a message of spiritual and moral uplift while entertaining the audience. Although San Francisco was the center of local culture, Sacramento, Stockton and Marysville also operated legitimate professional theatres. A legacy of the Gold Rush was to create a strong demand for mass entertainment. It was not until 1860 that Los Angeles opened a respectable playhouse, and this lack of cultural growth simply reflected the small economic and population base in Southern California.

It was a different atmosphere in San Francisco as the most noted writers, artists and actors settled in North Beach or on Telegraph Hill. Perhaps the best known actor to grace the San Francisco stage was Edwin Booth. His portrayal of Hamlet was a legend in the American theatre. In the 1880s Lillian Russell was the most noted actress due to her sensational revue, Babes in the Woods. This piece of ingenious theatrical production featured a beautifully choreographed dance sequence in which Ms. Russell used purple tights and a stylistic blouse to accentuate her figure. The public clamor over her performance created attendance records at San Francisco's twelve major music halls. What the theatre did for Californians was to remind them that progress and culture developed together in modern civilization.

Major Writers in Early California

It was not surprising that early literary themes centered around the Gold Rush. Perhaps the best example of this literature was a series of letters written by Louisa Clapp who signed her writings "Dame Shirley." These letters detailed the problems of a young, literate woman in a mining region. As the only woman in the small mining community of Rich Bar, Mrs. Clapp was privy to the feelings and thoughts of a large number of men. She was also an unusually perceptive observer of American manners and morals, and the letters that she sent to her sister in Massachusetts were filled with vivid images of frontier life. In 1854, the *Dame Shirley Letters* were published in a literary periodical, *The Pioneer,* and they immediately caught the imagination and interest of many Americans. As a lure for potential settlers and travelers to the mining regions of California they were an invaluable source, but they also provided a sensitive look into the rigors of frontier life.

The two writers who captured the western marketplace in literature were Francis Bret Harte and Mark Twain. In 1854, Bret Harte arrived in California an aspiring young poet, but he taught school for a short time in a mining camp. After some disastrous mining ventures, Bret Harte moved to Arcata and worked as a typesetter for a local newspaper. While in the Humboldt Bay region he witnessed the brutal killing of sixty Indians, mostly women and children, by a gang of local thugs. In a newspaper article Bret Harte referred to the killings as a prime example of open racisim, and he was forced to leave his Northern California home. It was in Arcata that Bret Harte became fascinated with violence, sexual repression and the hard life of local miners. While he glorified and romanticized the mining and logging communities, Harte did reveal a great deal about the everyday life of early California.

The strange success of Francis Bret Harte was due in part to the encouragement of Jessie Benton Frémont and other members of the Republican party. As a result Bret Harte became something of a propagandist for the Union cause. This led to a federal job as a clerk in the surveyor general's office and to a position in the United States mint. The actual writing span of Bret Harte's career was only about three years. As a contributor to the prestigious *Overland Monthly* in the late 1860s, he helped to recall the glories of the Gold Rush. In a prose style which loosely blended historical facts with fiction, Bret Harte produced a picture of a robust red-shirted miner who developed the California business impulse to new heights. To anyone familiar with the Gold Rush this stereotype bore little resemblance to the real mining community. But readers clamored for stories like "The Luck of Roaring Camp," which saw a gambler and a lady of the night sacrifice their lives to save a trapped snow party. It was this ability to mythicise gamblers and prostitutes which gave Bret Harte's literature a place in the American West.

In 1870 *The Overland* published Bret Harte's best known poem, "The Heathen Chinese." It was the tale of young gamblers who were cheated by a Chinese card shark. The poem became important because it concluded with some scathing comments on the use of cheap Chinese labor. Bret Harte detested racism, and he was unhappy that his poem was used to promote anti-Asian xenophobia. In 1871 Bret Harte left California to work as a feature writer for *The Atlantic Monthly,* and his literary reputation helped to establish San Francisco's national reputation as a leading cultural center. Although he never again attained the degree of literary success he had experienced in California, Bret Harte was a seminal figure in suggesting that self-sacrifice and hard work would produce a successful life. The qualities of frontier life were portrayed in Bret Harte's fiction, and he presented a view of California which made the faults of frontier life appear as virtues.

In San Francisco's early literary frontier Samuel L. Clemens or Mark Twain as he was known was the most heralded writer. Arriving in Virginia City, Nevada, in 1861 Twain witnessed the influence of the silver boom upon western manners and morals. In Twain's writings the dual themes of quick wealth and cultural change are woven through folk tales. It was as a humorist that Twain made his greatest contribution to western folklore. As a reporter for the Virginia City *Territorial Enterprise* Twain was fascinated by the mining camp and its history. As a result he was attracted to San Francisco which was the gravitational mecca for displaced miners and frontier characters. In countless bars and bordellos Twain matured as a thinker, and became friendly with many of the important writers of his day. But it was not long before Twain's manners and morals brought him into conflict with the San Francisco police. Although he hung out with the most disreputable characters and loved the color and excitement of San Francisco, nevertheless, Twain was an honest man who attacked police corruption and other social problems. Thus, it was Twain's integrity and a well developed sense of manners and morals which forced him to flee San Francisco for the mining country.

A brief trip led to a temporary residence at Angel's Camp in the Tuolomne area. For a period of time Twain read, wrote and mined for gold, but he spent many of his evenings at a nearby tavern listening to the tales of local characters. While sipping country whiskey Twain heard an intriguing story involving a frog derby. This tall tale led to the famous legend of the jumping frog of Calaveras County, and it created a legend in rural California. This simple story of a fixed frog race caught the American literary imagination, and it made Twain the most celebrated western humorist. Each year the citizens of Tuolomne County recreate the frog race, and it is one of the most enduring portions of American folklore. An equally important work is Twain's *Roughing It,* because this book realistically highlighted the problems of life in mining camps. Although it was a humorous vignette of mining life, nevertheless, serious historians and literary figures have quoted extensively from it. The significance of Twain's writing is to mirror the rough nature of California life and the unique contributions of the frontier upon the American character.

In Bret Harte's and Twain's writings the glories of frontier life were combined with the rigors of a new society to produce a romantic blend of fact and fiction. As a result increasingly large numbers of Americans were enticed westward to California. For those who remained in the east or middle-west the work of Bret Harte and Twain was the perfect piece of literature to explain the mysteries of California.

Poets and Artists in Early California

Another aspect of California's cultural renaissance was demonstrated in the work of poets and artists. With its multi-ethnic population, a fast pace of life and the availability of large sums of money, it was only natural for an artistic colony to emerge in San Francisco. Much of the art of the 1850s and 1860s reflected wealth, champagne tastes and the luxury of the new rich. It was not uncommon for theaters, hotels, saloons and brothels to have lavishly painted and decorated interiors. Mark Hopkins, the railroad baron, employed one person to continually polish the brass fences surrounding his Nob Hill mansion. The Hopkins residence was a three million dollar baroque castle which epitomized the garish wealth of California's new rich. It served as a fitting monument to the disparity in wealth and income that separated average Californians from the four hundred leading citizens who controlled San Francisco.

If the general artistic atmosphere appeared to encourage eccentricity, no poet better exemplified this feeling than Joaquin Miller. In 1870 Miller, whose real name was Cincinnatus H. Miller, arrived in San Francisco to publish a series of poems celebrating the cultural life of the American West. Miller's *Pacific Poems,* published at his own expense, was the type of literary anarchy which appealed to Californians in the late nineteenth century. Although his poetry was atrocious, Miller was a promotional genius who labeled himself the "Poet of the Sierra." When he was discovered it was not generally known that Miller had spent seven years searching for public acclaim, and he was an average writer filled with barroom tales. This combination of exotic stories and colorful western dress made Miller a national literary figure. In fact, he toured England and the European continent to the acclaim of many well-known literary figures. In a bright red shirt, baggy pants and a dirty fur coat, Miller extolled the virtues of his poetry and California's lifestyle.

Another aspect of Miller's career involved a poem glorifying the career of the legendary Mexican bandit, Joaquín Murieta. In 1869 a long and poorly written poem, "Joaquín," stirred bitter memories of the Californio-Anglo conflict of the 1850s. The poem glorified the Murieta legend, and it suggested that he was the last defender of Aztec pride. It was ironic that a writer of little or no talent who failed to understand the ethnic nature of California history would become one of the staunchest defenders of Spanish-speaking citizens. Often smoking two cigars at the same time, using crude language and barely being able to publicly read his own work, Miller was still an influential figure.

Perhaps the greatest compliment paid to Joaquín Miller was that he helped to popularize Bret Hart's and Twain's work by acting out mining literary and California quaintness. In the mid-1880s Miller built a garish house in the Oakland hills complete with statues of Moses, John C. Frémont, and the poet, Browning. His eccentric lifestyle became a means of continuing his prominence, and when he died in 1913 Joaquín Miller was proclaimed as one of California's literary giants. The truth is that he was a mediocre to disastrous poet who used his lifestyle to occupy a position of literary and artistic importance. The themes of western life were as important as the actual prose, and Miller's life was a living monument to successful bad taste. In many ways it was an interesting literary heritage that plagued many Hollywood writers in the twentieth century.

Women Poets in California

The large number of talented women poets and writers who traveled to California was an indication of the creative intellectual climate in the Golden State. The most successful early female poet was Ina Coolbrith who was a founding member of *The Overland Monthly*. Her family background was intriguing; she was born Josephine Smith, the younger daughter of the brother of the Mormon prophet Joseph Smith. There was a great deal of family conflict, an unhappy childhood in Southern California, and a bitter divorce in her early life. In the 1860s Coolbrith migrated to San Francisco and became close friends with Bret Harte. Her early writings were simplistic tomes about flowers, birds and the wind. To support herself she worked as a librarian in Oakland, and this helped her to introduce the finest literature to a number of aspiring writers. One was Jack London whom she took aside and directed a broad reading program for the teenage boy.

There was little doubt about the liberated nature of Ina Coolbrith. She boasted that she was the first female high school graduate in Los Angeles as well as the first divorced woman in Southern California. Whether or not any of these stories were true did not matter, they served to highlight her place in California letters. As a poet Coolbrith reflected the undeveloped, frontier nature of California society. Coolbrith's greatest contribution was to encourage poetry readings and the support of young writers, and she was recognized by the California legislature as the state's first poet laureate.

During the land boom of the 1880s a young midwestern woman, Mary Austin, migrated to Southern California. It was while living in the San Joaquin Valley from 1888 to 1904 that she matured as a thinker. One of the trademarks of her writings was to reflect on the poverty of the homesteader and to explore the themes of an unhappy frontier marriage. Living in the semiarid regions of Southern California she married, gave birth to a retarded child and quietly divorced. Much of her early writing reflected her observations of poor Indians and Mexicans, and her stories in *The Overland Monthly* were acclaimed for their descriptive qualities. Austin's personal philosophy was one which emphasized mysticism. After moving to Carmel in 1904 she began to experience what she termed "spiritual awakenings." One day while walking in a field she claimed to walk by poppies with an orange flame. She talked of a mystical God with whom she could communicate with through prayer. In two obscure books, *Christ in Italy* (1912) and *The Man Jesus* (1915) Austin wrote of two Christs, one who was in Italy and another who matured in the deserts of Southern California. These books led to a preoccupation with Catholicism, and she traveled to Italy to cure a mysterious illness. The result was to create a great interest in Roman Catholicism which she studied for some time in Rome. Although she spent an inordinate amount of time in the Vatican Library, Austin did not become a Roman Catholic convert. She was simply a mystical philosopher searching for meaning. What Austin represented to California letters was a combination of mysticism, religion, poverty and the problems the average person encountered coping with the rigors of an uncertain California lifestyle.

Perhaps the most theatrical of California's early women writers was Adah Isaacs Menken. She began her career as a dancer clad in flesh-colored tights, and this contrasted with her flaming red hair to produce a dazzling stage presence. The result was to make Menken one of the most popular dancers of the 1860s. In 1863 she was the only woman to play a leading role at the Tivoli Theater. She was also an extraordinary poetess who wrote emotional prose filled with themes of passionate conquest. Although the general public never responded to her poetry in a commercial sense, nonetheless, she developed a sense of artistic liberation that was unavailable to women in much of the American West.

Among the most successful early women writers was Gertrude Atherton. From 1890 until her death in 1948 at the age of 91, Mrs. Atherton was one of California's foremost amateur historians. In 1914, Harper and Brothers commissioned her to write a short history of California. With precise rapidity she hurriedly wrote, *California, An Intimate History;* this charming book re-created California's social history. Beginning her writing career in the late 1880s Mrs. Atherton was fascinated by the Spanish heritage, but she was also intrigued with the new California. In fact, her career included a brief stint as a Hollywood script writer for Samuel Goldwyn. Although born in 1857 in the Rincon Hill section of San Francisco to people of wealth, Mrs. Atherton was the most perceptive observer of the common person in California.

After an unsuccessful marriage, Atherton moved to San Francisco to pursue a career as a fledgling novelist. It was intriguing that she became a chronicler of the California traditions because she hated the men and surroundings in San Francisco. She often remarked that interesting people lived in Paris or London and certainly not San Francisco. It was Atherton's personal life style which attracted the greatest notoriety. She was in open protest against the conditions which enslaved women in the late nineteenth and early twentieth century. She argued that marriage was a form of intellectual castration, and she charged that if she had been a male writer her work would have sold much better. Although she was an excellent writer, Californian's overlooked much of Gertrude Atherton's best work and concentrated their attention upon her unusual lifestyle.

In recent years historians have discovered the quality of Atherton's historical prose. Much of her life was spent in New York and on the European Continent, and this caused Atherton to view the Spanish and Mexican periods as California's first aristocratic society. This was a way of striking back at the lack of intellectual stimulation which she claimed San Francisco failed to provide in her formative years. She spoke of the beauty of the Mission San José which stood near her Milpitas Ranch, and Atherton's prose evoked images of a simpler Spanish-Mexican civilization. There was a great deal of romantic fiction in her prose, but the descriptions of the tragically doomed Spaniards and Mexicans who founded California remain masterpieces of fiction. Her writing contains references to the so-called California dream; this tragic dream was a recreation of European society in San Francisco. It was an impossible task and it suggests the problems of novelists in a frontier setting.

There were a number of lesser known women writers who achieved some degree of success in early California. Ella Sterling Mighels was a sentimental writer whose prose caused members of the California legislature to label her California's foremost literary historian for her work on social and intellectual growth. While she was not the talent that Mrs. Atherton was, nevertheless, her prose demonstrated the growth of California culture and civilization. The tragedy was that her careful observations of California's unique historical growth went virtually unnoticed by contemporary critics.

The large number of talented women poets and novelists who turned out productive works in the period from the 1850s to the 1920s suggests that the emancipated female artist was allowed much more freedom in California than in much of the American West. It was also an indication that a fledgling woman's suffrage movement was in its embryo stages in the Golden State.

The Rise of Cultural Protest

The problems associated with the growth of the California economy attracted the attention of a large number of able writers and led to the growth of protest literature. In particular, the themes of railroad and land monopolies were topics which captured the general imagination of the public. An increasing interest in political reform was reflected in the writings of a large number of California literary and topical authors. In an effort to captivate the public mind, young writers realized that monopolistic business interests and the influence of immigrant groups like the Chinese were easy means of garnering literary interest.

In the early 1870s the Democratic party brought a young New York journalist, Henry George, to Oakland to edit the party newspaper. George had attracted the attention of local Democrats with a scathing anti-Chinese letter in a New York newspaper. His career in California was a dual one; he was a propagandist against Chinese labor and railroad monopolies. In a series of sophisticated articles George linked the use of Chinese labor to the growing wealth of the Central Pacific and Southern Pacific railroads. From his study of Asian labor, George concluded

Henry George, famous single tax journalist

Courtesy, The Bancroft Library

that it was the main reason that the railroad developed a land monopoly. The railroad barons and real estate developers, George argued, were not profiting from the benefits of their own labors. The long historical tradition of hostility to speculators and those who made large sums of money without hard work led to the massive success of George's writings. As editor of the *Oakland Transcript,* George was in a position to influence the rank-and-file working man about the dangers of cheap Chinese labor and unsavory businessmen.

One of George's favorite pastimes was to ride his horse in the Oakland Hills, and he used this time to think out his economic theories. On one idyllic day overlooking San Francisco bay George began to theorize that land prices were rising for reasons that he believed to be economically catastrophic. He speculated that the progress of the American economy was creating a dual partnership between wealth and poverty. In a moment of spontaneous reflection George believed that as progress and wealth increased in society a twin emerges in the form of poverty. Thus, George reasoned, one of the major problems with wealth is that it is created by a lack of hard work and this displaces many blue collar workers. The use of Chinese labor had driven wages down, but the real cause of poverty was land speculation. The rise in land values made it virtually impossible for the average person to purchase a home, or to successfully operate a small farm. The highest degree of western American labor, the ability to produce and market food, was being destroyed by huge rises in land values. The traditional mobility of the landowner was vanishing as land barons and corporate interests dominated the economy.

In a series of pamphlet's George suggested that the large land grants to railroads were unfair as they accentuated the drift toward monopoly. It was George's premise that a portion of public lands should be returned to the people. In the depression-ridden 1870s this was an unusually popular idea. This could be accomplished by a single massive tax on land speculation. In a finely argued piece of logic, George demonstrated that wages no longer had the purchasing power that they had in the past. In a time of spiraling inflation and declining wages, George's ideas titillated the popular spirit.

The most important weapon in Henry George's intellectual arsenal was a device called the Single Tax. It was a plan to tax the "unearned increments" on the rise of land values. In other words if a person held a piece of land for speculative purposes, there would be a stiff tax upon the land. In this way, George believed, free economic competition would remain a standard practice. One of the key elements in George's philosophy was the argument that the railroad's power was due to monopolistic practices aided by federal money and land grants. This was the perfect argument to exploit hostility to both the railroad and the federal government.

In 1879 George's best selling treatise, *Progress and Poverty,* popularized the single tax and sold a record breaking five million volumes. The natural distrust of corporate giants and the growing reaction against monopoly led to a large number of single tax converts. There was little sophistication in George's work. He asked a simple question: "Why should an individual be rewarded for simply selling land in an inflationary market?" This question was one that perplexed many Californians. It was also an indication that the dissatisfaction of California's working class population was reaching a new high. One of the best indications of local dissatisfaction was the public outcry in 1870 over land holding statistics. It was revealed that the State of California held 122 parcels of land which totaled more acreage than California's 23,602 small farms of five hundred acres or less. This slippery statistic was used to argue that not only were private business speculators causing inflation but that the state was a major land monopolist. This hostility to private business and government economic interests helped to create a new political impulse. The rise of protesting third party political movements reflected the increasingly radical nature of California politics. The vast majority of new political parties were insignificant ones, but all reform movements attacked the alleged coalition between business and government. Although the single tax was not a practical solution to California's economic ills, it did suggest that politicians and businessmen would soon have to become responsive to the wishes of the electorate.

Progress and Poverty represented the thoughts of a perceptive journalist and social critic who saw California as a lost civilization. The beauty of the San Francisco bay area had been destroyed by business practices and city government mismanagement, and George believed that the sturdy pioneer was no longer the backbone of the American West. In many respects George was describing the new industrial order which was beginning to transform California from a rural, agricultural state into an urban, industrial complex.

Cultural Anarchy in California Letters

As San Francisco lost its pioneer charm and became cynical over the triumph of business values, a new form of literature began to emerge. Suddenly bitter, acid-penned critics began to look at California civilization. The personal lives of any of these writers reflected the cultural anarchy which began to dominate California letters in the late nineteenth and early twentieth century.

Among the most interesting writers in California was a nasty, sharp-tongued short story artist, Ambrose Bierce. Arriving in San Francisco after a distinguished career in the Union army during the Civil War, Bierce became a well-known newspaper satirist. Although he hated novels and despised writers, artists, and reformers, Bierce was one of the most perceptive critics of California manners and morals. His life was living testimony to the new personal and cultural anarchy.

As a reporter for the *San Francisco News Letter,* Bierce wrote a titillating gossip column, "The Town Crier." The main thrust of his writings was to satirize the local intellectual climate and to report any form of scandal. He was threatened and beaten up for his newspaper accounts of San Francisco life. After four years as a gossip columnist, Bierce married a wealthy young San Francisco woman, and they embarked upon a four year honeymoon to Europe. It was in London that Bierce found the type of society and the quality of people he hoped to cultivate for the rest of his life. However, his homesick wife persuaded him to return to San Francisco. This was a mistake for he made his wife's life hellish, and he berated his two sons in a manner which suggested sadistic, psychological torture. One son was shot in an argument over a woman and the other died of pneumonia and alcohol. It seemed that Bierce was able to destroy virtually everything that surrounded him.

In San Francisco Bierce was known as an amorous lover, and his wife left him due to his extramarital pursuits. He spoke of San Franciscans as ignorant, lazy and unable to appreciate the finer qualities of civilized life. In a drunken stupor Bierce delighted in visiting local mortuaries to interview the dead. He spoke openly of his contempt for local ministers. He was frequently spotted on a street pulling a small pistol and killing a dog. Needless to say Bierce's reputation was a colorful one. Yet, to many people Bierce appeared little more than a mad man.

This all changed when William Randolph Hearst's *San Francisco Examiner* hired Bierce to become a journalist devil's advocate. His writings were ones which envisioned a new moral system.

View of San Francisco from north beach, 1880s

With shades of madness and self-disillusionment, Bierce was a critic of every aspect of California life. His wacky reporting caught on in an age of disillusionment. In 1911, Bierce's most famous work, *The Devil's Dictionary,* became an immediate best seller; it was a collection of ironic definitions and nonsense statements that appealed to the irrational thought process of many Californians. He defined birth as a disaster and suggested that suicide was every person's duty. In 1913 Bierce left San Francisco to join Pancho Villa's army and vanished in the Mexican desert. No one ever again heard from Bierce and the place and time of his death are not known. It was a fitting end for California's first anarchic intellectual.

The significance of Bierce's career is shown in his columns from 1887 to 1912 in Hearst's *San Francisco Examiner.* Despite the dubious literary merits of his work, Bierce established the necessity for an intellectual critic to purify San Francisco life. In doing so he established a literary and journalistic tradition that has persevered in California. The Golden State is one of the few self-critical areas in twentieth century America. It is also a trend setter due to this rapid rate of personal introspection.

Argicultural Reform and the Novel

The most effective critic of big business was a novelist who developed agricultural themes, Frank Norris. The product of a wealthy Chicago family, Norris' earliest interests were directed toward art. At fourteen his family moved to San Francisco, and a decade later he graduated from the University of California. After a year of studying creative writing at Harvard, Norris wrote a small novel, *McTeague*. This work established the young San Franciscan as one of America's foremost literary naturalists. The hero of this novel was a huge, beastly dentist with little professionalism and a minimum of intelligence. What Norris hoped to do with the character McTeague was to highlight the nasty side of modern urban life. McTeague was a repulsive character who married a young girl because she had won $5,000 in a lottery, and the marriage degenerated into sadism. Finally, McTeague murdered his wife, and he died when her cousin pursued him into Death Valley. Although urban themes dominated this work, nonetheless, the thesis was that the city was a foreboding place to live and work. The San Francisco lifestyle, Norris argued, was one which led to personality quirks and instability. The city corrupted in a manner which made it impossible for man to live.

Once Norris' writings caught the imagination of Americans, he conceived a trilogy entitled, "Epic of the Wheat." The first volume would discuss the problems of wheat in California, the second its distribution in Chicago, and the concluding novel would analyze its impact upon a European village. Although he met an untimely death at 32, Norris produced one of the most scathing attacks upon big business ever launched by an American writer. His epic novel, *The Octopus,* published in 1901, is a dissection of California ranching problems which highlighted the growth of large semi-feudal baronies, and the rise of conservative, agribusiness influences upon California civilization.

In *The Octopus* Norris was fictionalizing the Battle of Mussel Slough. In 1880 near Hanford in Kings County, local farmers and the railroad argued over homesteader claims. The Southern Pacific railroad had published a series of promotional pamphlets encouraging settlement on less than desirable railroad land. The Southern Pacific then ran a rail line through the San Joaquin Valley, and they confidently predicted that the influx of marginal land settlers would benefit the company. This land scheme was also to the railroads tax advantage, because to not take possession of the land meant delaying state land taxes. In a complicated legal maneuver the railroad reached a gentlemen's agreement with local homesteaders by which the farmers leased the land, but it was an extralegal agreement by which the Southern Pacific could evict the tenant farmers. The Southern Pacific promised that local farmers could eventually purchase the land for prices ranging from $2.50 to $5.00 an acre. For almost a decade industrious homesteaders worked the semiarid valley land and a productive agricultural settlement resulted.

Although local citizens often referred to the area as "Starvation Valley," there was little doubt that prosperity reigned on these lands. When the railroad demanded $25 to $35 an acre for the land, rebellion broke out. Local citizens argued that they had constructed an elaborate irrigation system, improved the land by constructing houses and barns, and brought prosperity to the railroad's valley. These points were overlooked for the law was on the side of the Southern Pacific. When railroad officials began the process of evicting the tenants violence broke out. After a bloody shooting a Settler's League was organized, and this led to sporadic riots. Finally, the railroad secured eviction notices for several of the initial settlers. This led to seven shooting deaths and eight wounded bystanders, which created a noticeable increase in public resentment against the railroad. Although Frank Norris' novel, *The Octopus*, fictionalized the Mussel Slough incident, it also helped to keep alive bitter memories of agricultural strife. When political reformers began to emerge in California politics the literature of Norris' trilogy was a powerful weapon for liberal reformers. Another well-known California historian, Josiah Royce, wrote a novel, *The Feud of Oakfield Creek*, in which he criticized the railroad in much the same manner as Norris. The popularity of both works attested to the strong feeling against the railroad, and the influence that literary figures had in generating this new feeling.

The Romantic Realist and Social Reform in the Novel

The realism of the American frontier combined with a romantic appeal was one of the reasons Jack London emerged as a successful California novelist. In his early years London burst upon the literary scheme as a chronicler of western adventure. In 1903 his *Call of the Wild* captured the American imagination because it beautifully described the virile frontier Alaska symbolized for many western buffs. In public interviews London spoke of physical culture as his God, and he glorified the rough, frontier nature of California life. London's early life was filled with heavy drinking bouts, arm-wrestling and exotic adventures in Alaska and the South Pacific. His travels as a hobo were recorded in *The Road*, published in 1907, and he delighted to being addressed as "Sailor Jack" or the "Frisco Kid." In the public imagination London was a romantic figure who wrote of the adventure and intrigue in California, Alaska and exotic tropical lands. In reality, London was a common drunk with a minimal writing talent and a public relations personality which brought him great success.

A native Californian, London's mother had been an astrologer and spiritualist and much attention was devoted to his illegitimate birth. The instability of London's early life, combined with a curious interest in history, produced a politically radical mind that was a mixed bag of Charles Darwin, Herbert Spencer and Karl Marx. Many early radical political ideas in the Golden State emanated from London's provocative pen and constantly prodding mind. In 1908 *The Iron Heel* firmly established London's radical credentials. It was a second-rate novel dedicated to advancing socialist propaganda, but the book was popular because it caught the strong feeling against big business. London used an impressive array of evidence to suggest that capitalism was enslaving blue-collar workers, and subterranean radicals proclaimed the birth of a new California socialism. To local radicals it soon became apparent that London was merely searching for a cause to absorb his energy, and this gave a hollow ring to his pleas for revolution.

Much of the watered down socialism of London's writings resulted from a brief educational stint at the University of California. In a highly autobiographical novel, *Martin Eden*, published in 1909, London spoke of the problems he encountered at UC, and he was particularly critical of the class-conscious attitudes fostered by the university. What is obvious in *Martin Eden* is that London could not accept the middle-class bent of educated people, and he was to continually search for the utopia of the adventurer. His dissatisfaction with traditional American values was displayed in *The Revolution*, published in 1910, which appeared with an alternative political structure to American democracy. This tract was an attempt to appeal to the radical labor union, the Industrial Workers of the World, and London donated large sums of money for an abortive radical campaign to invade Baja California. In sum, London was much like a little boy playing with a revolutionary spirit while living the personal life of a grand lord. It was an incongruous sight to see California's foremost literary radical dining nightly at San Francisco's finest and most expensive French restaurants.

A major turning point occurred in Jack London's life in 1910 when he began construction of his famous "Wolf House." This baronial palace was located in the Valley of the Moon north of San Francisco. It was a majestic structure with a swimming pool fed by a mountain stream and covered balconies highlighting the beauty of the Sonoma countryside. Almost like a medieval king, London presided over his estate from a lofty room in the tower of Wolf House. The significance of Wolf House was that London entered a new lifestyle as a country gentleman. He attempted to engage in scientific agriculture, the outdoor life, and he talked of patterns of leisure which would help his health return. In effect, London was physically sick, mentally fatigued, and he no longer dreamed of influencing social and political thought. This retreat to the countryside was an odd twist in London's career, but he believed that the countryside would reinvigorate his mental and physical capacities. On August 22, 1913, Wolf House burnt to the ground in a fire set by an arsonist's flame. Unable to speak, London lay on his bed for four days after the fire staring at the ceiling. For the next three years he engaged in an orgy of eating and drinking, and in late November, 1916, he took an overdose of morphine to end his life. At the age of forty London died an unhappy man, but he left an incredibly rich literary legacy. London's works beautifully reflect the tensions between urban and rural California values, the early dissatisfaction of blue-collar workers, and the search for a California past which would provide an idyllic civilization. His fifty books are filled with some of the best geographical and historical descriptions of California available to the common person.

Ecology and Wilderness Themes

The wilderness beauty of California attracted a number of writers. Typical of this nonfiction artist was John Muir. Born in Scotland in 1838, Muir immigrated to the Wisconsin frontier and became one with nature. A deeply religious man he read only ancient Latin and Greek works and the Bible. In March, 1868, young Muir arrived in San Francisco and three days later began a journey to Yosemite Valley. He fell in love with the natural beauty of the region and devoted the rest of his life working for established conservation policies. This began a lifetime of writing and lecturing on ecology, and Muir urged state and federal governments to spend money on wilderness preservation.

At the time of his death in 1914 Muir had composed sixty volumes of journals which had not been printed. He also wrote five books on wilderness themes, and his legendary public image popularized the necessity of ecological thought. It was not until he was fifty-six years old that his first book, *The Mountains of California,* revealed the full beauty of the Golden State. Muir's articles appeared in *Century Magazine,* and they influenced Congress to create Yosemite National Park in 1890. In 1892 Muir founded the Sierra Club as an organization dedicated to working for conservation-minded causes.

John Muir, founder of Sierra Club

Courtesy, The Bancroft Library

California Society: A Summary

The growth of California culture was celebrated in the Panama-Pacific Exposition of 1915. Although much of the world was in the midst of a war, San Francisco staged an impressive world's fair. In San Francisco the Panama-Pacific Exposition highlighted the recent link to the east through the opening of the Panama Canal. In addition, the first telephone connection was established between San Francisco and Chicago. It was a marvel of technology to see the latest devices which made living easier for the average Californian. This was a major turning point in California civilization as consumer goods were presented to a highly affluent, urban society.

One of the characteristics of the Panama-Pacific Exposition was the building of eleven gaudy plaster of paris palaces to house the exhibitions. They were regal palaces with a Disneyland motif. For a city with a well-established cultural heritage the Panama-Pacific Exposition provided a glimpse into a cultural future filled with pretentious artifacts.

Many Californians complained that it was no longer possible to buy the best wines or the finest meats. There were constant complaints of urban and rural overcrowding. As San Franciscans ate in the Palace Hotel or sipped a glass of Sonoma wine overlooking the ocean at the Cliff House they realized that urban congestion, industrial growth, and the increasing demands of a middle-class lifestyle were changing the base of the California dream. No longer would the major themes of California literature reflect ecology, realism or romanticism. The new literary emphasis would be upon the struggle of the individual to survive the California lifestyle. The machine age was descending upon California and would alter the major themes of local literature.

Bibliographical Essay

The best single volume on cultural change in the late 19th and 20th century in the Golden State is Kevin Starr, *Americans and the California Dream, 1850–1915* (1973). Franklin Walker, *A Literary History of Southern California* (1950) and *San Francisco's Literary Frontier* (1939) are model studies of cultural change. Joseph Henry Jackson, *Continent's End: A Collection of California Writing* (1944) is important for a variety of literary sources.

A brilliant essay on Josiah Royce is Earl S. Pomeroy, "Josiah Royce, Historian in Search of Community," *Pacific Historical Review,* XL (February, 1971), 1–20. For a study of other important historians see, Robert W. Righter, "Theodore H. Hittell and Hubert H. Bancroft," *California Historical Quarterly,* L (June, 1971), 101–110.

For biographical studies of key figures see, Richard O'Connor, *Ambrose Bierce: A Biography* (1967); Franklin D. Walker, *Frank Norris* (1932); Joan London, *Jack London and His Times* (1939); Richard O'Connor, *Jack London* (1964); Martin S. Peterson, *Joaquin Miller: Literary Frontiersmen* (1937); Helen M. Doyle, *Mary Austin: Woman of Genius* (1939); Edwin Bingham, *Charles F. Lummis, Editor of the Southwest* (1955); and Dudley Gordon, *Charles F. Lummis: Crusader in Corduroy* (1972).

The best work in Hubert Howe Bancroft the Golden State's first serious historian is John W. Caughey, *Hubert Howe Bancroft: Historian of the West* (1946).

There is a great deal of social history in Harold Kirker, *California's Architectural Frontier: Style and Tradition in the Nineteenth Century* (1960); and an equally useful study for social development is Edmond M. Gagey, *The San Francisco State, A History* (1950).

For women in the American West see, Dorothy Gray, *Women of the West* (1976); Joan Hoff Wilson and Lynn Bonfield Donovan, "Women's History: A Listing of West Coast Archival and Manuscript Sources," *California Historical Quarterly,* LV (Spring, 1976), 74–83; Elinor Richey, *Eminent Women of the West* (1975); and Mildred Crowl Martin, *Chinatown's Angry Angel: The Story of Donaldina Cameron* (1977).

An engaging tale of early entertainment is Constance Rourke, *Troupers of the Gold Coast: The Rise of Lotta Crabtree* (1928). A more sophisticated story is *Memories and Impressions of Helen Modjeska: An Autobiography* (1910).

On education see, William W. Ferrier, *Ninety Years of Education in California, 1846–1936* (1937); and Verne A. Stadtman, *The University of California, 1868–1968* (1970).

For a study of San Francisco's most elegant and stylish neighborhood in the 19th century see, Charles Lockwood, "Rincon Hill was San Francisco's Most Genteel Neighborhood," *California History,* LVIII (Spring, 1979), 48–61.

Photo Courtesy: Alan Kirshner

Blacksmith Shop, Death Valley

12

THE PROGRESSIVE MOVEMENT

Reform and Reaction: An Introduction to Modern California History

The birth of modern politics in California is commonly associated with the liberal reforms of the Progressive Movement. In 1901, Theodore Roosevelt ascended to the presidency and liberal reform politics became part of the mainstream of the American political system. In California, however, reform politics did not triumph until the election of Hiram Johnson as governor in 1910. Thus, the first decade of the twentieth century was spent in the attempt to organize a California based reform political coalition. The development of serious minded political reformers was the culmination of a reaction to half a century of corporate and political abuses stemming largely from two sources: the railroad interests and the city bosses. By 1900, for example, the Southern Pacific Railroad and its allied business interests still influenced a large number of business and political interests in California. The prospect of supplanting the railroad's control of California's political and economic development seemed an impossible task. Since the 1880s the railroad's power had declined, and from 1900 to 1910 California Progressives laid the groundwork for reform which broke the railroad's power in the Golden State.

Progressive politicians were a left-wing segment of the Republican party, and there was a small reform faction within the numerically weak Democratic party. They were generally young businessmen, newsmen, doctors, and lawyers who believed in direct popular democracy. The typical California Progressive argued that the voice of the people was no longer heard in state politics and vowed to bring back public opinion as a decision-making force. This appeal to the public consciousness was a shrewd one. While the voice of the people had never been significant in California politics, the timing was right for political rhetoric which emphasized the positive contributions of direct popular democracy.

To emphasize the lack of popular democracy, Progressives concentrated their rhetoric upon a unique feature of California politics—the political influence of the city. San Francisco and Los Angeles dominated state politics. California was more urban and less agricultural than other western states, and this produced two centers of political power. Distaste for the methods and morals of machine politics led to the rise of political reformers who fed upon the mass popular discontent directed toward the corrupt urban political machines.

Los Angeles and the Birth of Urban Progressive Reform

The earliest signs of reform politics in California emanated from Los Angeles. In the mid-1890s, Los Angeles was a small, sparsely populated city with a conservative tone. San Francisco chuckled at the pious announcement that the City of Angels had forbidden saloons to operate on

Sunday. Los Angeles newspapers constantly reminded citizens that there were more churches in their city than in any other similar-sized urban settlement in the United States. Despite the moral tone of Los Angeles, its city government was dominated by the Southern Pacific Railroad machine.

In the 1890s, Southern Pacific's president, Collis P. Huntington, attempted to prevent the construction of a deepwater harbor facility at San Pedro. When the railroad interests learned that the United States Senate was considering spending a quarter of a million dollars in San Pedro, the Southern Pacific began to search for land to control the commercial bonanza expected from the new port. After purchasing land in Santa Monica Bay, the Southern Pacific Railroad engaged in a smooth public relations campaign to denigrate the proposed San Pedro harbor site. Huntington believed that railroad control over the Los Angeles port was necessary to continued Southern Pacific influence in Southern California.

The Los Angeles free harbor controversy was a classic case of early Progressive confrontation with the machine. A study of the leaders who opposed the Santa Monica harbor site reveals that most Southern California Progressives organized to defeat the Southern Pacific Railroad's attempt to continue to monopolize Los Angeles' economic life. Led by Harrison Gray Otis' *Los Angeles Times,* Democratic United States Senator Stephen M. White and a local good-government organizer, Dr. John R. Haynes, the supporters of the San Pedro harbor site developed California's first successful Progressive political bloc. By the late 1890s, public pressure forced the Federal government to appropriate money for the San Pedro port site. This initial reform triumph whetted the appetite of Progressive reformers. Vice and graft continued to flourish in Los Angeles but the machine had been dealt one of its earliest significant defeats by reform politicians. It was during the 1890s, then, that the people's imagination was fired with the prospect of humbling the Southern Pacific.

In the midst of this atmosphere, Progressive reform politics was born in Southern California. Dr. John R. Haynes, who possessed doctorates in medicine and philosophy, lectured Los Angelans on the need to develop a philosophy of Christian Socialism which would eliminate poverty while encouraging the development of free enterprise capitalism. Although he was an ardent Socialist, Dr. Haynes was not a political radical. Rather, he feared developing class lines and a propensity to segregate people according to wages and occupation as a dangerous precedent. Dr. Haynes reasoned that political equality would bring social and economic changes. As a result of this belief, he founded the Direct Legislation League in 1895. At the turn of the century, thanks to the efforts of the Direct Legislation League, Los Angeles voters approved changes in the city charter which provided the citizenry with the power to initiate legislation, veto laws, and recall elected officials. These devices, the initiative, referendum, and recall, became the heart of the Progressive Movement. They provided politicians with the tools to appeal directly to the electorate with programs specifically designed to reform California politics.

The only problem was that the nominally Republican state was controlled by party bosses. Candidates for public office were selected in smoke-filled rooms through the caucus system. There were no primary elections, and it was difficult, if not impossible, for the average citizen to secure a spot on the ballot. As an extention of the Direct Legislation League, Dr. Haynes formed a Good Government League to elect a reform-minded mayor, and by 1906 Haynes' organization captured seventeen of twenty-three key positions in the Los Angeles city government. It was ironic that Haynes used the same technique of small, caucus-type meetings to take over local politics.

The experiences of Los Angeles' reformers were strengthened by successful recall campaigns aimed at a corrupt city councilman and the mayor. In addition, the Good Government League eliminated the use of ward politics, or neighborhood political clubs, which turned out the vote in return for specific political rewards. Still, Los Angeles reformers complained that they were unable to make any political changes in state politics. In 1902, Governor George Pardee was elected with Southern Pacific support, but by 1906, when he had begun to display a reformist mentality, he was replaced by James Gillett. Both Republican governors owed their elections to railroad money and influence. Clearly, the Southern Pacific Railroad still controlled the direction of California politics. The railroad was able to spend large sums of money to secure delegate votes for the nomination of political candidates. This practice annoyed reformers and they vowed to alter the structure of state politics.

From 1906 to 1913, Los Angeles Progressivism recalled Mayor Arthur C. Harper and served as a model of reform activity. It was the organizational skills of Los Angeles reformers which were important to the rise of a new political system. Changes in the political structure began in 1905 when prominent businessmen founded the Non-Partisan City Central Committee. Its stated purpose was to elect Progressives to city offices. As a result of this organization, two-thirds of Los Angeles' elected offices were occupied by Progressives in 1906, and the district attorney, Thomas L. Woolwine began investigating bribery charges against Mayor Harper. Angered by Woolwine's probing, Harper removed the district attorney from office. In February, 1909, the *Los Angeles Times* reported that racketeers had been paying off Mayor Harper. Public opinion demanded the mayor's recall, and shortly before the spring election of 1909, Harper resigned from office. Due to hostile public opinion political bosses remained on the periphery of Los Angeles politics, and a Progressive-Republican, George Alexander, was elected mayor by less than two thousand votes over a Socialist candidate. In this campaign the Socialist candidate was very similar to the Progressive, and both agreed that honest government was a necessity.

What was intriguing about Los Angeles Progressivism was the complete triumph of non-partisan politics. Mayor Alexander governed under a system of classless politics. He publicly boasted that the best men were selected for political appointments. However, Mayor Alexander neglected to mention that Progressives had excluded labor from the reform coalition; thus, growing hostility between labor and big business caused a middle and upper middle-class type of Progressivism to dominate Los Angeles politics. It was obvious to contemporary observers that Los Angeles Progressives interpreted democracy in terms of property rights and believed that social structures should be molded by the respectable and well-educated segment of the community. As a result, talk of "business efficiency" in city government was a common feature of Southern California Progressivism. Labor leaders spoke out against this conservative brand of political reform and continually emphasized the restrictive democratic nature of Los Angeles politics.

In spite of the non-democratic rhetoric of Los Angeles Progressives it brought vast improvements in the political system. In December, 1909, an initiative proposal was passed creating a Los Angeles Board of Public Utilities. This allowed the reformers to carefully monitor water, gas, electricity, and telephone services. By 1913, Progressive accomplishments included a partially renovated harbor, a municipal power system, expanded fire and police departments, and massive sewer and street construction. Yet, Mayor Alexander complained that these advances failed to draw complete voter support for the Los Angeles Progressive movement.

With the 1913 election approaching, Los Angeles Progressives believed that they would have to join forces with regular and conservative Republicans to retain control of city government. In the 1911 election, a Socialist candidate, Job Harriman, had come within an eyelash of being elected mayor. Labor had carefully organized itself and many Progressives believed a Socialist could be elected to lead Los Angeles government. Therefore, the decision to unite Progressive and regular Republicans appeared to be politically sound. During the 1913 election, however, liberal and conservative political elements found it impossible to unite effectively in a political campaign. As a result, an independent candidate aligned with neither Progressives nor regular Republicans, Harry Rose, was elected as Los Angeles' mayor. This ended Los Angeles Progressivism and splintered the reform coalition.

The disintegration of reform politics in Los Angeles was the result of divergent Progressive attitudes. Political unity had never been a strong part of Los Angeles reform politics. Consequently, debates over methods of public utility regulation, for example, tended to promote a Progressive split. This factionalism combined with strong opposition to reform from organized labor, regular Republicans and the business community, spelled an end to reform politics. Mayor Alexander's Progressivism was essentially an effort to inject efficiency and economy into city government. The most important change, however, was the destruction of the political machine, and thus, the development of a political atmosphere which forced candidates to appeal to the entire community. As an early example of reform-minded politics, Los Angeles provided a case study in successful urban change. The Progressive political philosophy was the most intriguing aspect of the reform mentality. Therefore, it is important to analyze the Progressives' political philosophy.

The Progressive Political Philosophy: An Analysis

In order to fully understand the complex nature of California Progressivism, it is necessary to examine the political premises which many reformers embraced. Most Progressives believed that industrial development had reached a stage in the United States which made the middle class dream impossible for a large segment of the country. Progressives pointed to increased emphasis upon class consciousness and dramatic economic differences among social groups to support this contention. The logical culmination of these differences, the typical Progressive argued, was to develop tensions between labor and capital and ultimately to create a revolutionary impulse in American politics. A large number of Progressives talked of the impending danger of a violent major confrontation between California's workers and employers. For this reason, Progressives were strong supporters of legislation granting labor rights. It was less the belief in labor's rights and more the conviction that they were removing the revolutionary ethos from American politics which prompted California Progressives to support trade union legislation. The cap to the Progressive political philosophy was the creation of "scientific government." To the California reformer, this meant creating a series of state agencies to regulate economic and political progress. The California Progressive envisioned a political program which would defuse the tensions threatening to destroy California's urban-industrial civilization.

City Bosses as the Catalyst to Public Acceptance of Reform Politics

It would have been impossible for the Progressive-minded politician to have garnered public support had it not been for the actions of city bosses. Since the 1850s, San Francisco had been the center of an Irish-Catholic political machine which provided a well-governed city with a free business climate which winked at moralistic and legalistic roadblocks. It had been customary for years for neighborhood political clubs to garner favors from city hall. Even honest, reform-minded mayors had to cooperate with ward politicians. Prior to 1900, political corruption had been minimal, but at the turn of the century a political boss emerged who was so blantantly corrupt that his behavior brought about a public demand for reform.

The background to the rising reform sentiment began in the late spring of 1901 when a teamsters' and waterfront strike was called by San Francisco labor. The steady advances of labor unions in San Francisco since the 1880s prompted big business to attempt to destroy the fledgling transportation workers' movement. The result was a lengthy strike during the summer of 1901. Business organized an Employers' Association and raised $200,000 to bring in special police and strike-breaking workers. There were numerous minor fights throughout the summer, but in July, the employers made it clear that they intended to break the back of the union movement through sheer violence and intimidation. After three months of minor disputes, a major riot broke out on September 29, 1901. The riot forced Mayor James D. Phelan, whose attempt to appear impartial had incurred the wrath of both sides, to ask the governor for help. A few days later, Governor Henry T. Gage sent in the National Guard. The reaction in San Francisco was one of hostility, and public criticism of the major political parties intensified. The time was ripe for a third party movement.

Abe Ruef, a minor Republican organizer in North Beach, took advantage of the turbulent times. He began to suggest that a union of laboring men organized into a political party would bring back the workers' control of San Francisco politics. Because of the strike Mayor Phelan's renomination was no longer possible and voters were lukewarm to most politicians who handled the strike. As a result of this feeling, Ruef quietly organized the Union Labor Party. In reality, it was a wing of the Republican Party. Seeing the immediate advantage of shunning the major parties, Ruef announced that the Union Labor Party was only a temporary expedient to clean up San Francisco politics and provide the laboring man with representation. He talked of ending class strife, even as he formed a political party which exploited the vote of the working man. The Union Labor Party became so powerful and so publicly corrupt that it ignited California Progressives.

The union interests which backed the Union Labor Party selected the president of the San Francisco musicians' union, Eugene E. Schmitz, to run for mayor. A close personal friend of Ruef's, Schmitz was an excellent candidate. A tall, articulate, well-dressed figure with a German-Irish ethnic background and close ties with the Catholic community, he possessed the political ingredients to appeal to the most populous segment of San Francisco voters. Since the 1850s, Irish-Catholic political interests had dominated San Francisco politics, and this made Schmitz a formidable candidate. In the 1901 campaign, Schmitz stressed the themes of economic justice and the necessity of ending class strife in San Francisco. In reality, however, Schmitz capitalized on the atmosphere which prevailed after the strike of 1901, because he subtly predicted the end of unionist influences in San Francisco politics unless he was elected mayor.

Union Labor Party Boss Abe Ruef

Mayor Eugene Schmitz

Courtesy, The Bancroft Library

In Schmitz' first two administrations from 1901 to 1905, there was only a modest level of corruption in the Union Labor Party. San Franciscans boasted that their city was the best governed urban center in the United States. In fact, the eighteen member San Francisco Board of Supervisors who governed the city-county government was not dominated by the Union Labor Party. Until 1905, only a few Union Labor members were successful in races for supervisor. This accounts for the minimal level of political corruption. It also forced Abe Ruef to wheel and deal in his promotion of Union Labor politics. From a booth in a well-known French restaurant, The Pup, Ruef nightly dispensed political favors and consummated shady financial deals. Ruef's desire for money was subordinated only to his political goal of obtaining a seat in the United States Senate. This often led him to make deals that were more political than financial. Thus there developed a potent alliance between a respected mayor and a covert and highly-skilled political boss.

Fremont Older, editor of the
San Francisco Bulletin

Courtesy, The Bancroft Library

Fremont Older's Liberal Crusade Against the Union Labor Party

The crusading editor of the *San Francisco Bulletin,* Fremont Older, spearheaded the early reform agitation designed to set San Franciscans against Union Labor politics. After experiencing a series of personal disagreements with Ruef and Schmitz, Older exposed every misdeed he could uncover involving the Union Labor Party. The revelations provided both humor and a sense of uniqueness to the vast majority of San Franciscans. Eventually, though, the scandals produced a reform-minded political core dedicated to replacing boss-dominated politicians. After Schmitz' reelection in 1903, the "moral fiber" of the Union Labor Party all but disappeared, and the control Ruef initially held over the machine began to vanish. Ruef became lazy and often did not keep close watch on his cohorts. The result was a series of well-publicized scandals.

In 1904, the *Bulletin* uncovered evidence that the Board of Public Works, under the direction of the mayor's brother, Herbert Schmitz, issued an order to repair city streets with blue rocks. Then came the comic opera revelation that the only firm producing blue rocks, the Gray Brothers

Quarry Company, had employed Abe Ruef as their attorney. San Franciscans did little more than snicker at Older's charges. This was a low level scandal which made San Franciscans boast that the city by the bay was the most colorful urban settlement in the American West.

Shortly after the blue rock scandal, the *Bulletin* uncovered a house of prostitution at 620 Jackson Street in Chinatown which seemed to have an official police blessing. The building inspector, sent out when construction began, reported that the structure could not possibly be used as a hotel since the rooms were too small; he suspected a house of prostitution was being built in Chinatown. Herbert Schmitz reprimanded the inspector, and Mayor Eugene Schmitz delivered a public speech defending prostitution as an innocent practice. In May, 1904, the Standard Lodging House opened for business, and Older reported that the small rooms were being rented to women at three dollars a day in two shifts. Finally, with the rise of public pressure, the police raided the hotel. The Standard Lodging House countered by filing for a restraining order in a San Francisco Municipal Court. Judge Seawell heard the testimony of both sides, but the conflicting opinions made it impossible to render a decision. In abject frustration, the Judge stationed himself in front of the Standard Lodging House on a Saturday night to see if the charges of prostitution were true. After his visit, Seawell ruled that the police were within their rights in raiding the establishment. But the decision only caused the San Francisco police to ignore illegal acts at the Standard Lodging House. Older called the incident the "Municipal Crib" scandal and charged that Ruef and Schmitz were coddling gamblers and prostitution. San Franciscans, however, were amused and showed even stronger political support for the Union Labor Party.

Soon though, more serious scandals emerged. The Standard Lodging House controversy had focused attention upon the San Francisco Police Department, and the *Bulletin* continued investigating. It was discovered that a recently-appointed police commissioner, Thomas Reagan, had opened an insurance agency to sell policies to saloons. Older charged that this was a legal form of extortion, and in reality, the saloons were buying Reagan's friendship. Using verbal persuasion, Older convinced Tom Ellis, a sargeant in the Chinatown division of the S.F.P.D., to turn $1,400 worth of protection money over to a San Francisco grand jury. The money, Ellis maintained, was one week's hush money from Chinatown gamblers. These accusations stirred the first serious interests in investigating the Union Labor Party.

Early investigations failed to turn up any substantial evidence of corruption. The only documented misdeeds were that Ruef and Schmitz were involved in extorting money from San Francisco's French restaurants in return for guaranteeing renewal of their liquor licenses. Since the Gold Rush, the French restaurants of San Francisco had become world famous. The twelve sumptuous three-story buildings housing the city's leading Gallic establishments had elegant public dining rooms suitable for family groups on the first floor; the second floor had luxuriously furnished dining rooms used to conclude business deals; and on the third floor were private supper bedrooms which catered to the businessman or tourist looking for a full evening. The French restaurants were a long and venerated tradition in San Francisco, and represented a million dollar investment for their owners. For their continued prosperity, the French restaurants depended upon the Union Labor Party. The city charter required a quarterly renewal of every liquor license by a majority vote of the police commission, and by 1904, it was public knowledge that members of the police commission were being bribed to renew the licenses. Since Commissioner Reagan was responsible for the renewal of liquor licenses, his actions brought the first attempts to organize a reform coalition.

Union Labor Power at Its Nadir and the 1906 Earthquake

There were a number of reasons for Fremont Older's initial inability to turn public opinion against the Ruef-Schmitz machine. First, there was very little substantial evidence of corruption. Second, San Franciscans lived in a well-governed and prosperous city. The taint of corruption was not easily detected by the average citizen. Third, past reform mayors, notably James D. Phelan, had created strong hostility to political change by failing to provide adequate city services and a smooth functioning government. As a result Mayor Phelan discredited the notion of Progressive political reform. San Franciscans clearly preferred political bosses and a well-oiled political machine.

In 1905, the Union Labor machine became careless when it selected candidates to run for office. When the election results came in, Ruef was pleasantly surprised to discover that all eighteen seats on the Board of Supervisors had been captured by Union Laborites. Moreover, every city government position of any importance was held by a member of Ruef's party. The use of voting machines in the 1905 election accounted for this success because most San Franciscans simply pulled the Union Labor Party lever, which, in turn, gave every Union Laborite a vote. But there were problems with the candidates elected in 1905, as Ruef had grown lazy in his selection process. District Attorney William Langdon was elected without prior knowledge of Ruef's machine. He was an honest politician and had no idea that bribery and graft were common features of the Union Labor Party. On the other hand, a newly elected supervisor, Andrew M. Wilson, chosen to represent smaller businessmen, viewed his election as an opportunity to engage in open bribery. Wilson had no idea that Ruef orchestrated the payoffs, and he openly solicited "campaign contributions" which in reality were bribes for political favors.

President Theodore Roosevelt worried about the future growth of the Union Labor Party. Abe Ruef's desire to go national was a well-known ambition; consequently, President Roosevelt met with Fremont Older to plan a means of exposing Union Labor corruption. William Langdon offered to cooperate in the search for evidence on San Francisco political corruption. A well-known millionaire, Rudolph Spreckels, pledged a quarter of a million dollars to underwrite the investigation. Roosevelt then assigned the head of the Secret Service, William J. Burns, to handle the behind the scenes gathering of evidence. Quietly, in January, 1906, more than one hundred special investigators moved into San Francisco to begin the arduous process of obtaining evidence for the San Francisco graft prosecution.

In the midst of the early planning to prosecute the Union Labor Party, a catastrophic earthquake shook San Francisco. On the morning of April 18, 1906, the tremor shook the city and ignited more than fifty fires. It was perhaps an ill omen that Dennis Sullivan, the fire chief, perished when rushing into his wife's bedroom, as the earthquake had collapsed that portion of his apartment and he fell to his death. The fire was impossible to contain because the city's waterline was laid on the quake fault. Furthermore, a large number of fire hydrants proudly displayed around the city had not been connected to the water supply.

One of the legacies of the 1906 Earthquake was that it provided Mayor Eugene Schmitz with an opportunity to exhibit a rare form of political leadership. His first act was to issue a handbill which prevented wholesale looting and mob violence. Schmitz then organized the Citizen's Committee of Fifty which fed, clothed, and housed the quake's victims. The Citizen's Committee began preparation for a rebuilding of the city, and Mayor Schmitz was an extremely important figure in maintaining public calm and restoring confidence. It was not surprising that when the graft trials began, San Franciscans demanded that Schmitz not be prosecuted.

Destruction after the San Francisco earthquake of 1906

Abe Ruef, however, used the earthquake and fire to enhance his own personal fortune. When businessmen applied for permits to reconstruct buildings, Ruef was available to secure emergency building locations and provide permits. It was alleged that any business which employed Ruef as an attorney, or admitted him as a stockholder, received special consideration from San Francisco city officials. Once the city was rebuilt and business returned to a normal course, there was clear contempt for Ruef's methods. His actions in the aftermath of the 1906 Earthquake may have been the decisive factor in bringing about his demise as a result of the San Francisco graft trials. Ruef was the only Union Laborite to receive a jail sentence.

The San Francisco Graft Trials and the Union Labor Party Decline

In the summer of 1907, Mayor Schmitz was convicted of extorting money from a French restaurant, and provisions in the city charter caused his removal from office. An appeals court overturned Schmitz' conviction, but this marked the end of the Union Labor Party. Abe Ruef was

Residential destruction during the San Francisco earthquake of 1906

tried in a series of spectacular trials and received a fourteen year sentence. It was the public trials from 1907 to 1909 which helped to create a Progressive political consciousness. As the Union Labor Party was dismantled, political reformers capitalized on the public's demand for change. The California Progressives in 1909 were ready to bring a revolution into state government. It would have been impossible to develop the Progressive reform mentality had it not been for the excesses of the Ruef-Schmitz machine. The Union Labor Party created an atmosphere conducive to liberal political change.

An ironical aftermath of the Union Labor prosecutions occurred when Fremont Older's *San Francisco Bulletin* launched a campaign to free Abe Ruef from San Quentin. Older believed that Ruef was the scapegoat for Union Labor corruption. The *Bulletin's* efforts led to a campaign which reduced Ruef's sentence to five years. After his release from prison, Ruef returned to the mainstream of San Francisco society. While never again an important political figure, nonetheless, Ruef was a respected citizen. In fact, he became something of a local folk hero. He died in 1936 in virtual bankruptcy, however, as his million dollar fortune had been appropriately depleted by fine food and wine.

Courtesy, The Bancroft Library

Abe Ruef is offered advice during the San Francisco Graft Trials

The California Progressive: A Profile of the Leaders

In order to understand the degree of political change which the Progressive Movement brought to California politics, it is necessary to profile the politicians who instituted liberal politics. What manner of man was the California Progressive? How did his beliefs concerning government bring change? Why were women visible in the Progressive Movement? What values emerged in the Progressive Era which were conducive to better government?

A profile of the typical California Progressive indicates that he was a relatively young and politically inexperienced individual. The Progressive was under forty, and his birthplace was generally in the Middle West. He came from predominantly Anglo-Saxon stock, and his father's career was often linked financially to the railroad. The typical Progressive was well-equipped to battle the machine. In terms of education, three of four were college graduates and were economically advantaged by early twentieth century standards. In sum, California Progressives were fortunate sons of the middle and upper middle class. Prior to the twentieth century, it was not the tradition for well-educated and economically successful professionals to enter the dark world of politics.

A major factor prompting the Progressive politician to emerge at the turn of the century was the specter of corrupt urban political bosses. By 1900 the revolt of the farmer and small-town businessman had matured, and the reform impulse passed to urban centers. By controlling San Francisco and Los Angeles' politics, big business directed the pulse of California civilization. It was not surprising, then, that the major thrust of reform politics would emerge at the urban level.

The real success of the Progressive Movement in California, however, was due to the dominance of the Southern Pacific Railroad. It served as the necessary symbol of corruption to bring political reformers together. Few states were as urban as California in the early twentieth century. Fifty per cent of the states population resided in four metropolitan areas; San Francisco, Los Angeles, Oakland, and Sacramento.

However, to assume that the California Progressive was interested solely in altering economic conditions, is to miss the overall significance of the reform impulse. Progressives believed that a more fluid social structure had to be developed in the Golden State. The conflict between capital and labor which the Progressive feared brought strong support for regulative government. It was the job of state government, the Progressive argued, to eliminate the conditions which produced conflict. Consequently, the Progressive felt that the correct goal of politics was to take the revolutionary impulse out of American society. In sum, the California Progressives held to a political philosophy which implied that a middle-class society that ensured a just distribution of consumer goods to all Californians was the ideal form of civilization.

The middle-class values of Progressives are reflected in their letters and speeches. References to "the better element, the good people, and the natural leaders" are phrases which reveal a form of heavy political morality. In many respects, California Progressives rejected the rapid technological change which twentieth century life brought into American politics. They looked with nostalgia to an older, stabler nation whose values and standards, emphasizing among other things "equal opportunity for all, special privilege for none," corresponded with their own views. Only when caught between militant labor and powerful business interests did the Progressive assume an active political stance. Then, Progressives adopted the tactics of the political machine and matched the organizational skill of the Southern Pacific Railroad. In using honest machine politics, the Progressive believed that the state was being rid of a worse evil—railroad and corporate abuses. The Progressives believed it was necessary to mold the continued conflict between labor and capital; this belief accounted for the often stuffy political rhetoric of the reformers. They were slaying the dragon of corruption and allaying the dreaded specter of class conflict.

Prelude to Reform: The California Legislature of 1909

In 1907, California Progressives organized a reform organization. The Lincoln-Roosevelt League as it was known, was a Progressive political club designed to organize reform politicians. It was an organization heavily infused with newspapermen, lawyers, doctors, and educators. The governor's mansion and control of the state legislature were the announced goals of the Lincoln-Roosevelt League. By 1909 its members were well organized and intent upon becoming the dominant force in California politics. The first signs of Progressive legislation emerged during the 1909 legislative session.

Despite opposition from railroad interests, a direct primary law was enacted in 1909. This enabled voters to select the party nominee. This was a significant reform because it made it easier for reform candidates to secure a position on the ballot. No longer could the Southern Pacific handpick political candidates. The railroad expended its last gasp of political power by excluding the United States Senate nominee from the direct primary law. The Southern Pacific was able to keep this position within party lines, thereby maintaining some semblance of the caucus system. Once the Progressives came to power at the national level, however, this changed. The 17th

Amendment to the United States Constitution in 1913 was the realization of an ardent goal of reformers for decades—the direct election of Senators. Progressivism at the state level now was being buttressed by national legislation. By 1914, California law provided that United States Senators would be directly elected and subject to primary election; viewed in retrospect, though, it is clear that 1909 had been the major turning point in California politics. The Direct Primary Law was an indication that machine politics were on the wane.

Another significant reform was the attempt to reform the Railroad Commission. Created during the constitutional revision of 1879, the Railroad Commission from 1880 to 1909 was a source of political controversy. Contemporary opponents of the Southern Pacific believed that the Railroad Commission was a tool of corporate interests. Recently, however, it has been shown that the commissioners were often conscientious, honest public servants. Their real problem was not that they were corrupt; they were unable to fulfill their duties due to lack of funds. In addition, regulation of big business was a new aspect of American history. To remedy the powerless nature of the Railroad Commission, a bill was passed which provided for specific powers. The Stetson Bill of 1911, allowed the commissioners to set absolute freight and passenger rates and provided still penalties for discriminatory shipping rates. While the Stetson Bill was not overly effective, it did indicate that the Southern Pacific's political influence was no longer the major factor in California politics.

The Triumph of California Progressivism: The Election of 1910

California Progressives were optimistic about the 1910 election. The Lincoln-Roosevelt League was well-organized in all parts of the state. Local clubs were prepared to turn out the vote for governor, but Progressives found it difficult to decide upon a gubernatorial candidate. After some searching, one of the minor prosecution lawyers in the Ruef-Schmitz graft trials, Hiram W. Johnson, of San Francisco, was selected as the Progressive-Republican nominee.

As a candidate for governor, Johnson was an intriguing figure. A small, heavy-set man with a jowly appearance, Johnson was an emotional and demagogic speaker. Traveling throughout the state in a red convertible, Johnson would stop along the side of a road or a city street corner, stand up on the back seat and ring a cowbell. The curious crowd was then treated to vague, but thunderous broadsides against the malfeasance of the railroad and big business. Shaking his chubby fist in the air, Johnson would assail the evil deeds of machine politics. The common man loved Hiram Johnson's rhetoric. The professional politician, however, complained that Johnson had no specific programs to remedy the corruption in state government. In addition, he had no past political experience. Even Progressives complained after talking to Johnson that he had no political philosophy, and even fewer ideas. An attractive candidate, he was unquestionably honest, and was an effective public speaker who was aided by a sympathetic press.

Johnson's political personality, however, contained some curious intellectual flaws. Once he adopted a position on a political issue, he never wavered from it. This unflinching viewpoint made it impossible for him to remain friendly with those who disagreed with him. As the August, 1910, primary election results came in, no one noticed Johnson's political assets or liabilities because the primary results produced an overwhelming victory for him. Johnson polled over one hundred thousand votes while the handpicked railroad candidate, Charles Curry, was able to garner only twelve thousand. One curious sidelight was Curry's victory in San Francisco and Sacramento

Courtesy, The Bancroft Library

Hiram W. Johnson campaigns
for governor in 1910

counties. It was Los Angeles County that provided Johnson's margin of victory by delivering one-fifth of his statewide vote. Johnson had greatly underestimated his voter support in Southern California, and, consequently, incurred heavy political debts to Southern Californians. It was a significant turning point in that the 1910 primary provided Los Angeles with its first major political influence in California's history.

The primary election results also produced a Democratic candidate for governor, Theodore Bell, who was a liberal-progressive. Bell had begun his political career as a Napa County district attorney. After one term in the United States House of Representatives, Bell unsuccessfully ran for governor in 1906. In that campaign, he created strong political support by recalling the anti-monopoly Democratic politics of the 1880s. Bell's theme in the 1910 campaign was that the railroad's domination of California politics must be ended. While Johnson and Bell were similar in rhetoric, Bell had developed a program of political reform. The Democratic candidate carefully spelled out how he would end the railroad's power. Among Bell's most appealing ideas were support for a national income tax amendment, a reorganized railroad commission, and suffrage for women. Bell's advanced Progressivism forced Johnson to develop a campaign package. In reality, Johnson parroted most of Bell's ideas. As the governor's race progressed into its final weeks, many contemporary observers believed it was too close to predict. Then, a bombshell occurred when William F. Herrin's Southern Pacific Political Bureau innocently endorsed Bell for governor in the *San Francisco Globe,* an in-house-organ of the Southern Pacific. Immediately Hiram Johnson charged that Bell had been bribed by the railroad interests. The charge was ludicrous, but the voters were swayed and returned a narrow victory for Johnson. Again, the voters of Southern California were instrumental in the Progressive-Republican triumph.

Hiram Johnson brought a revolution to California government. His six years as governor produced modern state government and curbed the malevolent influence of big business. But, the Progressive Movement produced an equally efficient political machine—one which was honest yet non-democratic. The irony of the Progressive Movement was the creation of a coldly efficient government. The impersonal revolution in California government produced a bureaucracy which became a major force in twentieth century California civilization.

The Triumph of Reform: The California Legislature of 1911

In January, 1911, the California Legislature convened with the chaplin's issuing an extraordinary plea, "Give us a square deal for Christ's sake." Politicians snickering from the floor delivered remarks suggesting that Governor Johnson would need all the help he could get in the next few months, but Johnson's critics underestimated his political skill. In ninety days, the 1911 California Legislature, with Governor Johnson as the guiding spirit, dismantled the railroad machine. Combining a demagogic appeal to public opinion with a shrewd political program, Johnson transformed the process of California government into one of the most efficient state machines in the nation. Johnson was responsible for introducing "scientific management" to California government. He reasoned that academic specialists without a direct interest in state politics would be the most logical civil servants. Like most Progressives, Johnson created a centralized state bureaucracy which exerted controls over the business community. Reliance upon commissions, hired experts and scientific facts took the human element out of state government. The Johnson administrations' devotion to efficiency and economy set the political tone for California politics in the twentieth century.

California Progressives displayed a mania for legislation. During the first week of the 1911 session, 156 Senate bills and 159 Assembly bills were referred to committees. Governor Johnson was determined to produce a prodigious body of reform legislation. This overzealous concern for legislation was a key cause of infighting among Progressives. Once the reforms of the 1911 legislature were completed, the Johnson administration lost its cohesion and the cooperation of fellow Progressives. Thus, the 1911 Legislature is the highpoint of reform politics. It is ironic that only ninety days of cooperation would exist among California Progressives, but the three-month session of the legislature produced one of the most enduring sets of changes ever experienced in California government.

Progressives believed that the greatest evils of the Southern Pacific machine could be remedied by reforming the Railroad Commission. Consequently, the first significant bill was to provide money to revitalize the Commission. In 1911, the Railroad Commission was given power to establish freight and passenger rates for all railroad and transportation companies. Many Californians believed that these new powers were inconsequential because the state government had tried unsuccessfully to dismantle the Southern Pacific since the 1880s. This time, however, there were very precise changes in California law, and the Commission was provided with enough money to function as a regulative body. Its powers were very specific ones. It could initiate an investigation if it felt a rate change was unreasonable or discriminatory, and it drew up a set of prescribed bookkeeping regulations and minimum standards of safety. What really made the Railroad Commission effective was that it now had enough money to operate, and its members were appointed, not elected. The popularity of new powers for the Railroad Commission was shown in a special initiative election in October, 1911, when voters amended the California Constitution to increase state regulation over the railroad.

The changes in the Railroad Commission were far reaching. The number of Commissioners was increased from three to five, and the governor appointed all Commissioners. In addition, the Railroad Commission was granted the power to regulate all public utility companies within the state except municipally owned utilities. In the regulation of the Southern Pacific and public utilities, the Progressives achieved their most noteworthy successes. Further, in controlling corporate abuses, Johnson lectured the Railroad Commission not to worry whether its actions were constitutional. Employing the same methods as the machine, the Johnson Administration did an outstanding job of regulating railroad abuses. An examination of the Railroad Commission's records indicates that between March 23, 1912, and October 1, 1914, more than 1,500 formal decisions were delivered. Only eight were challenged in the California Supreme Court. This resulted in a statewide reduction in passenger and freight rates, as well as a lowering of public utility rates in most California cities. Government regulations prompted William F. Herrin of the Southern Pacific Political Bureau to complain that Progressives had adopted the same political tactics as the Southern Pacific.

There were a number of other Progressive political reforms. In November, 1911, the initiative, referendum, and recall were written into the California Constitution. The people could now initiate legislation, or show approval or disappointment over state government action, and, if these measures failed, the corrupt politicians could be recalled from office. As these measures were incorporated into state law, it puzzled some of Governor Johnson's close associates when he privately mumbled that democracy was becoming too pervasive in California. Many Progressives wondered about the changing nature of Johnson's political thought, and a large number of Californians believed that he was a potentially dangerous demagogue.

Perhaps the most revealing piece of legislation, in reflecting Governor Johnson's need to monitor democracy, was the creation of the California Board of Control. It was a state agency headed by a twenty-six-year-old newspaper reporter, John F. Neylan. The purpose of the Board of Control was to act as a watchdog agency over state spending. This led to an eight million dollar surplus in state government funds by 1917. It also brought the indictment of sixteen state officials on charges of corruption. As a result of these reforms, Hiram Johnson received an inordinate amount of national publicity.

While it was harvest time for California Progressives, there were also signs of political trouble. Many Progressives believed that Hiram Johnson's power was becoming too enormous. There were also complaints about Johnson's personality. In 1912, Johnson compounded the complaint against him by running for the Vice-Presidency on Theodore Roosevelt's ill-fated Progressive Party ticket. It was not surprising that, with most of the essential reforms completed, California Progressives began to fight among themselves, and a liberal decline was noticeable in state politics. Still, the astounding record of the 1911 California Legislature in providing honest and efficient government cannot be discounted.

The Decline of California Progressivism

The decline of California Progressivism is a complex phenomena. In the beginning, Progressivism was a loose, makeshift political coalition with the common goal of ending Southern Pacific control of California politics. To all intents and purposes, this had been accomplished by the time the 1913 California Legislature, and the first clear signs of Progressive decline were evident to political observers.

As the 1913 legislature convened, Chester Rowell, editor of the *Fresno Republican* and a founding member of the Lincoln-Roosevelt League, commented that Progressive reforms were complete and that any further attempts to legislate reform would prove disastrous. Rowell was correct. Reform legislation in the 1913 legislature actually began the process of dismantling the Progressive political system. An effort to create a new set of reform goals placed great stress on the Progressive mentality, and the result was a legislative program that was ill-conceived. Progressivism took itself too seriously by 1913 and the result was the destruction of liberal politics.

One historian who has suggested that Progressives were "tired reformers" by 1913, has pointed to legislation that served no useful purpose. The innovative quality of California reform declined because the 1911 state legislature provided all the important legislation for honest and effective state government. The main thrust of the 1913 legislature was in creating new agencies to regulate the state. The Industrial Welfare Commission, the Industrial Accident Commission, and the Commission of Immigration and Housing were examples of the mania for regulation. Perhaps the most significant of these agencies was the Industrial Welfare Commission. Headed by Mrs. Katherine Phillips Edson, President of the California Federation of Women's Club and a Los Angeles reformer, the Commission investigated wages, hours, and working conditions for women and children. Mrs. Edson was instrumental in the passage of a minimum wage law in California, and she insisted that state law require a woman be appointed to the Industrial Welfare Commission. For many years, Mrs. Edson had worked diligently for the rights of working women. Because of her prodding, the Industrial Welfare Commission published well-circulated statistics which revealed that a woman in California must earn $500 a year or nearly ten dollars a week to live on a minumum subsistance level. In 1913, a study of women employed in California laundries indicated that they earned less than half that amount. Applying political pressure through women's political clubs, Mrs. Edson secured a minimum wage of sixteen cents an hour. By 1920, Mrs. Edson's efforts produced a number of compromises within California business. A minimum wage of $10 a week was more or less standard practice by 1920, and the Industrial Welfare Commission in 1920 indicated that more than fifty percent of the women workers in California were receiving a wage in excess of the minimum standard of living.

The women's movement during the Progressive Era reflected the problems that industrial-urban civilization posed for the family. It was not common from 1910 to 1920 to see women with large families employed in industry. In 1911, women achieved voting rights and were an important force in Progressive politics, but employers continued to take advantage of them. While minimum wage laws existed, there was little protection for women and children as hourly workers. Indeed, Mrs. Edson's persistent campaigning caused the 1923 California legislature to adopt maximum hour legislation. While these gains were much less than Mrs. Edson and her female Progressive cohorts demanded, nonetheless, they reflect the only bright spot in the latter stages of California Progressivism.

The Alien Land Law and Anti-Japanese Sentiment

The negative side of California Progressivism was shown when Governor Johnson quietly authored a bill to restrict Japanese land ownership. For two decades California judged the Japanese with the same racial stereotypes that they had used to intimidate the Chinese. The belief that the Japanese were unassimilable and lived in a substandard manner was not an easy argument to substantiate. Japanese truck farmers were unusually prosperous in the Sacramento and San Joaquin Valleys. The price of fresh fruits and vegetables declined as a result of Japanese agricultural productivity. The rice industry was virtually created by energetic Japanese farmers.

The long history of anti-Asian sentiment and the use of derogatory terms to describe the Japanese led to heavy voter turnouts and quick election to office. It was not surprising that most major California politicians pandered to this anti-Asian feeling. Governor Johnson was the most effective orator against the "Yellow Peril" and he quietly convinced the California legislature to pass an Alien Land Act of 1913. This highly discriminatory piece of legislation was an indication of the reactionary nature of California Progressivism.

The Alien Land Law of 1913 restricted land sales and the ownership of California lands by first-generation Japanese. The peculiarly worded law allowed land ownership for four years or less, but the law was easily evaded by the Japanese as they signed it over to family, friends, or Japanese-American relatives. The legacy of hatred toward the Japanese was amply demonstrated by the law, and California agribusiness applauded the restrictions which allowed for some land to be purchased at reasonable prices. What is ironic is that the Japanese government built an expensive pavilion at the San Francisco Panama-Pacific International Exposition of 1913, and the quiet and dignified protests of the Japanese government were ignored in the wave of anti-Asian xenophobia.

There were a number of Californians who defended Japanese business and land owning rights. Theodore Bell, Johnson's Democratic party opponent in the 1910 election, charged that the Progressives had made a mess of the land situation. Harry Chandler, editor of the *Los Angeles*

Times, called the law unwise and unfortunate. These were minor protests and most Californians applauded the measure as a necessary one. The strong feeling against the Japanese continued to smoulder until World War II when President Franklin D. Roosevelt signed Executive Order 9066 interning the Japanese in relocation camps.

California Progressivism: A Summary

The final triumphs of California Progressivism proved to be a mixed blessing. Manipulation by political parties prompted the Progressives to introduce devices to purify politics. Hiram Johnson believed that political parties were the source of a great deal of corruption in state politics. As a result, the Progressives secured legislation making judges, school officials, and county offices nonpartisan ones. The party system was further weakened with the introduction of cross-filing. Under the cross-filing law a candidate was permitted to appear on the ballot of more than one party during the primary election. Governor Johnson argued that voters were not interested in party labels. In reality, however, Progressive-Republicans were able to secure the Democratic nomination. It was no accident that the Democratic party virtually vanished in California politics after cross-filing became part of the political system. The Progressive succeeded in reducing the Democratic party to a minor force in state politics.

In 1914, Hiram Johnson decided at the last minute to run for reelection as governor. The reasons were primarily personal ones. It was assumed that Johnson would campaign for the United States Senate. However, Johnson learned that Francis J. Heney, the special prosecutor in the San Francisco graft trials, was intent upon running for either Senator or governor, and he vowed to block Heney's election. When Johnson was approached by Heney to support his candidacy for the governor's office, Johnson cooly remarked that he was seeking reelection, and this forced Heney to run for the United States Senate. The Johnson campaign then worked quietly behind the scenes to defeat Heney and elect the Democratic candidate for the U.S. Senate, James D. Phelan. By working against a Progressive-Republican colleague, Johnson was labeled a traitor by many reformers. By 1914 there was a disastrous split in Progressive-Republican political ranks.

In the midst of his second term as governor, Hiram Johnson announced that he would seek election to the United States Senate. In 1916 Johnson began to campaign but two incidents hurt his political image. The first was his heavy handed treatment of Republican presidential candidate Charles Evans Hughes. During his campaign trip into California in August, 1916, Hughes delivered a speech in a non-union San Francisco restaurant. A few days later Hughes and Johnson, unwittingly, checked into the same hotel in Long Beach. Neither candidate arranged a meeting with the other and the press reported that Johnson had snubbed Hughes. When the Republican candidate lost the presidential election, there was a rising chorus of bitterness against Johnson. Regular and moderate Republicans were taking charge of the party. The second incident which eroded Johnson's control of California Progressivism was the death of lieutenant-governor John Eshleman. A Southern Californian who was intensely loyal to Johnson, Eshleman was viewed as the heir apparent to Progressive politics. In a hastily worked out political compromise Johnson appointed a Southern Californian who had served three terms in the United States House of Representatives, William D. Stephens. Johnson never trusted Stephens. He accused the Southern Californian of undermining California Progressivism. After the November, 1916, election, Johnson refused to resign as governor of California. It was not until March 15, 1917, that Hiram Johnson delivered his farewell speech. It was an address filled with demeaning references to the Progressive faction Johnson was leaving behind to guide state politics. The insensitive tone of Johnson's speech spelled a final end to the California Progressive coalition.

Bibliographical Essay

The basic starting point for California Progressivism is George Mowry, *The California Progressives* (1951). An updated version of the Progressive Movement is Spencer C. Olin, *California's Prodigal Sons: Hiram Johnson and the Progressives, 1911–1917* (1968). For the activity of the Union Labor party see, Walton Bean, *Boss Ruef's San Francisco* (1952). Michael Rogin and John Shover, *Political Change in California* (1970) offers two interesting interpretations of California in Chapter 2, "Progressivism and the California Electorate," and Chapter 3, "The Progressives and the Working Class Vote in California."

The use of direct popular democracy is the theme of V.O. Key and Winston Crouch, *The Initiative and Referendum in California* (1939). A very sophisticated study of banking, utilities and business is Mansel G. Blackford, *The Politics of Business in California, 1890–1920* (1976).

The anti-Japanese impulse in the Progressive Era is brilliantly interpreted in Roger Daniels, *The Politics of Prejudice: The Anti-Japanese Movement in California and the Struggle for Japanese Exclusion* (1962).

An excellent reinterpretation of the Union Labor Party and political bosses is James P. Walsh, "Abe Ruef Was No Boss," *California Historical Quarterly,* LI (Spring, 1972), 3–16.

The career of Hiram Johnson is the subject of a number of important articles see, A. Lincoln, "Theodore Roosevelt, Hiram Johnson, and the Vice-Presidential Nomination of 1912," *Pacific Historical Review,* XXVIII (August, 1959), 267–284; Howard A. DeWitt, "Hiram Johnson and World War I: A Progressive In Transition," *Southern California Quarterly,* LVI (Fall, 1974), 295–305; Howard A. DeWitt, "Hiram W. Johnson and Economic Opposition to Wilsonian Diplomacy: A Note," *The Pacific Historian,* XIX (Spring, 1975), 15–23.

On the San Francisco Earthquake and Fire of 1906 see, William Bronson, *The Earth Shook, the Sky Burned* (1959); John C. Kennedy, *The Great Earthquake and Fire, San Francisco 1906* (1963); and Gordon Thomas and M.M. Witts, *The San Francisco Earthquake* (1971).

The confusion of the later part of Progressive politics and thought is examined in two excellent articles see, H. Brett Melendy, "California's Cross-Filing Nightmare: The 1918 Gubernatorial Election," *Pacific Historical Review,* XXXIII (August, 1964), 317–330 and Jackson K. Putnam, "The Persistence of Progressivism in the 1920s: The Case of California," *Pacific Historical Review,* XXXV (November, 1966), 395–411.

The changes in the electoral system are examined in Eric F. Petersen, "The Adoption of the Direct Primary in California," *Southern California Quarterly,* LIV (Winter, 1972), 363–378 and James C. Findley, "Cross-Filing and the Progressive Movement in California Politics," *Western Political Quarterly,* XII (September, 1959), 699–711.

An examination of anti-radicalism as a negative force on the decline of California Progressivism is in Howard A. DeWitt, *Images of Ethnic and Radical Violence in California Politics, 1917–1930, A Survey* (1975).

13

CALIFORNIA LABOR: THE FORMATIVE YEARS

Post Gold Rush Organization

In the 1850s California's first labor unions organized to demand increased wages or oppose a reduction in pay. The only city to support labor unions was San Francisco and a large number of organizations representing printers, bakers, bricklayers, stevedores, longshoremen, musicians, and teamsters met to discuss labor problems. The only other California city to possess a labor union was Sacramento, where printers formed a union. The early activity of San Francisco labor unions coincided with the level of unemployment and prosperity. When new industrial mining activity caused unemployment to decline temporarily in 1853, the labor union idea vanished. The depression of 1855 brought a resurgent demand for new labor organization.

The discovery of new mining wealth when the Comstock Lode was opened in 1859–1860 decreased the labor supply. It was not uncommon for wages of $6 to $7 a day to be paid during a labor shortage. The continual changes in wage and working conditions frustrated San Francisco workingmen and acted as a catalyst to permanent labor organization. The period from 1851 to 1859 saw the beginning of labor ideas, but it would not be until the 1880s that skilled craft unions would emerge as a potent factor in California. The key contribution of the 1850s is that virtually all trades were at least temporarily organized during the post-Gold Rush era. The general prosperity of the 1850s and 1860s would hinder the demand for changes in the relationship between the employee and the employer, but the demands for labor rights would dominate the minds of most workers.

The 1860s was a time of general prosperity in California with extensive employment in mining, agriculture, and manufacturing. From 1860 to 1870 the population of California increased from 380,000 to 560,200, and San Francisco's growth almost tripled in the decade. The general growth of California's labor force led to the creation of twenty-two workable unions by 1863, and there were a number of important strikes during the decade to demonstrate labor's new strength. One of the most important reasons for trade union activity in San Francisco was encouragement from workers in the eastern states.

In 1865 the eight-hour day became a labor demand. The ten-hour day was established in 1853 but neither the California press nor workers commented on it. In 1863 a tailors strike led to the formation of the state's first central labor organization, the San Francisco Trades' Union. Alexander M. Kenaday, a printer who had been elected president of the SFTU, was the strongest advocate of the eight-hour day, because he believed it would unite the working man behind labor unionization. Several San Francisco trades adopted the eight-hour day. The shipbuilding trade was the first to commonly follow the eight-hour day, and the Industrial League was formed in 1867 to promote a shorter work day.

The decade of the 1860s was a period of union growth amidst an atmosphere of prosperity and high employment. The economic development of the Golden State was less speculative, and the level of wages was high throughout the decade. Almost all skilled trades organized unions, and city and state central labor committees were formed to coordinate the California labor movement.

California's rapid commercial and industrial growth suffered a critical setback from 1873 to 1877 as a major depression caused wages and working conditions to suffer. The early optimism of the labor movement was replaced by a realistic belief that most of labor's future gains would be secured only after a hard struggle. In 1877 Denis Kearney's Workingmen's Party of California became the first California political movement to gain its legitimacy from labor. The Kearneyites organized as a result of a cut in wages by the railroad. The Workingmen's Party demonstrated that labor and politics could make a powerful combination, and the emotional issues behind the slogan, "The Chinese Must Go," were an important ingredient in labor unity. The Workingmen's Party persuaded Californians to rewrite the state Constitution, and they were instrumental in bringing about enactment of the federal law which banned Chinese immigration. Kearney's movement quickly faded into obscurity, but the lesson of labor strength and quick political action was not lost on early labor leaders. Kearney's emotional oratorical skills were copied by many union organizers to persuade lethargic workers to support the fledgling labor movement.

The slow recovery from the depression forced labor to regroup, and in 1881 Frank Roney became president of the San Francisco Trades Assembly. This was the only city-wide labor federation, and he was instrumental in the resurgence of labor power. An ardent Socialist, Roney believed that the rights of the masses could be protected only in a state where production was evenly distributed to the masses. This was an impractical but popular theme for many labor leaders in the late 19th century.

Another effective means of promoting labor unions was devised by the cigarmakers, who attached the slogan, "The Cigars Herein Contained Are Made By White Men," to the wrapper on union-made cigars. This helped to distinguish white-made from Chinese-made cigars, and the idea of labeling union products became an integral part of California labor strategy. Label goods were not always union-made products, though, as employers shrewdly and cynically imitated union labels to find larger markets for their goods.

The San Francisco Trades Assembly was in the forefront of anti-Chinese agitation, and there were also organized political campaigns to elect public officials sympathetic to labor. In 1882 Roney appointed a legislative committee to draft labor bills, question candidates about their political attitudes, and lobby for new labor legislation in Sacramento. The drive for free textbooks in public schools, weekly pay days, the abolition of child labor, and an employers' liability law were part of the early trade union drive.

In 1882 Burnette G. Haskell founded the Coast Seamen's Union, which quickly became the most important early force in organizing the San Francisco port. By the mid-1880s the CSU had negotiated a $40 a month wage, and a shoreside advisory committee tended to the day-to-day problems of sailor's rights. In 1891 the union merged into a large, more effective organization, the Sailor's Union of the Pacific. From the 1890s to 1915 Andrew Furuseth fought for the sailor's profession, and he encouraged the development of a craft union. It was Furuseth who convinced

White haired, cigar smoking Andrew Furuseth

the Federal Government to investigate the wages and working conditions of seamen, and this led to the LaFollette Seamen's Act of 1915. The Federal law ended imprisonment for desertion, stipulated specific working conditions, and ended the use of the arbitrary labor broker known as a crimp. The crimp system was a labor broker concept which allowed the employer to control all hired help. It prevented labor organizers and dissidents from gaining employment and approaching the other workers. The use of crimps led increasingly to demands for a union hiring hall.

The early trade union movement did not experience a great deal of success in California. Generally, working hours remained ten to sixteen hours a day for most non-union workers, and the continual readjustment of wages and working conditions reflected the controls which employers maintained over the labor market. Throughout the 1890s labor unions in every major California city held parades to display their degree of unity, but the truth was that labor was fighting for its very survival. In 1883 the larger employers in California formed the Merchants' and Manufacturers' Association to popularize the so-called radical nature of the labor movement and urge workers to discontinue their ties to trade union organizations. The rise of company controlled unions, known as blue book unions, was another indication that labor was in for a long fight. The idea of an open shop city was popular among many business leaders. This concept emphasized that each worker had a choice to either join a union or reject membership in one. In reality, the open shop was a means of destroying labor unions, because once a worker became a member of an established union he was usually fired from his job.

The Open Shop and Los Angeles Labor

The success of the open shop was obvious in Los Angeles. From the 1890s until World War I local business leaders destroyed the fledgling trade union movement in Southern California. Not until the 1960s did the wages and working conditions in Los Angeles equal those in the San Francisco Bay Area. The publisher of the *Los Angeles Times,* Harrison Gray Otis, was Southern California's most notorious opponent of trade unionism. After making a fortune in real estate, Otis began a crusade for workers' supposed freedom from labor unions. He believed that labor unions were meeting places for Socialist revolutionaries. Consequently, in the early 1890s, when the printers' union struck the *Times* for higher wages, Otis refused to negotiate with the union. The printers' union was forced to end the strike and accept a twenty percent wage cut. This was an early indication of the obstinacy that organized labor would face from powerful employers in twentieth century California.

The leading business interests organized an Employers' Association to harrass and intimidate the labor movement. The People's Store, a large Los Angeles mercantile firm, went so far as to advertise in eastern newspapers for non-union labor. In 1903 the Merchants' and Manufacturers' Association proclaimed that all unionists were susceptible to radical, unAmerican influences, and it urged a boycott against employers who dealt with labor unions. The prosperity during the early 1900s was an unwitting foe of labor unions as high wages created a large number of contented workers. The National Association of Manufacturers urged Californians not to recognize the right of labor unions to negotiate for better wages or improved working conditions.

The pressure in Los Angeles to prevent labor unions from organizing in Southern California sometimes led to violence and hysteria. Compared to the violence of the employers and the police there were only sporadic and isolated acts of sabotage by labor unions. There was a much greater degree of business violence. It was common for the Los Angeles Police Department to break up strikes with tear gas and dogs in direct violation of labor's civil rights. The violence which permeated California labor history was a reflection of Los Angeles' stringent opposition to trade unions.

San Francisco and Labor's Struggle

In San Francisco organized labor achieved a small degree of success in the late 19th century, and in 1892 the San Francisco Labor Council was founded to coordinate all union activity. By 1901 there were ninety unions in the Bay Area working with this central labor organization. The strength of San Francisco labor was felt by the business community and in the spring of 1901 a group of influential businessmen contributed a thousand dollars each to a fund to end union influences on Northern California.

The hostility of local labor prompted Michael Casey to organize the Teamsters Union. Local employers responded to this threat by demanding that all drivers who were members of Casey's new union quit it or their jobs. The firm of McNab and Smith was the catalyst to this demand, and it unwittingly served to strengthen the Teamsters Union. About two-thirds of McNab and Smith's drivers went out on strike, and by the end of one week more than 1,200 new members were recruited by the Teamsters.

For the next twenty years San Francisco business did everything possible to destroy the Teamsters Union. The success of Mike Casey's organization was a major step in legitimizing California labor. In 1901 a general strike in San Francisco demonstrated the new power of labor as teamsters joined with sailors and longshoremen to stage a successful waterfront strike. Mayor James D. Phelan was not particularly adept at handling the complaints from either labor or business. In fact, he alienated labor so badly that a new political movement, the Union Labor Party, was able to elect its candidate for mayor. Big business believed that Phelan coddled radical labor, and played into the hands of the new party by urging the voters to defeat the Democratic mayor.

The General Strike of 1901 solidified San Francisco labor strength and created a closed shop. The success of the union movement in the city by the bay was an important ingredient in the survival of organized labor in the American West. The degree of labor unity was demonstrated when Governor Henry T. Gage personally journeyed to San Francisco to settle the 1901 strike. After a series of mysterious, secret meetings, Governor Gage announced that the San Francisco strike had been settled to the satisfaction of both sides. It puzzled most local citizens when neither business nor the unions would reveal the terms of the settlement.

The right of labor to organize, make a series of demands, and strike to enforce these goals was recognized in the San Francisco General Strike of 1901. The result of the strike was to create a continuous power struggle between labor and big business. For the next decade there were many signs of violence, but the result of this struggle did not emerge until a spectacular dynamite explosion changed the course of California history.

The Bombing of the Los Angeles Times, 1910

At 1:07 A.M. on the morning of October 1, 1910, a suitcase of dynamite exploded in a narrow passageway linking the stereotyping and press rooms of the *Los Angeles Times*. The explosion killed twenty people and injured more than a hundred as one side of the *Times* building was reduced to rubble. The *Times* bombing was the outgrowth of a lengthy strike of two decades of labor-business differences over the trade union movement. Wages were often forty percent lower in Los Angeles than in San Francisco and most workers were paid twenty to thirty percent less than Northern California labor. After twenty years of demeaning treatment, some laborites feared that its members would employ violent acts as a means of achieving a semblance of social and economic equality.

After the turn of the century, the rise of mainstream labor interest in Los Angeles buoyed the spirits of local labor. The American Federation of Labor urged Southern California unions to resist the Open Shop movement. Edward W. Scripps, editor of the *Los Angeles Record,* was an early defender of labor who continually urged workers to stand up for their rights. The forces surrounding California life made labor militant. Unfortunately, militancy was also probably one of the contributing causes to the violent Times explosion.

The investigation by local police and private detectives indicated that the *Los Angeles Times* was blown up by three members of the International Association of Bridge and Structural Iron Workers. William J. Burns, the nationally known detective, had been employed by the city of Los Angeles for months to investigate labor violence. As a result Burns had a number of substantial leads on the bombing. He traveled to the Middle-West to arrest Ortie McManigal, James B. and John J. McNamara for the bombing of the *Los Angeles Times.*

In the aftermath of the blast labor leaders rushed to the defense of the three unionists. Samuel Gompers, president of the American Federation of Labor, staked his reputation on the innocence of the three men and the non-involvement of organized labor in the *Times* bombing. Most labor leaders blamed a well-publicized warning by the Los Angeles Health Department to fix a leaky gas main as the cause of the explosion. Otis struck back at labor's defense with a headline: "UNIONIST BOMBS WRECK THE *TIMES*." With public opinion becoming increasingly hostile to any hint of violence, the California labor movement faced a serious crisis.

The response from labor to the charges was overwhelming. A defense fund of more than a quarter of a million dollars was hurriedly raised by union rallies. Clarence Darrow, the country's best known lawyer for defending laborites accused of violence, was retained to head the defense. Despite the charge that labor was responsible for the *Times* bombing, the growth of unions continued at a rapid pace. In June, 1911, there were almost a hundred unions operating in Southern California. In the primary election of 1911 a Socialist candidate for Mayor of Los Angeles, Job Harriman, won a surprisingly decisive victory. If labor had continued to garner some public sympathy and vote as a bloc, Harriman might have been elected in the November, 1911, general election. During his campaign Harriman staked his political future on the innocence of the McNamara brothers and McManigal. He stated that he did not deserve election if labor was involved in the *Times* bombing.

On October 11, 1911, John J. McNamara's trial opened amid a great deal of speculation over labor's role in the violence. After seven weeks of courtroom battles between Darrow and the Los Angeles District Attorney, a stunned court heard James B. McNamara change his plea from innocent to guilty in the *Times* bombing. His brother John also pleaded guilty to dynamiting the Llewellyn Iron Works. Not only were the McNamara brothers apparently guilty of the *Times* explosion, but they were implicated in a number of other violent acts against big business. Any public sympathy for labor quickly vanished in Southern California as a result of these revelations.

During the trial the Los Angeles Police Department and the District Attorney's office harrassed the Darrow defense team. It is highly unlikely that a fair trial was possible in this tense atmosphere. One of Darrow's young assistants was arrested on a trumped up charge of attempting to bribe a juror. The use of surveillance detectives by the Los Angeles Police Department continued during the trial in direct violation of Darrow's civil rights.

The conviction of the McNamara brothers was due to the defection of the third suspect, Ortie McManigal. In a deal with the prosecution, McManigal was granted immunity for testimony which placed the McNamara brothers at the scene of the crime. After a temporary exile in Central America, McManigal returned to Los Angeles where he was employed as a maintenance man in the Los Angeles Hall of Records. It is ironic that he worked as a paid city employee in complete anonymity. James McNamara, who was convicted of planting the dynamite, was sentenced to life imprisonment; his brother John received fifteen years. In the 1911 general election voters responded to labor's misfortune by resoundingly defeating Job Harriman's bid for mayor. The *Los Angeles*

Times bombing was a major turning point in Southern California's hostility to labor growth. The Merchants' and Manufacturers' Association had crushed the union movement in Los Angeles by equating its actions and tactics with those of Socialists and other radicals.

The Industrial Workers of the World and Farm Labor

In 1905 the Industrial Workers of the World were organized as a Chicago-based union by Socialists, disgruntled members of the American Federation of Labor, and the Western Federation of Miners. The I.W.W. was organized as a union dedicated to representing seasonal and unskilled workers. As a result, its ethnic minority membership was extremely high. Many I.W.W. unionists were Japanese, Chinese, Filipino, Mexican, or recent European immigrants. The idea of organizing nonskilled workers was a unique concept in the fledgling labor union movement. Most unions represented skilled crafts and did not admit nonskilled workers. Members of the I.W.W. were nicknamed Wobblies. The origins of the term is uncertain, but it supposedly came from a distortion of a Chinese worker's comment, "I wobbly wobbly." Soon the use of Wobbly was common to describe member of the I.W.W.

Although the I.W.W. was often pictured as a violent union, its tactics were ones which emphasized nonviolence, and a great deal of prose and poetry by Wobblies emphasized ideals of nonviolence. The common tactics for the I.W.W. were to engage in work slow downs, free-speech fights, and striking suddenly while on the job.

In California the I.W.W. challenged a Fresno city ordinance which restricted public speeches by unionists. The colorful free-speech campaign caught the public eye and created the image of the Wobbly as a rugged frontier individualist. The Fresno free-speech fight of 1910–1911 attracted a large number of I.W.W. members, since about ten percent of all California cannery and agricultural workers belonged to this union. The romantic radicalism and moderate Marxism of the I.W.W. attracted a membership made up largely of college intellectuals, casual workers, and ethnic minorities. As members met on street corners or in parks, a little red song book, "I.W.W. Songs to Fan the Flames of Discontent," was pulled from the pocket as members burst into song.

In 1912 a free-speech fight in San Diego increased local membership and placed the I.W.W. in the public eye. As thousands of Wobblies rode the rails into Southern California, it appeared that the new union was on the verge of success. The major contribution of this fledgling union was to publicize the inhumane and degrading conditions which farm workers were exposed to in the California fields. The large growers labeled Wobbly criticism as sour grapes and called the unionists the "I Won't Work" movement. There was a steady increase in violence toward the I.W.W. organizers after the successful free-speech fights in Fresno and San Diego, and it was not uncommon to see fire hoses turned on union members as police units with dogs and rifles dispersed local Wobblies. Yet, the I.W.W.'s membership continued to grow as agricultural labor and nonskilled urban workers were attracted to a movement which offered leadership and hope for the future.

The Wheatland Riot of 1913 and the I.W.W.

In 1913 a confrontation between the I.W.W. and the leading hop producer in Northern California resulted from activity on a hop ranch owned by Ralph Durst, near the town of Wheatland in the Sacramento Valley. In a highly deceitful pamphlet, Durst advertised for 2,800 workers when his ranch needed only about 1,500 workers. The attractive brochure states: "A Bonus to All Pickers-helping us and doing satisfactory work. . . ." This clever advertising brought almost three thousand destitute workers speaking twenty-seven different languages into the Sacramento Valley. The motley crew of hobos, small farmers seeking extra money, city unemployed, and poor ethnic farm workers created a near riot in the drive for employment.

Once employed on the Durst Ranch, families found that if one wanted privacy it was necessary to rent a tent for $2.75 a week from the ranch. The temperature during the day was consistently over one-hundred degrees and water was a mile from the fields. The only drink available was a sour citrus concoction that workers were required to purchase from Durst's brother-in-law. Each week ten percent of the employees' pay was held back to purchase maggot-infested, high-priced food in Durst's company store. All workers were charged for transportation to and from the job. Only eight toilets were available for the workers. The highest wage was a dollar a day and the average was closer to seventy-eight cents for a ten-hour shift. These conditions, combined with humiliating treatment by overseers, prompted the I.W.W. to organize a unit on the Durst ranch a few miles southeast of Marysville.

Richard "Blackie" Ford, the I.W.W. organizer, demanded that Durst negotiate wages and working conditions. Ford used his oratorical skills to accuse Durst of fraud and waved the pamphlet in the air which had attracted most of the workers. The electric atmosphere surrounding the Wobbly organizational attempts led to an emotionally charged mass meeting in August 3, 1913. A lengthy list of demands was presented. They included higher pay, ice water in the fields, sanitary toilets, and sacks and weighing facilities to speed up production. Durst's response to these modest demands was to slap Blackie Ford in the face. Durst demanded that the local police disperse the crowd. When the Sheriff and the Yuba County District Attorney arrived on the Durst ranch, the hot weather and tension combined to produce a potentially violent situation. After some jostling a shot was fired in the air by a deputy sheriff who hoped to quiet the crowd. The result was a violent riot which left the sheriff, the district attorney, and two farm workers dead from bullet wounds. Governor Hiram Johnson called out the National Guard, and the I.W.W. was virtually destroyed as a viable farm labor organization.

As labor radicals fled from the Durst ranch, the William J. Burns Detective Agency was hired to hunt down the leaders. The arrests of Blackie Ford and Herman Suhr brought two men to trial who could not be linked to the murders. Although no evidence was produced to show that either man had participated in the killings, they were still convicted of second-degree murder due to their roles at the protest meeting. This was a warning to labor leaders that even legitimate organizational work which ended with potential riots could bring quick and lengthy jail terms.

The Wheatland incident focused attention upon the plight of the unemployed. Charles Kelley organized a march from San Francisco to Sacramento to protest high unemployment and inadequate public welfare. Kelley's Citizen Army was an expression of feeling against the depression of 1914. When the 1,500 unemployed marchers arrived in Sacramento, they were met by a large number of deputy sheriffs armed with clubs. The 800 deputies delighted in busting open heads and laughing at the destitute and unemployed. National attention was directed toward California. Governor Johnson was determined to meet the challenge, since unsavory publicity could ruin the Progressive reputation of California Republican politicians.

In 1914 Johnson attempted to reform farm labor conditions by creating the California Commission on Immigration and Housing to investigate and recommend reform in working conditions, housing, and services available to the farm workers. This humanitarian gesture failed to provide concrete improvements, but it did reveal the depths of California's farm labor problem. Local agribusiness arrogantly responded that low wages were only a means to deter hard drinking, fast living ethnic farm workers. The psychological racism practiced by California farmers indicated that farm labor problems would be a permanent part of twentieth century California agriculture.

The Preparedness Day Bombing and the Mooney-Billings Controversy

In 1914 World War I broke out in Europe and the American economy began to benefit from the heavy demands for war goods. As food products from the San Joaquin Valley were brought to the San Francisco port and gasoline was bought from the gushing wells of Southern California, a new form of prosperity inundated the Golden State. The San Francisco harbor bustled with wartime activity, but the longshoremen went on strike for increased wages. Local employers believed that the wartime emergency was the perfect excuse to end labor union strength. Most Californians resented the labor strike because it interfered with the growing prosperity. The San Francisco Chamber of Commerce held a mass meeting in which more than two thousand local citizens showed up to voice their disapproval over labor's militant actions. A vigilante-minded Law and Order Committee was formed to bring about the triumph of the non-union Open Shop.

President Woodrow Wilson's Preparedness program was designed to display America's willingness to go to war if provoked by Germany, but the leading California labor unions believed that this brand of patriotism was simply a convenient means of destroying organized labor. Consequently, San Francisco labor was extremely critical of the sale of war goods to Europe, because a great deal of the merchandise destined for foreign ports was manufactured by or conveyed through non-union shops. When President Wilson announced a Preparedness Day Parade for July 22, 1916, labor unions responded by holding an opposition celebration a week before the official display of national unity.

The San Francisco Chamber of Commerce was extremely critical of labor's position, and a new Law and Order Committee was formed to destroy union shops. From labor's viewpoint the Preparedness Day march was an anti-union event. This apparently systematic attempt to destroy the California labor movement was a catalyst to increased agitation between labor and capital.

On July 22, 1916, at 2:06 in the afternoon, a bomb exploded at Market and Steuart Streets just as the Preparedness Day parade was about to begin. The explosion killed ten persons and injured forty. The immediate reaction of public opinion was to cry out that "labor violence" was the reason for the bombing. The vivid memory of the *Los Angeles Times* incident continued to linger in the minds of Californians. The following day Thomas J. Mooney and Warren K. Billings were arrested for the Market Street bombing. Mooney and Billings were committed labor organizers who were associated with radicalism. Billings had served two years in prison for transporting dynamite, and Mooney was tried and acquitted of blowing up a Pacific Gas and Electric tower on the Carquinez Straits near San Francisco. In the San Francisco Bay area Mooney was a well-known left-wing Socialist who boisterously talked of strikes as a means of achieving a social revolution. In September, 1916, Billings was quickly tried and convicted on skimpy evidence. He was sentenced to life imprisonment in an emotionally charged atmosphere which made a fair trial

Tom Mooney talks to a reporter

a virtual impossibility. In January, 1917, Mooney was tried and convicted of the Market Street bombing. The key witness was F.C. Oxham, a right-wing Eastern Oregon rancher, who testified that he had seen Mooney place a small bag on the curb moments before the parade commenced. Several years later an investigation revealed that Oxham was in Indianapolis, Indiana, during the Preparedness Day explosion. Another witness, Estelle Smith, was promised a parole for her imprisoned uncle in return for testimony damaging to Mooney and Billings. The final witness, John McDonald, received a large sum of money from District Attorney Charles Fickert for his testimony linking the defendants to the violent act. Labor cried "Frame-Up," and defense funds were established in Russia, France, England, and the United States.

Symbolically, the Mooney-Billings affair was a perfect reflection of the nationwide shift from progressivism to conservatism. Hostility toward organized labor increased during World War I as big business linked trade unions to Communism, Socialism, and other radical events surrounding world history. Most Californians were unaware that a Federal investigation ordered by President

Wilson revealed that there was not a shred of evidence to convict either Mooney or Billings. In the aftermath of the trial it was also discovered that Estelle Smith was a drug addict and was mentally unstable. Her friends described her as a person who had "spiritual hallucinations" from drugs. This obvious miscarriage of justice outraged labor, and a two decade campaign began to free Mooney and Billings. In November, 1918, Governor William D. Stephens bent to public pressure by commutating Mooney's sentence from death to a life term, but he made it very clear that pardons were unthinkable to a conservative Republican politician.

World War I and the Drift to Conservatism

The mass hysteria which developed over alleged radicalism in California during World War I brought a dramatic readjustment in attitudes towards labor. Suddenly labor unions were forces of political radicalism in the minds of Californians. Governor William D. Stephens proclaimed that loyalty and patriotism were not traits of the California labor movement. The California Council of Defense, a temporary wartime investigative agency, labeled organized labor a friend of the Kaiser.

In addition to the hostility displayed toward traditional labor unions, Chicano and Mexican labor radicals were persecuted for opposition to the draft and for organizing boycotts to publicize the exploitation of Latin farm labor. Vincent Carillo, a Los Angeles Chicano leader, organized a community-wide protest to demonstrate that Mexican-Americans were drafted in greater proportions that their Anglo counterparts. Carillo served one year in the Los Angeles county jail for his efforts to publicize the problems faced by young Mexican-Americans in jobs, at school, and in the search for housing.

The fear of ethnic and radical labor violence created a reactionary political climate. Governor Stephens introduced a new dimension to California politics in his campaign to eradicate labor union influences. In 1919 the California legislature passed the Criminal Syndicalism law which limited free speech and hampered the use of dissent in public speeches. This law defined criminal syndicalism as occurring when anyone advocated any change in the political or economic system. This virtually ended any criticism of politicians or capitalism, and the prosecution of more than two-hundred labor radicals was an indication of the effectiveness of this measure.

The appearance of the Communist Labor Party in California politics was also a significant factor in the rise of anti-syndicalism legislation. A group of left-wing Socialists formed the Communist Labor Party in 1919 and held a state-wide convention in Oakland. During this meeting, Charlotte Anita Whitney, a prominent suffragette and social worker, urged the party to work through the ballot system to elect its candidates to office. Whitney was a well-known liberal spokeswoman for black equality as well as female rights. She was a strong advocate of improved wages and working conditions for women. Prior to her arrest the Oakland Police Chief, J. F. Lynch, had warned Whitney to discontinue her speeches favoring racial and feminine equality. When she persisted, the Oakland police arrested her for violating the criminal syndicalism law.

In reality Charlotte Anita Whitney was arrested for a series of political acts, but she had just delivered a speech on "The Negro Problem in the United States" when she was charged with violating the criminal syndicalism law. The trial of Mrs. Whitney was unique because of the wide-ranging public interest in it. The Whitney trial provides an excellent example of how the forces of anti-radicalism destroyed traditional civil liberties. One of the unfortunate aspects of Mrs.

Courtesy, The Bancroft Library

Mexican workers in tent city

Whitney's trial is that it opened in January, 1920, in the midst of the publicized Palmer raids. The United States Attorney General, A. Mitchell Palmer, carried out a series of spectacular raids arresting individuals he labeled as "Communists, Socialists, Anarchists, and Fellow Travellers." Public opinion was quick to convict anyone identified with radical causes. This made it very difficult for Mrs. Whitney to obtain a fair trial.

In January, 1920, Deputy District Attorneys for Alameda County, John U. Calkins and Myron Harris, presented a mass of evidence to document Mrs. Whitney's violation of the criminal syndicalism act. The focus of Mrs. Whitney's trial was on her loyalty. Among the witnesses was a seventeen-year-old reporter for the *Oakland Enquirer,* Ed Condon. He testified that a red flag was hung at a Communist Labor Party convention in front of the American flag. The defense countered by revealing that the red flag was in fact planted by an Alameda County employee of the District Attorney's office. The defense attorney, Thomas O'Connor, did an excellent job destroying the fabricated evidence against Mrs. Whitney, but the flu confined O'Connor to bed and he died during the last week of trial. The judge refused to declare a mistrial even though one of the jury members died the same week. A new defense attorney was appointed by the court. Under the circumstances this was tantamount to conviction.

The prosecution, due to O'Connor's death, showed a new confidence in linking the Communist Labor Party and Mrs. Whitney to a number of violent political acts. A number of pamphlets detailing I.W.W. sabotage were presented to the jury and the prosecution argued that violence was Mrs. Whitney's chief motive in her political actions. When Mrs. Whitney took the stand in her own defense, one observer remarked that she seemed more like a Christian pacifist than a Communist. This was a proper assessment of Mrs. Whitney's radicalism; she was concerned only with the plight of the poor and underprivileged. But 1920 was not the time to engage in left-wing political activity.

After deliberating for six hours the jury returned a guilty verdict in the Whitney case. After a motion for bail was denied, Mrs. Whitney was sentenced to from 1 to 14 years in San Quentin. She began a lengthy appeals process and in 1927 the United States Supreme Court ruled that Mrs. Whitney's conviction must stand. It appeared that prison was the next stop, but Governor C.C. Young commuted her sentence. The significance of the Charlotte Anita Whitney case is that it revealed the reactionary mood of California politics.

As the 1920s dawned, left-wing, liberal, and moderate Californians were intimidated by the rising tide of political conservatism. Mrs. Whitney's case was the only one which was well-publicized, but there were a large number of forgotten cases which allowed state law enforcement officials to silence critics of the system. In the final analysis, organized labor, political radicals, and the Democratic Party suffered from the excessive conservatism in postwar California.

The 1920 elections provides a case study of the difficulty which radical politicians faced in the Golden State. The Communist Labor Party virtually disappeared and only the Socialist Party remained to actively campaign for political change. The major political figures in 1920 campaigned on a platform which stressed the problems created by the influx of foreign migrant labor. The economic successes of Japanese truck farmers angered many Californians, and this helped to focus public attention on the growning number of Armenians, Turks, Hindus, Filipinos, and Mexicans who were working in the fields. Paul Scharrenberg, chief spokesman of the American Federation of Labor and the California State Federation of Labor, was one of the earliest union officials to worry about competition from foreign workers. Many union members also feared this competition because of the hostility of the employers to labor union demands. They, too, came to look upon minority workers as a form of cheap labor. Yet, in half a century the labor movement would welcome ethnic minorities in large numbers.

California Labor During the 1920s

The 1920s was a precarious time for organized labor. The American Plan under which employers sought to establish the open shop eroded the basic strength of labor unions. In San Francisco there was a vigorous attack upon the building trades, and anti-unionism triumphed temporarily during the 1920s. By attacking labor as a Communist front the employers were able to virtually decimate a number of important unions. The International Seamen's Union, for example, declined from 116,000 to less than 20,000 members between 1920 and 1933.

In 1920 the building trades struck over employer demands to cut wages and employ non-union workers. When the strike was placed before an arbitration commission, the future of California's trade union movement appeared bleak. On March 31, 1921, the arbitration board ordered a seven and a half percent cut in wages for seventeen building trade crafts. The San Francisco Building Trades Council angrily charged that a conspiracy to destroy the union movement was in progress. When the weakened unions accepted the cut in pay, the Builder's Exchange, an organization of big business interests pushing the open shop, countered with the demand that the workers could return to work only if non-union employees were allowed on the job.

Throughout the 1920s California labor declined as the open shop movement achieved enormous success. The new conservatism of local labor in retreat was shown when the California State Federation of Labor refused to allow Socialist activist Upton Sinclair to address its conventions. The organization even refused to endorse a resolution supporting a new trial for Sacco and

Vanzetti. As labor declined in membership and strength, organizations like the Better America Federation were able to attack any form of labor unity as a radical, Red supported conspiracy.

The Los Angeles based Better America Federation was a perfect example of a right-wing Republican, business oriented pressure group which sought to control public morals, direct the content of public education, outlaw radical political movements, and end the influence of labor unions in the state's economy. The BAF collected more than a million dollars to help elect a governor in 1922 who was anti-radical and conservative. Governor Stephens' defeat in the 1922 election was not due entirely to BAF opposition, but in an election won by 10,000 votes it was a determining factor. Friend Richardson, the new conservative Republican governor, benefited from the right-wing attitude of the BAF. It was obvious that an anti-radical politician was now the most acceptable kind in California politics.

Anti-Radicalism and California Labor

The rise of labor militancy during the 1930s was a natural response to more than a half century of intimidation by local police, business organizations, and opportunistic politicians. It is ironic that charges of Socialism, Communism, and Anarchism were leveled with such a high degree of intensity in the 1920s, because this attracted a miniscule number of radicals to the labor movement. While some labor leaders were Socialists, the majority of American labor were individuals with patriotic feelings and traditional Democratic or Republic Party political ties. The institutionalized anti-radicalism in California society, however, made it impossible for labor to receive a fair deal.

The early labor movement was split over the question of union membership for ethnic minorities. The American Federation of Labor tended to discourage minority members, but the Industrial Workers of the World and others vied for minority members. From 1926 until 1930 there was much concern over the newly organized Mexican and Filipino labor unions. Ethnic labor organizations were a new factor in California, and the exploitation of casual labor could not continue if they unionized. It was not until the Great Depression that the Filipino Labor Union and a number of Mexican unions began to seriously attract ethnic workers, but the genesis of minority labor unions began in the late 1920s.

There was very little radical political activity in the 1920s due to the success of anti-radical politics. Most radical political organizations were educational discussion groups or self-serving clubs. Among the organizations which carried on a piecemeal radical tradition were the Shelly Club of Southern California and the Fabian Society of Pasadena. In San Francisco the University of Vulcan was founded to explore Socialist ideas. The intellectual withdrawal by California radicals was a natural result of the police state tactics of local politicians and law enforcement agencies. It was also very difficult to interest the general public in change during a period of peak employment, high wages, and excellent consumer conditions.

The weakness of radical politics was shown by the actions of the Socialist Party. Its political influence was virtually unseen in the 1920s, and one contemporary critic laughingly remarked that only lumberjacks, backwoods drifters, and unskilled urban workers belonged to the Socialist Party. This disparaging remark was close to the truth as most Californians shied away from any form of political radicalism. In small California towns like Whitmore, thirty miles from Redding in the Shasta County mountains, or in Prather, a mountain community near Fresno, meetings were held

Early ethnic labor unionists demand change

in towns owned by Socialists. A sort of romantic, backwoods Socialism was practiced out of the mainstream of California life. As old radicals moved to the mountains, though, there was no longer a spirit of change in the Golden State.

What remained of labor radicalism in the late 1920s was confined largely to Chicano labor unions. The Benito Juarez Society of the Imperial Valley, for example, was one organization very critical of California agribusiness interests. The Chicano political and labor activist was also equally critical of the American Federation of Labor's unwillingness to accept Mexican-American members.

In 1928 Chicano and Mexican workers formed the Confederation de Uniones Obreros Mexicanos (CUOM) to unionize all Spanish-speaking field workers. The CUOM united with twenty-one other Mexican labor unions in an impressive convention in Los Angeles, and the question of ethnic labor unions was no longer a debatable one. Ethnic labor unions were surfacing with a new intensity and a strong commitment to obtaining better pay, improved working conditions, and recognition for ethnic labor organizations.

The first signs of serious labor action by a Chicano union occurred in May, 1928, when Imperial Valley cantaloupe workers struck at the Sears' brothers ranch near Brawley. The Union of the United Workers was formed by local workers to demand better wages and improved working conditions. The UUW did not plan its strike like a typical labor union. There were no strike threats, and local agricultural labor asked for very little in terms of wage increases. In many respects this movement was an attempt to gain the simple right to negotiate over working conditions. Ramon Mireles, the Union President, emphasized his law-abiding sentiments and urged the growers to negotiate with the union in good faith. On May 10, 1928, Imperial County Sheriff Charles L. Gillett closed the union office and banned future meetings due to the possibility of alleged labor violence. Sheriff Gillett charged that the Mexican union was a catalyst to violence and that it drew support from known radicals. In an attempt to combat this charge, the union changed its name to the Mexican Mutual Aid Society. The name change obscured the intense level of Mexican and Chicano agricultural unionization fever.

In Mexicali, just across the border in Mexico, a newspaper, *El Neuvo Mundo,* criticized Gillett for his actions and suggested that "democracy becomes a question of shade and color." The Imperial Valley cantaloupe strike of 1928 was settled with little concession for the workers and local employers continued to ignore the Mexican union. Yet, the strike was not a total failure as it planted the seeds of agricultural unionism firmly in the minds of ethnic workers. The strike did force the end of arbitrary pay periods and eliminated the practice of withholding 25 percent of the workers' wages until the season ended. This was the beginning of the ethnic farm labor consciousness which Cesar Chavez would build upon in the 1960s and 1970s.

Early California Labor: An Assessment

In the 1920s images of ethnic and radical influences upon the California labor movement led to a high degree of anti-radicalism. As early as the 1850s there had been immense hostility to organized labor; the use of highly inflammatory charges was a traditional means of destroying labor's power. But as the Great Depression descended onto California the labor movement regained its vitality. It had been weakened by the reactionary political climate of the 1920s. The Charlotte Anita Whitney case reminded workers of how much the Criminal Syndicalism Law of 1919 had done to destroy any form of criticism of California government. The influence of the Better America Federation and the popularity of the Klu Klux Klan were other indications of the general intolerance of the era. When ethnic labor unions arose there was increased violence and charges of Communism and subversive infiltration. The first signs of a "paranoid" political mentality began to appear in California politics. The tone and approach of Governor Richardson suggested the type of political mentality that Ronald Reagan adopted in the 1960s. The paranoid style restrained and intimidated political radicals, and it was an indication of the growing conservatism in the Golden State. As the New Deal coalition formed in California, it owed its birth to the anti-radical political debate which occurred from 1917 to 1930. If anti-radical politics had a legacy, it was to force the proponents of liberalism and radicalism to reorganize themselves into a vigorous, more effective political force. The irony of anti-radical labor politics was that it was so successful it produced an even stronger liberal tradition in California during the 1930s.

Bibliographical Essay

The best starting point for California labor history is David F. Selvin , *Sky Full of Storm: A Brief History of California Labor* (1975). A more traditional account is Ira B. Cross, *History of the Labor Movement in California* (1935). The best account of the Chinese and late 19th century labor is Alexander P. Saxton, *The Indispensable Enemy: Labor and the Anti-Chinese Movement in California* (1971). The influence of the California State Federation of Labor is an important feature of early labor development. See Philip Taft, *Labor Politics American Style: The California State Federation of Labor* (1968).

The important regional studies of California labor are Grace H. Stimson, *Rise of the Labor Movement in Los Angeles* (1955); Louis H. Perry and Richard B. Perry, *A History of the Los Angeles Labor Movement, 1911–1941* (1963); Robert Knight, *Industrial Relations in the San Francisco Bay Area, 1900–1918* (1960); and Jules Tygiel, "Workingmen in San Francisco, 1880–1901," (Ph.d. dissertation, U.C.L.A., 1977). The Tygiel study is a sophisticated examination of the blue-collar worker in the bay area.

There is very little intellectual history of California labor, but an outstanding master's thesis on the theory of labor ideology is Oscar Berland, "Aborted Revolution: A Study in the Formative Years of the American Labor Movement, 1877–1888, With Special Reference to the International Workingmen's Association of San Francisco," (M.A. Thesis, San Francisco State University, 1966).

Paul S. Taylor, *The Sailors' Union of the Pacific* (1923) and Hyman G. Weintraub, *Andrew Furuseth: Emancipator of the Seaman* (1959) are two excellent studies of early labor unionism.

For selected San Francisco labor topics, see Bernard C. Cronin, *Father Yorke and the Labor Movement in San Francisco, 1900–1910* (1943) and for an updated version of early San Francisco labor, see James P. Walsh, *Ethnic Militancy: An Irish Catholic Prototype* (1972). Frederick L. Ryan's *Industrial Relations in the San Francisco Building Trades* (1936) is a narrow but useful study of the labor attitudes of early trade members.

An excellent interpretation of California labor is Gerald D. Nash, "The Influence of Labor on State Policy: The Experience of California," *California Historical Society Quarterly,* LXII (September, 1963), 241–257.

For the I.W.W, see Robert L. Tyler, "The I.W.W. and the West," *American Quarterly,* XII (Summer, 1960), 175–187; Hyman Weintraub, "The I.W.W. in California, 1905–1931," (Unpublished M.A. Thesis, U.C.L.A., 1947); Howard A. DeWitt, *Images of Ethnic and Radical Violence in California Politics, 1917–1930, A Survey* (1975); Ronald Genini, "Industrial Workers of the World and Their Fresno Free Speech Fight, 1910–1911," *California Historical Quarterly* LIII (Summer, 1974), 100–114; Grace L. Miller, "The I.W.W. Free Speech Fight: San Diego, 1912," *Southern California Qarterly,* LIV (Fall, 1972), 211–238; Rosalie Shanks, "The I.W.W. Free Speech Movement, San Diego, 1912," *Journal of San Diego History,* XIX (Winter, 1973), 25–33; Woodrow Whitten, "The Wheatland Episode," *Pacific Historical Review,* XVII (February, 1948), 37–42; Joseph R. Conlin, *Bread and Roses Too: Studies of the Wobblies* (1969); and Patrick Renshaw, *The Wobblies* (1969).

For early agricultural labor see Carey McWilliams, *Factories in the Fields* (1939); and Howard A. DeWitt, *Anti-Filipino Movements in California: A History, Bibliography and Study Guide* (1976). A useful reinterpretation of the Wheatland episode is Cletus F. Daniel, "In Defense of the Wheatland Wobblies: A Critical Analysis of the I.W.W. in California," *Labor History,* XIX (Fall, 1978), 485–509.

The best account of the Mooney-Billings case and the Market St. bombing is Richard Frost, *The Mooney Case* (1968). Another account painted in purple prose is Curt Gentry, *Frame-Up* (1967). Woodrow C. Whitten, *Criminal Syndicalism and the Law in California, 1919–1927* (1969) is a brief, but useful account of anti-radical hysteria. See also Woodrow C. Whitten,"The Trial of Charlotte Anita Whitney," *Pacific Historical Review,* XV (September, 1946), 286–294. For a partisan view of the trial but a useful one, see Al Richmond, *Native Daughter: The Story of Anita Whitney* (1942). The right wing mentality of the Better America Federation is analyzed in Edwin Layton, "The Better America Federation: A Case Study of Superpatriotics," *Pacific Historical Review,* XXX (May, 1961), 137–148.

For key political issues influencing labor due to the rise of Communist labor see Ralph E. Shaffer, "Formation of the California Communist Labor Party," *Pacific Historical Review,* XXXVI (February, 1967), 59–78; and Ralph E. Shaffer, "Communism in California, 1919–1924," *Science and Society,* XXIV (Winter, 1970).

An interesting study of the eight hour day is Steven C. Levi, "The Battle For the Eight-Hour Day in San Francisco," *California History,* LVII (Winter, 1978/1979), 342–353. To understand the problems of labor organization in the 1890s see, William W. Ray, "Crusade or Civil War?: The Pullman Strike in California," *California History,* LVIII (Spring, 1979), 20–37.

14

CALIFORNIA BETWEEN THE WARS, 1920–1940

Since the 1920s California cultural and political ideas have reflected the influences of fads, cults, and demagogues. One recent interpretator of California life suggested that the mild climate of Los Angeles and San Francisco attracted peculiar personalities with get rich schemes, miracle health cures, and new religious messages. What was unique about many of the cultists is that they used religion and promises of financial rewards as the medium to recruit new followers. This form of religious quackery combined with the traditional morality of Presbyterian, Baptist, and Methodist churches brought a new social dimension to California life. Most recent migrants came to the Golden State from the Mid-Western and Southwestern regions of the United States, and they generally were prone to describe California as a land of sin. They clung to peculiar religious beliefs which mixed religion and politics. Another example of fanaticism was the emergence of the Ku Klux Klan in Orange County in the 1920s which eventually led to a widely publicized shootout between the KKK and the Los Angeles Sheriff's Department. The degree of radicalism in Los Angeles was illustrated when the KKK took over the Los Angeles public school board. The KKK used its power to denounce virtually anyone who disagreed with their definition of American democracy. The reactionary right-wing sentiment in California was reflected in the social-political development of the Golden State. The rise of fanaticism was expressed in a number of religious cults and social organizations.

The popularity of religious groups, which sprung up around fruit milk shakes, mushroom-burgers, and special protein diets, attested to the peculiar quirks of California society during the 1920s. An example of a popular sect was the Theosophical Society, which introduced a watered-down version of Buddism to young people, old people, anyone who would listen to the wisdom of the East. In the Ojai Valley, an Indian holy man presided over a flock of trendy, dim-witted, but financially secure, Americans. In sum, California was a veritable oasis for charlatans, faddists, and crackpots. There was a great deal of money to be made from religion, and the Los Angeles area was soon to produce new churches which emphasized wealth.

Sister Aimee and the Green Religion

This new religious group was the ingenious brainchild of the best known faith healer in Twentieth-Century California, Aimee Semple McPherson. A Canadian-born evangelical preacher, McPherson founded the Los Angeles-based Four Square Gospel Temple. In her five-thousand-seat Angelus temple, she often rode onstage astride a motorcycle, wearing a policemen's uniform, to arrest sinners in the name of the Lord. In 1927, *Harper's* magazine called McPherson's church the best show in town. Critics of the Four Square Gospel Temple charged that it preyed upon the aged, the widowed, and the recent migrant who felt homeless in California. There is little doubt its appeal was to the poor and elderly, who found the city a difficult place in which to live. Sister Aimee, as she was known, scattered pamphlets from airplanes, climbed into boxing rings to praise the Lord, and cured the elderly with her hocus pocus brand of fire-eating religion. Wearing a white dress, with gold braid, to suggest purity, wisdom, and concern for the poor, McPherson promised anyone who would listen a better life. From the $1.5 million Angelus Four Square Temple, she claimed to have converted half a million Americans to her brand of Christianity. For almost twenty years she spread the gospel over Los Angeles radio station KFSG, and her followers contributed millions of dollars to keep the golden voice of Sister Aimee on the air. It marked the beginning of entertainment and religion combining to produce the green religion—one that brought money and God together.

In the 1920s Southern California had a reputation for colorful religious figures and Sister Aimee provided lower-middle-class Californians with both entertainment and religious hope. Arriving in Los Angeles in 1922 with two children, a battered automobile, and one-hundred dollars in cash, McPherson collected more than a million dollars from her flock in the next three years, and she purchased more than a quarter of a million dollars worth of property. Historians have speculated on the reasons for the Four Square Gospel Temple's success in Los Angeles. The answer is that Hollywood wealth combined with the lure of real estate, oil, and oranges made Southern California a particularly wealthy spot for quakes and faith healers. Sister Aimee also had a strong sense of theatrical importance, as she staged sermons with elaborate settings. Another revolutionary feature of McPherson's religious appeal was her modern appearance, which included dyed, bobbed hair and stylish clothing. The local Los Angeles clergy constantly harrassed her, and during a tour of England a lengthy petition addressed British governmental authorities on Mrs. McPherson's immoral conduct.

In the mid-1920s an opportunity to discredit Sister Aimee's personal life occurred when she mysteriously disappeared from Ocean Park. After her May, 1926, disappearance, her flock announced that they would not give up hope, and in a few days a memorial seance raised $35,000 to conduct a search for her. After a six week unexplained disappearance, Sister Aimee walked in from the Mexican desert into the sleepy Sonoran town of Agua Prieta. After crossing the border in Douglas, Arizona, she spun an elaborate story of being kidnapped and forced to walk through the Mexican desert. No one questioned her story despite the fact that her black patent leather shoes were shiny and she failed to show any exhaustion from her desert ordeal. Arriving in Los Angeles, Sister Aimee was greeted by thousands of people who provided a carpet of roses for their heroine. Soon local newspapers charged that her kidnapping story was a hoax. In fact, Sister Aimee hid out for a period of time in a Carmel home known to local newsmen as the "Love House." She spent a quiet week with a radio operator who had worked for her at the Four Square Gospel Temple.

The Los Angeles Police Department issue a warrant for providing false information to law enforcement personnel. The charge against Sister Aimee was interfering with the orderly process of justice and this almost comic-opera-crime was one even the Los Angeles police could not successfully prosecute. After a great deal of publicity a trial began which ended with all charges being dropped against Sister Aimee. It appeared that middle-class hatred of her evangelical preaching had spurred the police to prosecute her. For the next few years the L.A.P.D. harrassed the Four Square Gospel Temple by bringing a series of minor charges against them. Despite the attempts to intimidate the Temple the movement grew to almost 50,000 by 1929.

The growth of religious cults in Los Angeles continued into the 1930s as 850 separate religious organizations sprang up outside the mainstream of Protestant and Catholic doctrine. Most of these religions practiced faith-healing and delivered sermons on the influence of climate and religion upon the soul. The high divorce and suicide rate was a reflection of the insecurity of Los Angeles social life. The hordes of Americans who arrived in Los Angeles to pursue a career as a movie star, worked for improved health, found renewed youth, or attempted to escape the structures of a small town were easy prey for evangelists like Sister Aimee. Much of the political quackery of the era emerged from Los Angeles. The large number of schemes to provide unemployment benefits, old-age pensions, and free land were Southern California ideas. A famous woman evangelist, Katherine Tingley, counted among her church members a dog whom she claimed was the reincarnation of her first husband. In summary, the religious antics and sermons which emanated from Los Angeles earned it the title of the "Capital of American Eccentrics."

There was a monetary reason for cultists and con artists to migrate to Southern California. In the 1920s an oil boom at Huntington Beach brought Standard Oil into California. In 1921, the Union Oil Company opened a large oil field near Whittier, and Shell Oil Company hit an economic jackpot with the Sugar Hill oil field in Long Beach. The new level of oil wealth was reflected in all phases of Southern California life, and the rise of conspicuous wealth created new social excitement. The degree of wealth was astonishing in the 1920s as almost two billion dollars were produced from Southern California oil fields. This new "gold rush" resulted not only in a great deal of wealth, but it was responsible for a revolution in the development of the automobile. The Los Angeles basin had the highest gasoline yield in the United States, and this acted as a catalyst to the mass production of the automobile.

The inexpensive Model T automobile developed by Henry Ford in 1908 helped to create pressure for highways, and the automobile revolution began to take over the nation. By 1920 mass motorization had transformed the Golden State into a highly mobile population center. The most notable influence of the automobile was to double the Los Angeles County population in the 1920s. In addition, the number of automobiles registered in Los Angeles was more than twice the national average for a major metropolitan city. The logical extension of this automobile mania was the rise of "tourist cabins" or "auto courts." Soon entire streets in Los Angeles were crowded with automobile dealerships. One enterprising Packard dealer, Earl C. Anthony, began to advertise his product over Radio Station KFI, and this combination of music and advertisements created a type of advertising reflecting the mass-consumption, mass-production mentality of the Roaring Twenties.

The Movies as Culture

The dreams of Californians were turned into huge profits when the small town of Hollywood was transformed into the capital of the movie industry. The initial development of the movies began on the East Coast in the early part of the twentieth century, but as a result of California's fine weather and the variety of geographical settings it moved west. As early as 1907 a major one-reel movie, *The Count of Monte Christo,* was shot in Los Angeles. But it was a series of western movies which popularized California's movies. In the small, rural town of Niles, thirty miles south of Oakland, The Bronco Billy series was shot and the movie's hero, Bronco Billy Anderson, became a major "star." From 1908 to 1914, the booming Niles movie industry produced almost four hundred westerns. It took a week to shoot a movie, and the profit margin was impressive. Charlie Chaplin, a young comedian with a hilarious gait, made a series of silent comedies which changed the tastes of the American public and the direction of the early movie industry. Chaplin's salary of $10,000 a week indicated that movies were making huge profits.

In the early days of movie production there were a number of legal battles over patent infringements on equipment. This is one of the reasons the Los Angeles suburb of Hollywood became the early movie center. It was easy to pack the cameras into an automobile and shoot a short film in Tijuana, Mexico. When this type of legal harassment ended, the movie industry stayed in Hollywood and brought a new, glittering world of entertainment to the masses, a source of employment to Southern California, and vast wealth to the investors and leading lights of the movie industry.

During the 1920s Hollywood was the capital of the entertainment business. By 1923 one out of five manufactured products in California was derived from the movie industry. In addition, movie owners found that with a small, five cents admission charge they were still able to make enormous profits. It was entertainment for the poor and middle-class American.

There was a great deal of publicity surrounding the private lives of movie stars. One well-known comedian, Roscoe "Fatty" Arbuckle, saw his career ruined when a young actress was killed in a gruesome Coca-Cola bottle murder in San Francisco. The murder, at a wild party in a San Francisco hotel room, was publicized as a typical Hollywood sex scandal. All of Arbuckle's movies were banned following the scandal, and President Warren G. Harding supported a censor for the movie industry. This led to the creation of the Motion Picture Producers and Distributors Association in 1922. Will H. Hays, a former postmaster general of the United States, was placed in charge of censoring the movie industry. The goals of Hays' office were laudable ones. They were to set up a motion picture code to instill morals and patriotism into the American public. Unfortunately, many producers and directors found this led to a decline in creativity as a happy ending was the only acceptable format.

In 1927 the movie industry was revolutionized when *The Jazz Singer,* starring Al Jolson, appeared as the first sound movie. With more than fifty million Americans a week paying twenty-five cents to attend a movie, there appeared to be no end in sight to entertainment profits. The major producers created lavish historical melodramas and inane comedies to appeal to mass audiences. Those shaping the taste of the masses, even as they reflected it, were enterprising men whose careers had begun by selling gloves, jewelry, and clothing in small stores in New York and throughout the Middle West. Louis B. Mayer, who was the best known movie producer of the day, began his career collecting rags.

Despite Hollywood's attempts to appeal to popular tastes, there were many great movies made during the 1920s and 1930s. There was a strong argument for peace in the 1930 version of *All Quiet on the Western Front,* a movie which effectively pointed out how war influences the culture of both sides. The vast majority of Hollywood movies failed to meet standards of literary or artistic achievement, but the money lured large numbers of writers to the Los Angeles area.

In 1941 Bud Schulberg satirized the movie moguls in *What Makes Sammy Run,* a brief novel which explored the callous manner in which the industry treated people. It was an examination of the breakdown in communication skills and the rise of mass production entertainment.

F. Scott Fitzgerald's unfinished novel, *The Last Tycoon,* written in 1941, was in a similar vein and it indicated how Hollywood consumed literary talent. Aware that continued profits were dependent on correctly gauging the public's taste, the studios then and since have rarely gambled, preferring the lowest common denominator to the uncertainties of elevation. Predictably, artistic standards and the artists themselves have been subverted. When World War II broke out there were more movie theaters than banks in California. The new entertainment medium had become the tastemaker for much of California and the nation, both the product and the purveyor of a mass production-consumer oriented society.

The Politics of Reaction: The 1920s

Newspapers, popular magazines, and the radio helped to perpetuate the image of California so often portrayed in the movies of the era, an image of social diversity and personal freedom, but the political reality indicated that the period between World War I and World War II was a time of strong political conservatism. The flapper, jazz bands, and wide-open speakeasies did not accurately portray the political climate of the decade. There were three political characteristics of the Golden State during the 1920s. First, the Democratic Party was virtually non-existent as its registered voters declined in between 20–35 percent. In elections to the United States House of Representatives, only one Democrat was elected in the 1920s from the eleven Congressional districts. In the 1924 presidential election 92 percent of the electorate voted for Calvin Coolidge. Since there was no effective Democratic Party, most elections were decided in the primary campaign. Second, there was a strong move by Southern California to reapportion the California legislature to provide equitable representation for the South. This was an indication that the traditional control of California politics by San Francisco was declining, and the balance of political and economic power had shifted to Los Angeles. Third, Progressive political attitudes continued to prevail but it now took the form of a watered down emphasis on business efficiency in government. Had it not been for the remnants of progressivism there would have been a politics of extreme reaction in California.

Scientific Progressivism in the 1920s

Although the 1920s was a period of reaction in the Golden State, most politicians continued to advocate progressive ideas, but it was a restrictive type of reform designed to maximize government services with a minimum expense. In fact, the Progressive Movement took on a form of scientific conservatism during the twenties. In 1921–22, Governor William D. Stephens launched a series of legislative recommendations which produced a second wave of Progressive reform. The reason for Stephen's legislative boldness was his election in 1918 without opposition. A quirk in California election law prevented the Democratic party from placing a candidate on the ballot in the general election. There was a cross-filing provision in state law which allowed candidates to run in both the Republican and Democratic primary elections, but there was a stipulation that a candidate had to win his parties primary to run in the general election. San Francisco Mayor James Rolph won the 1918 Democratic gubernatorial primary, but he failed to win the Republican primary. As a result, Stephens was the only candidate for governor in the general election.

In 1921 Governor Stephens revived the theoretical politics of the Progressive Movement, because he envisioned the rise of a new form of public opinion which would revitalize the reform impulse. Stephens constructed a carefully planned program to raise more tax money for expanded state government services. In his attempts to revitalize the liberal nature of California politics, he introduced a new type of progressivism. It emphasized that tax increases were an important factor in expanded governmental services. Yet, in many respects Governor Stephens appealed to the conservative side of California voters by suggesting that he intended for state government to become more efficient due to more scientific progressive legislation. Consequently the unpopular tax bill was passed by a divided California legislature, because it promised to provide funds for state government through a 35 percent increase in corporation taxes. The measure was one which prompted many major corporations to denounce Governor Stephen's administration, and right-wing resistance organized to elect a governor sympathetic to business interests.

In the spring of 1921, Governor Stephens secured passage of a Reorganization Act, which placed the functions of fifty-eight state agencies into five departments. This bill reduced the cost of state government while increasing the efficiency of social services. There was a strong reaction against reorganization from California conservatives who argued that state government was becoming too socialistic. The general consensus among professional Republican politicians was that Stephens was interested only in reelection. The cynicism of Republican Party bosses was reflected in the mild hostility to Stephen's political ideas.

To further compound Stephen's problems, members of the California Assembly and Senate came out in favor of new requirements for the initiative procedure so that it was more difficult to place a measure on the ballot. Many California politicians believed that popular democracy had reached epidemic proportions during the Progressive Era, and they advocated a political program which would curb the excesses of public opinion.

In 1922 the Better America Federation announced that it supported the Republican State Treasurer, Friend Richardson, for governor. The California Press Association, an organization of rural California newspapers, was another influential group to announce early support of Richardson's candidacy. Many Republicans believed he was an excellent choice for governor because Richardson theoretically identified with Hiram Johnson's brand of Progressivism. He also had a reputation for supporting stringent controls on the California budget. A big, swarthy, rotund man, Richardson was the editor of the *Berkeley Gazette,* and his political viewpoint reflected a rural, conservative bias which viewed labor, radicalism, aliens, and excessive state spending as dangerous elements in California democracy. Since 1914 Richardson's policy as state treasurer was to demand that school officials cut the cost of printing school textbooks and reduce funds which administer state services. These arguments were important ones in creating Richardson's responsible conservatism; he was a candidate who would not waste money nor pander to special interests.

As liberal politics declined, the attack upon labor unions increased to the point where non-union shops were becoming dominant in the Golden State. As businessmen and politicians united against the demands of the worker, the Los Angeles based Merchants' and Manufacturers' Association allied itself with the Better America Federation to promote the non-union, open shop or American plan. The California State Federation of Labor attempted to meet this reactionary challenge by supporting candidates who were sympathetic to the union idea, resulting in a large number of pro-labor politicians being elected to important state offices. While this failed to stem the reactionary tide, it was evident that some degree of liberalism remained as an integral part of California political philosophy. But it was a temporary feeling for reform and the conservative feeling dominated state politics.

In August, 1922, Friend Richardson won the Republican primary, a prelude to victory in the gubernatorial election. It was a close election; Richardson won because labor supported his candidacy. The fallacious reasoning of labor organizations was that Richardson's Quaker religious beliefs would result in a quick pardon for Tom Mooney. It was ironic that one of Governor Richardson's first public statements was to promise no leniency for labor radicals languishing in prison. The ten thousand vote majority for Richardson was the result of an editorial in the *Tom Mooney Monthly,* urging the election of a new governor. The main thought of Richardson's administration was to prevent the growth of labor, and it was a policy which reflected the feeling of a large number of Californians.

Friend Richardson and the Politics of Reaction

From 1923 to 1927, Friend Richardson's Republican administration created an anti-radical political machine in the mainstream of California politics. By pandering to fears of aliens, labor radicals, and the threat of third-party Communist and Socialist cranks, Richardson helped to create one of the most inhospitable climates for liberalism or change. In calling for a return to fiscal responsibility in state government, Richardson promised to end the "orgy of extravagance" in state government.

On February 1, 1923, Richardson submitted a budget for 1923–24 which purportedly would save Californians thirteen million dollars. Progressive-Republicans challenged Richardson's claim, arguing that the governor manipulated his statistics on fiscal spending to falsely document claims of economy in government. A number of Progressives were dismissed from important state offices for criticizing Governor Richardson's financial policies. Paul Scharrenberg, for example, was fired from the California Commission of Immigration and Housing for criticizing reduced state funds for agencies dealing with labor problems. While this type of political dismissal was not an uncommon tactic, the air of vindictiveness which the Richardson administration exhibited indicated that a reactionary turn had taken place in California politics.

In 1923, liberal Republicans organized the Progressive Voters League to combat the rising conservatism of Governor Richardson's regime. The significance of the P.V.L. was that it brought a mild revival of reform politics back into the mainstream of California Republican Party activity. In the 1926 campaign for governor, Progressives rallied behind Lieutenant-Governor C.C. Young. As the 1926 election approached, the question of liberal or conservative influences was a hotly debated topic in state politics. The decline of labor radicalism quieted many fears about left-wing causes. The subsequent election of C.C. Young as California's governor in 1926 brought back a form of scientific progressivism to California politics. From 1926 to 1930, Young revived liberal political ideas.

There was a new type of Progressivism in the late 1920s. Suddenly large bankers like A.P. Giannini were important political influences, and the branch banks of the Bank of Italy tripled during the Young administration. Business progressivism was also evident in the state government as a cabinet system was inaugurated under Governor Young to carefully plan state spending. In the final analysis, Young reversed the reactionary direction of California politics, but he failed to solve a serious problem facing state government. It was a controversy over water problems which created internal party divisions during the 1920s, and Governor Young received an inordinate amount of bad publicity for not being able to secure adequate water for Californians.

California Water Problems: A Summary

The politics of water in California were important long before the 1920s. The need for new sources of water for Los Angeles and San Francisco created a half century of legal and political battles. When San Francisco experienced a critical water shortage in 1901, Mayor James Phelan appointed a committee of engineers to explore a new source of water from the Sierra Nevada. The Hetch Hetchy Valley in Yosemite National Park was selected as the ideal site to supply San Francisco water. The Tuolumne River was to be flooded into the Hetch Hetchy Valley to create a water reservoir to supply Northern California. As a result of this proposal, John Muir began a public campaign to halt the Hetch Hetchy water project; but, Muir and his Sierra Club supporters were foiled in 1913 when the Federal government granted approval for the controversial water project. It was not until 1934 that the vast water system was completed, and it was an engineering marvel with 155 miles of aqueduct and a 25-mile long tunnel. In pumping water from the Sierra Nevada to San Francisco, the Hetch Hetchy water project provided much needed electrical power. As the controversial water project neared its final approval, many Californians blamed the Republican governors of the 1920s for it. The main concern over Hetch Hetchy was the expense and excess Federal government influences, and it was a reflection of the conservative political philosophy which dominated state politics.

The struggle in Southern California over water was an extremely bitter political and economic fight. The Owens Valley Water project was the main source of Los Angeles water. When the Los Angeles population exceeded 200,000 in 1905, there was a serious concern about the future water supply. The chief engineer for Los Angeles, William Mulholland, selected the Owens River on the eastern side of the Sierra Nevada as the best available source of water for Southern California. The residents of Owens Valley were incensed over the Los Angeles plan to pump their water supply into Southern California. Then a minor scandal broke out when the Owens Valley water project was exposed by the *Los Angeles Times* as an attempt by Fred Eaton, the city engineer for Los Angeles, to develop a water project which would aid his land holdings. Eaton was pinpointed as one of the major land owners in the Owens Valley area. The Owens Valley project would enhance his wealth and that of many of his business partners. There were a number of leading Los Angeles business leaders who had land holdings in the San Fernando Valley which would benefit a great deal of wealth once Owens Valley water was pumped into Southern California. In September, 1905, despite the hint of scandal and municipal corruption in Los Angeles, voters overwhelmingly approved the Owens Valley project. The mania for an adequate water supply prompted Los Angeles citizens to ignore the graft and corruption surrounding the Owens Valley-Los Angeles aqueduct.

The 233 mile aqueduct began construction in 1908 and in spite of the complaints of Owens Valley citizens the project was completed in 1913. Southern Californians proclaimed Mulholland a hero for his role in bringing in Owens Valley water. In the early 1920s a long dry spell caused problems with the Owens Valley water supply, and in 1924 a series of dynamite blasts began a decade of local sabotage to destroy the misguided water project.

As sporadic dynamite blasts went off, the bitterness of the Owens Valley dispute reached a new intensity. In 1928, agitation over the water aqueduct was ignited again when a dam William Mulholland had constructed collapsed near the town of Saugus. The death of 385 people from a flash flood prompted Mulholland to accept blame for the tragedy and he retired from public life. These were problems that Governor C.C. Young could not solve and the legacy of the Owens Valley project was one of bitter hatred between rural and urban Californians. Had Governor Young been able to mollify public opinion this intense hostility would not have influenced the Boulder Canyon Project, a Federally funded plan to build a huge dam to supply the California urban and rural settlements.

In the early 1920s the Owens Valley Aqueduct was no longer a sufficient source of water for Southern California. Los Angeles was growing at a rate of 100,000 citizens a year in the 1920s, and this caused a panic over the lack of adequate water. The city of Los Angeles demonstrated its panic by using Indian medicine men, magicians, and water-witching specialists to search for new water supplies. In 1922, the Boulder Canyon project was recommended in Congress, and in 1928, the Swing-Johnson Bill provided for construction of Hoover Dam. On March 1, 1936, the project was completed, and the Southern California water supply was assured. The rise in agricultural production after the completion of the Boulder Canyon project is a key to California wealth in the present day.

The Great Depression and California

In October, 1929, the Great Depression caused massive unemployment in California. This created a new economic-political atmosphere which revived labor union strength, popularized programs by political charlatans, and helped to add credence to utopian schemes. The unstable condition of the economy allowed Communists and Socialists to receive more attention than they were normally accorded in prosperous times. The changes in California were not obvious to the casual observer, but the Golden State in the 1930s was clearly a civilization in transition. The state's population underwent rapid change as Blacks, Oakies, and Mid-Western Democrats migrated into Southern California. While this migration led to impressive increases in Democratic Party voter registration, the lower, middle-class, blue-collar Democratic worker was prone to the appeal of social messiahs with new cures for California. It was the inability of Democratic and Republic Party politicians to cope with the changes in socio-economic conditions which created the atmosphere promoting Utopian schemes. Every imaginable type of politician emerged during the Great Depression; this was partially due to the public unrest over the state of the economy.

Early Republican Governors

The major reason for hostile public opinion in California was the indecisive leadership of the Republican Party. Since the 1890s Republicans had dominated state politics, but the Democratic Party quietly began to challenge the Republican organization. In addition, Democratic voter registration doubled during the 1930s; and this factor combined with the lack of legislative initiative from Republican Governors James Rolph, 1930–34, and Frank Merriam, 1934–38, served to undermine Republican politics. The Democratic Party was on the verge of reemerging as the major force in California society.

When James "Sunny Jim" Rolph was elected California's governor in 1930, he had a reputation for drinking heavily, chasing women, and neglecting the day to day operation of government. During his nineteen year reign as mayor of San Francisco, Rolph had ridden a white horse in Fourth of July parades and wandered about the City with a cheerful demeanor. This was hardly adequate training to solve the problems of the Great Depression.

As a conservative governor, Rolph prevented necessary tax reforms though he supported a food tax to raise revenue for state government. The increase in the state sales tax was necessary to finance public schools, and the creation of a special food tax prompted the small grocer to talk of "pennies for Sunny Jim." He completely discredited himself as a politician when he defended the lynching of two San Jose men in November, 1933. The two men, Harold Thurmond and Jack Holmes, had kidnapped twenty-two-year-old Brooke Hart, heir to a San Jose department store, and murdered him. The lynching prompted Governor Rolph's statement that he would not call out the National Guard against a lynch mob. Rolph publicly praised the mob and promised to pardon anyone who was arrested for the hangings.

On June 2, 1934, while campaigning for reelection, Governor Rolph slumped to the ground and died of a heart attack. The lieutenant-governor, Frank Merriam, a Long Beach businessman, ascended to the governor's office. He was an ardent foe of labor and one of his first public statements was to equate labor activity with Communism. He was elected governor in 1934, but Merriam's general lack of leadership and insensitivity to key socio-economic questions intensified hostile feelings toward state government. The Republican Party failed to provide adequate leadership during the Great Depression, and this was a factor in the turbulent nature of California society in the 1930s.

The Influx of Oakies and Arkies

One of the strengths of California's population was its diversity. Almost every ethnic group and region in America was represented in the Golden State. The prosperity of California was due to the continuing stream of able migrants to fill the job market. When the Great Depression broke, the migrants, known as Oakies and Arkies, faced a hysterical reception from Californians who believed that all newcomers from the Southwest were prone to welfare. As the Oakies streamed into California, a growing fear of overpopulation mounted. It was not until 1938 that the crisis reached its peak, and in 1939 the California legislature banned further Oakie immigration. The ban was unconstitutional and never enforced, but it reflected the alarm felt by swelling migration from 1935 to 1938.

The anti-Oakie phenomena is interesting because there was no other white migrant group which had ever experienced such a level of hostility. The attempt to exclude white Protestant-Americans indicated a new level of intolerance for the poor in the Golden State. The myths of California's wealth and sunny life style caused local citizens to jealously guard their state's resources. The Oakies were scapegoats for Californians who lashed out at the decline in agricultural production, the rise of urban problems, and the inadequacy of state government.

Utopian Schemers and the Depression

The rise of political and social quackery was one of the byproducts of the Great Depression. The seeming irresponsibility of the Republican Party, combined with the disinterest of the business

LOS ANGELES, CALIFORNIA   Monday, July 9, 1934

BAD BOYS THWARTED AGAIN

A highly sympathetic editorial cartoon supporting Upton Sinclair's EPIC program

Courtesy, The Bancroft Library

community in state affairs, led to a number of social and political messiahs who presented plans for a utopian future. The large number of retired and unemployed Americans in the 1930s were prime candidates for fast-talking promoters.

A highly respected literary figure and an amateur politician, Upton Sinclair, was the first important utopian. In 1934, Sinclair, who was a Socialist, ran for the Democratic Party nomination for governor. With two decades of political experience behind him, Sinclair constructed a unique platform entitled, "End Poverty in California." The EPIC plan was a tightly argued and logical means of combatting the depression. In an attempt to appeal to the retired population, Sinclair demanded a $50 monthly pension for the aged, widowed, and handicapped. To stimulate the economy, he proposed a state government program to create new jobs. There was a demand for increased taxes on idle wealth and speculation; and, Sinclair believed that the small homeowner should be exempt from taxation. In a final attempt to appeal to his radical colleagues, Sinclair suggested that state ownership of farms and factories might be a means of curbing unemployment and bolstering the economy. The philosophy behind Sinclair's EPIC program was similar to President Franklin D. Roosevelt's New Deal, but the national Democratic Party refused to endorse Sinclair's controversial program.

In the 1934 Democratic primary campaign, Sinclair cut an imposing path through state politics. He was a romantic, reform-minded crusader who had written almost fifty books critical of American capitalism. In 1933, Sinclair's futuristic novel, *I, Governor of California, and How I Ended Poverty: A True Story of the Future* (1933), wove a highly implausible tale of how Sinclair was elected governor and ended unemployment and poverty in a few years. The rise of massive dissatisfaction with state and Federal government prompted citizens to cast a vote for Sinclair as a protest against the system. In August, 1934, Sinclair won an overwhelming victory in the Democratic primary, but he was unable to defeat Frank Merriam in the general election. The EPIC plan faded into historical obscurity, but the nucleus of a movement remained in California politics.

The newest utopian charlatan was Dr. Francis E. Townsend, a retired physician and real estate promoter, who won the allegiance of the EPIC followers with a slogan emphasizing: "Youth for Work and Age for Pleasure." In 1934, the Townsend Plan proposed to lobby at the Federal level for a $200 monthly pension for every American over sixty years of age. The following year President Roosevelt's Social Security Act of 1935 was enacted, and Dr. Townsend eventually lost much of his national appeal.

The Townsend Movement grew to ten million members by 1937, and senior citizens became a major force in California politics. *The Townsend Weekly,* a newspaper organ of the movement, brought in thousands of dollars to aid the drive for the rights of senior citizens. It was ultimately discovered that Townsend embezzled funds, and he was cited for contempt of Congress for refusing to testify. What had attracted people to Townsend was the $200 a month pension. Sinclair called Townsend a madman, but the lure of a pension was a popular argument. While Sinclair and Townsend were important utopian politicians, there were also a number of minor social messiahs.

In 1938 the Ham and Egg plan suggested that a pension be awarded to every unemployed person in California over fifty. The slogan "Thirty Dollars Every Thursday," was a popular one among the large number of unemployed, middle-aged workers. The popularity of this scheme prompted a large number of vote-hungry politicians to support the program in the 1938 election. The measure almost passed despite its probability of causing further economic chaos. The Ham and Egg scheme is a good indication of how discontented Californians were with the nature of local economy. The dissatisfaction of the work force was reflected in the revival of labor union strength.

Labor in the Great Depression

The Great Depression brought large numbers of unemployed workers into California's major urban centers. Most transient workers were not members of labor unions, but the mass of unemployed job seekers spurred the dormant labor movement to reassert itself. An important factor in the revival of labor strength was the National Industrial Recovery Act of 1933, which contained Section 7a recognizing the legal right of employees to organize and bargain collectively with their employers. Section 7a was a signal for the renewal of labor organizations in San Francisco. The long history of bitterness between leading labor unions and local employers indicated that there would be a great deal of conflict.

In the early 1930s a young Australian immigrant, Harry Bridges, was the leading force behind the revival of the International Longshoremen's Association on the San Francisco water-

Police shooting teargas at strikers

front. A spellbinding orator, Bridges pointed out that employers used speed-up tactics to cut costs. He charged that a large number of accidents in longshoring were due to these tactics and to long hours and unsafe equipment. Bridges used his most vitriolic language on the company union, known as Blue Book unions. A labor broker selected only waterfront workers with the blue colored company books for employment, and Bridges condemned the favoritism and blacklisting built into the system.

During the summer of 1933, Bridges helped form a local of the I.L.A. which won the allegiance of virtually all waterfront workers. The I.L.A. presented a series of proposals: a dollar an hour wage, with a thirty hour work week, a union hiring hall, extra pay for overtime, and the creation of better working conditions. While these demands were not unreasonable, they were made in the 1930s when many strikes were more like civil wars than labor disputes.

In May, 1934, the San Francisco I.L.A. went on strike and the San Francisco Chamber of Commerce charged that union leadership was in the hands of Communists and could not be recognized. Local business leaders believed that the strike would be a brief one. They underestimated the strength and tenacity of the resurgent longshoremen's union. For eighty-one days the I.L.A. led 12,000 longshoremen on a successful coastwide strike against the open shop and the

Black member of the International Longshoremen's Association arrested during 1934 strike

Courtesy, The Bancroft Library

American Plan. The 1934 strike was not only a protest against the depression; but it was also a strong reaction to wage cuts, rampant unemployment, and small relief handouts. For fourteen years San Francisco longshoremen had experienced discriminatory hiring, low wages, and poor working conditions. The sight of grown men, many with families, lining up at the docks each morning depending upon employment from gang bosses who allowed unfair and oppressive work practices led to thousands of workers joining the I.L.A.

There was an almost magnetic style to Bridges' leadership of the I.L.A. The Australian longshoreman, who earned a reputation as a highly skilled waterfront worker, made an unsuccessful effort to revive the I.L.A. in 1924; and he continued to work night and day on the union effort until working conditions in 1933 helped him to reestablish the union idea on the San

Francisco waterfront. In early June, 1934, as Bridges' role as a rank-and-file strike leader was surfacing, local Teamsters announced that they would not carry cargo handled by strikebreakers. This action crippled the waterfront. The San Francisco Police Department stationed large numbers of men along the waterfront. Police cars began to cruise around Pier 38 where pickets gathered to continue the strike. On July 3, 1934, as eight police cars arrived at the pier to escort five trucks to work, pickets swung forth to protest and the police responded with lethal doses of tear gas. Suddenly a group of policemen mounted on horses rode into the area, and the pickets countered with stones, bottles, bricks, and fists. That day the heavily armed San Francisco Police Department escorted eighteen truck convoys to and from Pier 38. The sight of local police aiding the strike-breakers set the stage for a violent outbreak.

After two months of the longshoremen's strike, clashes between pickets and the police had become an almost daily affair. San Francisco Police Chief William J. Quinn received an extensive supply of tear gas from local business interests and this led to the charge that the police were

Violence during the 1934 San Francisco general strike

aiding the business community in breaking the strike. The arrogance of local business was shown on June 26 when the Industrial Association, an employer anti-union group, announced that it would reopen the waterfront. This was a direct challenge to union activists; and after two months of police intimidation, heavy use of strikebreakers, and charges of Communism in the union leadership, the stage was set for a violent confrontation.

The peak of the 1934 strike occurred on Blood Thursday, July 5, 1934, when a thousand San Francisco policemen attempted to remove five thousand pickets from the Embarcadero, the primary street on the waterfront, in order to allow strikebreakers to go to work. The violent confrontation resulted in thirty-one shootings and two deaths. Governor Merriam ordered seventeen hundred National Guard members into San Francisco over the objections of Mayor Angelo J. Rossi. As the guardsmen stood with fixed bayonets on the waterfront, Bridges had his strongest argument for unionization. The key element in the strike was the obvious unwillingness of the employer to negotiate with workers.

As an aftermath of the killings, a general strike of all unions took place from July 16–19, 1934. About 150,000 workers struck, the San Francisco area was paralyzed. The National Guard was used to protect state property, but the bitter legacy of the strike remained fresh in everybody's mind. The hostility over the strike forced the Federal government to intervene. The I.L.A. submitted a series of demands to a Presidential Longshoreman's Board, and in October, 1934, Bridges' organization won a number of concessions from local employers. The I.L.A. was granted increased wages and, most important, what amounted to union control over a newly created longshore hiring hall. Harry Bridges emerged from the 1934 strike as the leading figure in West Coast labor circles. He soon became head of the Pacific Coast branch of the I.L.A., and he would remain the model of a tough but scrupulously honest labor leader until his retirement in the late 1970s.

Recognition of the I.L.A. did not end labor difficulties in San Francisco. During the latter 1930s the teamsters and the I.L.A. engaged in a bitter jurisdictional fight over uptown workers that the longshoremen had organized. In time, Bridges' longshoremen merged with the Congress of Industrial Organizations, taking the name they still bear, the International Longshoremen's and Warehousemen's Union. From 1934 to 1938 the longshoremen's Warehouse Division organized the Northern California storage business in a tightly structured fashion which merged it with the waterfront. The development of a modern transportation-distribution system for goods made the waterfront and warehouses virtually indistinguishable from one another economically. The longshoremen helped freight handlers establish a small waterfront base, and the warehouse division then moved inland to organize storage centers.

Due to the militant unionism of Harry Bridges and the longshoremen's union, the California labor movement responded with a new vitality and became a permanent part of California's political and economic structure. The fight for power on the docks continued to rage for many years. In 1935 the maritime unions formally organized the Maritime Federation of the Pacific and staged a successful strike the following year. This was an indication of the potential strength of union activity on the San Francisco waterfront. The organization of labor unions in warehouses, shops, and on construction sites was the beginning of a triumphant period for the urban union movement. In 1937, a contemporary observer remarked that with the unionization of hotels, department stores, and restaurants, union membership had doubled in San Francisco.

Strikers march for ILA recognition, 1934

Farm Labor During the Great Depression

One of the most important changes in California during the Great Depression was the concern of the state government over the plight of migrant Mexican and Filipino workers. The well publicized nature of urban labor strength caused many Californians to ignore the rural farm workers' drive for unionization. It was during the 1930s that the first important ethnic labor unions arose in the Golden State. The main reason for ethnic labor organization was the unwillingness of California agribusiness to pay reasonable wages and provide adequate working conditions. A wage of twenty to thirty cents an hour was common during the 1930s when some teamsters in San Francisco were earning a $1 an hour. This created strong support for agricultural labor unions. There were also problems with housing, education, and cultural differences; and the rising militancy of Mexican and Filipino workers was due to these difficulties.

The cycle of Mexican and Filipino labor was characterized by the mass migration of workers to the San Joaquin Valley, the Salinas-Watsonville area, and the Imperial Valley. The deplorable

General labor parade after Bloody
Thursday, July 5, 1934

Courtesy, The Bancroft Library

living and working conditions led to a number of important strikes and labor stoppages. California's farms were factories in the fields, yielding three hundred agricultural items. The growth of agricultural monopoly resulted in about fifteen percent of the farms producing more than seventy percent of the state's farm income. The strongest period for agricultural consolidation by big business interests was during the Great Depression. This was one of the reasons for the rise of farm labor militancy.

In order to understand the growth of California agribusiness and the rise of ethnic farm labor unions, the strikes and work stoppages of the 1930s must be examined. In 1933 and 1934 labor organizers for the Communist Party began to form unions, and one of the most successful was the Cannery and Agricultural Workers' Industrial Union. This organization gained its credibility among Imperial Valley workers when wages were cut in 1934. The result was the C.A.W.I.U. strike of 1934 in the Imperial Valley. From January 7–12, 1934, national attention was focused upon California's fields as the first large scale Communist labor strike was carried out in Southern California. The immediate reaction to the striking farm workers was to equate Mexican and Filipino labor militancy with Communist subversion. Local growers argued that ethnic farm labor was being duped by sophisticated Marxists. The anti-union Associated Farmers of California urged all workers to return to the fields.

The C.A.W.I.U. was disbanded shortly after the Imperial Valley strike and farm labor won no important concessions. But the battle lines were drawn as the drive for agricultural unionization became one of the most important forces in California. The rise and growth of ethnic labor unions such as the Filipino Labor Union and the Mexican Labor Union was an indication that the casual migrant farm worker would not work under completely hopeless conditions.

In 1934 the Filipino Labor Union staged an important strike in the lettuce producing area around Salinas. It was during the Salinas lettuce strike of 1934 that the Filipino Labor Union firmly established its credentials as an important labor force. In late August, 1934, the F.L.U. in cooperation with a local American Federation of Labor affiliate, the Vegetable Packers Association, called for a general strike in the Pajaro Valley fields. After a week of solidarity between local white workers and the Filipinos, the leadership in both unions engaged in a power struggle, and the strike went to an arbitration commission. The rank-and-file members of the Filipino Labor

Courtesy, The Bancroft Library

Strikers calling for scab labor to leave the fields, 1933

Union voted to continue to strike. There was a great deal of violence as the Filipino Labor Union led local workers in a strike which resulted in the first important concessions to ethnic farm labor. In 1937 the Filipino Labor Union was granted an American Federation of Labor charter, and the major labor organizations began to take the force of ethnic labor seriously. The need for agricultural unionization after 1934 was obvious to Filipino and Mexican workers. The violence and open intimidation which characterized farm labor strikes in the 1930s made it imperative to speak out against farm fascism.

A conservative farm organization, the Associated Farmers of California, worked closely with local business interests and the police to prevent any form of agricultural unionization. Most county law enforcement personnel were either on the bankroll of large farmers or were ideologically predisposed to support any decision by local agribusiness interests. An anti-Communist journal, *The American Citizen,* warned of possible subversive influences in California's fields. The outcome of this type of publicity was to prompt most counties to pass anti-picketing ordinances. It was common to see strikers riding by the fields holding up signs urging workers to leave their jobs.

During Governor Culbert Olson's regime, Carey McWilliams, a young newsman and popular writer, was appointed to head the California Immigration and Housing Authority. McWilliams was a liberal journalist whose book, *Factories in the Field,* published in 1939, chronicled the grim story of migratory labor. For a few years McWilliams was instrumental in publicizing the filthy living conditions in farm labor camps. The Associated Farmers responded by passing a well-publicized resolution declaring McWilliams to be agriculture's number one problem. The publicity over farm labor problems created greater support for labor unions among Mexicans and Filipinos.

In the late 1930s young Mexicans known as pachucos attempted to cut their ties from the dominant Anglo cultural influence. Part of their defiance was in their mode of dress. The zoot suit, an exaggerated style of man's suit with baggy trousers narrowing at the cuffs and a long, draped, heavily shoulder-padded coat, usually worn with a big keychain swinging from the waist, was popular in Los Angeles and San Francisco. The pachuco was an indication of diversity in the Chicano community. A new generation of political and business leaders was coming to the forefront. This new leadership would include a young itinerant Mexican farm worker, Cesar Chavez, and a young Filipino unionist, Larry Itliong. As they grew up during the Great Depression, Itliong and Chavez recognized the diversity in the Mexican and Filipino communities, and they would come to be a driving force in farm labor unionization in post-World War II California.

The Resurgent Democratic Party

The social messiahs, labor troubles, and general decline of Republican leadership were key elements in the revival of the Democratic Party. After 1932 Democratic Party voter registration increased sharply, and State Senator Culbert L. Olson was the heir apparent to the growing Democratic strength. The Los Angeles politician, an experienced campaigner in local politics, was elected president of the State Senate in 1936.

In the 1938 gubernatorial election, Olson faced the incumbent governor, Frank Merriam, who had an extremely mediocre reputation. Early in the campaign it was revealed that Governor Merriam had aided Standard Oil in acquiring new oil lands in California, and this tie between the Republican governor and the monopolistic Standard Oil Company was extensively publicized. During the campaign Olson skillfully attacked Merriam's favoritism toward big business. There

Women strikers demanding food, 1933

was still not strong support for Olson's candidacy, and to overcome this he introduced Olson's New Deal for California. It was an ironic pledge because the New Deal was no longer an important part of national politics. By 1938 President Roosevelt's New Deal had declined before the threat of a European war and the reaction to the new militancy of American labor.

The strongest asset for Olson was the pledge that he could work closely with the Democratic State Assembly, and he suggested that the election might give the Democrats control of both houses. The Republican Party was alarmed by the increasingly strong campaign waged by the Olson forces. As a result, California Republicans used a United States Congressional Investigating body, the Dies Committee, to look into Olson's alleged radicalism. After two California Republicans testified that Olson fraternized with known Communists, the Democrat Party demanded proof of such accusations. The Republican Party responded with a list of Olson fund raisers who had allowed their names to be used by Communist front groups. On the list was the child movie star, Shirley Temple, and Olson responded to the charges in a Los Angeles speech that he was sorry that "Comrade Shirley" could not be there to address the audience. Manchester Boddy, the editor of the *Los Angeles News,* labeled the Republican political tactics as examples of unbelievable stupidity.

The key to the election did not prove to be the issue of Olson's alleged Communism. The labor vote was the determining factor due to the presence of Proposition 1, which would have made labor liable for any damages from picketing during a strike. Merriam wholeheartedly endorsed Proposition 1 and Olson urged its defeat. The labor vote was the difference in Olson's narrow election as California's first Democratic governor since the 1890s.

In a festive atmosphere, Olson began his administration by pardoning Tom Mooney and Warren Billings. After a week in office, Governor Olson collapsed and suffered a minor nervous breakdown. He had outlined a comprehensive program for state welfare increases, more funding for state government agencies, and an increase in aid to state education. Olson's health problems and a recalcitrant Republican legislature made it impossible for the Democratic governor to return a reform mentality in state government.

The impending war in Europe and the question of American participation brought new interests and attitudes to California society. No longer were labor problems, political messiahs, or thoughts of Communist influences important. The European war created a new consciousness which brought an international perspective to Californians.

Bibliographical Essay

The impact of Aimee Semple McPherson is shown in Lately Thomas, *Storming Heaven* (1970); and *The Vanishing Evangelist* (1959). The best study of the McPherson influence is David L. Clark, "Miracles for a Dime—From Chautauqua Tent to Radio Station With Sister Aimee," *California History,* LVII (Winter, 1978/1979), 354–363. For an analysis of the cemetary business as religion see Adela Rodgers St. John, *First Step Up Towards Heaven* (1959).

The early history of Hollywood is examined in Richard Batman, "D.W. Griffith: The Lean Years," *California Historical Society Quarterly,* XLIV (September, 1965), 195–204; Hortense Powdermaker, *Hollywood, the Dream Factory* (1950); Molly Haskell, *From Reverence to Rape; The Treatment of Women in the Movies* (1973); and Leo C. Rosten, *Hollywood, the Movie Colony, the Movie Makers* (1939). For movie censorship see Raymond Moley, *The Hays Office* (1945). The best biography of a Hollywood producer is Bosley Crowther, *Hollywood Rajah: The Life And Times of Louis B. Mayer* (1960).

For the politics of the 1920s see Howard A. DeWitt, *Images of Ethnic and Radical Violence in California Politics, 1917–1930: A Survey* (1975); Howard A. DeWitt, "Ethnic and Alien Images in California History: A Teaching Proposal," *Community College Social Science Journal,* II (Spring, 1978), 40–43; and Russell M. Posner, "The Progressive Voters' League, 1923–1926," *California Historical Society Quarterly,* XXXVI (September, 1957), 251–261 and "State Politics and the Bank of America, 1920–1934," (Unpublished Ph.D. Dissertation, University of California, Berkeley, 1956).

For the Hetch-Hetchy water controversy see, Elmo P. Richardson, "The Struggle for the Valley: California's Hetch-Hetchy Controversy," *California Historical Society Quarterly,* XXXVIII (September, 1959), 249–258; and Holway R. Jones, *John Muir and the Sierra Club: The Battle for Yosemite* (1965).

The best study of California water law is James Snyder, "Floods Upon Dry Ground: A History of Water Law and Water Resource Development in California, 1900–1928," (Unpublished M.A. Thesis, University of California, Davis, 1967). For the Lake Tahoe water controversy see W. Turrentine Jackson and Donald J. Pisani, *A Case Study in Interstate Resource Management: The California-Nevada Water Controversy, 1865–1955* (1973).

On the Owen Valley project see William L. Kahrl, "The Politics of California Water: Owens Valley and the Los Angeles Agueduct, 1900–1927," *California Historical Quarterly,* LV (Winter, 1976), 2–25; Norris Hundley, "The Politics of Reclamation: California, The Federal Government and the Origins of the Boulder Canyon Act," *California Historical Quarterly,* LII (Winter, 1973), 292–325.

There is a vast literature on California during the Great Depression. For the New Deal see Robert E. Burke, *Olson's New Deal For California* (1952). On the Oakies and Arkies see, Walter J. Stein, *California and the Dust Bowl Migration* (1973). For Utopian politics see Abraham Holtzman, *The Townsend Movement: A Political Study* (1963); and Charles E. Larsen, "The E.P.I.C. Campaign of 1934," *Pacific Historical Review,* XXVII (May, 1958), 127–148.

On labor see Charles P. Larrowe, *Harry Bridges: The Rise and Fall of Radical Labor in the United States* (1972) for an impressionistic examination of the longshoremen. A more scholarly work is Harvey Schwartz, *The March Inland: Origins of the I.L.W.U. Warehouse Division, 1934–1938* (1978). An interesting examination of the infighting among labor is Harvey Schwartz, "Union Expansion and Labor Solidarity: Longshoremen, Warehousemen, and Teamsters, 1933–1937," *New Labor Review,* I (September, 1978), 6–21.

An unusually analytical work on the California farm worker is Donald F. Fearis, "The California Farm Worker, 1930–1942," (Unpublished doctoral dissertation, University of California, Davis, 1971). The standard history of California farmers is Clarke A. Chambers, *California Farm Organizations, 1929–1941* (1952). The recent awakening in ethnic labor unions is examined in Howard A. DeWitt, "The Filipino Labor Union: The Salinas Lettuce Strike of 1934," *Amerasia Journal,* V (Winter, 1978), 1–22; Howard A. DeWitt, "Communism and the Appeal to Ethnic Minorities: The Cannery and Agricultural Workers Industrial Union in the Imperial Valley," Paper presented to the Pacific Coast Branch Meeting, American Historical Association, University of San Francisco, August 17, 1978; Howard A. DeWitt, *Anti-Filipino Movements in California: A History, Bibliography and Study Guide* (1976).

Although a United States Senator in this period Hiram W. Johnson was still an influential individual. For his career between the wars see, Howard A. DeWitt, "The 'New' Harding and American Foreign Policy: Warren G. Harding, Hiram Johnson and Pragmatic Diplomacy," *Ohio History,* LXXXVI (Spring, 1977), 96–114; and Howard A. DeWitt, "Hiram W. Johnson and Early New Deal Diplomacy, 1933–1934," *California Historical Quarterly,* LIII (Winter, 1974), 295–305.

The California Dream is not a reality for everyone

264

15

CALIFORNIA AFTER THE WAR, 1945–1962

World War II and the Black Migration

The economic and population growth of California during the 1940s and 1950s created a degree of prosperity which prompted many contemporary commentators to remark that a second Gold Rush was in progress. During World War II the Federal government spent as much as ten percent of its annual budget in California. In 1945 California's population was only about seven percent of the United States, but the per capital wealth of Californians was the highest in the nation. The image of a land of milk and honey with economic opportunity for everyone brought in large numbers of Black migrants and other ethnic groups from all parts of the United States.

In Southern California there had been a strong Black political consciousness for many years. The Los Angeles based newspaper, *The California Eagle,* had urged stronger political stands for Black Californians since the 1880s. During World War II the Japanese section of Los Angeles, known as "Little Tokyo" was inundated with almost 100,000 new Black settlers. The suburb of Pasadena, known across the nation as Rose Bowl City, was the chief housing area for Southern California's new black population.

In the San Francisco Bay Area the growth was most noticeable as the Oakland Army Base, the Oakland Supply Center, the Alameda Naval Air Station, and Treasure Island Naval Station all experienced massive growth. The availability of government money was important to the Golden State's economy. In Oakland, Henry J. Kaiser operated a multi-million-dollar war time shipyard, and there was rapid expansion of new shipyards in Richmond, Oakland, Sausalito, Vallejo and San Pedro in Southern California. During World War II more than a quarter of a million Californians worked in the shipyards. A large number of these new workers were newly migrated Blacks. In 1941 Blacks were a small part of California's population, but in the San Francisco Bay Area alone the Black population rose from slightly more than 1% to almost 14% during World War II.

It was during the 1950s that California's Black migration became an influential factor in the economic and political life of the state. In Los Angeles more than a thousand new Blacks arrived each month to pursue the economic dreams of California life. In the Los Angeles community of Watts, Blacks settled in what had been a lower-middle class Mexican and Anglo community. The reason for Black families moving to Watts was three low-income housing projects built during W.W. II. By 1946 Blacks comprised almost two-thirds of the Watts population. In the 1960s living and economic conditions would lead to rioting in Watts, and this was due to the problems faced by recent Black migrants.

Willie Stokes and the San Francisco Bay Area

Typical of young Blacks migrating to California was 27 year old Willie Stokes of Desha County, Arkansas. In June, 1943, Stokes, a former laborer on an Arkansas cotton plantation, was working at the Kaiser Shipyard in Richmond as a welder. His earnings of $10 for eight hours work seemed high to Stokes who had been paid $1.25 a day to pick cotton in 1941. During World War II Stokes lived in a four-room apartment, and he believed that the bay area offered him permanent economic opportunity. In June, 1946, Stokes was working as a laborer in a chemical plant for $6.40 a day, when he began to experience employment problems. As he moved from job to job and his wages declined, he was forced to borrow money and move into a smaller apartment.

In June, 1947, the California dream ended for Willie Stokes when he applied for unemployment compensation. Eventually his eligibility for unemployment expired and Stokes requested indigent relief from the Contra Costa County Department of Welfare.

There were many Blacks like Willie Stokes in the 1940s who came West for jobs. Suddenly, East Oakland, the Fillmore District in San Francisco, and the Santa Fe Tracks area in Richmond teemed with Black housing centers. The pattern of western migration, wartime employment, low paying post-war jobs, and eventually unemployment was a familiar story to young Blacks. Although only one of three Black workers was unemployed in the San Francisco Bay Area during the 1940s, this was a much higher figure than for White unemployment. In 1940 there were only 20,000 Blacks in the Bay Area, by 1947 there were 120,000.

The majority of California Blacks migrated directly from cities like Dallas, New Orleans and Memphis, and they found it difficult to maintain permanent employment in the late 1940s and 1950s. There were many reasons for Black inequality in the job market, but the most serious was the level of discrimination within the major labor unions. When Willie Stokes worked in the shipyard he joined an American Federation of Labor affiliate union, but it was an auxiliary or second-class union. Once Stokes' job at the shipyard terminated so did his membership in the A. F. of L. The rejection of Black workers by many major labor unions created serious racial problems in the 1960s and 1970s. The rise of organized Black politics in California was the direct result of problems encountered by the Willie Stokes' of the San Francisco Bay Area.

There were a large number of California Black professionals who arose to distinguish themselves in post-World War II California. The influence of Dr. Ralph Bunche, a United States State Department Official and representative of the United Nations, and Thomas Bradley, a Los Angeles City Councilman who eventually was elected Mayor of Los Angeles, attests to the political influence of Black Californians. Yet, the majority of Blacks were crowded into tenements and ghettoized, and this created a smoldering resentment toward the California dream.

Mexican-Americans and War Hysteria

The modernization of California agriculture was completed during World War II. The total increase in farm products was 300% during the war. The lack of available labor led the United States and Mexican governments to sign an agreement allowing Mexican workers known as braceros to immigrate into California's fields. The exploitation of Mexican workers during the war created rural racial strife and created a strong demand for a farm workers union.

As Mexican-Americans and Mexicans left the fields they crowded into East Los Angeles. Only Mexico City had a larger Mexican population than LA during World War II. The growing

Photo Courtesy: Howard DeWitt

Industrial worker in post World War II California

political sophistication of Mexican-Americans was demonstrated when a series of racial incidents broke out during W.W. II. For the first time Mexican-American leaders united to oppose Anglo racism. The first incident took place on August 2, 1942, when a young Mexican-American boy was found dead in a swimming pool. The resulting Sleepy Lagoon incident led to the arrest and conviction of 17 Mexican-American youths. The Los Angeles Police Chief reported that Mexicans were prone to violent crime, and the level of racial abuse was so obvious that the entire East Los Angeles community supported the young boys.

The defense for the Sleepy Lagoon youths was aided by Carey McWilliams, a writer and former state government official, and it was McWilliams' investigative and writing skills which prompted an appellate court to throw out the conviction and lecture the trial judge on the defendants' rights. The hostile feelings from the Sleepy Lagoon incident did not die out in the Mexican-American sector of East Los Angeles. There were numerous conflicts between Anglos and Mexican-Americans.

The climax of the tense racial atmosphere occurred on June 3, 1943, when a group of white sailors, soldiers, and civilians mobbed a group of young Mexican-Americans wearing zoot suits in downtown Los Angeles. For six days the Zoot Suit Riot of 1943 continued as a taxi cab brigade of servicemen roared around East Los Angeles looking for the suit that the young Mexican-Americans sported. The Los Angeles Police Department cooperated by never locating the brigade of ten taxicabs and sixty men.

The Zoot Suit Riot of 1943 was an important factor in the resurgence of Chicano political activism. The racial overtones behind the Sleepy Lagoon and Zoot Suit incidents prompted many formerly apolitical Mexican-Americans to demand a greater voice in government for Spanish-speaking Californians. The strong reaction against Chicanos was an indication of the tense racial climate in California. The most zealous anti-foreign sentiment was directed toward Japanese-Americans due to the hostilities created by World War II.

Japanese-American Relocation

On December 7, 1941, the Japanese bombed the American naval base at Pearl Harbor in the Hawaiian Islands. Following the declaration of war by the United States upon Japan, California was plagued by a hostile public reaction to Japanese-Americans. A Gallup Poll shortly after the bombing of Pearl Harbor described the Japanese as "sly, cruel, treacherous and war-like." These stereotypes did not disappear easily, even though Japanese-Americans time and time again demonstrated their unfailing loyalty to the United States during World War II. One of the reasons for the hysteria was the extensive aircraft and shipbuilding activities in California. In Los Angeles visitors commented on the extensive camouflaging around aircraft plants, and there was near unanimous opinion that Asian-Americans were potentially dangerous to wartime security. This attitude led to the incarceration of thousands of loyal Japanese-Americans in temporary relocation camps.

The organization of anti-Japanese pressure groups was not surprising considering the fear of the so-called "Yellow Peril" in California. The legacy of anti-Chinese sentiment was quickly transformed into anti-Japanese propaganda, but there had been more than three decades of political pressure placed upon Japanese-Americans. The Alien Land Law of 1913 restricted Japanese land ownership, but it also served as a psychological tool to allow California agri-business to attack the business activity of Japanese-Americans since 1921.

V.S. McClatchy, publisher of the *Sacramento Bee,* used his position as chairman of the California Joint Immigration Committee to agitate for further restrictions on Asian immigrants, and McClatchy conducted pseudo-scientific polls to develop racist propaganda concerning Asian health habits, living practices and working capabilities. The *Sacramento Bee* was instrumental in convincing Californians that Japanese-Americans were treacherous and must be incarcerated for the duration of the war.

California agri-business interests were eager to seize control of highly profitable Japanese truck farms. In 1940 Japanese-American truck farmers produced almost 7 million dollars annually in the fresh fruit and vegetable industry. Since 75% of all Japanese-Americans lived in California it was convenient to make the argument that they were dangerous to the wartime economy.

One of the most important forces behind Japanese Relocation was General John L. DeWitt, commandant of the Western Defense Command. A sixty-one year old career administrator, DeWitt lacked the most elemental leadership qualities, and he was simply pandering to the racial hostility toward Japanese-Americans. Most military and government officials preferred to use the Japanese-American community as a scapegoat for the bombing of Pearl Harbor. The real reason, however, was the military laxity in setting up an adequate security system around the Hawaiian Islands.

In January, 1942, DeWitt and Governor Culbert Olson discussed the Japanese situation, and they argued vehemently over the potential degree of Japanese disloyalty. Olson made it clear that he believed that most Japanese-Americans were loyal to the United States. DeWitt charged that Olson was a weak man, and Attorney-General Earl Warren supported DeWitt's contention that the Japanese must be placed in relocation camps. In February, 1942, President Franklin D. Roosevelt signed Executive Order 9006, which created the War Relocation Authority. The roundup and evacuation began in early 1942 with the Tanforan Race Track in Northern California and the Santa Anita Race Track in Southern California serving as processing centers for the California based Japanese-American population. Eventually 10 sand and cactus relocation camps were constructed throughout the United States. In Northern California, a camp at Tule Lake housed many politically active Japanese, and in Eastern California the Manzanar camp housed a diverse group. Many relocation camp leaders cooperated with the War Relocation Authority as they feared for the safety of their people. Mike Masaoka, national secretary of the Japanese-American Citizens League, stated that the camps would protect his organization's members from excessive American patriotism. He also emphasized that Japanese-Americans would overwhelmingly prove their loyalty from the camps. It was not long before many of the relocation camps were producing essential war items. Young Japanese-American scientists, who had the advantage of a college education, were allowed to conduct research experiments to produce synthetic rubber, while the older less-educated men willingly harvested sugar beets in Utah.

The wisdom of Japanese relocation was questioned by many important contempory Americans. Perhaps the most significant criticism came from the director of the War Relocation Authority, Milton S. Eisenhower. In a number of public speeches and statements Eisenhower stressed that internment was an unwise practice. He believed the loyalty of Japanese-Americans was generally excellent, and he urged President Roosevelt to release patriotic Japanese-Americans from the camps. In late 1942 a clumsily-handled loyalty questionnaire led to the release of selected college students and farm workers who were willing to work in the fields for wartime agricultural corporations. In 1943 about 17,000 Japanese-Americans reentered the mainstream of American life. Many permanently settled in the Middle-West and one young man wrote President Robert

Sproul of the University of California, Berkeley, that he found suprisingly little prejudice toward Japanese-Americans in Chicago.

The debate over Japanese-American allegiance prompted Secretary of State Henry L. Stimson to announce the formation of an all-Japanese-American combat unit. In 1943, the 442nd Regimental Combat Team and the Hawaiian 100th Batallion distinguished themselves on the Italian Front. The 442nd was the most decorated unit in American Military history and fought successfully in France and Italy.

On January 2, 1945, Japanese Relocation officially ended, but the scars and trauma of this monstrous injustice remained a part of California history. Governor Earl Warren and Attorney General Robert W. Kenney, a liberal Democrat, held a two day conference in mid-January, 1945, at the Palace Hotel in San Francisco to advise Californians on the necessity of bringing the Japanese-Americans back into the mainstream of state life. The conference was opposed by a number of anti-Asian bigots, and Los Angeles Mayor Fletcher Bowron suggested that Japanese-Americans could prove their loyalty by moving out of California. In the Imperial Valley, local police continued to arrest Japanese farmers. Eventually, the Attorney General prosecuted a number of deputies, stopping this practice.

Many Japanese-Americans returned to California society penniless. Law suits were filed on their behalf through the American Civil Liberties Union to recover their property, but only a small number of assets were returned. Numerous decisions made by the United States Supreme Court upheld the Federal Government's right to intern the Japanese, or other groups of Americans considered dangerous during wartime. In 1953, the Fukii vs. State of California case documented changes in attitudes when the Supreme Court of California invalidated the Alien Land Law of 1913. The loss in property and other possessions remains an incalculable figure and Japanese-American dissidents continue to suggest that the wartime tragedy was never fully resolved with direct financial compensation to those who suffered losses.

Post-war California Politics

One of the natural by-products of World War II was to create a conservative red scare in California politics. From 1946 to 1960, Red baiting and charges of Communist influences were commonplace in state politics. Another change was the rise of a vibrant Democratic party. For a century, Democrats had not fared well in this state, but the voter registration for the party increased to the point that in 1958 California was largely Democratic in its politics. As the war ended many politicians believed in a nonpartisan approach to state problems. This attitude would characterize the postwar leadership and adminstration of Governor Earl Warren.

His second term as California's governor began in 1946 with the promise to govern in a progressive, non-partisan manner. Earl Warren was a strong supporter of Hiram Johnson, and Warren believed that governmental reform was an important part of the political process. As a result, he stunned many conservatives when he recommended a compulsory state health insurance law. The California Medical Association and private insurance companies combined to defeat this proposal.

The following year Warren requested an increase in state gasoline taxes to finance the building of modern freeways. The oil and truck companies combined to defeat this proposal, and the lobbying interests in California displayed an inordinate amount of political power. During the late

40s and early 50s a three-hundred pound lobbyist, Arthur Samish, was responsible for a great many scandals and abuses in state government. A private investigator discovered that Samish bribed California legislature members, and the large oil companies were behind much of the resistance to change in the state tax structure. Samish represented truck lines, liquor interests, race tracks and major oil companies. In 1949 *Collier's* magazine exposed Samish's influence and he was banned from the floor of the California legislature. Samish was a colossal boaster and *Collier's* persuaded him to pose for a picture with a puppet labeled "Mr. Legislature" on his lap. It was shortly after this incident that he was banished from the scene of his great successes.

One of the changes in politics after World War II was the dominance of public relations firms in the political arena. In 1946 Governor Earl Warren selected the firm of Campaigns, Inc. to guide his reelection campaign. The brainchild of Clem Whitaker and Leone Baxter, Campaigns, Inc. used special marketing techniques to sell a candidate. By manipulating the media the Baxter and Whitaker team made it look as though their candidate was a reflection of public opinion. They never represented a candidate or campaigned for an issue that they did not support in their own politics. The rise of public relations firms specializing in political elections exploded in the 1960s and 1970s as a result of Campaigns, Inc. successes.

The Earl Warren Years: An Analysis

In 1950 Earl Warren was reelected for a third term as Governor of California. This is an amazing record considering the high Democratic voter registration. Governor Warren's reelection bids in 1946 and 1950 were due to a number of factors. The Republican headquarters worked harder because the majority of California voters were registered Democrats. Consequently, Republican candidates were well known public figures and the party financed their campaigns generously. Most Republican candidates were incumbents, and the crossfiling procedure which allowed voters to cross party lines aided the Republican party. The Republican party gerrymandered legislative districts to maintain control of the California legislature. The gerrymandering device is one which allowed the Republican-dominated state legislature to control the boundaries of legislative districts. In this way Republicans would dominate key areas. The final reason for Republican success was the California press. The largest and most influential newspapers were Republican oriented, making it easier to discredit Democratic candidates.

Warren's accomplishments in more than a decade as California's governor were important ones. Warren was unique because of his ability to work with the legislature. His non-partisan approach to politics created a working relationship with the California Senate and Assembly not experienced with other governors. Warren believed it was not the governor's prerogative to interfere with the legislative process, and he did not use lobbying techniques or a well-organized Republican party machine. Professional politicians believed that Warren was hurting the Republican organization, and he was criticized for not expressing a public preference for the selection of legislative officers or committee chairpersons in the state legislature.

One of the strengths of Governor Warren's nonpartisan political program was that he was forced to veto only 2% of all bills passed by the legislature. Governor Olson had vetoed 7% and Friend Richardson in the 1920s had vetoed 9% of the legislature's bills. As concrete accomplishments Warren secured: appropriations to begin urban development, special legislation to provide employment for returning servicemen, tax increases to build new highways, and cumulative state funding for hospitals and mental health centers. The public health insurance proposal Warren backed did not meet with success.

In 1953 President Dwight D. Eisenhower appointed Earl Warren to the United States Supreme Court, leaving California with a strong Republican party and a legacy of liberal accomplishments.

The main failure in Warren's years as governor was his inability to stem the growing anti-Communist mood in California. During the late 1940s and early 1950s this feeling began to change the manner of local politics.

Richard Nixon and the Birth of Anti-Communist Politics

In the post World War II California political climate there was a tendency to blame many of the rapid social and economic changes upon Communist influences. It was a time of high unemployment, declining Federal spending, and the beginning of demands for equality from labor unions and ethnic minorities. The rapid rate of change bothered many tradition-minded Californians who found it difficult to keep up with the new demands of society. This political atmosphere made California open for a demagogue. Such a man emerged in the 1946 Congressional election. He was Richard M. Nixon.

In the 12th Congressional district which included much of conservative Orange County, Jerry Voorhis had been the United States Congressman for a decade. In 1946 Republican party professionals believed that the liberal and extremely idealistic Voorhis was a vulnerable candidate. As the Republican party looked for a strong challenger they settled upon General George S. Patton, a World War II hero, or Dr. Walter Dexter, State Superintendent of Public Instruction. However, both men died before the Republican party met to select a candidate for Congress.

The person responsible for Richard Nixon's entry into California politics was Herman Perry, manager of the Bank of America branch in Whittier and a long-term family friend. Most Republicans agreed that the 33 year-old Nixon was an excellent candidate. A veteran's record, a law degree, a Quaker, and skills as a trained orator made young Nixon an appealing conservative Republican.

In the 1946 primary neither Nixon nor Voorhis faced opposition, and each was nominated with ease. This primary election vote resulted in some startling predictions as Voorhis' supporters dropped considerably from previous elections. At this point the Nixon campaign force decided to attack Voorhis as being too sympathetic to radical labor groups. Once Nixon began to hammer away at this sensitive issue, the charge of Communist infiltration was the next step in destroying his opponent's campaign.

As Nixon hammered away at radical labor support for Voorhis he failed to notice that the Political Action Committee of the C.I.O. and the National Citizens' Political Action Committee were the two key labor groups that did not support Voorhis. It is ironic that Nixon was able to effectively charge radical labor support for Voorhis, when in fact these organizations condemned both candidates. Harrison McCall, a Nixon aide, purchased advertisements in Southern California newspapers which stated the campaign office had proof of Voorhis' ties to Communist causes. This presented an opportunity perfect for debate between the two candidates at South Pasadena.

The Nixon-Voorhis debate easily swung the election to the young Republican. Voorhis talked of the need for social legislation, full employment, an internationalist foreign policy and the careful separation of governmental powers. This strange mixture of liberal and conservative political ideas did not appeal to Southern Californians. On the other hand, Nixon was reassuring with promises to recommend strong action against labor unions which hurt the economy, promises of ending red tape in government, and an attack on Harry Bridges, head of the International Longshoremen's Workers Union, for representing the type of people who were attempting to destroy the American way of life.

During the last stages of the election campaign Nixon was alleged to have hired a cadre of telephone solicitors who worked for $9.00 a day calling local voters and stating, "Jerry Voorhis is a Communist." There is not absolute proof of this accusation, but there are a number of important Orange County citizens who have described the phone calls. Whether or not this tactic can be blamed on Nixon is less important than the fact that the Communist issue suggests a new reactionary departure in California politics. Once in Congress Nixon continued to profit from charging others with Communist ties. As a member of the House Un-American Activities Committee young Nixon exposed what he believed to be a massive Communist conspiracy in the United States State Department. The fear of Communism focused California attention upon Hollywood.

Only Victims: Hollywood and Communism

In 1947 the House Un-American Activities Committee began its most publicized investigation into Communist infiltration of the motion picture industry. Richard M. Nixon sat on the HUAC panel as a stream of friendly witnesses elaborated on the Communist menace. The most effective California witness was the distinguished character actor, Adolph Menjou, who claimed to have read more than 150 books on Communist conspiracy notions. After a great deal of testimony, Menjou's less than intelligent suggestion was that all Communists be shipped to Texas. He reasoned that Texans would shoot them on sight. The ludicrous nature of Menjou's testimony, as well as a similar statement by Gary Cooper, was an indication of the hysteria surrounding the anti-Communist issue.

It proved to be difficult to make a sensitive, intelligent movie in the years immediately following World War II. Jack Warner's movie, *Mission to Moscow,* was attacked as a pro-Communist tract. It did not matter that the Warner movie was a production of former Ambassador to Russia, Joseph E. Davies memoirs, the movie was attacked because it dealt with Communism. The height of criticism came when a Tchaikovsky musical, *Song of Russia,* was injudiciously criticized for being too sympathetic to socialist politics. There were a number of young actors blacklisted, including Larry Parks, who had a promising career as a song and dance man. He had appeared in a movie of Al Jolson's life, but when he was called before the HUAC in 1951 he was destroyed by its intensive and politically minded members. It was not surprising that a number of writers and actors were blacklisted, and in 1947 hearings led to the infamous Hollywood Ten. This was a reference to ten unfriendly witnesses who were jailed for periods of six months to one year for contempt of Congress. The importance of the Hollywood Ten is that anti-Communists could point to the authenticity of revolutionary and subversive political activity in the movie industry. The ten creative artists who were jailed never furthered their literary successes. Dalton Trumbo's *Johnny Got His Gun* became a classic in the 1960s and 1970s because of its strong message to youth on the consequences of violence. The remaining writers, with the exception of Ring Lardner who continued to write and produce plays, never rose above the ranks of artistic mediocrity.

From 1938 to 1958 HUAC harrassed and intimidated any artist who displayed ideas and attitudes about American history that were out of the mainstream of California life. This forced the movie industry into adopting safe standards for motion picture entertainment and affected the creativity of many actors, actresses and screen writers. In the 1950s HUAC displayed a racist slant by forcing a Black actor sympathetic to Communism, Paul Robeson, out of the country. Robeson, a former professional football player and lawyer, was a marvelous actor and singer. He refused to bend to stereotypes forced on Black actors by the industry. Robeson graduated Phi Beta Kappa from Rutgers and earned his law degree at Columbia University Law School. He was an articulate man who created a sensation with his appearances in Othello, the Emporer Jones and Porgy and Bess in New York and Europe. On June 12, 1956, Robeson delivered a strong pro-Russian speech to the Committee and chided them for ignoring the plight of poor blacks. This ended Robeson's career in the United States and his European exile blunted the creative edge of his musical genius. There is little doubt that racism, and conservative Republican politics brought a new conformity to California thought. In addition to an obsession about Communist infiltration into the movie industry there was also concern over the issue of radicalism in the University of California.

The Loyalty Oath and the University

In 1941 the California legislature established a committee to investigate un-American activities in California. There were two important Los Angeles politicians in the early drive to uncover subversive activities; one was Jack B. Tenney, a state senator, the other was Sam Yorty, a Southern California Congressman. Both politicians built strong political machines by using anti-Communist rhetoric. In 1949 the Tenney Committee introduced a loyalty oath to be signed by university employees. Tenney's original idea was to submit a constitutional initiative to the voters which, once passed, would require the signing of a loyalty oath. The University of California pressured the Tenney Committee to reconsider and the result was a rebellion of faculty members.

The articulate response from the University of California, Berkeley, was one of the main reasons that President Robert G. Sproul asked the Board of Regents to repeal the oath. A former Progressive-Republican and onetime boy-wonder-bureaucrat, John F. Neylan, led a debate to cleanse the University of unsavory influences. The anti-Communism of the late 1940s and early 1950s clearly influenced the running of the State University.

In August, 1950, the University Board of Regents voted to dismiss 32 professors who had not signed the oath. It was not until 1967 that university professors were protected from the arbitrary loyalty oath. In 1971 James R. Mills, a liberal Democrat from San Diego, recommended the end of un-American activities investigations, and he displayed a number of files on State Senators who had voted against key bills. The anti-Communist scare ended at this point, but the loss in human productivity and the capricious nature of illegal government spying will never be fully known by Californians.

Richard Nixon and the Nader of Anti-Communist Activity, 1950

The most brazen use of anti-Communist rhetoric in California politics occurred during the 1950 United States Senate race between Congressman Richard M. Nixon and Congresswoman, Helen Gahagan Douglas. Mrs. Douglas, the wife of actor Melvyn Douglas, was a liberal-Democrat identified with liberal Hollywood causes. Her voting record in the House of Representatives was friendly to labor and the underprivileged, and she believed that government should take a strong stand against poverty and unemployment. This advanced liberalism was not in agreement with the political thought of 1950.

During the campaign Nixon referred to Mrs. Douglas as the "Pink Lady" and he prominently displayed a "Pink Sheet" listing 354 pro-Communist votes in the House of Representatives by Mrs. Douglas. He often referred to her inability to fully criticize the Communist political activity so prevalent in California, and he suggested that she was an unwitting agent of the Kremlin. These libelous tactics were beautifully tailored to the political climate of the day, and Mrs. Douglas' reference to Nixon as "Tricky Dick" was virtually ignored in the heated debate over her Communist leanings. Nixon denied that he was calling Mrs. Douglas a Communist and suggested that the term "Pink Lady" was a reference to one of her pink dresses. It was this perfect blend of sexism amd the use of anti-Communist rhetoric which persuaded the electorate to elect Nixon by almost 700,000 votes over Mrs. Douglas. For the next decade the conservative nature of California politics was due to Nixon's hegemony in local affairs.

Republican Problems and Rising Democratic Power, 1953–1958

On October 5, 1953, Governor Earl Warren resigned from the office of Governor of California to accept an appointment to the United States Supreme Court. The lieutenant-Governor, Goodwin Knight, succeeded him and the old political boss system of the early twentieth century returned to state politics. In his first two months as governor Knight delivered more than 80 speeches in an attempt to establish his bid for the governor's office in the 1954 election. It was not surprising that Knight was elected in 1954, but young Edmund G. (Pat) Brown compiled a spectacular voting record in his bid for the Attorney-General's office. Brown won both the Democratic and Republican primaries under the crossfiling law, and his showing in the 1954 election made the Democratic Brown the favorite in the next governor's election.

The Republican party began to fight internally as Vice-president Richard Nixon attempted to maintain control of the California State organization. Governor Knight stubbornly refused to appoint Nixon followers to important state positions. Consequently, Nixon and Knight fought openly for Republican patronage. Then in 1955 a series of political problems and a scandal clouded the effectiveness of Knight's leadership.

In 1955 the newly formed California Alcohol Beverage Control commission reported that the former top man in state alcohol law enforcement, William G. Bonelli, had embezzled large sums of money; by the time extradition papers were signed Bonelli was in self-imposed exile in Hermosillo, Mexico. The only communiques from Bonelli were ones instructing that his retirement checks be forwarded to his Mexican address.

Another sensitive political issue involved the Democratic Attorney-General, Edmund G. Brown, who ruled that prison authorities could prevent inmates from submitting manuscripts to prospective publishers. The author in question was Caryl Chessman, the alleged Red Light Bandit, who wrote *Cell 2455: Death Row* while appealing his death sentence. The twin issues of governmental corruption and capital punishment created important issues for liberal California politics.

The 1958 gubernatorial election created a great deal of interest in California politics when the Republican party replaced Governor Knight. On January 7, 1957, United States Senator William F. Knowland announced he would retire from politics to spend more time with his family.

This less than truthful exit from the U.S. Senate was an indication that Knowland, a strong supporter of Vice-president Nixon, was seeking the Republican gubernatorial nomination. Knight and Knowland were equally powerful in the Republican State Central Committee, and the press speculated on the obvious crisis in the Republican party. Sensing Knowland's political strength, Governor Knight did not run for reelection and he attempted to win the United States Senate seat recently vacated by Knowland. It is ironic that both Knowland and Knight lost their bids for public office. The Republican party went into decline and a liberal Democratic party consciousness permeated California society. In order to understand the reasons for Edmund G. Brown's success in the 1958 governor's race it is necessary to examine the change in Democratic politics.

The Democratic Organizational Revolution and the 1958 Election

In 1953 the California Democratic Council was formed to bring together amateur and professional party members to elect candidates to office. The CDC was an important force in turning out the vote, raising campaign funds and eliminating special interests in the selection of candidates. The high degree of internal democracy brought a new sense of commitment and a type of party unity necessary for success.

In the 1958 elections the Republican party virtually destroyed itself in California. William Knowland's Republican gubernatorial platform was extremely hostile toward organized labor. By supporting the right to work initiative, which was a major threat to the power of organized labor, Knowland forced labor unions to organize behind the Democratic party.

To complicate the 1958 campaign Knowland remained in Washington D.C. to conduct Senate business. Mrs. Knowland recorded speeches and pamphlets. When Brown's primary vote indicated that he would possibly be victorious in the general election, Mrs. Knowland sent a letter to 200 leading Republicans accusing them of pro-labor sympathies. As a result of Republican squabbling Edmund G. (Pat) Brown polled more than a million votes more than Knowland. In an incredible show of political strength Brown carried 54 of 58 California counties, and the Democrats won control of the senate and assembly. The years from 1958 to 1966 were ones of extraordinary Democratic party triumph after a century of virtually oblivion in California.

The Early Years of Governor Brown and Democratic Triumph

The changes in California governmental attitudes were apparent three days after Brown was inaugurated when the Fair Employment Practices Act was passed. The Fair Employment Practices Commission was set up to insure that California would be the first state in the American West to guarantee equal employment to all races. The strong commitment for increased government activity was shown when state inheritance taxes were increased, the upper levels of the state income tax expanded, and a new tax placed upon cigarettes and liquor. Brown maintained that he would provide "responsible liberalism" in spending new state funds. He advocated new welfare programs and a strong committment was made to all minority groups.

In 1960 Governor Brown's political fortunes began to decline as he failed to win support from the Democratic party as a favorite son in the California presidential primary. Another trouble spot was the Caryl Chessman case. Chessman had spent 12 years on Death Row at San Quentin for allegedly haunting lovers lanes in Hollywood and he was eventually convicted of intent to kidnap and the sexual assault of young girls. There were many issues raised by Chessman's attorneys, but the key part of his plea for executive clemency was that he had rehabilitated himself. There were also strong doubts about the legality of his confession and the continual references to Chessman's guilt in the local newspapers. Governor Brown attempted to sidestep the sticky political issue by granting Chessman a 60 day reprieve and demanding that the California legislature decide Chessman's fate. In March, 1960, the State Senate voted not to present a bill ending capital punishment, and this placed the Chessman execution back in Governor Brown's hands. Governor Brown's young son Jerry urged his father to grant clemency to Chessman but the execution took place.

The political problems of the early 1960s bothered Brown and he confided to close personal friends that he would not seek reelection. Waiting in the wings to return to California politics was Richard Nixon who had been defeated in the 1960 presidential campaign by John F. Kennedy. In a peculiar turn of events Brown announced that he would not seek the governor's office, but two months later Brown formally announced his candidacy for office.

California's 1962 Governor's Race: The Brown-Nixon Clash

The 1962 campaign was one of the dirtiest political events in California history. As Richard Nixon reentered California politics he was extremely vehement in his attacks upon Governor Brown's spendthrift approach to state government. Nixon accused Brown of being prone to radical influences, but the electorate laughed at these charges. To complicate Nixon's political problems the extremist John Birch Society offered eager support and in so doing influenced large numbers of voters in turn away from him.

There were a number of changes in California politics which reflected changes in the 1962 campaign. When Nixon suggested that welfare chiselers be dropped from state roles there was an outcry against Nixon's lack of compassion and humanism. Another problem with Nixon's campaign was his criticism of the press and his inability to answer media charges that he was using the California governor's race as a stepping stone to the White House. The campaign became so bitter that both sides filed law suits to prevent the distribution of derogatory campaign literature. The final comic opera touch to the 1962 campaign came when Nixon pledged to invoke the death penalty for large scale dope peddlers. Both candidates appeared to offer dated platforms and the cataclysmic changes in California society would soon bring in a new political feeling. Governor Brown was reelected by a surprising majority of some 300,000 votes. The day after the general election Nixon called a press conference in which he berated the press for their unfair treatment of him, and he announced that his political career had ended. As Nixon flew off to join a New York law firm, Governor Brown would, in his second term, experience some of his most difficult days.

Forces of Change in the 1950s

During the 1950s California underwent a silent change. The turmoil of politics was a reflection of general cultural revolution. Almost unnoticed in the early 1950s young poets and writers began to meet at the North Beach Cafe in San Francisco. One young poet, Paddy O'Sullivan, achieved immortality as part of a portrait known as "The Beat Madonna." The Beat Generation's painting

Assembly Speaker Jess Unruh, Governor Edmund G. Brown and President John F. Kennedy, 1961

of early Christianity offended many traditional citizens, but the literature of the Beats suggested a new direction in California culture. Jack Kerouac's, *On The Road,* published in 1956, became the Bible of the Beat generation as they listened to jazz, drank cheap wine, and talked of the virtues of marijuana. In dress, manners and morals they rejected post-industrial American life, but the vast majority of them came from wealth and were well-educated. Kerouac, for example, had been recruited by Columbia University as a football player, however he dropped out to pursue a writing career. Allen Ginsberg, one of the best known poets of the Beat Generation whose poem, *Howl*, talked of urban-industrial America in the 1950s, was also from Columbia University. A graduate from Columbia, Ginsberg was one of the early business oriented Beatniks. Lawrence Ferlinghetti and Ginsberg were partners in the City Lights Book Store at Columbus and Broadway in San Francisco. Lenny Bruce, a Hollywood comedian attracted attention from the Beats, and became the subject of movies and television shows. Bruce worked at the San Francisco Hungry I nightclub and learned appreciation for the new culture from the individualistic Beats. It was a movement which used drugs, talked of love and listened to new forms of music long before anyone heard of LSD, Haight-Ashbury or the Grateful Dead. California culture would take some strange turns in the 1960s and 1970s, in part because the Beat Generation began a revolution which paved the way for rapid change.

Bibliographical Essay

Much of the literature on postwar California is highly unsatisfactory. For an analysis of Governor Warren see Leo Katcher, *Earl Warren: A Political Biography* (1967); and Richard B. Harvey, *Earl Warren: Governor of California* (1969). For Richard Nixon see Earl Mazo, *Richard Nixon: A Political and Personal Portrait* (1959).

On postwar Communism and the loyalty question see, Ingrid Winther Scobie, "Jack B. Tenney and the Parasitic Menace: Anti-Communist Legislation in California, 1940–1949," *Pacific Historical Review,* XLIII (May, 1974), 188–211; and "Helen Gahagan Douglas and Her 1950 Senate Race Against Richard M. Nixon," *Southern California Quarterly,* LVIII (Spring, 1976), 113–126. On the 1946 campaign between Nixon and Voorhis see, Paul Bullock, "Rabbits and Radicals": Richard Nixon's 1946 Campaign Against Jerry Voorhis," *Southern California Quarterly,* LV (Fall, 1973), 319–359. The loyalty issue is examined in Edward L. Barrett, Jr., *The Tenney Committee* (1951); David P. Gardner, *The California Oath Controversy* (1967); John Caughey, "Farewell to California's Loyalty Oath," *Pacific Historical Review,* XXXVIII (May, 1969), 123–128; and R.L. Pritchard, "California Un-American Activities Investigations," *California Historical Society Quarterly,* XLIX (December, 1970), 309–327.

For Artie Samish see *Collier's,* August 13, 1949, 11–13, 71–73 and August 20, 1949, 12–13, 60, 62–63. Edgar Lane, *Lobbying and the Law* (1964) is an excellent study of how laws fail to control the lobbying process.

The role of public relations firms is examined in Robert J. Pitchell, "The Influence of the Professional Campaign Management Firms in Partisan Elections in California," *Western Political Quarterly,* XI (June, 1958), 278–300.

For California politics see Gladwin Hill, *Dancing Bear: An Inside Look at California Politics* (1968); Royce Delmatier, et. al., *The Rumble of California Politics* (1970); and Jackson K. Putnam, *Old-Age Politics in California from Richardson to Reagan* (1970).

On the role of the Beat Generation see the unusually provacative study by Marilyn M. Schwartz, "From Beat to Beatific: Religious Ideas in the Writings of Kerouac, Ginsberg and Corso," (Unpublished PhD Dissertation, University of California, Davis, 1976). Also see, John Tytel, *Naked Angels: The Lives and Literature of the Beat Generation* (1976).

For an early indication of ethnic problems in post-World War II California see, Charles Wollenberg, "Blacks vs. Navy Blue: The Mare Island Mutiny Court Martial," *California History,* LVIII (Spring, 1979), 62–75.

Photo Courtesy: Asemblyman Brown's Office

San Francisco Assemblyman Willie Brown

16

REFORM AND REACTION: CALIFORNIA IN THE 1960s AND 1970s

California in the 1960s

The turbulence of California civilization was never greater than during the 1960s as the forces of liberalism, radicalism, and conservatism all triumphed at one time or another. The increase of urban problems, ethnic political demands, student unrest, and social-economic change deriving from the new levels of consumer goods, created massive political and social change in the Golden State. In 1962 California became the most populous state in the Union, and the nature of economic opportunity appeared unlimited to most people. In 1966 Los Angeles County, the center of the Aerospace industry, passed the seven million population mark to become the largest county in America. But, a few years later an economic recession began to tarnish the California dream, and there were serious signs of dissatisfaction from local residents. In many respects the 1960s in California was a cycle of great promise, followed by a plateau of social-economic change, and ending in a political reaction by decade's end.

The Second Brown Administration and Signs of Unrest

The turmoil surrounding Governor Edmund G. Brown's second administration reflected the general conflict over the changing nature of California life. Although the media pictured the Golden State as a liberal and reform-minded society, there were serious signs of a great deal of divisiveness. The Vietnam war, the rise of Black political activism, and the demands of college students for change in their educational patterns tested the prevailing liberal pattern.

In 1963, Governor Brown proudly signed the Rumford Fair Housing Act which allowed anyone to purchase housing in California. The intent of the Rumford Act was to prevent discrimination by realtors in selling or renting homes to Blacks. In 1964 Proposition 14 was placed on the ballot by the California Real Estate Association; this measure was designed to institute a "right to sell" law. California's politically active Black community charged that Proposition 14 was a racist idea, but the measure was approved by voters with an overwhelming majority. Two years later Ronald Reagan was elected governor by almost the identical number of votes approving Proposition 14.

The United States Supreme Court eventually declared the Rumford Act unconstitutional, but the Black community believed that the act reflected racist white attitudes. On the hot, smoggy night of August 11, 1965, a white policeman attempted to arrest a young man for drunken driving, and an angry mob gathered on the streets of a Black Los Angeles suburb, Watts. After two days of heavy rioting, 14,000 armed National Guardsmen were deployed to Watts. After almost a week of riots, property loss was estimated at 140 million dollars and thirty-four people were dead, thirty-one of them Black. The dissatisfaction of the unemployed and low-income Californian was mirrored in the Watts riot. The Watts riot was the manifestation of the post-war hostility of Black Californians to high unemployment, poor housing conditions, and inadequate political representation. There were signs of a Black political revolution throughout the Golden State.

In Northern California there was a similar uprising in the San Francisco ghetto, Hunter's Point. Bobby Seale and Huey P. Newton founded the Oakland-based Black Panther Party in 1966, and the major state colleges and universities began to institute Black studies as a part of the curriculum. Nathan Hare, a San Francisco State College Instructor, founded *The Black Scholar* as a journal designed to create a new sense of Black awareness in the Golden State.

There were a number of Black politicians who rose to prominence in California during the 1960s and 1970s. When Wilson Riles was elected California Superintendent of Public Instruction in 1970, he began to demand better bilingual education and a greater emphasis upon early childhood studies. The result was a new level of personal interest by parents in California schools. Tom Bradley was elected mayor of Los Angeles over a three-term incumbent, Sam Yorty. One of the hallmarks of Mayor Bradley's leadership was to revitalize the economy of the City of the Angels and bring the 1984 Olympic Games to Southern California. Yvonne Braithwaite Burke was elected to the United States Congress and joined another Southern California Black, Augustus Hawkins, in that body. In 1974 State Senator Mervin Dymally was elected lieutenant-governor. By the late 1970s Black politicians were experiencing difficulty getting reelected to office. Yet, throughout the 1960s and 1970s Black Californians were elected to major state offices.

The most effective Black politician in the 1960s and 1970s was San Francisco Assemblyman, Willie L. Brown, Jr. In 1964 Brown, a Democrat, was elected to the state legislature from the 17th Assembly district. In the 1960s Brown represented a varied constituency of Blacks, Gays, Young People, and middle-class whites. His concerns as a politician reflected his broad based voter support as he became a leader in consumer affairs, workers' rights, health care, education, penal reform, fair housing, and civil rights.

Among Assemblyman Brown's legislative contributions are bills establishing Child Health Disabilities programs, the first state-funded urban park, and a law prohibiting discrimination in state government hiring practices. In 1978 Brown was a stabilizing force during the tragic assassination of San Francisco's Mayor George Moscone. His strong support for the new mayor, Dianne Feinstein, helped to smooth the way for the continuation of city government in a time of stress and uncertainty. In 1979 Assemblyman Brown was a strong critic of Governor Jerry Brown's presidential ambitions, and the two Democratic leaders appear on a collision course. For Black and White Californians alike Assemblyman Brown offers concrete leadership and a positive interest in the affairs of the Golden State.

It is ironic that Assemblyman Brown was a critic of Edmund G. (Pat) Brown in the mid-1960s and a skeptical observer of his son Governor Jerry Brown in the late 1970s. There is a continuity in this political opposition, because Assemblyman Brown believed that education and housing as well as equal employment are still important issues in California society. His concern for civil rights and employment advances were heightened during the events of the 1960s in Berkeley and San Francisco. An analysis of the University of California Free Speech Movement offers an insight into the forces shaping the political character of Assemblyman Brown.

The Free Speech Movement and the Student Revolt

In 1964 large numbers of University of California students had spent the summer registering Black voters in Mississippi. The means used to register Blacks was one often identified with civil disobedience. There was also a legalistic side to students in the early 1960s as they pointed out that the University could not constitutionally regulate their political activity. When a number of students complained that bongo drums were disrupting their studying, Vice-chancellor Alex C. Sherriffs ruled that it was no longer permissible to set up a table for political purposes on the twenty-six-foot wide strip of brick in front of the Student Union Plaza.

On October 1, 1964, more than three hundred students set up tables in the Sproul Plaza area, because five students had been disciplined for violating University regulations governing political activity. The leader of the students was a veteran of Mississippi voter drives, Mario Savio. When local police attempted to arrest Jack Weinberg, more than one-hundred students laid down in front of the police car. The police were stymied and Mario Savio asked to address the crowd. For the next thirty-two hours Savio and other Free Speech Movement leaders harrangued the policy of the University toward students. The Free Speech Movement was in full swing and it would bring lasting change to American education.

The real causes of the Free Speech Movement were a complicated set of political and educational goals which clashed with each other. The promises of American democracy seemed ludicrous to young students who watched fire hoses turned upon Blacks in the South. In 1964 the Republican National Convention was held in the San Francisco Cow Palace and Senator Barry Goldwater of Arizona appeared too conservative on most issues for students. He was not concerned with Black civil rights and he urged napalm and other chemicals to destroy the enemy in Vietnam. Bob Dylan's "The Times They Are a-Changin" provided the perfect backdrop to the new militant student attitudes.

A great deal of the ferment behind the Free Speech Movement resulted from poor teaching at the University of California. As young professors entered the system there were heavy demands placed upon them for publication, and this led to an enormous teaching load for young graduate students. The only contact many undergraduates had was with overworked and underpaid teaching assistants. The expansion of the University in the 1960s due to the post-war "baby boom" often led to rapid and poorly planned curriculum. In 1963 the University of California, Davis campus, inaugurated a Ph.D. program in history with only eight students. This type of premature academic planning and an apparent general disinterest in students created the attitudes which made the Free Speech Movement successful.

In December, 1964, a massive sit-in at Sproul Hall to protest the disciplining of student leaders forced Governor Brown to order state police onto the Berkeley campus and more than seven hundred students were arrested. When the University of California prosecuted 773 students, they responded by filing a series of damage suits totalling $4.5 million; the suits alleged police brutality and deprivation of political rights. Most Californians were not sympathetic to student demands, and a brief but highly publicized Filthy Speech Movement turned public opinion against the goals of college students. When Mario Savio appeared on Johnny Carson's *Tonight Show,* radical student leaders criticized the Free Speech Movement for selling out to the media. In addition, Governor Brown found it diffiuclt to control the growing right-wing reaction in California politics. It appeared that the Democratic party was too liberal and the cry of permissiveness could be heard from one end of California to the other.

Free Speech march through Sather Gate, 1964

As the 1966 gubernatorial election approached, Governor Brown was in political trouble. The leader of the California Assembly, a Democratic boss known affectionately as Jess "Big Daddy" Unruh, was in the forefront of a Democratic Party move designed to prevent the incumbent governor from seeking a third term. Unruh was using every political device to secure the nomination, and he destroyed what remained of Democratic Party unity. The Los Angeles mayor, Sam Yorty, challenged Brown for the Democratic nomination, and he made a strong showing in the primary campaign. The infighting between Democratic candidates was an indication that the party was in serious trouble with the voters. Yet, there was little doubt that California had undergone rapid change since Pat Brown was inaugurated in 1959. The Democratic governor had achieved a solid record of achievement during his two terms. The increase in minority employment, the end of housing restrictions, and the advances in public education produced a multi-ethnic society in the Golden State.

Ronald Reagan and the Creative Society

The new political messiah in California politics was a former Hollywood actor, Ronald Reagan. In 1964 Reagan gained prominence as a conservative spokesman for Republican presidential candidate Barry Goldwater. In his early years Reagan was a liberal Democrat and had served as President of the Screen Actors Guild. After his marriage to Nancy Davis he became a Republican and a staunch conservative. The General Electric Corporation employed Reagan to deliver a series of speeches to its employees and civic groups, and this experience in the early 1960s whetted his appetite for the political area. Using the demands of Blacks and students as his focal point for political argument, Reagan used a sophisticated campaign to appeal to the attitudes of middle-class taxpayers who believed that revolution was imminent in the Golden State.

The 1966 campaign was a contrast in style and argument. Reagan declared that he opposed the Rumford Fair Housing Act, because he believed that it was contrary to individual business rights. Brown countered that Reagan was a bigot. Yet, Governor Brown could not defend his inability to protect poor Mexican-American farm pickets from beatings and intimidation. The Chicano and Black communities were no more interested in Brown's call for civil rights than they were in Reagan's exortation that everybody should work in California.

Courtesy, The Bancroft Library

Mario Savio addressing students from atop police car

Free Speech Movement Women for Peace

The key argument which brought Reagan to the governor's mansion was the cost of state government. The Republican candidate vowed to cut government costs, and this led to almost a million vote majority for Reagan in the November, 1966, governor's race.

Implementing the Creative Society

One of the strangest events in California history took place at 12:02 A.M. on January 2, 1967, when Governor Reagan was inaugurated at the earliest possible moment, thereby preventing outgoing Governor "Pat" Brown from attending the ceremony. The usual procedure was to deliver the inaugural address on January 5, but the earlier address had allowed Reagan to exclude many Democrats and other dignitaries. As he entered the governor's office, Reagan referred to himself as a "citizen-politician." This pitch to the common person was a perfect reflection of California political attitudes and Reagan would remain a popular figure for the next eight years.

The first change under Reagan was the decline of state government services. He cut back funds for college and university education, reduced mental health facilities and funds, and cut back on medical and housing services for the aged and indigent. Despite Governor Reagan's protestations of economy the state budget rose from $4 billion in 1967 to over $10 billion in 1975. The announcement that he had saved California taxpayers $50,000 his first month in office by forcing state employees to use old typewriter ribbons did not square with the facts.

There were some positive accomplishments from the Reagan years. Much to the surprise of his Republican followers he signed a bill making abortion much easier. He also cut back on needless travel by state employees and reduced the cost of administering many state government programs. His fiscal conservatism appealed to business interests who believed that California's government should reflect stringent economy.

The individuals hardest hit by the Reagan years were college students, old people, and minority groups. The cost of a state college or university education rose in the 1960s and 1970s despite the lack of tuition. Fees, books, and living expenses made it difficult for many students to attend a four-year institution for higher learning. The California Community College system benefited from this change in public education, however, and a large number of junior colleges emerged to meet student needs. In 1967 Ohlone Community College in Fremont, for example, opened its doors to more than two thousand students in a community with less than a hundred thousand citizens. With more than one-hundred junior colleges, California's educational system reflected the diverse nature of the state. Senior citizens in the state were no longer able to collect from the Medi-Cal funds for much needed medical treatment. Reagan vowed to slash $210 million from Medi-Cal. It was a controversial program begun in 1966 to provide senior citizens and the financially disabled with medical care. From the moment he entered office, Regan was hostile to Medi-Cal, and he was often restrained by the California courts. Ethnic minorities were the hardest hit by the Reagan administration as the number of Blacks, Chicanos, and Asians in top level government jobs declined in the late 1960s and early 1970s.

The Haight-Ashbury Summer of Love, 1967

The staid and conservative nature of California politics was not reflected in the life style of its young people. In 1967 the "Summer of Love" emerged in a small neighborhood in San Francisco, the Haight-Ashbury. A placid, quiet little neighborhood next to Golden Gate Park, it featured low rents and a minimum of police interest.

There was another element to the San Francisco revolution—rock and roll music. For a decade Top 40 Radio had dominated the music industry, but in 1967 FM radio and underground hits began a new cultural revolution. At the Avalon Ballroom or the Fillmore Auditorium, Big Brother and the Holding Company, the Charlatans, the Quicksilver Messenger Service, the Jefferson Airplane, Country Joe and the Fish, or the Grateful Dead would hold forth in an orgy of rock music, cheap wine, and LSD. To many in attendance it seemed a fitting way of bypassing the complexities, frustrations, and disappointments of California politics.

There are a number of lessons from the Haight-Ashbury days. First, young adults were not just alienated from the system, rather they were forming alternative ideas and institutions on family, business, and social relationships. Second, the use of drugs and the problems of juvenile dislocation were serious problems. Third, the resistance of young people to corporate values had a positive side. The crusades to save the whales, end nuclear energy plants, provide greater ecology for California's natural resources and end poverty, crime, and racism all attest to the positive ferment of the Summer of Love.

Reagan and Reaction, 1971–1975

In the 1970s Governor Reagan's election for a second term was a mandate for change. The Democratic legislature had prevented Reagan from achieving a great deal of success during his first term. In 1970 the legislature reflected a Republican viewpoint, and this allowed for a great deal of fiscal conservatism in the early 1970s.

The welfare system was attacked as a public cancer, and the popularity of make-work projects for welfare recipients was an indication of the conservative public mood. The popularity of heavy cuts in government spending resulted in a barebones budget for the University and State College systems, the decline of welfare and public health services, and the lack of a cost of living increase for state employees. In December, 1971, Governor Reagan was forced to sign a new tax bill as a result of declining state government revenues. The critics of the Republican governor also pointed out that he had paid no income tax in 1969 and 1970 due to investments in a cattle ranch. Yet, Reagan's attitudes on government spending were representative of the Golden State.

One of the serious problems to confront Californians was the rise of financial problems in the public school system. In September, 1971, the California Supreme Court ruled in the Serrano v. Ivy Baker Priest decision that the system of financing public schools through property taxes was unconstitutional. The Court suggested that more than a thousand dollars per pupil was spent in Beverly Hills for public education whereas in the poor district of Baldwin Park approximately five-hundred dollars was spent on each student's education. The question of an equitable tax base and the financing of local education was an insoluble one in the 1970s.

The eight years in which Reagan controlled California politics were ones with attempts to reform the system. Generally, however, there was little change in California society. Although the Reagan years were ones of controlling state government spending, they were also a period of low employment, little change in job status, and held little prospect for the future of Black, Brown, and Yellow Californians. It appeared to be the 1850s or 1920s relived as a White Anglo-Saxon political machine ruled the Golden State. Nevertheless, there was a great deal of ethnic political and economic activity in California.

Cesar Chavez and Chicano Labor

In the early 1960s a young field worker turned union organizer, Cesar Chavez, began to attract attention to his independent union, the National Farm Workers Association. The new union called for a fifty dollar a week wage for casual farm labor. As a young man, Chavez had worked as a farm laborer in California and Arizona, and obtained his eight years of schooling in forty separate California public schools. Growing up in Yuma, Arizona, Chavez' family lost their land due to an inability to pay property taxes. While working in the California fields, the young Chavez witnessed first-hand the miseries of farm workers. He turned down a lucrative Federal job to pursue his desire to organize a farm workers union. Chavez recalled that the thought of his father, working from sun-up to sun-down, was a major factor in his decision to pursue lengthy farm labor strikes. The Delano strike is a good example of how Chavez' childhood experiences brought him extreme patience in dealing with California growers.

In August, 1965, Chavez' union joined a strike against thirty-three grape growers in the Delano area of northern Kern County, which continued for a year. Finally, during the summer of 1966, Chavez' National Farm Workers Association signed a series of agreements with San Joaquin Valley growers which recognized the Chicano labor movement. After a half century of poor wages, inadequate state government interest, and poor working conditions, the National Farm Workers Association achieved monumental success when Schenley, the second largest grape grower in the Delano area agreed to recognize Chavez' union. In San Francisco the longshoremen had refused to load Schenley Industry and DiGiorgio Corporation grapes and a nationwide boycott against Schenley's wines and liquors and DiGiorgio's S and W canned goods were major factors in the union's success.

After the Delano strike DiGiorgio issued a challenge to the National Farm Workers Association to allow elections for a field union controlled by Chavez or one headed by the Teamsters. Chicano and Filipino labor leaders formed a new organization known as the United Farm Workers Organizing Committee and became an AFL-CIO chartered union known as the United Farm Workers of America. The charismatic Chavez quietly campaigned for the United Farm Workers of America and local workers voted 530–330 for U.F.W. representation in California's fields. The Teamsters won the right to represent a small unit of shed workers and truck drivers. Despite these successes most local grape growers refused to bargain with Chavez' union. This led to another national boycott with the support of AFL-CIO, and from 1966 to 1970 the UFW pressured local growers for a union contract. California Governor Ronald Reagan defended the growers' rights and suggested that he would retaliate against any California community supporting the Chavez union. In the 1968 presidential campaign, Richard M. Nixon held a bunch of grapes in his hand as he informed a San Joaquin Valley audience that the Chavez boycott was illegal and un-American. The odds against U.F.W. successes were overwhelming, but the seeds of a century of farm labor discontent continued to buoy the spirits of the workers.

In 1970 the U.F.W. convinced a number of California table-grape growers to sign a union contract. The majority of the Coachella Valley grape growers began to place the "Thunderbird" label of the U.F.W. on their crates. In the Salinas and Santa Maria Valley contracts were reached with some local lettuce growers. A large number of Salinas lettuce producers signed agreements with the Teamsters Union which hampered the United Farm Workers.

During the 1970s Chavez' United Farm Workers experienced a great deal of competition from the Teamsters for migrant labor membership, and in 1971 Chavez and Teamster officials concluded a peace designed to end competition in the fields. The fighting between the Teamsters and United Farm Workers continued; however, and in December, 1972, the California Supreme Court ruled that Chavez' union could picket against Teamster controlled growers.

The American Farm Bureau Federation began to attack the United Farm Workers and many Chavez critics charged that pickets were already paid over $10,000 a year. Chavez laughed at these propaganda statements, and cited federal government statistics which indicated that the California field worker was paid $2.44 an hour. The strongest threat to Chavez' United Farm Workers was the Teamsters Union which controlled the lettuce crops. The leaders of the major union organizations backed Chavez, and George Meany, head of the AFL-CIO, charged that the Teamsters' were engaged in a conspiracy with growers to destroy the United Farm Workers.

Migrant farm worker in the 1960s

Courtesy, The Bancroft Library

Growers complained that it was virtually impossible to negotiate with Chavez, and the spectre of racism permeated California agribusiness in the mid-1970s.

In 1977 the long struggle between Chicano labor and the Teamsters ended when a five-year agreement was signed allowing greater United Farm Workers organizational activity. One of the reasons for this agreement was due to the sympathetic political influence of Governor Jerry Brown. Brown's interest was more a civil rights one than a labor dispute. The young governor was committed to equality for all workers, and he used the prestige of state office to shape an agreement which allowed the United Farm Workers to represent all field workers and the Teamsters to serve cannery workers and truckdrivers. The success of the Chavez movement in the California fields has led to livable wages and improved working conditions. The force of local agribusiness is no longer an arbitrary and oppressive feature of California life.

Women in California

The influence of women in recent California is a complex and interesting reflection of the changing lifestyle and attitudes in the Golden State. With women comprising more than forty percent of the work force, the drive for equal pay and equal rights in the 1960s led to a number of important women emerging in public life. The most recognizable women were society figures who served on the University of California Board of Regents. Dorothy Buffum Chandler, for example, was a regent from 1954 until 1970 and served as vice-chairman for a time. Catherine Hearst was a regent from 1956 until 1976 when personal family problems over her daughter Patty led to her resignation. Governor Jerry Brown appointed a Chicana, Wilma Martinez, to succeed Mrs. Hearst. This was the first sign that women with serious political attitudes were being considered for appointments to state office. The tragedy of California women was that they were viewed as subservient political volunteers who filled in where needed, but this changed in the 1970s when a number of women were elected to important public offices.

Perhaps the most controversial woman in the 1970s was California Supreme Court Chief Justice Rose Elizabeth Bird. A young, energetic legal figure, she was much too liberal and reform-minded for big business. In 1978 an attempt to oust her from office was defeated, and the traditional independence of the California Supreme Court was preserved from right-wing political attack. In the mid-1970s March Fong Eu was an important voice for women's rights as Secretary of State, and in 1976 Rose A. Vuich of Dinuba became the first woman ever elected to the California Senate. As an observer pointed out in 1979, women were still grossly underrepresented in California politics.

In the 1970s the controversy over the Equal Rights Amendment to the United States Constitution forced Californians to reexamine their attitudes on sex discrimination. When March Fong Eu supported a move to eliminate pay toilets for women, she was emphasizing the level of discrimination against women in public places. Despite the number of jokes in poor taste, Mrs. Eu succeeded in publicizing her broader point of equal rights for women. In 1972 the California Senate held hearings which set up rules to prevent sex discrimination and Senator James R. Mills prematurely proclaimed that all sex bias had ended in California.

In 1979 women were no longer in a minority as California voters, and this suggests that the drive for women's rights in the future will be an intense one. There are still areas of great discrimination in university teaching positions, law firms, medical schools, and skilled union memberships; but the new awareness toward sex bias is ending one of California's most perplexing problems.

Mayor Dianne Feinstein of San Francisco provided positive leadership in the aftermath of the mass suicide by members of the People's Temple in Guyana. She was particularly skillful in answering charges that San Francisco was the "kook center" of America. Mayor Feinstein proved to be a hard working administrator during her first year in office. In 1971 and 1975 she had unsuccessfully bid for the mayor's office, and Moscone's death brought the San Francisco Board of Supervisors squarely behind her appointment as mayor.

Her record was an impressive one in the first few months after the November, 1978, assassination of Mayor Moscone and Supervisor Harvey Milk. A growing concern for the plight of senior citizens prompted Mayor Feinstein to make the Tenderloin section of San Francisco safer through increased police patrols. A city ordinance regulating the number of pornography shops helped to reduce local crime. Since 1969 when Mrs. Feinstein was first elected to the San Francisco

Board of Supervisors she had displayed an extraordinary interest in the small person and the underrepresented minority. Her elevation to the Mayor's office was an indication of one type of political change abroad in California in 1979.

Bibliographical Essay

For Ronald Reagan see, Bill Boyarsky, *The Rise of Ronald Reagan* (1968); Joseph Lewis, *What Makes Reagan Run?* (1968); and Lou Cannon, *Ronnie and Jesse: A Political Odyssey* (1969). On Jerry Brown see Robert Pack, Jerry Brown: The Philosopher Prine (1978).

On Cesar Chavez see, Jacques Levy, *Cesar Chavez: Autobiography of La Causa* (1975); Peter Matthieson, *Sal Si Puedes: Cesar Chavez and the New American Revolution* (1969); John G. Dunne, *Delano: The Story of the California Grape Strike* (1971, ev. ed); and Joan London and Henry Anderson, *So Shall Ye Reap* (1970).

The Free Speech Movement and campus rebellion in general is examined in Seymour M. Lipset and Sheldon S. Wolin, editors, *The Berkeley Student Revolt: Facts and Interpretations* (1965); Steven Warshaw, *The Trouble in Berkeley* (1965); and Terry F. Lunsford, *The Free Speech Crises at Berkeley, 1964–1965: Some Issues for Social and Legal Research* (1965).

17

FROM JERRY BROWN'S CHAMELEON POLITICS TO THE S.F. CITY HALL KILLINGS, 1970 TO 1984

Jerry Brown: The Philosopher-Prince Enters California Politics

In 1969–1970 Jerry Brown entered the mainstream of California politics and revived the drab political image of the Golden State. There was no indication in Jerry's background that he possessed political ambition, and at the age of 32 Brown did not appear to be politically motivated. However, as the son of former Governor Edmund G. (Pat) Brown, young Jerry grew up in the midst of partisan political activity. After witnessing his father's crushing defeat by Ronald Reagan for a third gubernatorial term in 1966, Jerry began to consider his own political options. It was the strong disdain for Reagan's intellectual deficiencies which prompted Jerry Brown to become involved in the political arena. In 1968 he was active in the anti-war movement in Los Angeles, and he was an alternate delegate for Eugene McCarthy at the 1968 Democratic National Convention in Chicago. It was McCarthy's youthful, peace-oriented campaign for the presidency which shaped Brown's political attitudes. As a result of this campaign, Jerry's earliest political philosophy emphasized the belief that the governmental process must be orderly, and a model politician must not succumb to demagogic tactics. The irony of Jerry Brown's early ideas is that he failed to follow his own rules for political success.

There were a number of important events in Jerry Brown's life which shaped his political character. Jerry had once been a student in a Jesuit seminary, and some felt that this experience emphasized a cold, stoic side of his character. After leaving the seminary Jerry graduated in 1961 from the University of California, Berkeley with a degree in Latin and Greek. By 1964 Brown had completed Yale Law School; however, he failed the California bar exam. After extensive tutoring in the governor's mansion, young Jerry passed the bar and quietly left Sacramento to practice law in Los Angeles. It was while living in Southern California that Brown initially ran for elective office, campaigning for a seat on the Los Angeles Community College Board of Trustees. Although there were 133 candidates running for seven seats on the college board, Brown's politically potent name provided for an easy victory.

It was while Brown served on the LA Community College Board of Trustees that he developed his penchant for attracting publicity. He criticized the LA Community College District for spending $23,000 for press agents, and he continually informed the press that college administrative costs were too high. Brown challenged the junior college district's decision to offer such non-academic courses as flower arranging, and he urged Los Angeles voters to take an active interest in community college affairs. This aggressive stance on college spending, coupled with the moralistic piety of a priest, made Brown an attractive political personality. He also displayed radical chic by defending unpopular causes. For example, conservative Republican members of the Los Angeles Community College Board cast enough votes to fire an English instructor, Deena Metzger, for reading a poem, "Jehovah's Child," which the board considered to have "abnormal" sexual overtones. Brown opposed Metzger's firing and criticized his colleagues for their unwillingness to respect First Amendment freedoms. The California Supreme Court reinstated Metzger with back pay, and this case made Brown the darling of liberal Democrats. Always ready with a quote or an interesting anecdote, Brown found himself praised by the press and courted by leading Democratic politicians. His youth and gaunt good looks were an asset, and his political stands attracted a cross-section of voters.

As Ronald Reagan dominated the headlines in his quest for a second term as California's governor in 1970, Jerry Brown quietly announced that he would run for the Secretary of State's office. Since 1911, Frank Jordan and subsequently his son, Frank, Jr., had held the Secretary of State's job. After Frank Jr. died, his wife, Alberta, declared that she would run for public office to keep the family tradition alive. (One veteran Sacramento political observer wryly remarked that the only apparent function of the Secretary of State was to keep the Jordan family employed.) Brown recognized that the Secretary of State's office would be one that he would have little trouble winning. Alberta Jordan was an unknown political figure and Jerry Brown was the son of one of California's most popular governors. It was a shrewd political move by Brown to run for this office.

In the spring of 1970 the Democratic party primary was Brown's first major political test. His Democratic opponent, former State Senator Hugh Burns, was not a formidable foe. The *Los Angeles Times* reported that Burns supported revised state insurance laws which increased his personal wealth by a half million dollars. Although there was no immediate evidence of wrongdoing newspapers reported that the California Legislative Ethics Committee would not investigate the case. Since Burns was the chairperson of the Legislative Ethics Committee, cartoonists and editorial critics sarcastically suggested that Burns was serving two masters. This mild hint of scandal aided Brown's campaign. What helped even more was the size of Brown's campaign war chest. As the primary campaign progressed, young Jerry spent $24 in political advertising to every $1 spent by Burns.

Brown was able to raise large amounts of money thanks in part to his father's former political supporters. The San Francisco hotel magnate Ben Swig was typical of the "Checkbook Democrats" who held fried-chicken fundraisers to launch Jerry's fledgling political career. Swig allegedly began one fundraiser by announcing that the doors to the bathroom would be locked until donations were received for Brown's campaign. But Brown also attracted funds because of his political views. Jerry spoke out privately against the anarchist-minded college students of the 1960s. He also attacked the college community for not enforcing rules, and he vowed to expel any students who refused to obey college regulations. This law and order pitch impressed traditional Democrats.

As Jerry Brown campaigned in 1970, he perfected the technique of identifying with a number of different political causes. In Los Angeles' Watts District Jerry was a civil rights advocate. In the cafeteria on the University of California, Los Angeles campus he talked about the problems of the selective service system and proclaimed his righteous indignation with the Vietnam war. In downtown San Francisco he spoke of reviving the business community. In the San Fernando Valley he sipped herbal tea and talked about high taxes and crab grass. In Marin County there were small encounter groups designed to foster voter awareness. Jerry was a politician for all seasons, and he became the perfect political caricature of the "me generation" of the 1970s.

In the November, 1970 general election not only did Brown defeat his Republican rival, James Flournoy, by 300,000 votes, but he was also the only Democrat elected to a top-level state office. The Democratic party soon began to view Jerry Brown as an important challenger for the governor's office in 1974.

Once he assumed the office of Secretary of State, Brown himself also began planning a campaign to secure the governor's office. He hired an aide to function as an "idea" man. This individual was a mysterious Frenchman with a shaved head, Lorenzo Jacques Barzaghi, who proved to be a practical political observer. The 29 year old Barzaghi was a French citizen who visited Los Angeles with his American born wife in 1968 and promptly fell in love with California chic. His wife filed for divorce and returned to Paris after Barzaghi announced his intention to move permanently to Hollywood. A dashing figure with the girls, he married again and quickly divorced. In 1971 the U.S. Immigration and Naturalization Service informed the Svengalilike figure that he would be deported.

After meeting Jerry Brown at a party, Barzaghi visited the Secretary of State's office for advice on his immigration problems. In order to obtain a green card guaranteeing permanent resident status, Barzaghi requested Brown's help. Finding Jerry Brown wearing jeans and sitting with his feet on a desk, Barzaghi told his tale of immigration woes. Soon the two young men found out they had mutual interests in Zen Buddhism, American movies and styles of political leadership.

Beginning as a trainee clerk in 1971, Barzaghi eventually was placed in charge of television commercial production for the 1974 governor's race. After that he was named both a cabinet secretary and a special assistant for the arts. Many of Brown's political programs were the direct result of Barzaghi's influence. In particular, Barzaghi was influential in convincing Brown that British economist E. F. Schumacher's book, *Small Is Beautiful,* was an original theoretical treatise which could solve California's economic problems. Schumacher believed that small, human-scale industries would replace large industrial plants. A Buddist economist, Schumacher emphasized the importance of the spiritual over the material. It was the sound of the phrase "Small is Beautiful" which appealed to Brown, and he traveled to London to consult with Schumacher. It was Brown's ability to coin catchy phrases, popularize obscure ideas, and to appear non-establishment, but honest, which made him an important political figure. When Brown was elected to the Secretary of State's office in 1970 he began a career that led to national political prominence.

Brown as Secretary of State Training for the Governor's Office

From 1970 to 1974 Jerry Brown was a politician who was in the forefront of California's major political battles. Brown's skill in dealing with the media impressed most California political observers, but few people realized how important A. Thomas Quinn was to Brown's political machine. Quinn, the son of Joe Quinn, a United Press International News executive, met Brown in 1969 and began to help plan Brown's political future. On March 2, 1970, Brown announced his candidacy for the Secretary of State's office with a carefully concocted press release written by Quinn. Much of Brown's future political success was due to Quinn's able handling of the media.

The duties of Secretary of State were dull and mundane, and Brown delegated to his staff the functions of managing state archives, keeping all state records, issuing commissions to notary publics, and granting charters to corporations doing business in the state. Jerry concentrated on politics. Shortly after taking office, for example, he challenged Attorney General Houston Flournoy's decision to force college students to vote in their parents' district. When Flournoy argued that students could take over a University town, Brown scoffed at this suggestion. In praising the vote for 18–year-olds, Brown clearly believed that he would profit in future elections because of the youth vote.

The most dramatic political act during Brown's term as Secretary of State occurred only three weeks after he took office when he filed a suit alleging that a number of major corporations had made illegal campaign contributions. Within three days Gulf Oil admitted giving $20,000 secretly, and Standard Oil of California stated that it had made an anonymous $45,000 donation. After eight months of investigation, Brown publicly reprimanded 134 candidates (including, ironically, a number of his father's political allies) for failing to fully disclose campaign contributions. Brown made it very clear that state laws governing the reporting of campaign contributions would be strictly enforced. None of the threats resulted in prosecutions and convictions, but the spectre of an obscure Secretary of State lecturing the most important figures in California for not filing timely and accurate campaign contributions reports gave Jerry Brown the image of a fearless Don Quixote tilting at the powerful windmills which controlled state politics.

The campaign to expose corruption continued in March, 1973, when Brown reported that employees of his office were denied access to public records by the legislature's Lobbyist Control Committee. On April 10, 1973, Brown, with help from the public lobby groups, Common Cause and the People's Lobby, succeeded in placing the Fair Political Practices initiative on the June, 1974 ballot. This measure provided that campaign reports be meticulously audited to detect any conflict of interest. California legislators were furious with Brown's proposal, particularly its requirement that lobbyists spend no more than $10 a month on an individual legislator. However, the Fair Political Practices initiative got enough voter signatures to become "Proposition 9" on the 1974 ballot, and it passed. This initiative confirmed Brown's public image as a no-nonsense politician who did not condone the "good old boy" politics of the past.

The Gubernatorial Election of 1974: The Politics of Limits

As he considered his political future, Jerry Brown faced a difficult decision: whether to run for governor in 1974 or wait until 1978. California Democratic Senator John Tunney cautioned Jerry to proceed slowly, believing that Jerry should follow in his father's footsteps and run for the Attorney General's office. However, when Watergate broke and President Richard Nixon resigned in disgrace, the political atmosphere seemed ready made for a gubernatorial candidate with morality and integrity.

A number of Brown's close political advisers, notably Marc Poché, still urged Brown not to run for governor. Poché was a Republican who had become a Democrat when his San Jose law partner, John Vasconcellos, was elected to the state assembly in 1966. Poché argued that it was not logical for Brown to consider jumping from the Secretary of State's office to the governor's mansion. Like most other political observers, he did not believe that Brown could defeat Assembly Speaker Bob Moretti or San Francisco Mayor Joe Alioto in the Democratic primary.

Mayor Alioto was the candidate of organized labor, but Brown's political supporters shrewdly negotiated a deal with the AFL-CIO's Committee on Public Education (COPE) to free labor from specifically supporting one candidate in the primary election. As a result many unions provided Brown with the same campaign contribution that Alioto received, and Alioto lost his initial advantage. Brown went on to easily win the primary by deemphasizing traditional politics and playing upon the strong desire for political change in the Golden State. One observer called Brown's 1974 primary campaign a lesson in confusion which avoided issues and concentrated instead upon the candidate's honesty and good looks.

Brown took a similar approach in his general election campaign, avoiding issues and creating a cult of personality. Pamphlets and ads focused, for instance, upon Jerry's distinguished family and their contributions to the Golden State, extolling his father's positive accomplishments as California's governor and his ancestor's contributions to the state. The media also paid much attention to Brown's personal life. He was continually questioned about his lifestyle and bachelor status. He answered his critics by replying: "I think the governor's job is incompatible with marriage." The Republican candidate, Houston Flournoy, spent an inordinate amount of time criticizing Jerry's carefree bachelor living, and this seemed to increase voter interest in Brown's candidacy.

Flournoy, Brown's opponent, was not the strongest Republican candidate. The favorite had been Ronald Reagan's Lieutenant Governor, Ed Reinecke. However, he was indicted for perjury by the Watergate grand jury in 1974. Ironically, Reinecke was later vindicated, but his political career never recovered. As a result State Controller Houston Flournoy won the Republican primary. Flournoy was an inept campaigner with a dull speaking voice and a lackluster political style. He took a moderate stand on most issues and differed on many points with then Governor Reagan. As one political observer commented, "Flournoy seemed to be a recycled Democrat who has difficulty explaining his programs."

As Jerry Brown's strength in the general election campaign increased, he made two mistakes. One was to appear overly-confident. The other was to make statements that he was the head of the California Democratic Party. This seemed to be arrogant, and it caused many political veterans to take another look at Brown's candidacy. The other mistake was to stop his television advertising for one week. A Gallup Poll taken three months before the November, 1974 election indicated that Brown had a strong lead over Flournoy, and it seemed pointless to Brown to spend huge sums on TV ads with such a large lead in the polls. This lack of advertising permitted Flournoy to surge as the election approached and Brown barely escaped with a narrow victory.

Once Brown was elected there was a great deal of interest in his novel political programs. On election night, for example, Jerry Brown announced that austerity in government spending was necessary to combat the excesses of the past. Taking advantage of the anti-government feeling following the Watergate crisis, Brown cancelled the inaugural ball as a needless extravagance. He also labelled the new governor's mansion as a "Taj Mahal," and replaced Governor Reagan's official Cadillac with a blue Plymouth sedan. Political cartoonists had a field day characterizing Brown's politics, and he was suddenly the hottest media political figure of the mid-1970s.

A good example of the media's curiosity about Brown occurred when it was reported that he traveled to the Tassajara Hot Springs to meditate. This Monterey County Zen Center, one newspaper reported, emphasized that truth is outside of words. After a weekend of meditation, Governor Brown responded to this Zen maxim by announcing that he was removing all the symbols of power from his office. Brown also refused to authorize an official portrait of himself, and he rented a $250 a month downtown apartment. He even proudly announced that his bed sheets came from the Napa State Hospital. A disgruntled Republican remarked that Brown's political ideas bore a resemblance to the same state facility.

Yet Jerry Brown was a shrewd politician. His 1974 Plymouth Satellite became the symbol of the California governor's austerity. He loved to tell reporters that it did not have air conditioning or power windows. The average voter identified with a governor who shunned a police escort, refused to spend money on a limousine, and was seen walking in from the San Francisco Giants parking lot to watch a ball game.

The Politics of Vision: Jerry Brown's Early Years, 1974–1976

The amateur nature of Brown's politics was demonstrated in an innocuous 9 minute inaugural address which revealed that the governor had no idea about the future of California politics. Veteran San Francisco political observers labelled Brown a politician with a penchant for cliches. But Brown shrewdly realized that criticism of inefficient government, excessive state spending and bungling bureaucracy was a means of appearing independent-minded. Consequently, he spent an inordinate amount of time condemning past political practices. The *Sacramento Bee* humorously reported that Governor Brown's frugality was so excessive that he refused to provide the free briefcases traditionally given to state workers. After Brown cut his own salary 7%, he announced that a new philosophy of state government was taking shape in the Golden State.

Part of Governor Brown's new philosophy included the appointment of women, ethnic minorities and the handicapped to state jobs. In June, 1977, Yritada Wada became the first Asian-American appointed to the University of California Board of Regents. Fred William Gabourie, a former actor and American Indian, was appointed as a judge to the Los Angeles Municipal Court. Mario Obledo, a forty-five-year-old Mexican-American was named Secretary of California Health and Welfare services. When he was a child, Obledo's parents were on welfare, and he announced that the system would be completely overhauled. Ed Roberts was named to head the Department of Rehabilitation, and he emphasized that his own quadriplegic status would make him sensitive to the needs of handicapped Californians. A black lawyer, Wiley Manuel, was named a California Supreme Court Justice and Adriana Gianturco, a former *Time* magazine reporter and transportation aide in Massachusetts, was named the director of the State Department of Transportation (Cal-Trans). Gianturco's appointment resulted in a barrage of politically-motivated criticisms about her qualifications. Governor Brown brushed these comments aside by quoting from Suzuki-Roshi, the founder of the San Francisco Zen Center. Brown informed the bewildered press that a beginner's mind has more flexibility and intelligence than that of an expert. Brown's detractors remained unconvinced, and Gianturco remained a controversial figure.

The most important accomplishment of Jerry Brown's first term was the enactment of Agricultural Labor Relations Act for farmworkers. In his inaugural address, Brown urged state legislators to consider a bill to include farm workers within the bounds of state unemployment insurance. The governor also spoke of extending the rule of law to the agricultural fringe and establishing a state-guaranteed right to secret union elections for farm workers. For a century abuses surrounding farm labor had tarnished the liberal image of California society. Chinese, Japanese, Mexican, Filipino and East Indian laborers were exploited decade after decade, and the major growers had prevented effective farm labor unions from organizing in the California fields.

On June 5, 1975, Brown signed a model bill guaranteeing the Golden State's quarter-of-a-million agricultural employees the right in secret elections to decide which union they wanted to join. The Agricultural Labor Relations Act (ALRA) was the first of its kind in the United States, and this law further enhanced Brown's reputation as a liberal. The farm labor legislation was also an indication of Cesar Chavez' influence with Governor Brown.

Assemblyman Willie Brown, a San Francisco Democrat, was extremely critical of the Agricultural Labor Relations Act. Brown called the ALRA a "corruption" of what the legislative process shall be. Governor Brown put the farm labor bill together before it was introduced and announced that there would be no amendments to it except those which he approved. Willie Brown was furious with Governor Brown's dictatorial attitude, but the creation of the ALRA indicated that the governor had matured as a politician.

By late July, 1975, Governor Brown's five appointees to the Agricultural Labor Relations Board began planning to oversee farm worker elections. During its first five months the ALRB conducted 359 elections. The United Farm Workers of California, Cesar Chavez' union, won 195 and the Teamsters won 120. Also, 19 small unions were victorious, and 25 elections resulted in no union receiving a majority. Then the ALRB ran out of funds on February 6, 1976, and it ceased to function. Consequently, the United Farm Workers of California organized an initiative known as Proposition 14, which became the most controversial measure on the November 1976 ballot. Proposition 14 guaranteed the Agricultural Labor Relations Board state funding, and Governor Brown swung his entire political machine behind this measure. Brown was joined by President Carter and Senators Alan Cranston and John Tunney in supporting the measure, but the voters were not happy with the open warfare between the UFW and the Teamsters unions. Californians defeated proposition 14 by an overwhelming 62% no vote. The voters also sent Senator Tunney into retirement, and he bitterly blamed his defeat on the backlash vote against Chavez' farmworkers.

The Agricultural Labor Relations Board continued to function and in April, 1977, the United Farm Workers and the Teamsters Union signed an agreement recognizing the UFW's jurisdiction over all field workers in the 13 western states. The California legislature approved a law which extended unemployment insurance to farm laborers. Governor Brown's support for California's farm workers was a courageous political stand because he lost votes on this issue. San Joaquin Valley agribusiness interests donated a half a million dollars to the campaign of Assemblyman Ken Maddy of Fresno in 1978, hoping that the Republican candidate could unseat Governor Brown.

From the Presidential Election of 1976 to Space Day

In 1976 Jerry Brown dabbled in national policies when he challenged Jimmy Carter for the Democratic presidential nomination. As one of 15 candidates attempting to unseat the favored Georgian, Brown defeated Carter in three of six presidential preferential primaries. In California, Brown won a resounding 59% of the vote to Carter's 21%, and he also won in Maryland and Nevada. In New Jersey and Rhode Island, Brown campaigned successfully for uncommitted slates to back his presidential candidacy. The Oregon primary was one Brown did not officially enter, but he appealed to the ecology-minded state workers. When Brown informed students at the University of Oregon that he had prepared a California law limiting the amount of water that a new toilet could hold he was greeted with thunderous applause. Brown then boldly announced that California toilets would no longer drain Oregon's water supply. This inane type of campaigning was cheered in Oregon, and Jerry Brown received 23% of the Democratic vote in the state primary although his name wasn't officially on the ballot.

While campaigning for the Democratic presidential primary in New York in July, 1976, Governor Brown stayed in the budget-rated McAlpin hotel. Brown's attempt to impress New York voters by using this delapidated hotel as his campaign headquarters backfired. Most New Yorkers were amused but not impressed with Brown's political posturing. The California governor's attempt to challenge Jimmy Carter there was a dismal failure.

Brown's inability to make a respectable showing in the 1976 Democratic presidential contest had dramatic results in California politics. The *Los Angeles Times* charged that Brown had ignored serious financial and academic problems in the California public schools. The business community also complained that major corporations were leaving California or simply not expanding their operations in the Golden State because of restrictive state policies. Groups like the San Francisco Chamber of Commerce pointed to agencies like the Air Resources Board and the California Energy Commission as examples of unnecessary enforcement of environmental standards. The Dow Chemical Company shocked the major investment firms and banks in 1977 when it announced that it would not construct a large-scale power plant in California due to bureaucratic interference. The *Wall Street Journal* then reported that California was 47th among the states in terms of business environment.

There were also charges that Brown's closest political advisers were anti-business. This charge seemed accurate when one observer remarked that intellectuals constantly occupied the governor's attention. Individuals such as the poet, Gary Synder, the economist, E. F. Schumacher, and the Zen philosopher, Baker Roshi, who ran the San Francisco Zen Center, were constantly advising Brown. Perhaps the most bizarre example of Brown's non-traditional policies occurred during the January, 1976 Governor's Prayer Breakfast when Jacques Barazaghi convinced the governor to invite Marin County's Sufi Choir to sing and dance for the 1400 government workers and guests. Most observers stared in amazement as the Sufi Choir swirled around the capital. This strange melange around Brown included Stewart Brand, a former member of Ken Kesey's Merry Pranksters, a group which had gained notoriety in the mid-1960s riding around in a psychedelic bus handing out LSD laced Kool-Aid, and listening to the music of the Grateful Dead.

Stewart Brand founded and edited the *Co-Evolution Quarterly,* which was hip combination of *Popular Mechanics* and the *Scientific American.* By 1977 Brand was part of Governor Brown's brain trust, and he developed new plans for promoting California's economic expansion while maintaining the state's environmental beauty. Each Thursday Brand drove from Marin County to Sacramento to inform the governor of his latest ideas. One result of the collaboration was to suggest that California serve as a launching pad for space colonization. Soon former astronaut Rusty Schweickart, who had circled the moon on Apollo 9 in 1969, was advising Governor Brown about a Space Day for the Golden State. On August 11, 1977, the day before the U.S. Space Shuttle made its first flight, Brown held his well-publicized Space Day.

The Space Day celebration was a perfect example of the trendy political issues in California politics. It was the space debate which provided Brown with the political slogan he would develop in the 1978 gubernatorial campaign. When Brown called the Space Age "an era of possibilities," this slogan became the rallying point for his second gubernatorial election campaign. Republican Senator Barry Goldwater of Arizona was one of many politicians who spoke glowingly of Brown's new ideas. In January, 1978, Governor Brown proposed that the California legislature appropriate six million dollars to launch the first state-owned communications satellite and to establish a space institute at the University of California. Before he abandoned the colonization of outer space as too expensive, Brown spent an inordinate amount of time arguing that space exploration would provide the technological basis for solar power. As one critic suggested, only Governor Brown could announce that the day of Astronaut Ethics had arrived in California politics.

The Gubernatorial Election of 1978 and the Era of Possibilities

In the 1978 gubernatorial election, it was obvious that Jerry Brown had grown in political stature and that he was now a skilled and seasoned politician. Although he continued to commit non-traditional political sins, there were strong indications that this type of political behavior attracted California voters. In eight years of public service Brown had also built up a loyal political following, and he had skillfully used his appointment powers to build voter support among women, ethnic minorities, young people, and organized labor. Brown was not too busy, however, to realize that California political attitudes were changing, and his 1978 governor's campaign was a masterful lesson in the politics of reversal. During the course of the campaign Brown became a political chameleon who turned from a liberal, anti-business politician into a conservative, establishment-oriented figure concerned about inflation, housing and the job market. Jerry Brown's political skill lay in reading the voters' minds and adapting his policies to their ideas.

The Republican Attorney General Evelle Younger was Brown's opponent in the 1978 election. For twenty years, Younger had easily defeated all rivals for political office. In 1974, Younger was the only successful Republican candidate for state-wide constitutional office. As the Attorney General he was respected for his environmental policies and his vigorous protection of consumer rights. Neither Governor Brown nor Attorney General Younger faced significant opposition in the June primary elections. Younger's only opponent was former Los Angeles Police Chief Ed Davis, an arch conservative who did not appeal to a wide range of voters. Younger won handily. Brown had no well-known opposition and won without much effort.

The most significant issue in the primary was an initiative, Proposition 13. Howard Jarvis and Paul Gann, veteran political lobbyists and sporadic candidates for public office, conducted a well-organized campaign to reduce property tax assessments and cut back on state spending. Initially, few California politicians took the Jarvis-Gann initiative seriously. Jarvis, a Los Angeles based real estate investor and business tycoon, had failed in every previous political effort. Gann, a former used-car salesman, looked, acted, and talked like he was still selling used cars. The success of "Proposition 13", as the Jarvis-Gann bill was known, resulted from the tremendous grass-roots response by California's voters. In every city and county taxpayers walked the streets to garner signatures for the initiative. The measure qualified for the ballot with an overwhelming 1.2 million signatures.

The Jarvis-Gann initiative was both a radical and conservative solution to California's economic problems. It set property taxes at no more than 1% of the market value of a piece of property, but since it applied to business property as well there were huge tax savings for landlords and business interests. Governor Brown believed that Proposition 13 had little chance of passing, and he predicted that the voters would decisively defeat it. What Brown failed to realize was the level of anti-government feeling in California. In the aftermath of the Watergate scandals, voters were suspicious of government policies. Californians not only demanded a new accountability from the state, but they also advocated extensive cuts in education, libraries, parks and general public services. No longer was just welfare cheating an issue: suddenly politicians found themselves defending all government services as well.

In June, 1978 Proposition 13 was approved by a landslide margin of almost 2 million votes. Jerry Brown had campaigned extensively against the Jarvis-Gann initiative and his Republican opponent Evelle Younger strongly supported it. The success of Proposition 13 was the first sign that Governor Brown was in political trouble. He had badly misjudged the tax-cutting ideas of California voters, but Brown responded instantly to this unexpected shift in the political winds. In one of the most dramatic turnabouts in California politics, Jerry Brown not only immediately endorsed Proposition 13, but also vowed to carry out its every provision. He appointed a commission to propose ways of making California government more efficient and to suggest economy minded reforms for the state.

To demonstrate his support of a new economy in government, Brown imposed a freeze on state hiring, banned pay raises for California employees, cut cost-of-living increases for welfare recipients, and urged the state legislature to use surplus funds to help finance local government projects. Brown also wisely disassociated himself from the heavy spending policies of his father Governor Edmund G. (Pat) Brown. Another important change in Brown's politics occurred when he began campaigning for the fall election in grass roots cities like Eureka, Santa Cruz, Santa Rosa, Susanville and Pismo Beach. Startled restaurant patrons looked up one evening in Grover City's Quarterdeck restaurant and found an animated Jerry Brown explaining his programs to a group of local ranchers.

In the 1978 general election campaign Governor Brown took a strong law and order stand. He also spent an inordinate amount of time defending his appointment of minorities, women, and political newcomers to state office. Labor leaders were reminded that Governor Brown supported legislation requiring stronger safety measures and equal employment guidelines. In fact, Governor Brown developed such a conservative political image that the Americans for Democratic Action, a liberal pressure group, openly accused him of political opportunism. His opponent Evelle Younger maintained that Brown was the worst governor in California history, citing Brown's appointment of liberal justices like Rose Bird to the California Supreme Court, his failure to construct new freeways or repair old ones, and his no-growth economic policies which had alienated large segments of the California voting populations.

Brown's sudden change of political philosophy worked. Despite Younger's criticisms, Brown was reelected by an overwhelming plurality of 1.3 million votes. The majority of Democratic candidates for public office fared well. However, Brown's lieutenant-governor, Mervyn Dymally, was defeated by Republican candidate Mike Curb. A recording executive for MGM records who became a millionaire record producer, Curb was an arch-conservative with the good looks of a Hollywood movie star. Jerry Brown and Mike Curb disagreed on almost every major political issue and when Jerry Brown left the state to campaign in national politics, Curb made appointments and set policies as if he were the governor. This warfare hampered the political career of both politicians. As one knowledgeable critic remarked: "The Jerry and Mike show was a lesson in juvenile politics, and the voters sent the governor and lieutenant-governor into early retirement." This comment reflected the growing unhappiness with Brown and Curb's policies and suggests the main reason that both candidates were defeated in the 1982 election.

Jerry Brown's Second Administration: The Politics of Lowered Expectations, 1978–1982

Governor Brown began his second term convinced that political conservatism was necessary to survive. As a result Brown lectured state employees on the need for reductions. He proposed that 5000 jobs in state government be eliminated, and he suggested increases in state spending well below the inflation level. The California State Employee Association charged that Governor Brown was using civil servants as a whipping post, and soon public unions opposed many of the governor's programs. In his second inaugural address, Brown remarked: "We are going to squeeze and cut and trim until we reduce the cost of government." Assembly Speaker Leo McCarthy complained that the governor was mortgaging the state's future to guarantee his own political success. In an abrupt political turnabout, Brown complained about welfare chiselers and vowed to implement a business-minded approach to state government. There was no doubt that Jerry Brown was preparing his political machine for the United States Senate election in 1982. Senator S. I. Hayakawa, elected to the United States Senate in 1976 as the first Californian of Japanese ancestry, had no support from the Republican party, and Jerry Brown believed that he could easily win the U.S. Senate seat. But before he could convince the voters of his national political merits, Brown was faced with four tough years as California's governor. The task proved to be a difficult one, and in 1982 the voters retired Jerry Brown from public office. It was Brown's inconsistent political behavior in the late 1970s and early 1980s which doomed him politically.

The unpredictable nature of Brown's politics was demonstrated when he asked the California state legislature in 1979 to support an amendment to the U.S. Constitution requiring an annually balanced budget. It was presumptious for a governor to suggest such an amendment, and it reflected Brown's insatiable quest for political recognition. The federally balanced budget was a popular political issue, and one designed to win a number of voters. In fact, Brown believed that the federally balanced budget was the main political issue of the 1980s. This shift in ideology prompted liberals to attack Governor Brown for pandering to the conservative mentality in California politics. The California legislature, however, dealt Brown a resounding defeat by voting against his proposal and scolding the governor for advocating programs that were beyond his constitutional prerogatives.

Jerry Brown was building another presidential challenge, and to some national Democrats he seemed a viable alternative to President Jimmy Carter. But Brown soon learned that it was not possible to play both presidential and gubernatorial politics without weakening his state support. California Republicans began attacking Brown as a political opportunist because they were worried that he might effectively challenge Ronald Reagan for the presidency. Because of Brown's national political ambitions, the California legislature turned on him and vetoed a number of his bills. The legislative vetoes were designed to embarrass Brown and to call attention to his failure to deal with the problems of the Golden State.

In 1979 Brown was concerned that his former liberal constituency might desert him because of his new positions on many issues. Consequently, he appointed Tom Hayden, a former organizer for the Students For A Democratic Society organizer and now a community organizer, to two state commissions. Hayden's wife Jane Fonda was nominated to serve on the California Arts Council, and a partisan political debate broke out in Los Angeles because of her involvement in the anti-Vietnam war movement. The Hayden-Fonda appointments backfired because they were not popular with either liberals or conservatives, and Governor Brown's blatant use of patronage to woo liberal defectors rankled his former followers. The sudden emergence of a conservative political philosophy in Brown's governor's policies bothered his closest political advisers.

By 1979 Governor Brown's rhetoric and political positions were very similar to those of Governor Reagan in 1967. Brown talked like a fiscal conservative, and he began wearing three piece suits with Wing-Tip shoes. Political cartoonists poked fun at Brown's inability to maintain a consistent political stance on most issues. The *Chicago Sun Times* columnist Mike Royko nicknamed Brown "Governor Moonbeam" and shrewdly pointed out that Jerry Brown didn't listen to his political advisers. In the "Doonesbury" cartoon strip, Gary Trudeau criticized Brown's penny-pinching attitudes by suggesting that the governor was going to hire the Mafia because they were "cost efficient." Trudeau's strip labeled Brown as a "flake" and constantly made fun of Brown's policies. In a more sensitive vein, Trudeau criticized California's governor for not giving straight-forward answers to important political questions.

Prior to challenging President Carter for the Democratic nomination, Brown took a vacation to Africa with rock singer Linda Ronstadt. Although there were rumors about the couple's impending marriage they were no more than good friends. When Brown and Ronstadt arrived in Nairobi, reporters were waiting impatiently to cross the border to Uganda to cover the overthrow of dictator Idi Amin. Suddenly the bored news media descended upon Brown and Ronstadt, and they were world-wide news. Ronstadt, an intelligent singer-businesswoman, voraciously read the *Wall Street Journal* and *New York Times* European edition on the trip. She also disagreed with many of Governor Brown's ideas. During their relationship the press often criticized Ronstadt as an "air-head" who was just along for the fun. During the African tour it was Brown who appeared frivolous when he left Ronstadt to meditate and talk politics. She was so disgusted with the so-called "vacation" that she rarely saw Brown after returning to Los Angeles. The significance of the African trip is that Brown received an inordinate amount of negative political press. The Democratic party was also concerned that by traveling openly with an unmarried woman he was endangering his chances for the Democratic presidential nomination.

The Politics of Failure: Jerry Brown's 1980 Presidential Campaign

In January, 1980 Jerry Brown launched his campaign for the presidency. He entered the Iowa Caucus debates against President Carter and Massachusetts' Senator Teddy Kennedy. The strategy devised by Brown's campaign managers hinged upon debating President Carter, but the Iranian hostage crisis forced the President to cancel the debate. Brown then flew from one small Iowa town to another, exorting the citizens to support his people-oriented campaign. In Dubuque, citizens seemed to reflect the opinion of most Iowa voters when they made it very clear that they had no interest in Brown's candidacy. As he left the Dubuque high school auditorium Brown remarked: "Well, if you don't feel you can vote for me . . . at least don't vote for those other two (Carter and Kennedy)." Ignored by midwestern voters, Brown brought his arguments to New Hampshire. At candidate nights in New Hampshire cities, the voters response was colder than the weather. After receiving only 10% of the New Hampshire vote, Brown boarded a Greyhound bus for the trip to Maine.

Brown's closest friends and political advisers urged him to drop out of the presidential race. Ignoring the advice of professional politicians, Brown hired movie producer Francis Ford Coppola and rock promoter Bill Graham to produce a TV special designed to win the Wisconsin presidential preferential primary. Coppola and Graham's extravagant half-hour TV special preempted a Peter Cottontail cartoon special. Rather than eliciting support, the slick Brown TV show brought in more than 100,000 letters protesting the lifting of a children's holiday program for politics. The

Wisconsin primary was appropriately held on April Fool's Day, and Brown received 8% of the vote. In a deadpan gesture, the California governor remarked: "The lesson I take from the 1980 campaign is that the voters feel I am not ready to be President."

The 1980 presidential primaries were a disappointment to Governor Brown. In virtually every area his campaign failed to excite the voters. A good example of his inability to capitalize on popular discontent occurred when Brown sued the Three Mile Island nuclear plant for violating safety procedures. Brown's action was viewed as a public nuisance and neither the courts nor the general public accepted Brown's ideas.

When he returned to California, Brown found that his political approval rating in a Field Poll was the lowest of any governor since Culbert Olson in 1942. What Brown failed to realize in 1980 was that it was impossible to campaign for the presidency without funds, a large staff, and careful attention to detail and organization. As he traveled about the country, Brown appeared to be a bumbling political amateur whose roots were in the "flower power" revolution of the 1960s. Perhaps Brown's greatest flaw was his belief that he was singularly correct on most political issues, often despite evidence to the contrary.

The San Francisco City Hall Slayings: A Barometer of Political Change

On Monday, November 27, 1978, Mayor George Moscone drove his family station wagon to Babe Zanca's garage for minor repairs. Zanca promised the Mayor he would have the car ready that evening. They walked outside Zanca's garage and stood on the corner of Broadway and Polk, and Moscone smiled at the memories his old neighborhood brought back. The Mayor used to play basketball in the adjacent playground, but now the area was filled with singles bars like Lord Jim's with ornate, imitation Tiffany lamps, antique furniture and ferns displayed in the window. In this pleasant neighborhood a number of gay bars operated alongside the Bank of America, a record and book store, a string of restaurants, and other assorted businesses which were typical of San Francisco's neighborhood development. There seemed to be nothing unusual about this Monday morning, but, later, at 10:56 the Mayors' bodyguard called the San Francisco Police Department to report that Mayor George Moscone had been assassinated. The killer was ex-supervisor Dan White, who had calmly walked down a city hall corridor after killing Moscone and shot Supervisor Harvey Milk as well. The slayings of Mayor Moscone and Supervisor Milk provide an important example of changes taking place in California society. The tragic city hall slayings occurred as a result of the alternate life style of many San Franciscans and the tensions which resulted from this demographic revolution.

When Dan White shot Moscone and Milk, he imagined that he was John Wayne riding in from the range to free San Francisco from the gays, ethnics, and alternate lifestyle folks who infested the city. White, a native San Franciscan, acted out a fantasy which many Californians talked about, bringing back the good old days. Consequently, much of the controversy over the Moscone-Milk slayings centered around the new political forces in California.

In order to understand the significance of the Moscone-Milk killings, it is necessary to analyze the political background of the people involved in this tragic event. Dan White, a native San Franciscan, was an Irish-Catholic who the city rewarded with police and fire department employment. It seemed traditional for the Irish to somehow finish a little better than anyone else in city government tests. George Moscone, an Italian-Catholic, once remarked to his barber that his hair must be cut so he didn't look so Italian. This remark indicates Moscone's preference of appealing to all groups. Soon Moscone became a part of the century old tradition of Italian involvement in city government. Harvey Milk, a transplanted New Yorker, was one of San Francisco's leading gay politicians, and his career was illustrative of the changes coming over city politics. The careers of these three politicians reveal a great deal about the new California in the late 1970s.

George Moscone and the Italian Catholic Democratic Tradition

Like many San Franciscans George Moscone grew up in an Italian family that prided itself on sending their sons and daughters to St. Ignatius High School and then to the University of San Francisco. Eventually, young George graduated from the Hastings College of Law and entered private practice. He married a local girl, Gina Bondanza, and began a successful law practice. It was John Kennedy's entrance into national politics which persuaded Moscone to run in 1963 for a seat on the San Francisco Board of Supervisors. By 1966 Moscone was elected to the California State Senate, and he soon established an excellent reputation as a liberal Democrat committed to civil rights. For eight years Senator Moscone served with distinction in Sacramento, and he developed into a mature and shrewd politician. During his second year in the state senate, Moscone was chosen as the floor leader by the Democratic majority, and he became an articulate spokesperson against Governor Reagan's conservative political ideas.

In 1975 Joe Alioto was completing his second term as San Francisco's Mayor, and George Moscone actively sought the Democratic party nomination to succeed Alioto. After a hotly contested election Moscone was forced into a December, 1975, runoff in which he defeated archconservative John Barbagelata. In January, 1976, Moscone took office pledging to keep the streets safe and return the warmness of the "old San Francisco." Crime increased so dramatically during Moscone's first year as Mayor that by February, 1977, metal detectors and window bars made the San Francisco City Hall appear like an armed fortress. Moscone governed a city unsure of its political future and badly divided over the proposed solutions to its problems.

Another important political figure in this period was Dianne Feinstein. When the Milk-Moscone assassinations took place she was President of the San Francisco Board of Supervisors, and she was selected to act as the Mayor after the killings. In 1979 Feinstein became the first woman elected as the city's chief executive. Her wide range of political interests, coupled with an intricate knowledge of city politics, made Feinstein an important figure. In the aftermath of the tragic assassinations, she held the city together with her calm stewardship.

The tragedy of Moscone's candidacy was that he represented the old-style San Francisco politician. By 1975 ethnic minorities, gay activists, Irish-Catholic pressure groups, and traditional business interests were all vying for political influence. The back-slapping patronage of the past was no longer a significant part of San Francisco's political climate. The mayor now had to be an individual who could balance many interest groups and still retain a consensus of local political opinion.

George Moscone's election was the result of a coalition of blacks from the Hunter's Point district, the Fillmore and the Western Addition, the Spanish-speaking vote from the Mission district, and gay voters from the Haight Ashbury and Noe Valley. Although Moscone was elected Mayor by only 4,443 votes, it was his liberal, ethnic-oriented political campaign which brought him to power.

As San Francisco's Mayor, George Moscone was not the leader and politician that Joe Alioto had been in the late 1960s and early 1970s. After a year in office, Moscone's only real accomplishment was preventing the San Francisco Giants baseball team from moving to Toronto. In fact, Moscone was so inept that during the summer of 1977 John Barbegelata presented a petition to recall the Mayor. The right-wing political mentality which guided Barbegelata's thinking prompted him to argue that the city's worst elements were behind Mayor Moscone. The voters responded by overwhelmingly defeating the recall petition. Mayor Moscone was usually seen drinking at Henry Africa's bar and pub crawling on Union Street, or eating in one of his favorite restaurants rather than engaging in city business. One political observer was astounded to find out how little Moscone knew about San Francisco government. Yet, this was the historic role of the San Francisco Mayor. From the 19th century, when city bosses such as David Broderick and Blind Chris Buckley controlled the destiny of San Francisco, into the colorful 20th century when mayors Eugene Schmitz and James "Sunny Jim" Rolph ignored San Francisco politics, there was a long established tradition of benign neglect. San Francisco Mayors were not expected to mind the store, and George Moscone followed this venerable political tradition.

Harvey Milk: The Queen of Castro Street

Harvey Milk, a New Yorker, arrived in San Francisco in 1969 following his lover Jack McKinley. Milk, experienced in business, had a dramatic, artistic temperament. His hair was shoulder-length in the fashion of the 1960s, and he wore love beads. Harvey settled among the remnants of the hippie subculture in the Haight-Ashbury. Milk fit easily into the free-thinking milieu surrounding the city. In 1970 Harvey tired of the city and he returned to New York. The move was a temporary one, and Milk followed his new lover, Scott Smith, back to San Francisco. They set up housekeeping in the Italian dominated North Beach section and were no different than thousands of other gay couples living openly in San Francisco.

At about the same time a political revolution was quietly taking place at 18th and Castro in San Francisco as a gay business and political community emerged. Harvey Milk, with a one thousand dollar investment, opened Castro Cameras and became a small businessman with no apparent interest in politics. One day while watching the Watergate hearings in the summer of 1973, Harvey began considering a political career. It was a ludicrous thought, Milk stated to a friend, for a 42 year old Jewish homosexual with a ponytail and a small business to consider running for public office.

But Harvey Milk was concerned that gays were not receiving fair treatment in the city. After unsuccessful campaigns for supervisor in 1973 and 1975, Milk ran a third time in 1977. By this time supervisors were elected by districts, and this was the catalyst to Milk's political success. As a candidate in District 5, Milk ran in an area embracing the Haight-Ashbury, the Duboce triangle, Noe Valley and the Castro neighborhoods. It was a young, predominantly gay area populated by well-educated, financially secure, professional people. Milk ran against Rick Stokes, who Mayor Moscone supported, and the winner was to be the first openly gay city official in America. Stokes was a formidable candidate, but Milk concentrated upon the declining civil liberties for gays. The *San Francisco Chronicle* endorsed Milk's campaign, and he proved to be a tough campaigner. The Reverend Jim Jones of the People's Temple also supported Milk's election bid, and People's Temple workers distributed Milk's campaign literature in the Haight Ashbury. After an overwhelming victory, Harvey was troubled by the adulation and he humorously called himself San Francisco's "number one Queen."

The Harvey Milk who was sworn in at City Hall was a remade person. The pony tail and the rumpled clothes were replaced by a short haircut and conservative, if somewhat threadbare, suits. Milk announced that he no longer smoked marijuana or frequented the gay bath houses. With the vigor of a recent convert, Milk threw himself into San Francisco politics. Milk developed organizational skills and the ability to swing votes in the direction of his causes. Within a year the Castro Supervisor gained a reputation as a knowledgeable tough-minded politician.

Dan White: The Blue Collar City Servant

Dan White decided to run for the San Francisco Board of Supervisors, because he believed that the blue collar, Irish-Catholic worker was not properly represented in the city's changing social-political climate. White attended St. Elizabeth's Grammar School and Riordan High School, and like many young San Francisco Irish-Catholics he eventually became a city policeman. Later he switched to the Fire Department.

During his years at Riordan High, White developed a reputation as a tough guy and an exceptional athlete. While attending high school White often fantasized about eventually living in Ireland. It was White's fascination with the Irish mystique which offers an important insight into his character. He could not accept many of the changes coming over San Francisco, and the Irish fantasy was a convenient means of ignoring the new forces.

Another important change in San Francisco politics which affected Dan White's career was the election of supervisors by district. The demand for district elections was largely the work of Calvin Welch, a Haight Ashbury political activist, who reasoned that local neighborhoods were not receiving a fair share of city services. Welch organized the Citizens for Representative government, and in November, 1976, district elections were approved by San Francisco voters. In District 8, the area that would elect Dan White, there was a 56% vote for district elections. District 8 was a strange mixture of neighborhoods divided by two freeways. It included Visitation Valley, Crocker-Amazon, the Portola and the Excelsoir. These areas were blue collar, lower middle-class neighborhoods either forgotten or ignored by city government.

By the time he decided to enter San Francisco politics, Dan White was a fireman with liberal tendencies in local politics. White was also shrewd enough to realize that he could not be elected without professional political advice. As a result White sought out Goldie Judge, a middle aged woman, who was a political activist in Visitation Valley. For years Judge was a minor league political boss in local politics, and her power was demonstrated when Mayor Moscone cultivated her friendship. In May, 1977, a friend introduced Goldie to Dan White, and they discussed his chances to be elected a supervisor. It was after meeting Dan's wife Mary Ann that Goldie realized Dan White could be elected a supervisor. Not only was White a native San Franciscan, but he had the boyish good looks and a record of city service that would appeal to local voters.

By mid-June, 1977 13 candidates were actively campaigning for the supervisor seat in District 8. The district had 60,000 residents but only 28,000 were registered voters. Dan White's closest rival, Len Heinz, had been Dan's English teacher at Riordan High School. Heinz soon raised the issue that White did not live in District 8, and this precipitated a major debate on the question of White's residency. But this change did not dissuade District 8 voters from electing White.

The supervisor's position paid only $9600 a year, and when Dan White resigned his $18,000 a year job in the San Francisco Fire Department he did not realize that it would precipitate a serious financial crisis. In a well-publicized ceremony, White informed Chief Andy Casper that "It saddens me to turn my badge over to you." After he had won the supervisory seat a number of White's close friends counseled him on the financial consequences of public service. These financial problems eventually forced White to resign as a supervisor.

Once he settled into his supervisor's job White was uncomfortable with political power. He was also easily persuaded by Quentin Kopp and Dianne Feinstein to support their political programs. It was not so much that White was easily manipulated, but he had a "good old boy" mentality which prompted him to do anything for a friend. Supervisors Kopp and Feinstein recognized this character trait and exploited it. White was impressed with Dianne Feinstein who was elected President of the San Francisco Board of Supervisors. Not only was she a brilliant politician with a strong sense of local issues, but she displayed a graciousness and charm which attracted the lower-middle-class, blue-collar mentality of Dan White.

Seventeen Days in November, 1978: The City Hall Killings

Although the White's had opened a restaurant, the Hot Potato, in the tourist infested Pier 39 complex, there were still financial problems from the start of White's career. After more than a year as a supervisor, the pressures of finances, fatherhood and an inept political record led Dan White to resign his seat as a San Francisco supervisor on Friday, November 10. That evening Dan and his wife Mary Ann went out to dinner and celebrated, but the mercurical temperament and inconsistent behavior of Dan White soon set a series of events in motion which resulted in the killings of Mayor George Moscone and Supervisor Harvey Milk.

White's resignation provided Mayor Moscone with the opportunity to appoint someone from District 8 who would support the Mayor's programs. White seethed with rage as he watched Mayor Moscone benefit politically from his resignation. But White's dramatic departure from San Francisco politics was soon swept off the front pages by the tragic events surrounding the Reverend Jim Jones and his one thousand followers who had fled to a remote section of Guyana. For years Jones had received favorable treatment from liberal Democrats like George Moscone. Jones' People's Temple was considered a model program in rehabilitating drug addicts. There were rumors about Jones' strange behavior for many years, but he organized his followers to crush any opposition to his religious schemes. San Francisco's liberal-radical community had been co-opted by Jones, and when Representative Leo Ryan of San Mateo, an area just South of San Francisco, announced that he was going to investigate the People's Temple, there was a rush to cover the story. Dan White was upset that during his biggest political moment he was suddenly old news.

Dan White was an amateurish politician who found it difficult to operate in the jungle of San Francisco politics. He was so inept that Mayor Moscone's advisers reasoned that it would be political suicide to reappoint White to his old seat. White's followers began a series of demonstrations in front of San Francisco's City Hall.

San Francisco Mayor Dianne Feinstein

However, on Sunday, November 19, the news that Representative Ryan had been killed in Guyana upstaged White's fight to reenter city politics. Sunday's normally placid television coverage became a media event as a massacre of the Congressman and his party was reported, followed by suggestions of a mass suicide by Rev. Jones People's Temple followers. It was a horrifying story which riveted attention on a well-known local white preacher with a predominantly Black congregation who had apparently gone insane.

That evening Dan White met two of his close political aides at the Hot Potato and stuffed envelopes with requests urging his supporters to pressure the Mayor into reappointing Dan White to his former seat. The following morning the *San Francisco Chronicle* confirmed that hundreds of members of the People's Temple had stood in line to commit suicide by drinking a cyanide-mixed Kool Aid. Dan White was busy in the midst of this news, seeking a restraining order to prevent Mayor Moscone from appointing someone else to his seat. The controversy over the People's Temple and Dan White's change of heart subsided over the Thanksgiving weekend. During that time Mayor Moscone confided to his old friend, Assemblyman Willie Brown, that he was fearful that a crackpot would take his life. Little did Moscone realize that one of his close political colleagues would assassinate him.

After a relaxing four-day weekend George Moscone returned to work on November 27, 1978 to resume directing San Francisco's city business. There was no longer any question that Mayor Moscone would reappoint White. The political consensus was that Dan White was a liability and that he would hamper the Mayor's future political objectives. This decision prompted Dan White to shave meticulously, shower, dress, load his gun and calmly enter City Hall shortly after 10 A.M. to assassinate Mayor Moscone and Supervisor Milk. The tragic deaths of these two San Francisco politicians, however, was a small part of the continuing drama. In White's subsequent murder trial, San Francisco politics, not justice, influenced the course of California history.

The Trial of Dan White: The Lessons of Big City Politics

When Dan White's trial for the murders of Mayor Moscone and Supervisor Milk began, five months had elapsed since the tragic murders. Once the trial began it was plagued by an inept San Francisco Police Department investigation and a timid prosecution. In fact, both the prosecution and the defense had a number of problems presenting an error-free case.

The earliest prosecution error occurred when Dan White turned himself into the North Station branch of the San Francisco Police Department. After he was disarmed, White was taken into an interrogation room and handcuffed. A call was made to the SFPD Homicide office, and Dan White waited for Inspector Frank Falzon to begin the investigation. Falzon asked Inspector Eddie Erdelatz to witness the proceedings. It was a strange moment as the two Inspectors were placed in the uncomfortable position of investigating a murder allegedly committed by a former San Francisco policeman.

The initial investigation by Falzon and Erdelatz was sloppy and imprecise because they believed that it was a perfect case. Although both inspectors acted in a highly professional manner and were exceptionally competent investigators, they were lulled into poor police work by what they believed to be Dan White's obvious guilt. In addition White was extraordinarily cooperative with the investigators. Rather than asking tough questions, Falzon asked obvious ones. The Inspector also interrupted Dan White and often added personal comments as the interrogation proceeded, and this prevented White from giving a full confession. Once the trial started, White's defense team was able to pick apart the sloppy police work. As Dan White's trial began, no one, except his defense team, believed that he had a reasonable defense. The spectacular trial, however, demonstrated how incorrect local observers were when they predicted that Dan White would escape with no less than a life sentence without the possibility of parole.

It had been Mary Ann White's responsibility to find her husband a defense attorney. Mary Ann hired Douglas Schmidt to represent Dan. Schmidt had previously represented a young Chinese boy accused of a sensational gang-related killing spree at the Golden Dragon restaurant in San

Francisco's Chinatown. All of the gang members were found guilty of first degree murder and given life sentences, except for Schmidt's client who was convicted of a lesser charge. Schmidt was only 32 years old, a transplanted Michigan resident who had practiced law almost for a decade in San Francisco.

After talking with Dan White, Schmidt was uncertain about his defense strategy. White was not mentally deranged, he was able to distinguish right from wrong, and he had not killed in self-defense. Clearly, Schmidt needed some time to consider his defense strategy. White's closest advisers urged him to get rid of the young attorney, but Schmidt carefully prepared a number of pretrial motions which would buy some time to investigate the crime further.

Once the jury was selected, Dan White's trial began. After a lengthy description of White's character by the defense including some examples of heroism while a fireman, and a list of his contributions to city government, the Prosecutor Tommy Norman then described the events leading up to White's resignation as a supervisor and the financial strain which prompted the killings. The description of Dan giving up his job as a fireman, Mary Ann's pregnancy and the long hours needed to run the Hot Potato restaurant by the defense touched a responsive chord with the jury. They could identify with Dan White's problems and understand the forces which triggered the crime. The prosecution was never able to match the defense attorney's skill.

In quiet, almost understated tones, Schmidt informed the jury that White had no intention of harming anyone, let alone committing murder. It was the prosecution who would have to prove that Dan White acted out a well-planned and premeditated scheme to kill Mayor Moscone and Supervisor Milk. The prosecution presented a dull case. As Prosecutor Norman painstakingly re-created the events which led to the murders, Dan White showed no sign of emotion. Whether he was mentally ill, as some court room witnesses believed, or was simply acting out a grand court-room charade was difficult to decide.

As the evidence was presented, Prosecutor Tommy Norman did a methodical but competent job. He guided Mayor Dianne Feinstein carefully through the day of the killings. He presented the physical and circumstantial evidence for a first-degree-murder conviction, and he was careful not to antagonize the jurors. The trial, however, took a turn against the prosecution when Frank Falzon testified about White's confession. Judge Walter Calcagno allowed the prosecution to play a tape recording of White's confession, and Prosecutor Norman sat in stunned silence listening to the grotesque litany of events which led to Moscone and Milk's deaths. The Jury's reaction to White's tape was not one that helped the public prosecutor. The choking, emotional tones of White's voice prompted the jurors to wonder what really made Dan White kill Mayor Moscone and Supervisor Milk. Norman's case had not remotely touched on the reasons for the killings. The prosecution's case did little to sway the jurors aginst Dan White.

When Inspector Falzon took the stand, Defense Attorney Schmidt asked a number of questions which aided White's defense. Falzon described his old friend as a person who ticked like a timebomb. In a startling admission, Falzon speculated that revenge might have been a motive in White's actions. This statement hurt the prosecution's case as one of its chief witnesses suggested a reason for White's action. Prosecutor Norman sat in stunned silence as the case's chief investigator turned into a strong witness for the defense.

After calling 19 witnesses, Prosecutor Norman finally called a criminologist who clinically described how White killed George Moscone and Harvey Milk with shots to the head from a range of six inches. When Prosecutor Tommy Norman finished presenting the evidence, he was confident of a guilty verdict.

When Doug Schmidt began presenting the defense, there was a great deal of curiosity about his courtroom tactics. No one paid much attention when Schmidt asked one defense witness what type of food White ate or if he drank or smoked. Then the defense attorney concentrated on White's sporadic preference for junk food. As Schmidt presented testimony, he painted a sorrowful picture of Dan White's problems. Prosecutor Norman countered by raising questions about White's personal relationship with his aide Denise Apcar. This tactic alienated the jury and produced a great deal of sympathy for White.

It was during the second week of the trial that Schmidt's defense pinpointed why Dan White killed Mayor Moscone and Supervisor Milk. It was Twinkies, Chocolate Cupcakes, and cokes which had changed White's personality, the defense contended, and the media soon responded with mocking criticism of the killer cupcakes. In the courtroom, however, it was serious business as Dr. Marty Blinder, a brilliant Marin County forensic psychiatrist, took the stand to testify concerning Dan White's crime. Blinder's field of forensic psychiatry dealt with the relationship between law and psychiatry.

Dr. Blinder's testimony combined the intelligence of a medical doctor with the storytelling ability of a gypsy fortune teller. Blinder's description of how White gave up his usual pattern of good nutrition and exercise to feast on junk food produced the startling conclusion that the Twinkies had induced the murders. To bolster Dr. Blinder's testimony, another psychiatrist Dr. George Solomon was called by the defense. Dr. Solomon was an important figure in Dan White's defense since he had interviewed the defendant three times prior to the trial. Unlike Dr. Blinder, Solomon was a nervous man with a tendency to talk to himself. He did not have the commanding personal presence of his counterpart. But Solomon was a brilliant witness, testifying that White did show remorse for the killings. In addition, Solomon believed that White did not have the mental capacity to premeditate a deliberate act of murder. It was Dr. Solomon's testimony which placed the "killer cupcakes" or the "white sugar syndrome" into the center of the courtroom as the real killer. State law contained a provision allowing for a defense of temporary insanity due to the effects of diet.

Another important witness was Stanford University Professor Donald Lunde. Dr. Lunde, author of *Murder and Madness,* was a psychiatrist who was considered one of the best in the nation. Dr. Lunde concluded that the defendant was suffering from a form of mental illness which brought about a depressed mental state. This completed the psychiatric testimony for the defense, and Dr. Lunde provided a legal means for the jury to decide on a reduced crime.

During the fifth day of the jury deliberations a note was sent to Judge Walter Calcagno requesting the court transcripts so that the jury could review Dr. Martin Blinder's testimony. The result of this testimony was to convince the jury that White was guilty of voluntary manslaughter in the deaths of Mayor George Moscone and Supervisory Harvey Milk. The verdict was a triumph for the defense, and Schmidt broke into a broad smile after the decision was read.

It was the aftermath of the Dan White trial which revealed how San Francisco had polarized over the voluntary manslaughter verdict. Once the 5:30 news began reporting the decision in the White case, there was a strong reaction in the gay community. In the Castro an irate gay heard someone on a police band radio singing "Danny Boy," and there was a strong feeling that White's verdict was influenced by Milk's open homosexuality. An hour later an ugly mood developed in the Castro district. Harry Britt, the person who was selected to fill Milk's seat on the Board of Supervisors, called the verdict "obscene." A riot soon began. Before the night was over more than 120 people were injured. An angry mob smashed doors and windows at City Hall, and the San Francisco TAC squad aggressively cleared the area surrounding the city government buildings.

California in 1984: Was George Orwell Right?

By the summer of 1984 Republican Governor George Deukmejian was midway through his first term. A tough politician in the mold of former Governor Ronald Reagan, Deukmejian typified the California brand of conservatism which demands a high degree of accountability from government officials. In 1984 the budget submitted by Governor Deukmejian reflected careful and detailed planning. Deukmejian's $265 billion dollar proposal, the largest state budget in America, provided that more than 75% of state funds be appropriated to aid local government. Only one of every five dollars in the 1984 state budget was to finance state services. In sum, Deukmejian's fiscal package was just adequate enough to keep the state running, and this philosophy seemed to perfectly suit California's fiscally conservative mentality in the 1980s.

Although Jerry Brown is no longer an important figure in California politics, he remains an ideological free spirit. He heads an independent political pressure group in Los Angeles and continues to study public policy. There is little doubt that former Governor Brown is planning a political comeback. This seems an impossibility in 1984, but California's ability to resurrect politicians who have suffered humiliating defeats in an intriguing facet of the state's history. Since Brown continues to advocate pioneer political ideas, there is no doubt that he may once again become an attractive candidate.

As Californians prepared for the Democratic National Convention in San Francisco in the summer of 1984, strange controversies swirled about in state politics. In San Francisco there was a campaign designed to close gay bath houses because they were instrumental in spreading the dreaded disease AIDS. In Los Angeles there was concern over security and housing problems caused by the 1984 Olympic games. San Diego citizens argued that they were being overlooked by the state because their port and local transportation facilities were not up to par. The *Sacramento Bee* noted that Californians were no longer as optimistic about the future, and the once-young population of the state seemed to be settling into middle-aged conservatism. San Francisco Mayor Dianne Feinstein summed up the feeling of many Californians when she suggested that the mid-1980s was a turning point in the Golden State's history. The eternal optimism and belief in progress which had characterized much of California's past, was replaced by a new cynicism. No longer were Californians confident that they could conquer the future, and this negative feeling was reflected in the political-economic climate in the state. Old political radicals like labor leader Harry Bridges, now living in comfortable retirement, were amazed at the reactionary side of the blue-collar worker. No longer was California the liberal bastion of reform and progress in America. The 1980s had taken a toll on the liberalism, the innovative tendencies and the pioneering spirit of the California character.

Bibliographical Essay

The role of Jerry Brown in California politics is covered in a number of important books. The best book on Brown is Roger Rapoport, *California Dreaming: The Political Odyssey of Pat and Jerry Brown* (1982). Also see, Robert Pack, *Jerry Brown: The Philosopher Prince* (1978) for a particularly good analysis of Brown's first term and the people who shaped his political philosophy. For a disillusioned liberals view of Governor Brown see, J. D. Lorenz, *Jerry Brown: The Man on the White Horse* (1978). An excellent analysis of Brown's first gubernatorial campaign is Mary Ellen Leary, *Phantom Politics; Campaigning in California* (1977). The editors of *California*

Journal have analyzed Brown's career in depth and a compendium of articles and viewpoints from this journal is presented in Ed Slazman's, *Jerry Brown: High Priest and Low Politician* (1977). Jerry Bollens and G. Robert Williams, *Jerry Brown: In a Plain Brown Wrapper* (1978) is an interesting analysis of Brown's political performance through 1977.

An excellent examination at recent California history is Jackson K. Putnam, *Modern California Politics, 1917–1980* (1980). In addition a number of articles are important in analyzing recent trends in California history, see, for example, Ed Salzman, "The Brown Record," *California Journal,* IX (June, 1978), pp. 173–176, Alexander Cockburn and James Ridgeway, "The Not-So-Flaky Candidate: Tracking the 'New' Jerry Brown," *San Francisco Bay Guardian,* January 10, 1980; Leo Rennert, "Does Jerry Brown Have A Future," *California Journal,* XI (May, 1980), p. 211; and Jamie Wolf, "Looking for Jerry," *New West,* VI (April, 1981), pp. 89–93, 149–151.

An excellent analysis of California government is Charles P. Sohner, *California Government and Politics Today* (1984). On California government see, Winston Crouch, John Bollens and Stanley Scott, *California Government and Politics* (1977), John H. Culver and John C. Syer, *Power and Politics in California* (1980); James D. Driscoll, *California Legislature* (1978), Thomas R. Hoeber, Ed Salzman and Charles Price, *California Government and Politics Annual 1982–1983* (1983), and Anthony T. Quinn and Ed Salzman, *California Public Administration* (1982).

On the George Moscone, Dan White and Harvey Milk controversy see the excellent book, Mike Weiss, *Double Play: The San Francisco City Hall Killings* (1984). For cultural change in California during the 1960s, 1970s and 1980s see Howard A. DeWitt, *Van Morrison: The Mystic's Music* (1983), Blair Jackson, *The Grateful Dead: The Music Never Stopped* (1983) and Barbara Rowes, *Grace Slick: The Biography* (1980).

18

CALIFORNIA IN THE 1980s: THE GOLDEN STATE IN THE AGE OF REACTION AND FISCAL DOOM

In 1980, Ronald Reagan was elected President of the United States. As the former California governor was inaugurated in January 1981, the Golden State faced an atmosphere of economic crisis and demographic change. At President Reagan's inaugural celebration the subject of federal aid to California came up in light hearted conversation. President Reagan chuckled: "If more federal aid isn't funneled into the state it will face fiscal doom." This remark contained an element of truth. In a more serious vein, Reagan commented on the orgy of spending bankrupting California. Unwittingly, President Reagan's remark was an accurate forecast of the Golden State's future.

As the 1980s dawned political reaction and fiscal problems clouded prospects for California's growth. It was Governor Jerry Brown who sabotaged California's future. In 1980 during the last two years of his second term, Brown was more interested in the next phase of his political career than in solving California's social-economic problems. For the first time in history the richest and most populous State in the Union was on the verge of bankruptcy.

The shifting political fortunes of California political parties was another problem. The state's Democratic and Republican organizations were weak and lacked adequate campaign funds. One of the main reasons for California's difficulties was strong political personalities. Since statehood in 1850, the cult of personality had dominated politics in California. The candidate who mesmerized the electorate gained access to public office. In 1913, Progressive Governor Hiram Johnson became the first modern demagogue when he highlighted the dangers of Japanese immigration. After World War II, Richard Nixon ran for Congress exploiting the public hysteria toward Communism, radical labor unions and the unsavory influences of Hollywood. This type of politics, which was a reminder of California's past history, resurfaced in the 1980s.

Republican Governors George Deukmejian and Pete Wilson were subtle demagogues who criticized welfare, immigrants, feminists, gays and labor unions. As classic demagogues, they fueled public fears. The Democratic Speaker of the California Assembly, Willie Brown, frequently charged racism and favoritism when he criticized his Republican opponents, but they had the voter's ear.

As a result, California politics were emotional and volatile. The numerous ballot measures which targeted illegal aliens, AIDS carriers and supporters of Affirmative Action perfectly reflected the conservative political climate. Proposition 187 was the best example of this mentality. In 1995, this ballot measure attempted to control the flood of illegal aliens. The result was a heated political controversy which tore the state apart.

Willie Brown was the staunchest critic of Proposition 187. In 1980, when Brown became the Assembly Speaker, one of the themes of his leadership was to maintain the quality of life in California for the poor, ethnic minorities and immigrants. This viewpoint prompted Brown to square off in the 1980s with Republican Governor George Deukmejian. Brown represented the liberal, urban, multi-ethnic and progressive faction of Democrats, whereas Deukmejian and his successor, Governor Pete Wilson, were the spear carriers for conservative, anti-government forces. They hoped to cut taxes, state services, education and government bureaucracy.

The Reagan Mafia and Its Economic Influence Upon California in the 1980s

When Ronald Reagan was elected President and came to office in January 1981 he did everything he could to help his Republican friends. Almost a hundred Californians were appointed to top jobs in the Reagan Administration. What impact did this have upon California?

President Reagan vowed to make up for Democratic President Jimmy Carter's neglect of the Golden State. While Carter was President, he seldom consulted California politicians and very little federal money was awarded to the Golden State. Californians paid more money in federal taxes than they got back in government benefits. In the final act of humiliation, President Carter scrapped the California made B-1 bomber and announced it was no longer needed in the American military arsenal, but the Reagan Administration made plans to award massive defense contracts.

It was the Bechtel Corporation, a California company and the largest major government contractor, that received more federal funds than any other defense contractor. George Schultz, Reagan's Secretary of State, and Caspar Weinberger, the Secretary of Defense, eventually went to work for the Bechtel Corporation after leaving their government posts. By lobbying the Reagan Administration, Bechtel helped to revive the sagging local economy.

The electronics business was a new industry that benefited from Reagan's presidency. To promote the rapidly growing electronics field, the Golden State Round Table, a group of some fifty major corporations and twenty lobbyists, held monthly luncheons with members of Congress. They quickly secured lucrative government contracts. TRW, a major defense contractor, had thirteen lobbyists urging the Reagan Administration to fund their needs. FMC had eight major law firms and six lobbyists on retainer to secure government contracts. The Rockwell Corporation, the company that built the B-1 bomber, had four lobbyists, two law firms and a consultant working for federal funds. The pressure worked as California had more federal contracts awarded in the 1980s than any other state.

This is partially because California had more lobbyists, law firms and staffers working for federal funds which paid off as California was constantly near the top in federal funding. This was not surprising as three of the four men closest to President Reagan were Californians. The majority of Californians appointed to federal offices stayed on a short time and then returned to work as lobbyists to secure federal money. "The Reagan Mafia is well and alive in Washington, and we see them everywhere in California," Assembly Speaker Willie Brown remarked.

Some of President Reagan's appointees had other missions to carry out in the Golden State. The environment was dramatically affected by Reagan appointees. Secretaries of the Interior James Watt and Don Hodel allowed Yosemite Park to fall into disrepair, and they threatened the future of the redwoods. While neither Cabinet member worked for a California firm, they did support laws and government programs that benefited large California corporations. They also supported policies which tied the hands of environmentalists. Reagan appointees hurt California by favoring big business. Still, others pressured for cuts in welfare and education.

The Golden State benefited from a number of federal programs. President Reagan secured millions of dollars for water research. There were major tax breaks for the entertainment industry. The Reagan administration increased its defense spending and, as a result, the B-1 bomber and the Trident II missile were built at California's Lockheed facilities. In addition to numerous military contracts, the Bechtel Corporation benefited from President Reagan's huge peace time government contracts and substantial federal tax breaks. The old pork barrel political system of rewarding the Republican business supporters prompted Reagan to funnel millions of dollars into Governor Deukmejian's state.

The impact of the California Mafia, as Reagan's advisers were dubbed, created a mammoth defense industry. As one critic suggested, "water, guns and money" is what the Reagan

The California environment: Will it survive the Republicans in the 1980s?

Photo Courtesy: Alan Kirshner

administration showered upon California. It was enough to keep the economy prosperous and the voters conservative. But political change was in the air.

Dianne Feinstein: The 1980s and the First Decade of the Woman

On November 29, 1978, Dianne Feinstein stood before a stunned crowed outside San Francisco City Hall and eulogized Mayor George Moscone and Supervisor Harvey Milk. Just two days earlier they had been murdered by an ex-policeman turned San Francisco Supervisor, Dan White, and there was a bitter, acrimonious air in San Francisco. Feinstein's words of conciliation echoed throughout the city. She reminded the audience that like the earthquake of 1906, the city could be rebuilt from this tragedy.

Her career began in 1969 when Feinstein was elected to the San Francisco Board of Supervisors. With her electoral victory, Feinstein began redefining the role of women in California politics. She would lose two bids for the Mayor's Office before she became San Francisco's thirty eighth mayor.

By the late 1970s, Dianne Feinstein's skill as President of the San Francisco Board of Supervisors made her a logical choice for higher office. In the aftermath of Mayor Moscone's assassination, Feinstein burst into the state and national media with her thoughtful remarks on the tragedy. As a result, she was publicly endorsed for the San Francisco Mayor's position by every important local politician.

As the President of the San Francisco Board of Supervisors, Feinstein was Moscone's successor. The decade of the woman in California politics began with her ascension to the Mayor's Office. The *San Francisco Chronicle* wrote of Feinstein: "She provided a voice for the city's sorrow...she was reassuring and strong."

Feinstein attacked her job with zeal. San Francisco has a wide ranging political constituency. Downtown business people were often pitted against the neighborhoods. The ethnic minorities, the gay community and the straights all besieged City Hall with special requests. Feinstein attempted to listen to everyone. Each night she had two police officers carry a sack of mail to her car and at home she read through as many letters as possible. Feinstein realized that the error of her predecessors was in not pressuring the federal government for funds to continue city expansion.

Feinstein ingratiated herself with President Jimmy Carter. She used one of her political advisers, Dick Blum, to help her gain federal funds. The influx of federal funds helped to modernize the waterfront, expand the freeway system, accommodate tourists and modernize the jail and court systems. In 1979, she married Dick Blum, and his wealth became an asset in future campaigns.

San Francisco was a city beset with problems. The assassinations of Mayor Moscone and Supervisor Milk continued to plague the city. The gay community was outraged with the manner in which the district attorney handled the case against former police officer Dan White. There were numerous demonstrations in the predominantly gay Castro District and then on May 21, 1979, when White received a lenient sentence (seven years and eight months for the two murders) a riot broke out.

White Night was the term used to describe the violence which inundated San Francisco in the aftermath of White's conviction. When the police moved into the Castro District and beat up every gay and straight in sight, there was a major confrontation. But the gay community was not intimidated. At 11:00 P.M., a mob set fire to a row of police cars parked near City Hall. The police then cleared the Civic Center Plaza and dispersed the crowd. The police were out of control as they rampaged against gay spectators.

Mayor Feinstein met with San Francisco Police Chief Charles Gain and tried to end the violence. The White Night riot occurred on what would have been Supervisor Harvey Milk's forty-ninth birthday. It prompted Feinstein to play close attention to the needs of the gay community. Not only did Feinstein realize that there were serious differences between the gay community and the police, but she actively began a program to reeducate the police. Homophobia was a problem for the SFPD and Feinstein was determined to provide a bridge to the gay community. But she found herself criticized by the police for doing too much and by the gay community for doing too little. It was a no win political situation

The fallout from the White Night riot was a blow to Mayor Feinstein's political career. Supervisor Quentin Kopp announced that he would run in the 1979 San Francisco Mayor's election. Feinstein had already lost two previous mayoral elections, but in November 1979, she entered the Emerald Ballroom of the Hilton Hotel to give a victory speech. She had finally been elected San Francisco Mayor but it was a hollow victory. Feinstein won the election but had blown a thirty-five point lead in the polls to finish first. However, she had failed to win a majority of the voters and faced a runoff election.

A gay candidate for mayor, David Scott, drew enough votes to force the runoff. In the five weeks before the runoff, Feinstein courted the gay community. When the final election results came in Feinstein edged Kopp 42% to 40% in the runoff.

A series of delicate negotiations took place with David Scott and the gay vote swung behind Feinstein. Finally, on December 11, 1979, she was elected mayor on her third try 54% to 46%.

As the 1980s dawned, Mayor Feinstein's career was on a bumpy road to success. The gay community demanded the passage of city sponsored domestic partnerships which would allow gays health insurance and other benefits that spouses in traditional marriages enjoyed. Finally, in 1982 the domestic partners bill passed.

The following year Feinstein began her reelection campaign. The November 1983 campaign was a rocky one. Seven months before the election a recall movement resulted in a special election. The $400,000 special election was the result of hostility towards her support of the gay community, senior citizens programs, women's rights and her non-traditional appointments. The recall failed when 80% of the voters kept Mayor Feinstein in office.

After winning her second term as San Francisco's Mayor, Feinstein brought the 1984 Democratic National Convention to the city. The Democratic presidential candidacy of Walter Mondale was a disastrous one, but the San Francisco Democratic Convention caused Feinstein to emerge as a candidate for the Vice Presidency. A story in *Time* magazine listed Feinstein's strengths and weaknesses and asked the question, "Why Not A Woman?" The Democrats eventually nominated New York's Geraldine Ferraro. In her own way, Mayor Feinstein helped to launch women in national politics as she pushed the Democratic National Committee to nominate a woman for vice president.

When the 1984 presidential election resulted in a forty-nine state Republican landslide, Mayor Feinstein was the winner. She benefited because the press identified her as "a responsible and far sighted Democratic leader."

For the remainder of the 1980s Mayor Feinstein's administrative skill and personal political touch increased her popularity. During her nine years as San Francisco Mayor she was known as a hands on administrator. As she rode around the city, Feinstein wrote in a small notebook and turned out the "Mayor's Action Memos."

Mayor Feinstein steered San Francisco toward the political center and helped lay to rest many of the controversies dividing the city. The city grew from 670,000 to 750,000 and young, white professionals replaced the Italian, Irish-Catholic, Mexican-American, Asian and Jewish families that dominated the local economy. Few people knew that Feinstein paid weekly visits to Hunter's Point to visit with black school children.

Crime was another San Francisco problem. Feinstein had a long standing fascination with law and order. As a result, she placed 350 more police on the streets, campaigned for controls on handguns and presented a detailed research package to the California Legislature on law and order problems. It was common to see Mayor Feinstein riding in a police car to answer a reported crime. Citizens were astonished to see her at crime scenes.

Among her most publicized policies was the handling of the AIDS crisis. Randy Shilts, a *San Francisco Chronicle* reporter, began publicizing the "gay cancer" and there was a strong outcry for research funds. Mayor Feinstein ordered a shutdown of the gay bathhouses and the city's director of public health services helped to launch a $20 million educational and health program.

The strongest aspect of Mayor Feinstein's years was her handling of city finances. In September 1978, Feinstein discovered a $77 million gap in the city budget. In just three months she ordered a hiring freeze and delayed city construction thereby quickly balancing the budget.

A few weeks after Mayor Feinstein left office, the California Democratic Party organized a pool of women to run for political office. Dianne Feinstein was ready to plunge into the 1990s as a candidate for major public office. In time, she would win a U.S. Senate seat and continue the decade of the woman into the 1990s.

Political Changes in the 1980s and Onward

During the 1980s, cataclysmic changes in California society altered the direction of the Golden State. The most obvious change was the rise of a young, conservative electorate. The "baby boomers" were coming of age in a declining economy. The generation born in 1946 and beyond found it difficult to make incomes stretch into a comfortable life style. The cost of housing, the instability of the job market, the crisis in immigration and the decline in government services made this generation skeptical of the future.

What the term baby boomers defined was a highly educated segment of the population who believed they would have a greater income than their parents. When they entered the job market they found out quickly that they could not achieve their parent's success. So they compensated by living highly and spending money by using their credit cards.

As a result, the baby boomers had little allegiance to political parties. Neither Republican nor Democratic values influenced them. They lived an ostentatious life style bringing back expensive suits, cocktail music and a demand for less government. Suddenly welfare, education and social security were under attack. The baby boomers saw the job market shrinking and people working longer. They found it difficult to purchase homes in the inflated California real estate market. Boomers criticized social security, employment tenure and expanding welfare programs.

What these attitudes resulted in was political support for the conservative and often ethnically unfair politics of Governor Deukmejian. By the early 1990s, baby boomers flocked to Governor Pete Wilson who played to the prejudices and preconceived notions of the baby boomers. One important contribution of the boomers was to point out excessive government spending.

One example of a needless expenditure of funds took place on January 6, 1982 when California's legislators returned to the Assembly and found brand new mahogany desks, lush green draperies, expensive crystal chandeliers and other furnishings to make their chamber comfortable. Even the bathroom had been renovated and the comfort of each Assembly member was assured. A silver toilet paper holder was the final touch in the Assembly bathrooms. Immediately, Republicans complained that Speaker Brown was abusing his fiscal power.

Speaker Brown didn't apologize for spending the money. "We need to be comfortable to do our work," Brown informed the press. This incident was a good indication of the charming, often arm twisting, political style of the Democratic Assembly Speaker, and it also suggested his penchant for taking credit for any change, major or minor, in state government.

Jesse Unruh, the former Democratic Assembly Speaker, gave Governor George Deukmejian some advice when he told him to give Brown the credit for some of California's advances. "You'll work with Brown better if you let him take some of the limelight," Unruh remarked. Not only did Deukmejian take the advice but he hammered out a workable political relationship with Brown. With the Democrats controlling the Assembly, Governor Deukmejian let it be known that he would compromise.

So when the Assembly convened, Speaker Brown talked about the need for bipartisan cooperation to bring the state out of its economic quagmire. Brown had been the Speaker for a little more than a year when he faced some difficult problems. The most serious of which was imminent bankruptcy. There had to be an immediate plan to reorganize state finances. But there were other problems.

Reapportionment was another difficulty facing the Democrats. In 1980, as the census mandated, legislative districts were redrawn. Both Republicans and Democrats played politics with reapportionment. As California redrew its legislative districts, Speaker Brown used his power to create a Democratic advantage in California's Congressional districts. Many of Brown's friends in the California Legislature ran for and won these new Congressional seats. When Democrats Howard Berman, Mel Levine and Rick Lehman were elected to the House of Representatives in 1982, they thanked Willie Brown for his help.

With the exception of the Governor, the Assembly Speaker is the most powerful person in California government. After serving a long apprenticeship, Brown made a run for Assembly Speaker. He was a protégé of former Speakers Jesse Unruh and Bob Moretti, and, as a result, he was able to solicit both Republican and Democratic votes successfully before he was elected Speaker. To maintain that power, however, Brown had to continually modify his stand on political, economic and social issues. The key issues were invariably financial ones.

California Politics: Financial and Political Problems on the Eve of the 1982 Election

In 1982, Republicans nominated George Deukmejian for governor, and they were confident of victory due to the Golden State's financial crisis. The two term incumbent Democratic Governor Jerry Brown left the state house with California near bankruptcy. Not only had Brown ignored the dwindling economic plight of the Golden State, but he also evolved from a staunch liberal into a middle of the road conservative.

Governor Brown was a self-centered politician who had little interest in California's future. He was self righteous, judgmental and prone to making emotional statements. Brown had rhetoric but never substance. The cult of personality fit Brown's style and his demagogic appeal got him elected governor twice. His behavior was so destructive that he was never able to win another important California political office. The voters saw Brown for what he was, an opportunist.

One of the problems with Brown's years as governor was his frequent absences from state business. Invariably, he was off running for the United States Senate, and he had little time for state business. This led to internal political dispute with Lieutenant Governor, Mike Curb.

The Lieutenant Governor's Office is one of symbolic power not of substance. He has few duties but he does fill in for the governor when he is out of state or busy with other affairs. Mike Curb had the good looks of a movie star, a political position just to the right of most Republicans and a penchant for calling contentious press conferences. A mogul in the entertainment business, Curb was known for his shrewd business deals in the recording and movie industries. While producing movies like "Hot Rods To Hell" and records like the Hondells' "Go Little Honda," Curb became rich and politically connected. Soon he was the darling of the radical right.

When Governor Brown left Sacramento, Curb stepped in to sign or veto bills, to act ceremonially as governor and to offer political advice. Curb attempted to use the Lieutenant Governor's office as a stepping stone to the Republican gubernatorial nomination. He failed miserably. But during the Brown Administration, Curb acted as the governor for more than 200 days. However, neither the Republican Party nor the voters paid much attention to this Los Angeles based demagogue.

The Curb-Brown feud created a California which was more like a comedy act than a political arena. Lieutenant Governor Curb loved to veto bills that Brown would have signed and sign bills that he would have vetoed. In this comic opera political atmosphere, Brown frequently hurried back to California to overturn what the Lieutenant Governor had done to change the direction of Democratic politics.

Californians were becoming increasingly conservative and didn't care for the Democratic message of spend, spend, spend or welfare, welfare, welfare. Conservative Republican and Democratic lawmakers responded to the voter's plea for responsibility in government.

This resulted in cuts in education, mental health facilities, roads, state parks and welfare funds. Who was responsible for the mess? Most critics suggested that Governor Jerry Brown destroyed Democratic chances for electing a governor due to his handling of the budget. When San Francisco Democrat Willie Brown tried to bring the governor back into the budget fray, there was a behind the scenes power struggle. Governor Brown refused to deal with Speaker Brown, and a political impasse resulted. Finally, the Democratic leadership gave up and passed a budget contrary to the governor's wishes. It was time for new political leadership and the Republican Party recognized the change in voter sentiment. It only had to find a strong candidate to retake the governor's mansion.

George Deukmejian: The Early Political Years and a Grinding Conservatism

Who was George Deukmejian? This was a question that many Californians asked. He had been a prominent, if somewhat invisible, figure in California politics for two decades. In 1982, he became the leading Republican candidate for governor. There were many positive sides to Deukmejian's candidacy. The most obvious strength was that he had an immigrant background and also succeeded in making a name for himself, thereby allowing the Republican party to advertise him as a "self made man."

George Deukmejian was the first Armenian politician to win a major office in the Golden State. He was a transplanted New Yorker who understood the fickle ways of state politics. Deukmejian moved to the Golden State in 1955 to practice law, although he demonstrated no interest in politics. For a time, he worked as a corporate lawyer and then became a Los Angeles county deputy counsel. This was followed by a brief stint in a private law firm.

Soon Deukmejian established a base in the Republican Party. It was the civil rights issues of the early 1960s which prompted Deukmejian to enter politics. He believed that there was a law and order crisis in the Golden State. So he vowed to run for office. His political career began in 1962 when he won a seat in the Assembly. He represented Long Beach and for sixteen years was an accomplished Assemblyman.

Deukmejian's early political career revealed a conservative politician. He voted against the Rumford Fair Housing Act of 1963 and was critical of civil rights legislation. In 1966, Deukmejian was elected to the California Senate. In time, he became the Republican Senate Floor Leader.

In 1967, when he aligned himself with Governor Ronald Reagan, Deukmejian's political star began to rise. Shortly after Reagan's gubernatorial inauguration, Deukmejian was selected to carry the Republican tax package through the California Senate. During the battle over the 1967 budget, Governor Reagan and Assembly Speaker Jesse Unruh became locked in a battle over a withholding tax. The Governor insisted that withholding money from citizens was taking advantage of the tax payer while Assemblyman Unruh believed it would balance the budget and allow the state to ferret out tax cheats. Deukmejian was an important participant who supported Reagan's plan to prevent a withholding tax.

Governor Reagan depended upon Senator Deukmejian to negotiate a budget that didn't allow a withholding tax. As he brokered the compromises between Reagan and Unruh, Deukmejian learned important political lessons. He also recognized that Reagan's conservative, anti-tax stance helped the Republican Party establish a solid electoral base. As Deukmejian's star rose, he fashioned a well-defined political position. As a result, Deukmejian was identified by voters as an outspoken conservative who fought for tough gun laws, strict enforcement of capital punishment and a rewriting of the judicial code to create stronger sentencing guidelines.

With the help of Governor Reagan, Deukmejian sponsored three bills raising the minimum sentences for violent crimes. He also sponsored a bill that created a Crime Council to formulate plans for computer enhanced crime detection, and he helped to establish a research foundation to implement the latest crime fighting technology. The press quickly picked up the issues that Deukmejian supported, and he was thrust into the political mainstream.

In 1977, George Deukmejian received an inordinate amount of newspaper publicity for his stand against the "punks and hoodlums" who were terrorizing California. He sponsored the California law restoring the death penalty and the "use a gun, go to prison" law that made him a favorite to be elected as California's top law enforcer-Attorney General. This office is the state's top cop and is regarded as the second most powerful position in state government. Earl Warren and Edmund G. "Pat" Brown used the Attorney General's office as a springboard to the gubernatorial mansion. This fact was not lost on Deukmejian.

While California's Attorney General, he de-emphasized environmental protection, increased the state budget to fight urban crime and was a strong opponent of Governor Brown's liberal policies. Deukmejian attacked Brown for "coddling criminals" and was critical of decisions made by the California Supreme Court. The Chief Justice of the California Supreme Court, Rose Bird, was a favorite Deukmejian target. After Governor Brown appointed Bird Chief Justice, she reversed all twenty-seven death sentences that had come before the court. Deukmejian's political stock soared when he attacked the Chief Justice's policies.

Many Republicans were skeptical of Deukmejian's appeal. He was a poor pubic speaker. His idea of a good time was to spend the weekend in his Long Beach home mowing the lawn, drinking iced tea and cleaning the garage. His wife Gloria told the *Los Angeles Times* that her husband's only weakness was for jamoca almond fudge ice cream. Deukmejian's friends called him "Corky" but his campaign manager insisted on the nickname "Duke." As he prepared to run for the Governor's Office, the Republican Party hired a voice coach.

The main reason for Deukmejian's Republican gubernatorial nomination was that Lieutenant Governor Curb was unacceptable to the Republican mainstream. He had a great deal of charisma but a low political IQ. Good looks and Hollywood connections no longer mattered.

In the June, 1982 Republican primary, George Deukmejian easily beat Mike Curb. Deukmejian's stand on crime won him the Republican nomination. He hit a strong nerve with California voters when he suggested that he would once again make the streets safe. The notion of appointing tough judges, rewriting the criminal law code to put teeth in sentencing and the promise to build new prisons vaulted Deukmejian into the Republican Party forefront. But Deukmejian still had to face a tough Democratic candidate in the general election.

The 1982 Gubernatorial Campaign: A Strange Conservative and Liberal Mandate in the Golden State

As the 1982 gubernatorial campaign progressed, Deukmejian stressed his law and order background. It quickly became the most significant electoral issue, but there were other concerns. Voters complained about government spending, immigrants, law and order difficulties as well as the state economy.

The Democratic gubernatorial candidate, Los Angeles Mayor Tom Bradley, was the first African American elected mayor of a major California city. He had also been the LA police chief. An experienced politician with a long record of public service, Bradley was an excellent candidate for the governor's office.

As a campaigner, Mayor Bradley described himself as a moderate who had governed Los Angeles effectively. But Bradley, like Deukmejian, was not an arousing public speaker, and his reputation was that of a political plodder. He lacked the spark and charisma of a candidate running for a major public office. The Democratic Party was so skeptical of Bradley's lack of voter appeal that it took out ads which proclaimed: "Tom Bradley. He doesn't make a lot of noise. He gets things done."

Mayor Bradley's key Democratic advisers were so concerned with his performance that they seized upon one of the revolutions of the computer age. The California Democratic Council authorized funds for target mailing. For half a century mailers had been part of California politics. Routinely, the CDC sent brochures to registered Democrats prior to general elections. In the closing days of the 1982 governor's race, the CDC sent out half a million letters targeting women. The clear message: "Tom Bradley was committed to women's issues, whereas the Republican Attorney General, George Deukmejian was not." This mailing made no difference in the election.

Despite Bradley's ineffectual campaigning, California newspapers, right up to election day, predicted his victory. The *San Francisco Chronicle* headlined: "First Black Elected Governor." It was an embarrassing mistake as George Deukmejian won by 0.8% of the vote. It was the narrowest gubernatorial victory in California history.

The reason for Mayor Bradley's defeat was a simple one. Governor Jerry Brown had bankrupted the state during his two terms, he failed to quiet public fears regarding crime and was unable to solve the budget crisis. While Bradley distanced himself from the egomaniacal Brown, Deukmejian reminded voters that nothing would change with a Democratic governor.

As Governor Deukmejian prepared for his inauguration, he talked at length about the dangers of illegal immigration, the increase in drug use and the perpetual welfare fraud which drained the state budget. These were issues near and dear to California hearts and were designed to win a large segment of the voters. The 1982 election forced the Democratic Party to change its direction.

San Francisco's Willie Brown and the New 1980 Style Democrats

The Democratic Party was in trouble. Since the 1950s, Democrats had spent enormous sums on welfare, schools, roads, the environment, state parks and local government. By 1982, this trend angered the voters and turned the Golden State into a conservative, Republican bastion. No one understood the mood of the voters better than San Francisco Assemblyman Willie Brown. In the 1980s he single-handedly kept the Democratic Party in the mainstream of Golden State politics. His flashy dress, highly personal politics and bon vivant, good time attitude obscured his shrewd and calculating political moves. But Brown's political personality couldn't hide Democratic difficulties.

Democratic political troubles had developed over time. The popular reaction against the Democrats began in 1966 as Governor Reagan blamed the Party for the University of California at Berkeley's Free Speech Movement. Then he tied state difficulties to the money spent controlling student dissent. Reagan was a fiscal conservative with a strong aversion to big government. As governor he limited state finances and cut back funds for state and local government. Because of declining state revenues, Reagan convinced the California Legislature to reform the welfare system and cut spending for schools, mental health facilities and other state services. When Reagan left office, California had recovered from the orgy of Democratic spending. But the old liberal ways returned in 1974 when the Golden State elected a Democrat, Jerry Brown.

During the Reagan years, Willie realized the need to reorganize the Democratic Party in order to meet the changing times. With gusto, Brown became not only a major party fund-raiser but a link to the ethnic, liberal and labor votes. When Jerry Brown was elected California's governor he owed a great debt to Willie Brown's influence.

As governor, Jerry Brown was a mixed blessing. He appointed women, gays, ethnic minorities and labor leaders to important political positions. The California courts experienced a complete overhaul. Governor Brown appointed Rose Bird as the Chief Justice, and she began a crusade to liberalize the law. The Chief Justice of the California Supreme Court has enormous power. Chief Justice Bird was too controversial for most Californians. Her decisions created the image that she was "coddling" criminals and her opposition to the death penalty incensed conservatives. She became a major campaign issue that George Deukmejian exploited during the 1982 gubernatorial election.

The Democrats had other problems. Willie Brown was frustrated with Governor Brown's condescending attitudes. When he spoke on African American issues, the Governor would show up in Hunter's Point and hold a preachy press conference in San Francisco's festering ghetto. Willie Brown preferred Governor Brown support public funds for housing, playgrounds and increased police protection in Hunter's Point. In an interview with public television station, KQED, Brown remarked: "It's always harder to work with liberals…they think they know about your community." Despite his negative feelings for Governor Brown, the San Francisco Assemblyman supported the Democratic Party leader.

In 1982, Brown raised $2.2 million for Democratic Assembly candidates. Four years later, Brown raised $6.6 million. During the 1986 election, Brown gave more than half a million dollars to two rookie legislative candidates who spoke of supporting Speaker Brown. Both candidates lost. He also forced other Democratic legislators to donate sums from $15,000 to $45,000 to party campaign coffers.

Brown was able to induce the California Applicant Attorneys Association to donate $38,000; the California Society of Industrial Medicine presented a check for $19,500, and the Atlantic Richfield Company quietly sent $10,000. However, Dan Sanford, of the California Fair Political Practices Commission, suggested that legislators were raising too much money.

The *Sacramento Bee* coined the phrase Willie Inc. to describe Speaker Brown's fund raising successes. Republican politicians joined in to criticize the Democratic Speaker's fund raising, and this so infuriated Brown that he vowed to retaliate. The Speaker responded by vowing to excuse Republicans from key committees. The stage was set for a political tiff between newly elected Republican Governor Deukmejian and the irrepressible Assembly Speaker Brown.

The key to Brown's power was in consolidating the functions of the Speaker and raising campaign funds so that it was virtually impossible to get elected to the California Senate or Assembly without Brown's political approval and financial support. The Democratic National Chairperson checked with Brown before making any political moves in the Golden State. "The person who has the money is the person who controls the California Legislature," Ruth Holton, the executive director of California Common Cause, observed sagely.

Despite his power, Brown retained his sense of humor. He talked movie director Francis Ford Coppola into giving him a walk-on part in the opening segment of the blockbuster movie "The Godfather, Part III." Brown came on the screen for a few seconds and thanked Mafia don

Michael Corleone for the campaign contribution. Herb Caen in the *San Francisco Chronicle* used this and other incidents to remark that Willie Brown was a politician who still liked to have fun.

Governor George Deukmejian and the Era of Law and Order, Anti-environmentalism and Silicon Valley Business

On January 3, 1983, Deukmejian was inaugurated as California's governor with the message that he would appoint common sense judges, cut welfare spending, reform the educational system and control big government. The promises of a new governor were quickly dampened by the revelation that he didn't have a place to live. The Democratic Party had sold the governor's mansion.

Before Deukmejian could begin his duties, Speaker Brown persuaded the California Legislature to sell the governor's mansion. It was too expensive to maintain, Brown argued, and a conservative, Republican governor would want it that way. It was Speaker Brown's way of letting Deukmejian know that he was in for trouble. It also slowed the Republican small government message.

California newspapers picked up the story. Soon voters knew more than they cared to about the eleven thousand-square foot, eight bedroom, Spanish-style house in Carmichael. This was a Sacramento suburb and the sumptuous mansion had been built by Governor Reagan's wealthy supporters. His wife Nancy shuddered at the old downtown mansion. She refused to live in it. So Los Angeles based Republicans raised money for the home under the stipulation that state funds maintain it. This quickly turned into a dollar drain that Democratic party legislators would not approve.

When Jerry Brown was governor he was so uncomfortable just standing inside the mansion's foyer that he dubbed it the "Taj Mahal." To show disdain for this luxurious residence, Brown lived in a downtown apartment and drove an old car to work. By selling the mansion, Willie Brown let Californians know that the Democratic Party had a no nonsense, frugal approach to state government. It was also a means of getting even with the newly elected governor.

So Deukmejian and his family lived in a condominium on N Street some five blocks from the Capitol. Eventually, wealthy Republican benefactors bought Deukmejian a townhouse in the suburbs. This comical housing controversy suggested that Deukmejian needed to reach a compromise with Speaker Brown if he was to govern California effectively. A consummate politician, Deukmejian soon came to a political truce with Speaker Brown.

As Governor Deukmejian came into office, the state borrowed $400 million dollars to pay its bills, because Governor Brown had left California teetering on the edge of bankruptcy with a $1.5 billion dollar deficit in the $27 billion dollar state budget. The surplus of the 1970s was spent and a recession cut deeply into state revenues. Then a New York stock brokerage firm announced that it was lowering the value of California bonds. Investors were wary. The *Wall Street Journal* predicted serious financial problems. This prediction materialized when the State of California paid a small portion of its bills with warrants rather than cashable checks. The warrants were in fact an IOU from the state, and this further intensified fears over California's economic future.

The budget crisis continued, and this gave Governor Deukmejian and Speaker Brown time for further budget cutting. They agreed to $638 million in immediate budget cuts and then they delayed construction and maintenance projects in order to stem the flow of money from state coffers. Eventually, a one per cent state sales tax increase was implemented. State finances creaked back to life and California was once again solvent.

The irony to the budget compromise was that Governor Deukmejian's Republican supporters suddenly became his biggest critics. The conservative Republicans argued that the Governor was too close to the Assembly Speaker. Brown compounded these feelings by standing up in the Assembly and shouting: "Give the Duke a vote." Incredulously, the Republican Party swung in line behind a sales tax increase which in reality was a tax hike.

For the remainder of Governor Deukmejian's first term the economy continued to be a major problem. Once Deukmejian's second administration began, the California legislature passed the 1986-1987 budget and the governor responded by vetoing more than $1.2 billion of it. Then Deukmejian demanded a "rainy day" surplus of one billion dollars. It was approved and California's finances were once again in order. But then state revenues fell by $500 million and the state welfare and corrections program spent $380 million over budget. The spiral of economic problems continues as the Governor looked for ways to keep the state solvent.

After consulting Willie Brown, Governor Deukmejian ordered a two percent cut in state expenditures and a ten percent cut in Medi-Cal. This recouped more than $160 million and stabilized state finances. It was with the help of Speaker Brown and a shift in the nation's finances that California once again became solvent. This new financial boon was due to the rise of the business oriented Silicon Valley.

California's Silicon Valley to the Rescue: Business Bails Out the Golden State

In northern California, the fiscal crunch was eased when the Silicon Valley began expanding its economic base. The businesses that made up the Silicon Valley were located from San Jose to Palo Alto. The Silicon Valley was an area of scientific work which owed its birth to Stanford University engineering professor Frederick Terman. After encouraging his best graduate students to form their own businesses, Terman watched in awe as one successful electronics and engineering firm after another made a new fortune. The scientific and business skills emanating from the Silicon Valley were a tax boom to California government.

The revenues from the revived business atmosphere also made many young men rich and none more so than William Hewlett and David Packard who shortly after graduating from Stanford founded the Hewlett Packard Company. Because of their close relationship with Republican President Dwight D. Eisenhower, Hewlett Packard received lucrative government contracts. By 1953, the Stanford Industrial Park included Hewlett Packard as one of its main tenants and the Silicon Valley was on its way to riches.

The growth of high technology business created a thirty year boom in California. As the electronics industry grew, housing prices, the cost of living and educational and governmental costs increased. Then after years of unprecedented prosperity, the Silicon Valley experienced problems. In 1983, the first in a series of bankruptcies took place and then many major corporations began reducing their work forces. The most notable was Atari, a major producer of video games, which laid off almost two thousand employees. By 1985, the Apple Corporation announced that it was experiencing problems and began lay offs as well.

When Governor Deukmejian took office, the Silicon Valley was made up of more than fifty industrial parks that had created a high tech revolution in the Golden State. The more than six billion dollar, high tech payroll helped to bail out Governor Deukmejian during the later stages of his first administration.

By 1986, the California economy temporarily revived and Governor Deukmejian no longer needed a tax increase. Despite flush financial times the Governor decreased state revenues for the University of California, the California State University system and the 106 community colleges. To make up for the decrease in educational funds, Deukmejian forced through a bill charging $50 tuition for community college students. Historically, the community college had provided free tuition. The immediate result was the decline of African American, Mexican American and immigrant students.

A resurgent conservatism caused Deukmejian's popularity to exceed that of any recent governor. It was one of the most astonishing comebacks in California political history as Deukmejian went from a governor who faced certain defeat in his reelection bid to a sure winner. The volatile California economy had rebounded to rescue the Republican Party. In the midst of Deukmejian's first term the Presidential election of 1984 took place and the California governor supported President Reagan's reelection bid. The praise that President Reagan heaped upon Governor Deukmejian added to his renewed popularity.

The 1986 Election: Governor Deukmejian, the Rise and Fall of Rose Bird and a New Republican Majority

In November 1986, Deukmejian was reelected in an anticlimactic campaign. The incumbent governor began his campaign with a large lead in public opinion polls. His opponent was once again Los Angeles Mayor Tom Bradley. Much like the previous election, Bradley proved to be an ineffective candidate. Although Bradley was a four-term Mayor of Los Angeles, he was not well known outside his home town. A poll one month prior to the election showed that 30% of the voters didn't know that Bradley was an African American.

There were some important political issues in the 1986 election. The most significant was a battle over Supreme Court Chief Justice Rose Elizabeth Bird. In 1977, Governor Jerry Brown had appointed Bird as Chief Justice to the California Supreme Court. Her tenure was a controversial and non-traditional one.

She was a Democrat, a graduate of the prestigious University of California, Boalt Law School and a former Secretary of the Agriculture and Services Agency in Governor Brown's administration. An ardent feminist with a strong personality, Bird had little judicial experience. She was also only forty years old, and this was twenty years younger than the average California Supreme Court appointee. She was also the first woman selected for a seat on the California Supreme Court.

Because Rose Bird wasn't from the legal establishment there was an immediate outcry over her performance. The aging, white, male dominated California court system was challenged. One critic charged that Brown was using the 3-B Plan for justices: "Blacks, Browns and

Broads." Governor Brown appointed more than seven hundred Hispanics, Blacks and women to the state courts. The Chief Justice was the most visible and she was subjected to constant criticism.

Rose Elizabeth Bird's liberal politics and her ideological direction as Chief Justice intensified partisan debate. Political passions over her alleged leniency toward criminals, support for gay rights, fair treatment for immigrants and tough minded ideas about business malfeasance brought Chief Justice Bird enemies throughout the Golden State.

Unlike justices in most other states, the California constitution mandated that Rose Bird be confirmed by the voters. The justices are confirmed by the voters and a full term on the Supreme Court is twelve years. As a result, justices had to face the voters for reelection. In November, 1978, a heated electoral campaign took place with the Republican party, agricultural interests, big banking and law enforcement urging Bird's rejection.

Her critics found an unlikely ally when a liberal magazine attacked her judicial decisions. *New West* magazine accused Bird of anti-feminist behavior when she ruled that rape did not constitute "great bodily harm." The reaction to the Caudillo rape case suggested that Chief Justice Bird was "soft on crime."

To counter these charges, the Democratic Party raised half a million dollars to win her confirmation. Funds from labor, women's groups, consumer advocates and liberal supporters of Governor Brown provided advertising funds. Increasingly, the Rose Bird for Chief Justice issue was fought in the press. When the vote came in Rose Bird won 51.7% of the vote which was the narrowest margin of any judge in California history.

After her election, the press charged that Rose Bird had suppressed controversial decisions until after the election. She responded by assigning the Commission on Judicial Performance, the agency which monitors the California judiciary, to investigate her behavior. In June 1979, the Commission concluded there was no evidence of wrongdoing.

The Rose Bird controversy continued into the 1980s. When Chief Justice Bird led the Supreme Court in allowing state funds for abortions there was an immediate outcry. She also voted against placing Proposition 9 on the ballot. This proposal was a sweeping law and order initiative mandating stricter sentencing procedures. In 1982, the Rose Bird Court voted four to three to approve the Democratic reapportionment plan. Assembly Speaker Willie Brown now had power to draw up federal legislative districts, and this increased his power dramatically.

In the four years following her confirmation as Chief Justice of the California Supreme Court, there were four recall drives. Recall was a progressive political reform inaugurated in 1911 to allow voters to get rid of an elected official, but all four recall moves against Chief Justice Bird failed. She succeeded in beating her enemies, but the Democratic Party was destroyed by the fallout.

Rose Bird stood for reelection to the California Supreme Court in 1986 and she was finally defeated. Now, Governor George Deukmejian was able to appoint a new Chief Justice. He selected his old law partner Malcolm Lucas. When Lucas was appointed to the California Supreme Court in 1984, he was subject to confirmation by the voters. After Lucas earned voter approval, he earned the nickname "Maximum Bob" for his heavy handed criminal sentences. He also upheld the death penalty more than any Justice in California history. The Rose Bird era was over.

During his first administration, Governor Deukmejian had frequently attacked Chief Justice Bird. Deukmejian not only opposed her decisions, but he also charged that she was violating the California constitution. Her decisions, Deukmejian argued, were contrary to the constitution. The Governor was incensed when Chief Justice Bird ruled that Proposition 24 could not be implemented. This was passed by the voters to decrease the size of state government. The brainchild of Paul Gann, one of the authors of Proposition 13 which regulated property tax, Proposition 24 was an electoral device to regulate state spending by controlling the Speaker's power. Willie Brown charged that because he was an African American, Gann was targeting his power. "No one heard from Gann about the power of the Speakership when whites held the post," Brown roared. But Rose Bird put an end to this attempt to control the Assembly Speaker's power and Willie Brown remarked: "Thank you, Sister Rose and the Supremes."

The continual controversies with the California Supreme Court helped Deukmejian's Republican policies with dissatisfied California voters. The result was that he easily defeated Mayor Bradley in the general election receiving more than 4.3 to his opponents 2.7 million votes.

As California politics progressed, the partnership between George Deukmejian and Willie Brown continued until the 1990 election. It was a strained relationship that seemed always on the verge of breaking down. But both were pragmatic politicians who realized that they each needed to govern California.

From 1986 to 1990 California was a strange mixture of liberal and conservative attitudes. Although Governor Deukmejian had been an anti-environmental politician, Speaker Brown convinced him to sign AB 2595 which would cut down smog emissions. The governor also signed a number of Democratic bills that surprised his Republican colleagues. When Deukmejian announced that he was signing AB 357 and SB 292 which banned the sale of automatic weapons in California, there was an uproar from the Republican right. But these types of actions also drew in large numbers of middle of the road Democrats and made the Republican Party unbeatable at the polls. The politics of the 1980s were dominated by Deukmejian and his careful reading of public opinion.

Willie Brown: Still Triumphant in the Middle of Republican Power

Willie Brown remained in the middle of California politics. He kept the Democratic Party coffers filled with campaign funds by acting as a large fund raiser. By 1990, Brown was the titular head of the Democratic Party. However, as the 1990s dawned, opposition to his power in the Assembly and his political tactics threatened his position. To counter these moves, Brown helped politicians launch their careers. So, forcing Willie Brown to give up the Speakership was not going to be an easy task.

Los Angeles Assemblywoman Maxine Waters began her political career with Brown's help. During her campaigns for public office, Brown acquired campaign funds and appeared at rallies in her behalf. Once Waters was elected, she repaid Brown's support. Waters served as Assembly Democratic caucus chair from 1984 until her election to Congress in 1990. She was a strong supporter of Brown's political program, but she remained independent of him in her dealings regarding state government. Waters served on the budget conference committees helping Brown control the budget process. "I was the gatekeeper and the protector of resources...."

Yet, there was very little the Republican Party could do because Brown controlled much of California's financial direction in the midst of Republican rule.

Willie Brown didn't have one gatekeeper but many in California governmental circles. Gloria Molina was a good example of Brown's political acumen. She began her career as an aide in his office and by 1990 she was a Los Angeles County Supervisor. The *Los Angeles Times* labeled Molina as California's most powerful Hispanic politician. Then she was elected to the California Assembly and helped Brown withstand the onslaught of Republican rule. By the late 1980s, Willie Brown created a multi-ethnic political coalition which kept him and the liberal dream alive.

The Gang of Five: The Attack on Willie Brown and the Rise of Redneck Democrats

There was also strong opposition in the Democratic Party to Speaker Willie Brown. In 1987-1988 five newly elected Democratic Assembly members began an alliance to end his power. Because of their political machinations, they were dubbed the Gang of Five. They met nightly at Paragary's Bar and Oven, a trendy California cuisine restaurant about a mile from the Capital. The Gang of Five included Rusty Areias, Steve Pace, Gary Condit, Jerry Eaves and Charles Calderon, and they all had something in common. They were Democrats who were elected from small and politically insignificant Democratic districts. Calderon and Eaves represented suburbs east of Los Angeles. Pace was from a district which included San Diego suburbs and rural portions of the Imperial Valley. They were all Reagan Democrats. In their meetings and public statements there was no doubt that they were incensed about an African American rising to a position of power. But despite that, it wasn't as much a question of racism as it was of legislative impropriety. Willie Brown did not fit their concept of a leader and they were determined to replace him as Assembly Speaker.

There was a red-neck tone to the politics of the Gang of Five. However, the voters in their districts approved and they appealed to a conservative, often reactionary, political element. The Gang of Five was tough on criminal law; they opposed abortion; they talked at length about welfare fraud and they pilloried the illegal immigrants. The Gang of Five were young conservatives who believed that California's Democratic Party was too heavily influenced by liberals. Willie Brown was at the top of their list. Their list included welfare reform, putting an end to liberal politics and preventing African Americans like Brown and Waters from ascending to positions of power. As the Gang of Five argued, Brown was simply too easily influenced by Democrats like Tom Hayden. In typically conservative fashion the Gang of Five saw a conspiracy between Hayden and Brown. To support their thesis they suggested that Hayden, who headed the Assembly Labor Committee, was giving Speaker Brown anything that he desired. The Gang of Five was determined to break Brown's commitments to labor.

What made the Gang of Five unique is that they held important positions on Assembly committees. These assignments were due to Speaker Brown. Because the California Assembly was composed of 44 Democrats and 39 Republicans, the Gang of Five reasoned that they could overthrow Brown by switching their allegiance to the Republican Party.

The political war that followed was an indication of Brown's political tenacity and skilled leadership. To let their displeasure with Brown be known, the Gang of Five opposed Brown's no-fault auto insurance bill. This placed the Gang of Five squarely in support of the insurance companies and they also urged one of Brown's largest campaign contributors—the California Trial Lawyers Association—to reduce their campaign funds. For more than a decade this organization pumped millions of dollars into Democratic campaign coffers. The payback for this campaign money was the passage of the no-fault auto insurance bill. When the Gang of Five charged Speaker Brown with unethical behavior, he took quick action.

Brown stripped the Gang of Five of key Assembly committee positions. Since the Gang of Five felt persecuted, they attacked Brown on the Assembly floor. They used a number of parliamentary motions to pull bills out of committees and force votes on them. Then they conceived a plan to strip Brown of the Speakership.

At boisterous and often drunken dinners at Paragary's, the Gang of Five tried to induce others to join them. Suddenly Willie Brown was worried about losing his enormous power. He announced his hopes of reaching a compromise and met with the recalcitrant Democratic Assemblyman Eaves's apartment. But when Brown arrived, he had changed his mind and told them that he would fight them in the Assembly.

The attempts to remove Brown from the Speakership in May 1988 failed. However, the political infighting exposed Democratic Party weaknesses. But in the 1988 election the Democratic party picked up three more seats and had a six seat cushion over the Republicans. They now had even stronger control over the California legislature. This hurt the Gang of Five's attempts to destroy Speaker Brown's power. Shortly after the November 1988 election Brown was once again confirmed as Assembly Speaker.

Bibliographical Essay

To understand Ronald Reagan's legacy to Governor George Deukmejian see Lou Cannon, *Ronnie and Jesse: A Political Odyssey* (New York, 1969) and for the politics leading up to the era see, Jackson K. Putnam, *Modern California Politics, 1917-1980* (San Francisco, 1980).

For Willie Brown's career see, James Richardson, *Willie Brown: A Biography* (Berkeley, 1996). Also see Richard Edward DeLeon, *Left Coast City: Progressive Politics in San Francisco, 1975-1991* (Lawrence, 1992). For a the role of Mayor Dianne Feinstein see, Jerry Roberts, *Dianne Feinstein: Never Let Them See You Cry* (New York, 1994). A good study of the political turmoil in California in the 1970s and early 1980s is James R. Mills, *A Disorderly House: The Brown-Unruh Years in Sacramento* (Berkeley, 1987).

For the term "Brown Inc." and general criticism of the Speaker's power see, John Jacobs, "The Rise and Fall of Willie Inc.," *Sacramento Bee*, June 4, 1995 and Richard A. Clucas, *The Speaker's Electoral Connection: Willie Brown and the California Assembly* (Berkeley, 1995).

For the revolt of the Gang of Five see, for example, Amy Chance, "Willie Brown Fights To Keep Control," *Sacramento Bee*, February 21, 1988; Arnold Hamilton and Bert Robinson, "Willie Brown: A Legacy of Power," *San Jose Mercury News*, March 6, 1988 and James Richardson and Herbert A. Sample, "Assembly Seething on Inside," *Sacramento Bee*, April 10, 1988 and Leo C. Wolinsky, "Sacramento Feels Impact of 'Gang of Five,'" *Los Angeles Times*, April 11, 1988.

For biographical information on Deukmejian and Brown see, Dan Walter, editor, *California Political Almanac, 1989-1990 Edition* (Santa Barbara, 1990).

An excellent is John Jacobs', *A Rage of Justice: The Passion and Politics of Philip Burton* (Berkeley, 1995). For Willie Brown's attitudes on Governor Jerry Brown see, for example, "Willie Brown Hits Jerry's Race Relations," *Sacramento Bee*, May 11, 1975.

For the Rose Bird controversy see, Preble Stolz, *Judging Judges: The Investigation of Rose Bird and the California Supreme Court* (New York, 1981); Gale Cook, "Judging the Bench Brown Built," *San Francisco Examiner*, July 8, 1979; Kenneth Kahn, "Rose Bird and the Politics of Rape," *New West*, July 31, 1978, pp. 28-31 and Bob Egelko, "The Court's National Stature Has Waned Under Bird," *California Journal*, 17, no. 9 (September, 1986), pp. 428-429.

On gay rights and politics see Randy Shilts, *The Mayor of Castro Street: The Life and Times of Harvey Milk* (New York, 1982) and Randy Shilts, *And The Band Played On: Politics, People and the AIDS Epidemic* (New York, 1987).

An excellent examination of California politics is Terry Christensen's and Larry N. Gerston's, *Politics in the Golden State: The California Connection* (Boston, 1988). Also see Cary McWilliams, California: *The Great Exception* (Westport, 1971, reprint).

On the 1982 campaign see, "Bradley Ms. Mailing Seeks Female Vote," *Los Angeles Times*, October 26, 1982; "Are You Planning to Run for Political Office? Then a Political Consultant is a Must," *National Journal*, January 16, 1982, p. 101; Michelle Willens, "The Real '82 Opponents: Garth, Haglund and Rietz," *California Journal*, 12. no. 12 (December, 1981).

19

PETE WILSON: A REPUBLICAN FOR THE 1990s AND THE ROLLER COASTER RIDE TO CONSERVATISM

As the 1990s dawned, California was in a precarious position. A growing conservatism, heightened by an economic downturn, and strong reactions against Asian immigrants and illegal aliens caused the Golden State to begin a roller coaster ride toward conservatism. The political mood was one which demanded government cuts in welfare spending. The result was the passage of Proposition 187 in 1994 by California voters. This measure was aimed at restricting the rights of illegal aliens by denying them state services. Once again, ethnic politics dominated the mainstream of the Golden State. The primary reason for the rise of conflict in California was the economy, the drop in property values and uneven Silicon Valley business prosperity.

When California went into the worst economic decline since the Great Depression, the result was that the Republican Party received ready made voter approval to cut educational and welfare spending. Simultaneously, federal spending cuts further hurt the state. By 1994, San Francisco's Presidio was closed and other California military bases and national parks were threatened with closure or a reduced role because of a lack of federal funds. San Francisco Mayor Frank Jordan was inept and offered little hope for saving the high level of employment in the federal sector.

Finally, a city politician emerged to challenge the federal cuts. In the House of Representatives San Francisco Democrat Nancy Pelosi fought for federal funds to keep the Presidio open. She was appointed to the House Appropriations Committee and this committee was responsible for funding the Presidio as a national park. Almost single handily Representative Pelosi kept the Presidio open by helping to secure legislation making it a national park. She also fought attempts to sell Presidio land to private developers. For a time, this controversy obscured the ugly confrontation over illegal immigrants. But the issue soon resurfaced.

Proposition 187 became the focal point of the divisive politics of the early 1990s. California voters had passed the Proposition to deny public education, non-emergency health care and social service benefits to illegal immigrants. Governor Pete Wilson was a strong supporter of the initiative, claiming that California spent more than two billion dollars per year providing public support for illegal aliens.

Politicians with an eye for reelection were aware that Proposition 187 had passed 59% to 41%. As a result, in subsequent elections most candidates supported restricting aid to illegals. The opponents of Proposition 187 argued that it violated the basic laws of human nature as well as

Photo Courtesy: Walter Halland

Professor Walt Halland leads a group of students in discussing California history.

the United States Constitution. The constitutionality of Proposition 187 was questioned because it seemed to violate the 14th amendment of the U. S. Constitution which forbids any state from denying any person "equal protection of the law." If the courts found that Proposition 187 was illegal, the state would have to fund benefits for illegal immigrants. Governor Wilson argued that if President Bill Clinton wanted illegals to have government services, the Federal Government should provide the funding.

Public opinion polls indicated widespread support to cut off health benefits and public education to illegal immigrants. This attitude was used by Governor Wilson to blame California's problems upon illegal immigrants. Critics of immigration contended that newly arrived immigrants were likely to be heavy users of state services and, as a result, a burden to Californians financially. Supporters of Proposition 187 pointed out that foreign households received 32% of all public cash assistance. This argument was countered by a Claremont Graduate School study which argued that illegal immigrants paid more to California in taxes than they cost in government services. However, Californians remained divided on the illegal immigration issue.

The reaction against illegals brought a strong defense of seasonal labor from small agricultural communities. In Lamont, California, a small town in the San Joaquin Valley, almost 25% of the population consisted of illegal farm workers. They had been welcomed to Lamont for half a century and by 1990 were paid $4.25 an hour to pick grapes, carrots and lettuce.

Lamont celebrated a "Weekend of Diversity" each year to commemorate the role of farm workers. The passage of Proposition 187 and resulting controversy over illegals prompted Juan Rivera, President of Lamont's Chamber of Commerce, to remark: "When we were prospering we closed our eyes to illegal immigration...." He continued by suggesting that tough times necessitated stronger border controls, but he believed that there was a double standard working against illegal immigrants.

The day after Proposition 187 was passed eight law suits were filed in state and federal courts to prevent its implementation. A San Francisco superior court judge ruled that the measure could not be enacted. A similar order was granted to public colleges and universities, which allowed the community college and state university systems to provide aid to students regardless of their resident status. The future of immigrants continued to be a mainstream political issue. As Governor Wilson suggested: "3.4 million illegals requiring state services placed California on the verge of bankruptcy."

Governor Pete Wilson: The Background and Rise of a Conservative Republican

By 1990 the Republican Party had a new and controversial leader, Governor Pete Wilson. He began his political career in the 1960s in the California Assembly. Who was Pete Wilson? He was the forerunner of a growing California conservatism. In examining Wilson's background, he was typical of the post World War II American who migrated to the Golden State.

He was born in an upper middle class, mid-western home in 1933. His mother always referred to him as the favored son. An older brother, James, was something of a trouble maker and "Petey," as his mother called him, was groomed for success. He not only attended private schools but was always the best dressed kid.

As he grew up in a lush suburb near St. Louis, Missouri, in a family with traditional values, Wilson developed the ingrained conservatism of the self-made aristocrat. His father, a well-paid advertising executive, sent his son to the most prestigious universities. Wilson attended Yale, and he was so intent upon pleasing his father he even joined his dad's former fraternity. At Yale, Wilson was an English major who friends described as "a library grind."

His only extracurricular activity at Yale was a three year ROTC commitment to the U.S. Marines. Young Pete desperately hoped to become a lawyer. In preparation for a legal career, he took the Law School Aptitude Test twice to achieve the highest possible score. Eventually, he was admitted to both Harvard and the University of California Boalt Law Schools. Wilson selected Boalt Hall because he hoped to live in the Golden State. Wilson was a top flight law student who possessed excellent grades, but his classmates remember him talking incessantly about using the law to protect "American values."

Yet, for all his rhetoric, Wilson hated law school. The courses were tedious, and he blanched at the mock law court arguments. When he graduated, Wilson found it difficult to study for the bar exam. He flunked the bar three times, before he passed, and he demonstrated little interest in any specific field of law. When he finally passed the bar, Wilson was a mediocre lawyer. He simply didn't have a passion for law. It appeared that Wilson went to law school for no other reason than to become a politician.

As a young man, Wilson was a fierce defender of establishment values. He also identified with policies and politics of tough minded Republicans. It was only natural that California's

Richard Nixon was his earliest political influence. When Nixon ran for the House of Representatives an adolescent Pete Wilson kept a scrapbook on the campaign.

Many of Wilson's colleagues and friends urged him to forgo a political career, because as a young man, Wilson kept to himself and was devoid of personal charisma. They reasoned that his personality wasn't well suited to the political arena. He had a mid-western monotone to his speech and a harsh, unfriendly look. His clenched jaw suggested a rigid personality. In his Brooks Brothers suit with his carefully styled hair, Wilson looked like a liberal. But his politics were those of the white, middle class with a reactionary viewpoint. He was also much too close to his family. His father, James Boone Wilson, Sr., as late as 1995 at the age of ninety three, was still giving Governor Wilson advice. His father's primary message was to keep immigration from destroying the California dream. The negative aspects of Wilson's personality turned out to be a plus in the local political climate because he seemed to be protecting the California dream.

In his personal life, Wilson had limited experiences with fatherhood. He has been married twice to women with children from previous marriages. He spent little time with his stepchildren and on the campaign trail few people realized that he had a family. Politics dominated Wilson's life and he had little time for outside activity. His focus was the California Dream. This was a vision of the Golden State which drove Wilson's political career to exclude minorities, illegal aliens and those who did not fit into his pattern of upwardly mobile citizens.

This obsession with illegals can be traced to Wilson's family moving to southern California. When Wilson arrived in the Golden State, shortly after the conclusion of World War II, there was a booming economy and a strong feeling for progress. When illegal immigrants, foreign business interests and ethnic minorities began changing the nature of California history, Wilson became a strong critic of California's multicultural direction.

The roots of Wilson's anti-immigrant politics were formed during his earliest years in California politics. When he left the U.S. Marine Corps, Wilson went to work as an advance man for Richard Nixon during his ill-fated 1962 gubernatorial campaign. While working for Nixon, Wilson began looking for a community which reflected his political values. It was Nixon's political mentor, Herb Klein, an ardent right wing conservative, who urged Wilson to move to San Diego where he quickly established a solid political base. Klein was the editor of the *San Diego Union*, and not surprisingly the newspaper endorsed Wilson as a promising politician.

In 1964, Wilson was a strong supporter of Arizona Republican Senator Barry Goldwater. The Goldwater for President campaign brought Wilson to San Francisco's Cow Palace for the Republican National Convention and he hob nobbed with party big wigs. Soon Wilson was a favorite of the right wing faction of the Republican establishment. Wilson let everyone know that he was a businessman's Republican. He was tough on fiscal issues, staunchly anti-union and ardently anti-tax. This political package brought him widespread support, and he was urged to run for public office.

In 1966, Wilson ran for the California Assembly and easily won a seat representing San Diego. He became the chairperson of the Committee on Urban Affairs. The problems of the city were ones that Wilson had many solutions for and he became known as a city reformer. The next step was to become the mayor of a major California city.

In 1971, Wilson was elected San Diego Mayor with the Nixon White House supporting his candidacy. Few people took him seriously when he talked of becoming governor, United States Senator or President. To his close friends Wilson described himself as an executive and not as a politician.

By 1982, Wilson won a seat in the United States Senate. As a U.S. Senator, he was ineffective. He was not as ease making political deals. Wilson found it difficult to compromise his viewpoints. For six years he was visibly uneasy with his colleagues. He also displayed little interest in his constituents and his record of absenteeism was amongst the highest in the U.S. Senate. He had one of the lowest ratings of any senator in California history.

He was also perpetually in the shadow of his Democratic colleague Senator Alan Cranston. On occasion when Wilson appeared on NBC's *Meet The Press*, he displayed little knowledge of national affairs. But he continued to display an obsession with illegals. President Ronald Reagan labeled Wilson a politician with "a limited vision," but the President recognized Wilson's views were popular among Californians.

Senator Wilson envisioned conspiracies everywhere in the Golden State. Feminists, gays, illegal immigrants, welfare cheaters, legal immigrants, labor radicals and liberals were all at one time or another a target for Wilson's venomous barbs. However, Wilson didn't look or act

Photo Courtesy: Alan Kirshner

A Californian relaxes in the 1990s.

like a fanatic. He had a choir boy demeanor which hid a vicious right wing conservatism. His calm, relaxed personality caused him to come across very well on television. He had the looks and talked like the average suburban Californian. Equally important, he appealed to the demagogic prejudices of the white, middle class voter. At no time in California history was the state more divided along racial lines than during Wilson's political career.

What made Wilson an extremely successful politician was a group of advisers who began working for him in the 1960s and were still on the payroll in the late 1990s. His advisers had a peculiar vision of California politics. It was one which envisioned the need to control the forces of change and this led to conflicts with liberals, feminists, the gay community, labor unionists, the media and various ethnic communities, especially the African American and Mexican American political organizations. The end result was that these interest groups often labeled Governor Wilson a racist.

Wilson's advisers included Chief of Staff Bob White who never married nor seemed to have a life outside of Republican politics. Otto Bos, an ex-newspaperman, who helped to mold Wilson's political image through public opinion polls. It was Bos who concentrated upon southern California's conservative, Republican areas to produce flattering poll results. The most significant political brain was George Gorton, because he had a sense of the key electoral issues. It was Gorton who convinced Wilson that the illegal immigrant issue and excessive government spending were the key to attracting voters. Few politicians have had the dedicated and loyal staff that brought Pete Wilson victories in major elections. As Wilson prepared to ascend to the Governor's Office, a newspaperman remarked that "the Pete and Willie act would be a strange one for Californians in the last decade of the twentieth century." This reference to the differences between Governor Wilson and Speaker Brown suggested the degree of hostility between them.

The Pete and Willie Act in the 1990s: California Politics in the Age of Reaction

Wilson's political nemesis, Assemblyman Willie Brown, supported Dianne Feinstein in the gubernatorial race. With unusual candor, Brown suggested that Wilson's emphasis on race, crime and excessive welfare spending was due to his conservative, anti-ethnic attitudes. Or perhaps, as Brown suggested, there was a subtle racism.

Despite Brown's opposition, Wilson remained the perfect California politician. He dressed and looked like a liberal, and he had the political message of a right wing moderate. Wilson was in favor of welfare reform and demanded that the Federal Government help finance the illegal alien problem. He decried the new immigration for changing the balance of California society.

Although Wilson and Brown had a political relationship which went back to 1966, they never liked one another. When Wilson represented San Diego in the Assembly, Brown was often critical of his urban planning ideas. Wilson retaliated by preventing Brown's rise to power in the Assembly. In 1969, when Wilson was assigned to head the new and prestigious Assembly Urban Affairs and Housing Committee, Brown was appointed to govern over Wilson's objections. Wilson ignored Brown's impute and they clashed frequently in committee meetings. The NAACP responded by suggesting that Wilson needed a "racial adjustment."

But Wilson also had his defenders. In San Diego, a California Police Officers Association Conference gave Governor Wilson a rousing hand. His speech on the problems in California society received thunderous applause. In a reception after the speech, one police administrator remarked that Wilson came across much better in person. "He was a genuine and sincere person," a police chief from northern California remarked. Most people were favorably impressed with Wilson after meeting him. The media presented a picture of Governor Wilson that was quite different from the one suggested by those who had interacted with him.

San Francisco Democratic Assemblyman John Burton remarked that "Wilson had some kind of goddamned arrogance." For years, Burton pointed out, Wilson was dangerous to the state and he urged the Democratic Party to elect a forceful speaker. Everyone knew what Burton was up to; he was promoting his good friend Willie Brown for the Speakership. In 1980, when Brown was elected Assembly Speaker, Burton's support was a key reason for Brown's rise to power.

The decade that Willie Brown spent as Assembly Speaker did little to slow Wilson's rise to political prominence. What is important about the Brown-Wilson political tiff is that it was in the grand tradition of California politics. Since 1850 the liberal-conservative split in the Golden State had guided local politicians. Brown represented the progressive liberals who favored welfare spending, increased educational opportunity and affirmative action, while Wilson was the voice that controlled spending, low taxes and reduced welfare. It was a classic political stand off typical of California.

During the January 1991 inauguration, Governor Wilson brought Speaker Brown to center stage. A private celebration was held where Wilson acknowledged Brown's power in the Assembly and offered a truce. It was a sincere gesture but one that Brown could not accept.

As legislative business began in early 1991, there was bad blood once again between Wilson and Brown. Because Governor George Deukmejian had spent eight years sharing power with the Speaker, they had worked out a harmonious relationship. This was not to be the case between Wilson and Brown.

As Wilson was inaugurated the California economy was in a state of decline. Not only were state revenues down but Silicon Valley businesses were fleeing to the Sun Belt cities. Declining business revenues and reduced taxes led to decreased government spending. Unfortunately, the $7.7 billion dollar budget in 1991-1992 was the largest in state history, but Wilson was having trouble convincing a Republican legislature to support it. His program was one of cutting government services and subtle tax increases.

Republicans were opposed to any tax increases. The economy was hampered by reductions in federal spending. The federal budget for military bases and the defense industry had been reduced each year since Reagan's presidency began. Democratic President Bill Clinton continued this trend. In 1992 the California Legislature needed $10.7 billion dollars to balance a $57 billion budget.

The problem with the California budget was that state law automatically locked money into a prearranged spending schedule. Half of the budget goes to schools because of Proposition 98. This ballot measure approved by the voters and backed by the California Teachers Association gave schools a defined level of financial support. As a result, education took up 50% of the state budget and another 33% was mandated for health and welfare services. The governor and the legislature, due to the changes in the law, had little room to make spending cuts.

So Governor Wilson proposed a $2.6 billion cut for the schools. The California Teachers Association turned on him with a vengeance. CTA pointed out that the cost of living increases for educators legged far behind private industry. Governor Wilson ignored these comments.

Willie Brown entered the fray by taking the teachers' side. The budget was delayed. Governor Wilson and Speaker Brown continually told the press that their differences were not personal but political while California operated without a budget and teetered on the brink of bankruptcy.

Then Governor Wilson made a serious political mistake when he proposed to cut the budget for kindergarten education. The CTA once again marshaled its vast resources and organized a large group of five-year-olds with sad eyes to show up at Wilson's Capitol office and protest the proposed kindergarten cuts. The press had a field day with this issue, and it caused Wilson's popularity to plummet.

After a sixty-four-day budget impasse, Governor Wilson backed down and dropped his suggested school cuts. The budget was passed with a number of compromises. As the 1992 general election approached, a shift in voter attitudes took place.

Surprisingly, the November 1992 election continued the Democratic majority in the California Legislature. As a result Brown's power increased in the eighty seat Assembly. Speaker Brown was now free to pursue his own agenda. However, Brown's power was illusionary. The declining economy, the passage of term limits and the growing hostility over illegal immigrants did not bode well for the Democratic Party.

Before he left the California Assembly, Brown did complete his program for California. He created a workable Affirmative Action program; he pushed through legislation benefiting labor unions; he supported bills guaranteeing women and minorities a share of state government contracts and he was a tireless worker for civil rights. These issues were not popular ones, but Brown was committed to making them a part of the California dream.

In April 1993, Willie Brown celebrated his fifty-ninth birthday in the splendor of the Fairmont Hotel ballroom. This famous old hotel was a symbol of San Francisco's old money. Although Brown was still Speaker of the Assembly, his career would soon head back to San Francisco politics.

As Ray Charles sang "America The Beautiful," Brown looked over a group of guests who had paid $10,000 to celebrate his birthday. It was a pleasing moment, and Speaker Brown was still at the top of his power. However, he was already making plans to become San Francisco's Mayor.

The Fall of Speaker Brown and the Emergence of Mayor Brown:
Back to the Source of Power

In the early 1990s, the term limit law was approved by voters. Brown was California's most powerful legislative politician, but he was no longer eligible to run for the Assembly. When the Democratic Party failed to overturn the term limit law, Brown had to leave the Assembly.

Sacramento newspaper columnists and politicians speculated on Brown's future. There was a rumor that he would run for the Chair of the California Democratic Party. His close friends urged him to seek a United States Senate seat. This was impossible as the 1992 election brought two Democratic Senators, Dianne Feinstein and Barbara Boxer to Washington. But Boxer had been elected to fill the remainder of Senator Alan Cranston's term, and she would have to stand for reelection in 1994. Brown could not bring himself to challenge Boxer, and he turned down overtures to run for the U.S. Senate.

In March 1994, Brown turned sixty and was feted in a series of birthday parties. His health was excellent; he was thin and never drank more than half a glass of wine with dinner. Brown's energy was that of a man half his age. At the pinnacle of his political career, Brown still had a great deal left to accomplish in California politics.

In his last few years in the Assembly, Brown lived through one of the most reactionary periods in California history. The Republican Party, under the national leadership of Newt Gingrich had a "Contract With America" which not only put them in control of Congress but they dominated conservative California politics. Brown was determined to stand up to this onslaught. The new Republicans were a reactionary group prone to demagogic name calling.

The worst demagogue was Santa Barbara Republican Michael Huffington. He spent $29 million of his own money in a losing U.S. Senate race against Dianne Feinstein, and he continually criticized welfare cheaters and those who abused the law. Huffington called for a law and order oriented California. The product of hereditary wealth, there was a demeaning attitude in Huffington's politics which caused California voters to reject him. Huffington's wife, a best selling author and an amateur psychic, led the charge for her husband. She held teas and fund raisers which pandered to right wing Republicans who believed that the Golden State was in decline. Wisely, California voters retired the Santa Barbara Republican. But Huffington did represent the conservatism taking over one segment of California politics.

There were many Republicans who couldn't wait to replace Brown as Assembly Speaker. Jim Brulte was a young Republican who quickly challenged Brown's power. He was a second term Republican Assemblyman and a seasoned politician. Brulte had been part of the campaign organization which elected U.S. Senator S.I. Hayakawa, and he was an advance man for President George Bush. The hopes for a new Republican majority finally materialized in the 1994 election. The Democratic Party lost eight Assembly seats as voters turned out incumbents. Some of these Democratic candidates who lost did so by just several hundred votes in predominantly Democratic districts. Voter discontent was high. When the smoke cleared the Republican Party had a 41 to 39 majority in the Assembly.

Brulte ordered champagne and held a press conference predicting the end of Brown's power. When Brulte urged Brown to step down as Assembly Speaker, he refused. Brown stated that until someone else had forty-one votes he was still the Speaker.

Then Brulte held another press conference and accused Brown of bluffing. Brulte announced he would seek the Speaker's post. The Assembly chamber was packed to start the new legislative session. After fourteen years, the Republicans were gloating that Brown's power was about to end. But the celebration proved premature, Brown still had some political leverage.

For a month Brown had talked with Assembly Republicans looking for someone who would bolt the Party. He had to find one Republican dissenter to maintain his power. Finally, on a cold December morning, Speaker Brown struck a deal to retain his power.

Paul Horcher, a dissident Republican, agreed to cross party lines to vote for Brown. Horcher had been on the outs with Republican leaders for four years. As a reward for his defection,

Brown named Horcher the vice chairperson of the Assembly Ways and Means Committee. Brulte was furious. In the Assembly, a jubilant Horcher slammed his fist on his desk and hollered: "Brown for Speaker." Once again Brown had pulled off a political coup.

The Assembly was deadlocked 40 to 40 and the Republicans could not elect Brulte as Speaker. There was one more parliamentary move used by the Democratic Party when they forced Assemblyman Richard Mountjoy to resign from his seat. He had been elected to the California Senate in a concurrent special election, and the Democrats would not allow him to hold two legislative seats. So Brown was elected 40 to 39 and retained the Speakership. But his power was on the decline.

For a brief time Brown retained the Speaker's powers. He realized, however, that the end of his state power was near. So Brown made the decision to run for Mayor of San Francisco. It was the term limit law that forced him to leave office. Suddenly, Assembly careers were limited to six years and state senate careers to eight. Although Brown was reelected Speaker in 1995, it lasted only six months. It was time for Brown to seek a new political challenge. The mayor's job in San Francisco was an especially appealing position.

Da Mayor: Willie Brown's Triumphant Return to San Francisco Politics

When Willie Brown announced in June 1994 that he was entering the mayor's race, *San Francisco Chronicle* columnist Herb Caen remarked that Brown once said he would never become mayor because all you dealt with was "street lights, dog-doo and parking meters." Caen, in his daily column, devoted an entire page to Brown. It was the beginning of a campaign in which Brown defeated the heavily funded incumbent mayor, Frank Jordan, and proved that he was still among California's most powerful politicians.

The city still loved Brown, and he had a well-organized and dedicated staff that promptly began combing every neighborhood for votes. Brown reminded San Franciscans that their city was built on the strength of local neighborhoods. He appealed to the self interest of the Asian, the Irish Catholic, the gay, the Jewish, the African American, the Mexican American and the recently arrived immigrants who were making San Francisco their home. The city, Brown preached to the electorate, was made up of many interest groups, and they all deserved special consideration.

During the fall of 1995, Brown's campaign was better financed than that of his opponents. He was a savvy politician who understood city politics. Another advantage was that Brown was better known to San Francisco voters than the incumbent, Mayor Frank Jordan. Although he was not involved there were a series of sexual harassment scandals in the police department which cast aspersions upon the Mayor's leadership. Since Jordan had been the San Francisco Police Chief, the media had a field day charging that he might have overlooked sexual harassment. This wasn't true, but Jordan found it difficult to defuse these charges. His wife, Wendy Paskin, also received a great deal of negative newspaper publicity and she was often referred to as "the lady who ran the city."

Frank Jordan was also a poor campaigner. He was a balding man with an unfriendly personality who easily lost his temper and political focus. Jordan appeared ill at ease with the various ethnic groups which made up San Francisco's voting population. His personal style was

Mayor Willie Brown

the good old boy school of politics which emphasized a slap on the back. This out-of-date political approach didn't appeal to San Franciscans.

Because he was a political amateur, Jordan made too many mistakes. He alienated large segments of the community. The Jewish vote was concerned about his civil rights record. The gay vote was a crucial one, and Jordan had trouble supporting gay rights. The African American and Mexican American communities complained about police abuse, and Jordan simply ignored their concerns. Jordan also failed to mend political fences with his rivals.

Roberta Achtenberg, a former member of the San Francisco Board of Supervisors and a lesbian activist, was the candidate for mayor who was most critical of Mayor Jordan. Achtenberg controlled the 20% gay vote, and Jordan was never able to reach an accord with her. Brown needed the gay vote to win the election, so he began to bombard Achtenberg with information on his politics. The result was that the gay community swung its support to Brown. Achtenberg was a formidable candidate who had a serious list of concerns. At the top of her list was regulation of police behavior and a more active community review board. She also lectured the SF Board of Supervisors on the need for spousal benefits for same sex living situations. Jordan didn't seem to understand the gay community but Brown did.

When the *San Francisco Chronicle* reported Brown's rise in the polls, Mayor Jordan realized that he was in political trouble. So he began attacking Brown's integrity. The strategy was to suggest that Brown was serving too many San Francisco interest groups. Jordan never called Brown a crook, but he implied it.

Clint Reilly, a San Francisco political consultant, was hired to smear Brown. For years, Reilly had been a Brown hater. When Reilly told a national magazine that Brown was a poor role model for African Americans, Brown countered with charges that racism motivated his opponent. The sight of a black man in the Mayor's Office, Brown charged, was more than Reilly could bear. To counter these smears, Brown hired Jack Davis as a political consultant. It was Davis who turned the election around by organized campaign appearances, bringing Brown into neighborhoods to address community needs. The multi-ethnic neighborhoods heard what they wanted from Brown and swung behind his candidacy. Brown was also able to appease big business by promising tax breaks and a friendly business atmosphere.

Another reason for Brown's appeal was that he reeducated himself about San Francisco's needs. Where he was once a prominent figure in restaurants or having a martini with *San Francisco Chronicle* columnist Herb Caen, Brown was now a fixture at political fund raisers, community dinners and social events.

In North Beach, San Francisco's Italian enclave, Brown could be found playing bocce ball in the afternoons. During the evening, he was often in Chinatown having dinner. This was followed by a group of meetings with downtown business interests at the Fairmont Hotel. By the morning, Brown could be spotted having coffee in the predominantly Irish Catholic Sunset district, followed by another coffee in the Mexican American Mission district. Brown understood the fragmented nature of city politics and played to the varied interests.

There were some tense moments during the campaign. The press bothered Brown with their inquires about his personal life. When a reporter for the *Washington Post*, William Claiborne, asked Brown if he was worried about Mayor Jordan's personal attacks, Brown responded: "I'm not into this bullshit about my integrity."

The media predicted Brown's defeat. Then ten days before the election Mayor Jordan posed nude in a shower with two radio personalities, Mark Thompson and Brian Phelp. The *San Francisco Examiner* positioned the photo on its front page. With his flabby stomach and silly grin, Jordan turned off voters. His wife, Wendy Paskin, took the blame for this publicity stunt, and it cost Jordan the election. Suddenly, he looked like the village idiot. The newspapers quickly forgot about Brown's alleged lack of integrity and criticized Mayor Jordan's lack of common sense.

When he appeared on a number of radio shows, Brown was asked questions while the host played Bobby Darin's "Splish Splash." Everyone had a good time ridiculing Mayor Jordan while emphasizing his inability to lead the city.

Brown's campaign for mayor was a textbook example of well-organized politics. Armies of supporters walked the streets turning out voters. On November 7, 1995, the voters went to the polls and Brown finished two percentage points ahead of Jordan. But Brown failed to receive 50% of the vote. So a runoff election was scheduled.

In order to win the runoff election Brown had to convince Achtenberg and her supporters to throw their votes to him. She had little choice as Mayor Jordan was never able to deal with the gay community. In the runoff on December 12, 1995, Willie Brown was elected San Francisco's forty-first mayor and became the first African American to lead the city.

Brown vowed to run the city efficiently. He talked at length about good city services, low municipal taxes and a renewed business community. Prosperity and good times were Brown's goals. As *San Francisco Chronicle* columnist Herb Caen observed: "Da Mayor gets what he wants." Mayor Brown wasn't the only headline grabber. California women were in the forefront of state politics. The decade of the woman ready to enter the 1990s with new levels of success and achievement was on its way.

Dianne Feinstein: The Decade of Women, Part II: The 1990s

In 1990, Dianne Feinstein was a nationally known politician. She was no longer considered the ex-Mayor of San Francisco but a voice for liberal Democratic politics as well as a force in the Party. The "Year of the Woman" is how *Time* magazine described the electoral activity of female candidates. Feinstein's name was prominent in this press coverage. She was the ex-Mayor of San Francisco in search of elective office. When she announced that she hoped to become governor, there was a wave of Democratic euphoria.

An experienced politician, Feinstein realized that she faced a tough task. To further her quest for elected office, she hired two political consultants, Bill Carrick and Hank Morris, to begin organizing her gubernatorial campaign. Although she failed to beat Pete Wilson in the 1990 gubernatorial race, this contest was an important training group for two successful United States Senate elections.

Feinstein's advisers discovered that television was an important political tool. Her political consultants produced a thirty second TV commercial demonstrating how Feinstein took charge of San Francisco in the aftermath of the George Moscone-Harvey Milk killings. This TV ad boosted her popularity, and the Democratic Party prepared a campaign which would elect Feinstein California's governor.

The 1990 California governor's race was a major turning point in Golden State politics. Since California had the sixth largest economy in the world, a history of Democratic legislative controls and a belief in a multi-cultural society, it was assumed that Feinstein was the electoral favorite. But there were changes taking place in the Golden State. Both the economic and Democratic Party organization faltered. Then the illegal immigrant questioned strained the racial tolerance of Californians.

As politicians geared up to seek the governor's job, Feinstein was the only candidate without an office. In the primary election she faced Attorney General John Van De Kamp and beat him 52% to 45% for the Democratic gubernatorial nomination. Clint Reilly, the old Willie Brown hater, was the force behind Feinstein's Democratic primary victory.

However, the disagreements between Feinstein and Reilly doomed her general campaign. Reilly cautioned her to relax and not be so obsessed with detail. Feinstein warned him that a slipshod campaign would result in an embarrassing loss. As they fought, Feinstein's health declined, and she eventually had to undergo major surgery.

Feinstein's general campaign for governor never got off the ground. She was ill with fibroid tumors and put off the surgery her doctors recommended. Reilly urged her to travel the campaign trail a little harder. She was a private person and didn't tell her staff the full extent of her illness. Finally, in July 1990, Feinstein secretly went into the hospital for a hysterectomy. It wasn't until late August that she resumed serious campaigning. By then it was too late. Her campaign organization was in shambles and another chief aide, Hadley Roff, had to go to the hospital for surgery.

Feinstein found Wilson a formidable candidate. His Republican political career was a twenty-five year one, and he was a seasoned campaigner. One of Feinstein's advisers told the *San Francisco Chronicle* that running against Wilson was like walking on a sidewalk where someone was throwing marbles at you.

Wilson's television ads suggested that he combined fiscal conservatism with a plan for smaller government. However, Wilson was not a typical conservative Republican; he also supported abortion rights and environmental controls. Wilson was also a shrewd politician who could capitalize on Feinstein's mistakes. When Feinstein suggested hiring quotas for women, Wilson turned her comment into a major campaign issue. Unwittingly, Wilson hit upon a sensitive issue—Californians would not support quotas or Affirmative Action.

Sensing that she was running behind Wilson, Feinstein's political opinions became increasingly conservative. While Feinstein was pro-choice on abortion, she did her best not to raise this question. Feinstein never mentioned the large campaign contribution from the California Abortion Rights Action League. As a result, she was able to convince conservative and church oriented voters that she had a responsible attitude on the abortion issue.

When the vote came in for governor in 1990, Feinstein was beaten. On election day Democratic voter registration was down 30,000 and Republican registration had gone up 50,000. The final electoral results were not surprising as the lowest voter turnout in California history brought Wilson into the Governor's Office. What made Wilson's victory a close one was that he had beaten her by 240,000 ballots with six million cast. The 240,000 ballots were absentee ballots which the GOP had concentrated upon and they turned out to be the margin of victory.

A few months after the ill-fated gubernatorial campaign, Feinstein began planning her campaign for the United States Senate. On January 13, 1991, she made formal announcement that she would seek Wilson's Senate seat.

During Feinstein's campaign for the United States Senate, she courted the ethnic vote. The Hispanic, African American and the Asian communities responded to her civil rights oriented campaign. Since Hispanics were conservative on the abortion issue, Feinstein shrewdly took a middle of the road stand. Hispanic men were a problem for Democratic women as the patriarch factor made it difficult for them to cast their vote for females. Feinstein overcame this by calling upon Los Angeles political activist Gloria Molina and a local lawyer lobbyist Tony Zamora. Feinstein was able to win the vote with a strong commitment to better education and jobs.

The Asian vote was a complicated matter. It was a conservative and often Republican mentality. Los Angeles City Councilman Michael Woo was critical of Feinstein for not spending enough time courting southern California Asians. Although she eventually won 52% of the Asian vote, Feinstein never made serious inroads into the community outside of San Francisco. One of the lessons of political change in the 1990s was that Hispanics and Asians warmed slowly to Feinstein's candidacy but eventually did give her their vote in the 1992 Senate election. Like Hispanic voters, Asians had difficulty supporting a woman.

In the 1992 Democratic primary, Feinstein had faced formidable opposition from Gray Davis. He was a young and highly ambitious politician who made his mark as Chief of Staff to Governor Jerry Brown. Initially, Davis was the odds on favorite to win the Democratic Senate nomination because he was closely connected to the party money sources. But what Davis and the Democrats didn't realize was that more than 50% of Golden State voters were female and almost a third of the male vote was sympathetic to Feinstein's candidacy.

In San Francisco, the National Organization for Women took up Feinstein's candidacy but used a low key approach. A NOW campaign tract pointed out that Feinstein had been a strong supporter of the ill-fated Equal Rights Amendment and had appointed more women to San Francisco city government positions than any other mayor. The most applauded Feinstein appointments were those of San Francisco Treasurer Mary Callahan and Supervisor Willie Kennedy.

The 1992 Democratic Senate race brought Feinstein up against John Seymour who had been selected to fill the remainder of Pete Wilson's term. Seymour was a carbon copy of Senator Wilson. He was an obscure legislator from Orange County who was a staunch conservative with little charisma. His public speeches were poorly delivered, and he was uncomfortable in front of crowds. In ideology and hard line conservative politics, Seymour was a political double of the governor. He was also a former Marine, a hard line conservative on financial matters, a strong opponent of abortion and a staunch anti-immigrant politician. He was also abusive toward Feinstein during the early days of the campaign. She maintained her class by not engaging in name calling contests with Seymour. Soon the voters realized that he was too inexperienced a politician for the job.

She easily won the 1992 election against John Seymour and became a United States Senator. But there was only two years left in the term formally occupied by Alan Cranston. So Feinstein began planning to run again in 1994.

Her Republican opponent in the 1994 election, Michael Huffington, provided little opposition, and she ran away with the election. Despite the prospect of an easy electoral victory, Feinstein waged a hard and fair campaign. The name calling and nasty tactics of Governor Wilson made her determined to conduct a campaign based on the issues.

The 1994 United States Senate campaign was a major turning point in California politics. Feinstein was identified as a middle of the road Democrat with a penchant for supporting mainstream feminist issues. Delaine Eastin, a Democrat who was elected California Superintendent of Schools, commented that Feinstein made the "so called women's issues respectable." Nancy Pelosi, San Francisco's Democratic Congresswoman, echoed these sentiments: "The gap of understanding between men and women grows narrower."

California was proud of Dianne Feinstein and Barbara Boxer. Not only were they first rate politicians, but they made history as the first two women to represent their states in the U.S. Senate.

Willie Brown in 1997: The SF Mayor after One Year on the Job

A year after being elected San Francisco's Mayor, Willie Brown had reason to celebrate. He was in the middle of a 525 million dollar election debate over a proposed retail mall and S.F. 49er football stadium, which passed by a narrow margin. He was the picture of the energetic mayor protecting his town's major sports franchise. Everything Brown did was directed toward reviving the city economy and attracting tourists. He held a major press conference when $22,000 lampposts were constructed outside the Moscone Convention Center. One day he rode the city buses with reporters and announced that he was solving the public transit problems. Or at least this was the impression he gave the voters.

Much like his career as Assembly Speaker, Brown was taking quick action. By beautifying San Francisco, providing special tax breaks for the major sports franchises and maintaining good city services, Brown was living out his vision of the city. It was also one designed to maintain his power.

"How a city looks is very much a part of the pride people have in it...." Brown remarked. Then he announced a plan to redo Union Square. He ordered extra garbage trucks to clean up downtown's Market Street and he proposed moving the Academy of Sciences and the deYoung Museum downtown to allow greater public access. "The city is open to everyone, and we have to make it accessible," Brown quipped.

Brown's critics were aghast at the proposed changes. San Francisco's traditional Society 400 normally make the suggestion and plan such changes. Brown, always the Populist, made it clear that a new brand of Democracy was inundating the city. The look of the city had to be as precise as that of Mayor Brown. He also hoped to explain the cultural horizons for everyone.

This controversy prompted Wilkes Bashford, the San Francisco clothing magnate, to observe: "Willie cares about how things look, whether it's a room, the city or his suit." Other close friends suggested that the environment was just as important to Mayor Brown as a downtown beautification program. "I want the city to look better than Paris," Brown said after returning from Paris. He also talked of extensive trade with the Far East and a commitment to business.

In the midst of these successes the San Francisco City garbage workers staged a wildcat strike. They walked off the job in late April, 1997 without notice. Mayor Brown stepped in and negotiated a settlement. The three day strike did little to lower Mayor Brown's image since he negotiated the quick settlement. The Teamsters Local 350 signed the agreement at City Hall where Brown held a press conference. "I'm not looking for credit," Brown said. But Mayor Brown was upset with press reports indicating that he may have ignored, at least for a brief moment, the demands of San Francisco's powerful union movement. But Brown suggested that he was never concerned about the strike.

Yet, Brown remains thin skinned and does not take criticism well. "I've got to be prepared to fight the fights to move the city in my direction," Brown stated. To keep the city in the mainstream of state politics, Brown negotiated a truce with Governor Wilson. By May 1997, public opinion polls placed Mayor Brown as California's most popular political figure. The San Francisco economy, public safety and voter content were higher than anywhere else in the Golden State.

Pete Wilson: The Governor Walks the Line in 1997

In the middle of his second term as Governor, the sixty-four-year old Wilson blamed California's problems on liberals and crime. Although the California economy was in good shape, there were social problems that plagued the state. Welfare spending, illegal immigrants and rising gang violence hampered the Golden State.

As Governor Wilson declined in public opinion polls an issue arose which restored some degree of his former popularity. The University of California Regents, the governing board for the University system, announced that the fairness of Affirmative Action and special admission procedures were in question. So they began studying the admission process and the University of California with more than 120,000 students became the focus of a national struggle. The issue was whether or not to continue a special admission program. As the nation's largest public higher education system, the University of California was a trendsetter. A nasty argument broke out over admissions and the University modified its politics to discount race as an admission criteria. With 40% of the student body admitted for reasons other than pure academic merit, there was criticism from a large segment of the population.

Governor Wilson hoped to use his opposition to Affirmative Action and special admission quotas as a springboard to the Republican presidential nomination.

When the California voters passed Proposition 209 striking down Affirmative Action at the University of California, Governor Wilson was a strong supporter of the measure. After it passed, however, northern California chief federal judge Thelton Henderson, a former civil rights lawyer, blocked its implementation in December 1996. Judge Henderson ruled that Proposition 209 violated the 14th amendment and banned its enforcement.

In April, 1997 the Ninth U.S. Circuit Court of Appeals ruled that Proposition 209 was legal. The Ninth Circuit Court cited the almost five million people who approved the so-called California Civil Rights Initiative as a voice for a more democratic future. Attorney General Dan Lundgren jumped on the anti-Affirmative Action bandwagon and praised the decision. Not surprisingly, Lundgren was a major candidate for the Republican gubernatorial nomination. The issue of where Affirmative Action fits into the fabric of California society is one which is still being debated. Civil rights lawyers are challenging the implementation of the law.

In 1996, Governor Wilson was unable to interest the Republican Party in his presidential candidacy. He suffered a major setback when his ex-wife admitted that they had hired an illegal alien as a housekeeper. They hadn't paid her social security tax and the media had a field day criticizing the governor. In an indignant statement to the press, Governor Wilson defended his actions. It was Wilson's advocacy of gay rights, his lukewarm support for abortion rights and his call for a ban on assault weapons which estranged him from the Republican party mainstream. He was simply too California for traditional Republicans

Robert Gunnison, a *San Francisco Chronicle* reporter, suggested in February 1997 that Governor Wilson's image was at its low point. A Field Poll supported this observation as Wilson received a 51% unfavorable rating which was the lowest in his career. The reaction was due to Wilson's propensity for immigrant bashing and ethnic insensitivity. Surprisingly, Californians rated Wilson's job performance satisfactorily.

Governor Wilson's plan to cut welfare programs remained popular despite the reaction against his politics. His new program outlined by the Governor was designed to reduce 600,000 families from welfare roles by 2000. By setting limits for adults receiving welfare, Wilson argued, and forcing the able bodied to work, there would be a dramatic reduction in welfare spending. The California Legislature didn't agree with the Governor and the issue turned in a nasty partisan, political debate. Elizabeth Hill, California's legislative analyst, was critical of Wilson's welfare proposal, and she called the work incentive program a "poor compromise."

Hill's criticism centered around the notion that workers could keep only fifty-four cents of every dollar earned while on welfare. She believed that this reduced the incentive to work. As California cruises toward the year 2000 the arguments over welfare reform will escalate. It will continue to be one of the issues in the Golden State.

Dianne Feinstein: The United States Senator in 1997

By late 1990s, Senator Dianne Feinstein occupied a prominent place in the United States Senate. She was an important member of the Senate Foreign Relations Committee and remained a strong voice for women's rights. Her membership on the foreign policy body brought her into a position where she helped to bring Chinese and general Far Eastern business to California. In San Francisco, there was a great deal of appreciation for Feinstein's ability to cut through the federal red tape to make trade with China easier.

One of the negatives to Feinstein's economic bridge to the Far East was an FBI report that the Chinese were donating large sums of money to members of the United States Senate. In a series of sensationalized newspaper articles, a number of major newspapers speculated on whether or not Feinstein accepted illegal campaign contributions. The source for this story was an FBI report which revealed that Feinstein had been warned about illegal campaign contributions. She had turned down $12,000 from the Lippo Group, an Indonesian banking firm and real estate corporation with ties to the Chinese Government. She was never part of this developing scandal but she demonstrated her political integrity by turning down any suspicious campaign contributions. Feinstein also demonstrated excellent self control by not publicly condemning the FBI for its leak.

On a more positive note, by March 1997, as the fallout over President Bill Clinton's fundraising activity dominated the press, Feinstein continued to bring in large sums of federal money to modernize the port of San Francisco, extend the Bay Area Transit System and provide assistance to Los Angeles and San Diego city government in modernizing their transportation systems. Feinstein was the consummate politician who understood the need to continue growth and progress in the Golden State.

As a United States Senator in the 1990s, Feinstein demonstrated excellent work habits, independence from any political faction and the skills necessary to represent Californians. She had spent thirty years in politics but standing on the Senate floor in November 1992 she summed up her feelings: "I wish my father could have seen this...my father would have been proud. My uncle would have been proud." Californians felt the same way about Senator Feinstein and demonstrated it by making her California's most popular federal politician.

Judge Richard O. Keller: A Jurist for the 1990s

Law and order remains one of the most visible issues of the 1990s. Since the Rodney King incident in Los Angeles there has been a renewed interest in the court system. The O.J. Simpson trial focused attention on the role of the trial judge and Lance Ito received an inordinate amount of criticism. The Republican party has suggested that the governor appoint judges with an even handed, but firm, approach to law and order. The stability of California society depends upon seasoned judges.

Judge Richard O. Keller

Photo Courtesy: Richard O. Keller

As a result of the intensified public interest in the legal system, one of Governor Pete Wilson's most important mandates was to appoint skilled Municipal Court Judges to handle local legal problem. The governor is able to shape the direction of the court by appointing judges with a philosophy similar to his law and order mandates.

The role of the Municipal Court Judge is one where the presiding judge deals with a wide variety of cases. Former California Supreme court Justice Stanley Mosk reminisced that the Municipal Court was responsible for maintaining the precarious balance of local justice. "I believe that the toughest appointment a governor has to make is that of the Municipal Court Judge," Mosk remarked.

The road to this Court is a complicated and politically involved one. The candidate for a judgeship must obtain a wide range of legal and personal recommendations, informally campaign for the court appointment and meet with various representatives of the governor. His or her qualifications are reviewed by various members of the bar. There is also a Judicial Nominee Evaluation Commission of the state bar which by statute reviews all judicial applicants. So by the time a judge is appointed, he or she has gone through a long and tedious process.

Governor Pete Wilson once remarked that Municipal Court Judges are his most difficult appointments, because there so many qualified lawyers. What Wilson failed to add was that most of these lawyers worked diligently for his election. So there is a chance of political fallout every time the governor appoints a judge. Governor Wilson has often remarked that these judges are the heart and soul of the judicial system. Before a Judge is appointed, Governor Wilson's staff makes sure that the candidate makes his or her opinions known on a wide variety of topics usually including civil liberties, abortion and the death penalty.

When Richard Keller appeared before John Davies, the judicial appointments secretary for Governor Wilson, he underwent an hour interview on his legal views. In a very cordial, but pointed, meeting, Davies asked Keller for his opinions on a wide variety of subjects. The questions were ones in which the governor had a philosophical interest. Keller's answers were ones which the governor found acceptable and he was appointed to the Municipal Court.

Once Judge Keller was appointed, he began to establish a solid record. Most Municipal Court Judges are appointed to fill out the term of a Judge who is moving to another court or who is retiring. As a result, Keller filled out the term of Judge Joseph Jay who retired. Under California law, Keller was required to stand for election at the end of Judge Jay's normal term.

Judge Keller's route to the Fremont-Newark-Union City Municipal Court followed a long and varied legal career. The road to a California judicial appointment invariably begins with the candidates education. It was during Keller's undergraduate education that he became interested in government and politics. As an undergraduate political science major at Emory University, he spent four years as a top flight student with an option for graduate or law school. Keller selected the law.

After graduating from Emory University Law School in Atlanta Georgia in 1967, Judge Keller entered the United States Air Force where he was a Captain and Judge Advocate. After his discharge in 1972 he began a distinguished legal career which led in 1981 to the opening of his own firm, the Law Offices of Richard O. Keller in Fremont, California. He developed a wide range of specialties with Real Property, Business and Corporate Law, Family Law, Probate and Estate Planning occupying his time. This was the perfect law practice to train a Municipal Judge.

Jim Snell, a partner in Broun, Norris, King, Grasskamp and Snell, hired Keller after his discharge from the Air Force. He found him not only to be an outstanding lawyer but a bastion of community service. Snell remarked: "For more than two decades Judge Keller was a respected lawyer with a wide variety of legal specialties. I have confidence that he will be an extraordinarily competent Judge." This opinion was echoed by a large number of lawyers in Southern Alameda County.

The variety of legal problems handled by Judge Keller's law office was excellent training for a court appointment, but his courteous and professional courtroom demeanor also attracted attention. As a result of his work, Judge Keller drew the attention of local Republican politicians and a number of other Judges. In time he was recommended for appointment as an Alameda County Municipal Court Judge. But this appointment was also due to his splendid record of community service.

The fifteen years that Judge Keller spent developing his own law practice was sprinkled with public service. He was elected to the Governing Board of the Fremont-Newark Community College District in 1976 and remained in this position until his appointment to the bench.

One of the reasons that Judge Keller was appointed as a Municipal Court judge was his long history of service to the local community. He was active in the Washington Township Bar Association as an officer and member, and he was a Judge Pro-Tem in the Municipal Court.

The Judge Pro-Tem is a temporary position where an attorney is appointed by the presiding judge to hear cases on a limited basis. This helps to relieve court congestion. He was also active in many local service organization. Keller was generous with his time to the community. Governor Wilson recognized his two decades of local involvement with the court position.

Judge Keller's Judicial appointment capped a long and distinguished legal career. He has shown an even handed judicial personality in handling a wide variety of legal issues. As a result, Judge Keller is well respected by all the attorneys who appear before him. Judge Keller typifies the Municipal Court judge, he is dedicated to fairness and serving the best interests of the local community.

Bibliographical Essay

For Willie Brown's career see, James Richardson, *Willie Brown: A Biography* (Berkeley, 1996). On Brown's miraculous retention of the Speaker's position see, John Jacobs, "The Two Secrets That Helped Willie Win," *Sacramento Bee*, Forum Section, February 8, 1995. Also see Richard Edward DeLeon, *Left Coast City: Politics in San Francisco, 1975-1991* (Lawrence, 1992) and Chester Hartman, *The Transformation of San Francisco* (Totawa, New Jersey, 1984). For the role of Mayor Dianne Feinstein see, Jerry Roberts, *Dianne Feinstein: Never Let Them See You Cry* (New York, 1994); Carol Pogash, "Mayor Feinstein's Twelve Rules for Getting Ahead," *Working Woman* (January, 1986), pp. 84-85 and Susan Ware, *American Women* (Belmont, 1989).

On Feinstein's electoral strategy see, Celia Morris, *Storming The Statehouse: Running for Governor with Ann Richards and Dianne Feinstein* (New York, 1992). The best sources from the contemporary press on Feinstein are Sidney Blumenthal, "A Woman of Independent Means," *The New Republic*, August 13, 1990 and Garry Wills, "Guv Lite!" *California*, November 1990. Also see, "Campaign '90: A Look Back At The California Governor's Race," Institute of Governmental Studies, University of California, Berkeley, January 18-19, 1991. On the Feinstein campaign fund allegations and the FBI role see, Bob Woodward and Brian Duffy, "Donors Targeted Feinstein," *San Jose Mercury News*, March 9, 1997, pp. 1, 24A.

For biographical information on Willie Brown, Pete Wilson and Dianne Feinstein see, Dan Walter, editor, *California Political Almanac, 1989-1990 Edition* (Santa Barbara, 1990).

An excellent biography of a close Willie Brown friend is John Jacobs, *A Rage of Justice: The Passion and Politics of Philip Burton* (Berkeley, 1995). On gay rights and politics see Randy Shilts, *The Mayor of Castro Street: The Life and Times of Harvey Milk* (New York, 1982) and Randy Shilts, *And The Band Played On: Politics, People and the AIDS Epidemic* (New York, 1987).

For California politics see Terry Christensen and Larry N. Gerston, *Politics In The Golden State: The California Connection* (Boston, 1988).

On Willie Brown's election as San Francisco Mayor see, John King, "King of the Hill," *San Francisco Chronicle*, February 13, 1997, p. 17A, 20A. For Governor Wilson's decline in public support see, Robert E. Gunnison, "Wilson's Image Takes Clobbering in New State Poll," *San Francisco Chronicle*, February 20, 1997, pp. 13, 21A.

On Pete Wilson see Howard Fineman, "Riding The Wave," *Newsweek*, May 22, 1995, pp. 19-21; Howard Fineman, "The Rollback Begins," *Newsweek*, July 31, 1995, p. 30 and Jon

Meacham and Andrew Murr, "Undecided: Will California's Lead Dog Run?" *Newsweek*, March 6, 1995, p. 29 and Jordan Bonfante, "Campaign 96: New York or Bust," *Time*, September 25, 1995, pp. 31-32.

For Senator Barbara Boxer see Barbara and Nicole Boxer, *Strangers in the Senate: Politics and The Revolution of Women in America* (Washington D.C., 1994).

On the settlement of the San Francisco garbage strike see, Ray Delgado, "Mixed Feelings on Garbage Contract," *San Francisco Examiner*, April 27, 1997, pp. A1, A15 and Rob Morse, "Garbage In, Garbage Out," *San Francisco Examiner*, April 27, 1997, p. A2.

Appendix

The Mission System: A Chronology

San Diego de Alcalá, July 16, 1769
San Carlos Borroméo (Carmel), June 3, 1770
San Antonio de Padua, July 14, 1771
San Gabriel Arcángel (the mother of Los Angeles), September 8, 1771
San Luís Obispo de Tolosa, September 1, 1772
San Francisco de Asis (Dolores), October 8, 1776
San Juan Capistrano, November 1, 1776
Santa Clara, January 12, 1777
San Buenaventura, March 31, 1782
Santa Barbara, December 4, 1786
Purisima Concepción, December 8, 1787
Santa Cruz, August 28, 1791
Neustra Senora de la Soledad, October 9, 1791
San José de Guadalupe, June 11, 1797
San Juan Bautista, June 24, 1797
San Miguel Arcángel, July 25, 1797
San Fernando Rey de España, September 8, 1797
San Luís Rey de Francia, June 13, 1798
Santa Inés (or Ynéz), September 17, 1804
San Rafael Arcángel, December 14, 1817
San Francisco Solano (Sonoma—the only Mexican established mission) July 4, 1823

Spanish Presidios

San Diego, July 16, 1769
Monterey, June 3, 1770
San Francisco, September 17, 1776
Santa Barbara, April 21, 1782

Spanish Pueblos

San José, November 29, 1777
Los Angeles, September 4, 1781
Branciforte, 1797

Spanish Governors

Gaspar de Portola, Governor of the Two Californias, 1767–1770
Felipe de Barri, Governor of the Two Californias, 1770–1775
Felipe de Neve, Governor of the Two Californias, 1777–1782
Pedro Fages, 1782–1791
Jose Joaquin de Arrillaga, 1792–1794
Diego de Borica, 1794–1800
Jose Joaquin de Arrillaga, 1800–1814
Jose Dario Arguello, 1814–1815
Pablo Vicente Sola, 1815–1822

Index

Adelantados, 16
Aguirre, Martin, 132
Alcalde, in the California Mines, 93
Alemany, Joseph, 184
Alexander, George, 203–204
Alien Land Law of 1913, 220–221, 270
Almonte, Juan, 75
Alta California, discovery of, 19
Alvarado, Juan Bautista, 63–69, 129–130
American-California, early days, 71–86
Anderson, Bronco Billy, 244
Anthoney, Earl C., 243
Anti-Communism in California, 233–235, 257–262, 272–277
Anza, Captain Juan Bautista de, 28, 34
Arbuckle, Roscoe "Fatty," 244
Arguello, Luis, 54–57
Arrillaga, Governor Jose de, 44–45, 47–49
Atherton, Gertrude, 190–191
Audiencia, Spanish Court in New Spain, 16
Austin, Mary, 189
Australian Ballot, 105
Ayuntamientos, 54
Aztec Indians, 15–16

Bandit Stereotype (Mexican-American), 124–129
Bank of California, 1875 Suspension, 152–156
Bank of Italy, 247
Barclay, John S., 125–126
Bartleson, John, 75–76
Battle of Old Woman's Gun, 82
Battle of Olompail, 79
Battle of San Pascal, 83
Baxter, Leone, 271
Beale, Edward F., 164–165
Bear Flag Republic, 78–80
Beat Generation (1950s), 277–279
Begg, John and Co. (English Merchants), 55, 72
Bell, Theodore, 217, 220
Benton, Senator Thomas Hart, 244–246
Berryesa Family, 114
Better America Federation, 236–238, 246–247
Bidwell, John, 75–76
Bierce, Ambrose, 159
Big Brother and the Holding Company, 287
Bigelow, Mayor Harden, 134–135
Bigler, Governor John, 169
Billings, Warren K., 231–233, 262
Bird, Chief Justice Rose, 291
Black Californians, 29, 38, 76, 109–111, 168–169, 182–185, 265–266, 281–282, 292–293
Boddy, Manchester, 261

Bolanos, Francisco de, 19
Bonelli, William G., 275
Booth, Governor Newton, 131–132
Borica, Diego de, 42–44
Bouchard, Hyppolyte de, 49–50
Boulder Canyon Project, 249
Bowron, Fletcher, 270
Bradley, Mayor Thomas, 266, 282
Branciforte, 42, 65–66
Brannan, Sam, 90–91, 112, 114, 116, 134
Bret Harte, Francis, 181, 186–188
Bridges, Harry, 252–257, 273
Broderick, David, 105–120
Brown, Governor Edmund G (Pat), 275–278, 281–286
Brown, Governor Jerry, 277, 282, 291–293
Brown, Willie L., 282, 292–293
Bruce, Lenny, 278
Bryant, Mayor Andrew Jackson, 171
Bryant and Sturgis Company of Boston, 72
Bryce, James, 157
Bucareli, Viceroy Antonio do, 27–28
Buchanan, President James, 119–120
Budd, Governor James, 160
Bunche, Dr. Ralph, 266
Burke, Yvonne Braithwaite, 282
Burlingame Treaty of 1868, 171
Burnett, Governor Peter, 102
Burns, William J., 210, 228
Butterfield, John, 142–143

Cabrillo, Juan Rodriguez, 8, 20, 50
Cahuenga, Treaty of, 110, 152, 180
Cahuilla Indians, 8
Calafia, Queen, 19
California Democratic Council, 276
California Eagle (Black Newspaper), 265
California Indian Education Association, 167
Californios, schizoid heritage, 133
Californios, second-generation, 129–133
Calkins, John V., 234
Canby, General E.R.S., 165–166
Cannery and Agricultural Workers' Industrial Union, 258–260
Carillo, Vincent, 233
Carlos, Martha, 125–126
Carpentier, Horace, 137–138
Carrillo, Jose Antonio, 82, 100
Carson, Johnny, 283
Carson, Kit, 73, 76, 82
Casey, James, 116–119
Casey, Michael, 227–228
Castillero, Andres, 132

Castro, Jose, 63, 67, 76–77, 81–83, 114, 129–130
Castro, Marina, 118
Central Pacific Railroad, and new growth, 271–273
Central Pacific Railroad, transportation advances, 145–150
Chandler, Dorothy Buffum, 291
Chandler, Harry, 221
Chaplin, Charlie, 244
Chapman, Civil War ship, 255
Charlatans, 287
Charles V, King of Spain, 16
Chavez, Cesar, 260, 288–290
Chessman, Caryl, 275–277
Chico, Mariano, 63
Chinese, Building the Central Pacific RR, 148–150
Chinese, Exclusion Act of 1882, 171
Chinese, Geary Act of 1892, 171
Chinese, in early California, 169–175
Chinese, in the mines, 124–125
Chumash Indians, 8–9
Church Influences in Mexican-California, 56–63
Church Influences in New Spain, 30–31
Civil War in California, 141–142
Clapp, Louisa (Dame Shirley), 95–96
Coast Seamen's Union, 224–226
Cole, Cornelius, 110–111
Coleman, William T., 117, 172–175
Colored Citizens of California, 168
Colton, David C., 157–158
Colton, Water, 84, 98–99
Communist Labor Party, 233–235
Comstock Lode, 153–155
Condon, Ed, 234–235
Cone, Joseph, 174
Confederation de Uniones Obreros Mexicanos, 237–238
Constitution of 1849, 98–103
Constitution of 1879, 173–174
Cooke, Sherburne, 5
Coolbrith, Ina, 189
Cooper, Gary, 273
Cora, Charles, 117–119
Coronel, Antonio, 88
Cortes, Hernando, 15–19
Country Joe and the Fish, 287
Covarrubias, Jose M., 100
Crabb, Henry, 111, 113–114
Crabtree, Lotta, 96–98, 185–186
Crespi, Father Juan, 25
Criminal Syndicalism Law, 233–235, 238
Crocker, Charles, 92, 146–152
Croix, Teodoro de, 34
Curry, Charles, 215

Dame Shirley Letter, 95–96, 124
Dana, Richard Henry, 55
Darrow, Clarence, 227–229
DeWitt, General John L., 269–270
Dexter, Dr. Walter, 272
de Young, Charles, 174–175

Diego, Bishop Garcia, 63–64
Diggner Indian Stereotype, 5
Diputacion, Mexican-California legislature, 54–55, 58–59, 61, 63, 65, 67
Direct Legislation League, 202–204
Divisionist Movement, 111
Donner Party, 94
Dorr, Ebenezer, 44
Dorsey, Caleb, 128
Douglas, Helen Gahagan, 275
Downey, Governor John, 141
Drake, Sir Francis, 20
Durst, Ralph, 229–231
Dutch Flat railroad scheme, 144–146
Dwinelle, John W., 169
Dylan, Bob, 283
Dymally, Mervin, 282

Earthquakes, 4, 210–222
Eaton, Fred, 248
Echeandia, Governor Jose, 46, 57–61, 72
Edson, Katherine Phillips, 177–178, 219–220
Education, 166–167, 169, 182–185
Eisenhower, Milton S., 269–270
Ellis, Tom, 209
Emigrant's Guide to the Gold Mines, 94
End Poverty in California, 250–252
English explorers in Spanish California, 20–21
Eshleman, John, 221
Estevanico, 17
Estrada, Jose Mariano, 57
Estudillo, Jose G., 132
Estudillo land grant, 137
Eu, March Fong, 291
Exploits of Esplandian, 19

Fabian Society, 236
Fages, Eulalia de Callis, 34–35
Fages, Pedro, 26–28, 34–35
Fair Employment Practices Commission, 276
Farm Labor, 1920s, 236–238; 1930s, 257–260; 1960s–1970s, 288–290
Feinstein, Dianne, 282, 291
Ferlinghetti, Lawrence, 278
Fickert, Charles, 232
Figueroa, Governor Jose, 61–64
Fillibustering (1850s), 111–114
Filipino Labor Union, 258–260
Finney, Senator Sheldon, 169
Fitzgerald, F. Scott, 245
Flint, Timothy, 73
Flood, Noah, 169
Flores, Jose, 82–83
Flourney, Houston, 292
Foltz, Clara, 177
Ford, Richard "Blackie," 230–231
Foreign Miners' Tax Law of 1850, 123–129
Fort Gavilan, 77
Fort Gunnybags, 119

Fort Ross, 45–48
Foster, Mayer Stephen, 116
Free Speech Movement (1960s), 282–287
Fremont, Jessica Benton, 75–85, 135–136
Fremont, John C., 75–85, 135–138
Friedlander, Isaac, 152
Fugitive Slave Law, 109–111
Fukii v. California, 1953, 270
Furuseth, Andrew, 224–225

Gable, Clark, 4
Gage, Governor Henry T., 205, 227
Gale, William, A., 72
Galvez, Jose de, 23–24
Geography, influences of, 1–2
George, Henry, 191–193
Giannini, A.P., 247
Gili, Bartolome, 39–40
Gillespie, Archibald, 78–83
Gillett, Charles, 203–204, 238
Ginsberg, Allen, 278
Glenn, Dr. Hugh, 152
Gold Rush in California, 87–97
Gompers, Samuel, 228
Graham, Isaac, 65–67
Grateful Dead, 279, 287
Green Thomas Jefferson, 109–111, 124–129
Guerra, Pablo de la, 100–103, 114
Guzman, Nuno de, 16
Gwin, William, 101, 105–120, 135–137

Haight-Ashbury Summer of Love, 1967, 287–288
Halleck, Henry W., 134–135
Hallidie, Andrew S., 155
Ham and Egg Pension Plan, 252
Hancock Park (LA), 4
Haraszthy, Agoston, 3
Hare, Nathan, 282
Harper, Arthur C., 203–204
Harriman, Job, 203–204, 228–229
Harris, Myron, 234
Hart, Brook, 250
Hartnell, William, 55–56, 71, 76
Haskell, Burnette, 224–225
Hastings, Lansford, 75, 94
Hawkins, Augustus, 282
Hawks Peak Incident, 77–78
Haynes, Dr. John R., 202–204
Hays, Will H., 244–245
Hearst, Catherine, 291
Hearst, Patty, 291
Hearst, William Randolph, 158–159, 193–194
Heney, Francis J., 221
Herrin, William F., 160, 217–218
Hetch Hetchy Water Project, 248–249
Hijar, Jose Maria, 62–63
Hill, Dr. John, 109
Hinds, Tom, 184
Hollywood, 243–245, 273–274

Holmes, Jack, 250
Holmes, Rachel Hobson, 73
Hoover, Herbert C., 185
Hopkins, Mark, 92, 144, 146–152
Hounds, vigilante organization, 114–116
House UnAmerican Activities Committee, 272–274
Hughes, Charles Evans and 1916 election, 221–222
Humphrey, Isaac, 91
Huntington, Collis P., 92, 146–152, 155–161, 202
Huntington Library (San Marino), 155–156
Hupa Indians, 7

Ide, William (Bear Flagger), 79–80
Independent Taxpayers Party, 161
Indian Clothing, Food and Dwellings, 8–9
Indian Cultural Areas, 6–8
Indian, Digger Stereotype, 5
Indian, education 1850–1920s, 166–167
Indian life on the Missions, 34–41
Indian Religion, 9–10
Indian Reservation System, 163–167
Indian Slavery, 56–57
Indian Society, 10–11
Indian, Stone Age Concept, 5
Indian, temescal, 7–9
Indians, 1850–1900, 163–167
Indians, in Mexican-California, 56–63
Indians, pre-Spanish, 5–12
Industrial Workers of the World, 229–231
International Longshoremen's Association, 252–257
Irrigation, Spanish, 2–3
Itliong, Larry, 260

Jack, Captain (Modoc Indian Leader), 165–166
Jackson, Helen Hunt, 36, 165
Jalauehu, Francisco, 37
Jansen, C.J., 115
Japanese-American Relocation, 268–270
Jefferson Airplane, 287
Jenkins, John, 116
Jesuit Order in New Spain, 17, 23–24
Jesuits, Influence upon California Settlement, 23
Johnson, Governor J. Neely, 108–109, 118
Johnson, Hiram W., 174, 178, 201, 213–222, 230–231, 246
Johnston, William G., 164
Jolson, Al, 244, 273
Jones, Commodore Thomas, 66–67
Jones, Sandy, 109
Jones, William Carey, 135–136
Juanita, hangins of first woman, 126
Juarez, Benito, 129
Judah, Theodore, 144–146

Kaiser, Henry J., 265–267
Kalloch, Isaac, 174–175
Kearney, Denis, 172–175, 224
Kearny, Stephen W., 83–84
Kelley, Charles, 230

Kelly, William, 164
Kelsey, C.E., 166
Kelsey, Nancy, 75
Kenaday, Alexander, 223
Kenney, Robert W., 270
Kerouac, Jack, 278
King, James, 116–119
King, Thomas Starr, 141
Kino, Father Eusebio Francisco, 17, 23, 24
Knight, Goodwin, 275–276
Knights of the Golden Circle, 141
Know-Nothing Party, 108–109
Knowland, William F., 276–277
Kroeber, A.L., 5

Labor, post Gold Rush, 223–226
Labor, 1870–1920, 224–235
Labor, 1920s, 235–238
Labor, 1930s, 252–260
Labor, 1950s–1970s, 288–290
La Brea Tar Pits, 4–5
LaFollette Seamen's Act of 1915, 225
Land Law of 1851, 123, 133–138
Langdon, William, 210–212
La Purisma Concepcion Mission, 56–57
Lardner, Ring, 274
Larkin, Thomas Oliver, 77–84, 101–103
Lasuen, Father Fermin Francisco de, 39–42
Latham, Governor Milton, 141
Lee, Archy, 110–111
Leidesdorff, William (Black Leader), 76
Limantour, Jose Yves, 135–136
Lincoln-Roosevelt League, 214–215, 219
Literature, ecology and wilderness themes, 197–198
Literature on the California frontier, 185–199
Literature, romantic, realist and social themes, 196–197
Literature, themes of agricultural reform, 195–196
London, Jack, 196–197
Lonshoremen's Strike of 1934 (ILA), 252–257
Lopez, Francisco, 87–88, 131
Los Angeles, Blacks in 19th Century, 169
Los Angeles County Art Museum, 4
Los Angeles, early capital, 64
Los Angeles, founding of, 29
Los Angeles in the 1960s, 281
Los Angeles and the Open Shop, 226
Los Angeles, Progressive Reform in, 201–204
Los Angeles Times, bombing, 1910, 227–229
Los Angeles, vigilantes in 1850s, 116
Love, Captain Harry S., 128–129
Loyalty Oath Controversy, 274
Lux, Charles, 152
Lynch, Chief J.F., 233

Manila Galleons, influence of, 20–22
Mansur, Abby, 176
Maritime Federation of the Pacific, 256
Marsh, Dr. John, 74–75
Marshall, Colonel Robert B., 3

Marshall, James W., 89
Martinez, Jose Longinos, 4, 43
Martinez, Vilma, 291
Masaoka, Mike, 269
Mason, Colonel Richard B., 83, 90–91, 99
Mayer, Louis B., 244–245
McCall, Harrison, 272
McCarthy, Leo, 292–293
McClatchy, V.S., 269
McCullough, Hugh, 55
McDonald, John, 232
McDougal, Governor John, 111
McKinney, Sheriff Joseph, 135
McManigal, Ortie, 228–229
McNamara, James B. and John J., 228–229
McPherson, Sister Aimee, 241–243
McWilliams, Carey, 260, 268
Mendoza, Antonio de, 19
Menjou, Adolph, 273
Menken, Adah Isaacs, 189–190
Merchants' and Manufacturers' Association (LA),
    225–226
Merriam, Governor Frank, 249–250, 256, 260–261
Mexican-American Influences on the 1849 Constitution,
    100–103
Mexican-American labor, 1920s, 237–238; 1930s,
    257–262; 1950s–1970s, 288–290
Mexican-American, Schizoid Heritage, 133
Mexican-American, second generation political impulse,
    129–133
Mexican-Americans, women in recent politics, 290–291
Mexican-Americans and World War II, 266–268
Mexican-California, 53–69
Mexican-California and American-Mexican hostility,
    75–78
Mexican-California, early American frontiersmen,
    71–75
Mexican War and California Annexation, 80–84
Micheltorena, Manuel, 63, 66–67, 75–80
Mighels, Ella Sterling, 190
Milk, Supervisor Harvey, 291
Miller, Henry, 152
Miller, Joaquin, 188–189
Miller, John F., 173
Mills, James R., 274, 291
Mining, ethnic conflict in, 93, 123–129
Mining, legal claims, 92–93
Mining, Spanish and Mexican claims in early Gold
    Rush, 91–92
Mining, technology, 90–93
Mireles, Ramon, 238
Mission System, 26–30, 59–63
Modoc Indians, 8, 165–166
Mojave Indians, 10
Monterey, Conde de, 22
Monterey Constitution Convention of 1849, 98–103
Monterey Constitutional Convention of 1849, Spanish-
    speaking influences, 99–100
Monterey, mission and presidio, 24–28

Montesclaros, Marques de, 23
Montez, Lola, 96–98, 185–186
Montezuema, Aztec ruler, 15–16
Mooney, Thomas J., 231–233, 247, 262
Morehead, Joseph, 112
Morrison, Judge, 109
Moscone, Mayor George, 282, 291
Moulder, Andrew Jackson, 168, 183
Movies as culture, 243–244
Muir, John, 197–198, 248–249
Mulholland, William, 248–249
Murieta, Joaquin, 127–129, 188
Murray, Judge Hugh C., 170

Nativism in the 1850s, 108–109
Natural Resources and California's Economy, 2–3
Neve, Governor Felipe de, 28–30, 33
New Laws of 1542, 16–17
Newton, Heuy, P., 282
Neylan, John F., 219, 274
Nixon, Richard M., 272–277, 289, 292
Niza, Fray Marcos de, 19
Nootka Sound Controversy, 43–44
Norris, Frank, 195–196

O'Cain, Joseph, 44–45
O'Connor, Thomas, 234
Ohlone College, 287
Ohlone Indians, 8–10
Older, Fremont, 208–212
Olompali, Battle of, 79
Olson, Governor Culbert, 260–262, 269, 271
O'Sullivan, Paddy, 278
Osuna, Friar, 133
Otis, Harrison Gray, 202–204, 226
Overland California Mail Act, 142
Owens Valley Water Project, 248–249
Oxham, F.C., 232

Pacheco Rancho, 126–127
Pacheco, Romulado, 131–132
Pachucos, 266–268
Pacific Appeal (Black Newspaper), 168–169
Pacific Electric Railway Company, 155–156
Pacific Railroad Convention of 1859, 144–145
Pacific Republic Idea, 75, 111–114
Padres, Jose Maria, 60, 62–63
Palace Hotel, San Francisco, 153–154, 199
Panama-Pacific Exposition of 1915, 198–199
Pardee, Governor George, 203
Park, Alice, 177
Parks, Larry, 273
Pattie, James O., Personal Narrative of, 73, 176
Pellett, Sarah, 177
People's Party (1850s), 119
People's Protective Union, 171
People's Temple, 291
Peralta land grant, 114, 137–138
Perez, Juan, 43

Perkins Case (Slavery), 109–111
Perouse, Comte Jean de la, 36, 43
Perry, Herman, 272
Phelan, James D., 205, 227
Pico, Andrés, 108, 111, 142
Pico, Pio, 53–54, 65, 67, 81, 114
Pig-Tail Ordinance of 1854, 170–171
Pindray, Charles de, 112–113
Piper, Alice, 166–167
Piper vs. Big Pine, 1924, 166–167
Polk, President James K., 78, 80, 83, 90, 94–95
Pony Express, 143–144
Populist Party, 282–283
Portola, Gaspar de, 8, 24–26
Preparedness Day Bombing, 231–233
Progress and Poverty, 191–193
Progressive Era, politics, 201–222
Progressive Voters League, 247–248
Progressivism in the 1920s, 245–249
Proposition 1 (1938), 261–262
Proposition 9 (1974), 292
Proposition 13 (1978), 293
Proposition 14 (1964), 281

Quicksilver Messenger Service, 287
Quinn, William J., 255

Railroad Commission, 215–216
Ralston, William C., 153–156
Ramona, popular novel on Indians, 36, 165
Rancho Camulos, 130–131
Rancho Mariposa, 83
Rancho San Antonio, 137–138
Rancho San Rafael, 131
Raousset-Boulbon, Count Gaston de, 113
Reagan, Ronald, 238, 284–288
Reagan, Thomas, 209
Red Light Abatement Act of 1913, 219
Reglamento, Spanish law code, 29–30
Regulators, vigilante organization, 114–116
Reorganization Act of 1921, 246
Reyes, Inocencia, 82
Rezanov, Nikolai, 45–46
Richardson, Friend, 236, 246–248, 271
Richardson, William, 116–119
Riles, Wilson, 282
Riley, General Bennett, 99, 102
Rivera, Captain Fernando, 24–27, 34
Robeson, Paul, 274
Rolph, James, 245, 249–250
Roney, Frank, 224–225
Ronstadt, Linda, 292
Roosevelt, Theodore, 210–212
Rose, Harry, 204
Rossi, Angelo J., 256
Rowell, Chester, 219
Royce, Josiah, 133, 176
Royce, Sara, 176
Rubi, Mariano, 39–40

Reuf, Abe, 205–213
Rumford Fair Housing Act, 281–282
Russell, Lillian, 186
Russian-American Company, 45–48

Salvatierra, Father Juan Maria de, 23
Samish, Arthur, 271
Sanchez, Father Jose Bernardo, 72
Sanderson, Jeremiah, 168, 183–184
San Jose, founding of, 28–29
San Diego, settlement of, 24–26
San Francisco Bay, exploration of, 24–26
San Francisco Earthquake of 1906, 210–211
San Francisco General Strike of 1901, 205, 226–227
San Francisco General Strike of 1934, 252–257
San Francisco graft trials, 211– 213
San Francisco labor and the closed shop, 226–227
San Francisco Vigilante Committee of 1851, 114–116
San Francisco Vigilante Committee of 1856, 116–119
Savio, Mario, 283–286
Scharrenberg, Paul, 235
Schmitz, Eugene, 205–212
Schmitz, Herbert, 208–209
Schulberg, Bud, 244
Scott, Daniel, 184
Scott, Rev. W.A., 118
Scripps, Edward W., 227
Seale, Bobby, 282
Secularization, 59–63
Semple, Dr. Robert, 100–103
Serra, Father Junipero, 24–31, 35–36, 39, 41
Serrano decision (school financing), 288
Seven Cities of Cibola, legend of, 17–18
Sharon, William, 153–154
Shelly Club of San Francisco, 236
Sheriffs, Alex C., 283
Sherman, General William Tecumseh, 118–119
Shinn, Charles, 133
Sierra Nevada range, 1–2
Silliman, Benjamin, Jr., 153
Sinclair, Upton, 235, 250–252
Slavery and the Democratic Party, 109–111
Sleepy Lagoon Incident of 1942, 268
Slidell, John, 76, 78, 80
Sloat, John D., 80–84
Smith, Estelle, 232–233
Smith, Jedediah, 60, 71–72
Sola, Governor Pablo Vincente, 49–51
Solis, Joaquin, 58
Southern Pacific Political Bureau, 160
Southern Pacific Railroad, 150–151
Southern Pacific Railroad and Lawyers, 150–151, 160
Spain, background of early explorations, 15–16
Spain, governmental institutions, 16–17
Spanish-California, foreign intruders, 44–51
Spanish-California in transition, 1790s, 42
Spanish-California, isolation and foreign intruders, 33–34

Spanish-California, last days of 1800–1822, 47–51
Spanish Church influences in New Spain, 17
Spanish exploration, myths essential to it, 17–18
Spanish settlements, early colonies in California, 24–28
Spreckels, Rudolph, 210–212
Sproul, Robert G., 269–270, 274
Stanford, Leland, 157–160
Stanford University, 185
Steinbeck, John, 3
Stephens, Governor William D., 221–222, 233, 236, 245–246
Stetson Bill of 1911, 215
St. Mary's College, 184
Stockton, Robert Field, 81–86, 98
Stokes, Willie, 266
Stovall, Charles, 110–111
Strait of Anian, myth of, 18
Strauss, Levi, 96
Strong, Daniel, W., 145
Studebaker, John, 144
Suhr, Herman, 230
Sullivan, Dennis T., 210
Sunset Magazine, 152
Sutro, Adolph, 158
Sutter, John A., 47, 67, 75–80, 88–90, 102, 134, 163
Swett, John, 168
Swing-Johnson Bill, 249
Sydney Ducks, vigilante organization, 114–116

Taylor, Zachary, 80
Teamsters Union, 227–228
Temperance Reform Party, 161
Temple, Shirley, 261
Tenney, Jack B., 274
Tenochtitlan, Aztec capital, 15–16
Territory of Colorado scheme, 111
Terry, David, 119–120
Thomas, Judge, 109
Thurmond, Harold, 250
Todd, William, 79
Torre, Joaquin de la, 79
Townsend, Dr. Francis E., 252
Tracey, Spencer, 4
Transportation Revolution (1850), 142–151
Treaty of Cahuenga, 67, 83
Treaty of Guadalupe-Hidalgo, 87, 100, 102, 133–135
Trumbo, Dalton, 273
Twain, Mark, 186–188
Two Years Before the Mast, novel, 55

Ulloa, Francisco de, 18–19
Union Labor Party, 205–212
United Farm Workers, 288–290
University of California, 184, 282–287
University of San Francisco, 184
University of Santa Clara, 184
University of Vulcan, 236
Unruh, Jess (Big Daddy), 284

Vaca, Cabeza de, 17–18
Valle, Ygnacio del, 130–131
Vallejo, Mariano, 47, 63–69, 79, 114, 129–131, 133, 163
Vancouver, Captain George, 43
Van Ness, Mayor James, 118–119
Varela, Servulio, 129
Verdugo, Don Julio, 130–131
Victoria, Manuel, 60–61
Visalia Colored School,
Vizcaino, Sebastian, 21–23
Voorhis, Jerry, 272–273
Vuich, Rose A., 291

Walker, William, 113–114
Ward, Mary Francis, 169
Warner, Jack, 273
Warren, Earl, 270–273, 275
Water Controversies, 248–249
Watts Riot of 1965, 281–282
Weinberg, Jack, 283
Wells Fargo, 143–144
Wheatland Riot of 1913, 229–231
Whitaker, Clem, 271
White, Stephen W., 202

Whitney, Charlotte Anita, 178, 233–235, 238
Wilson, Andrew M., 210
Women, California Equal Suffrage Association, 177–178
Women, Constitution of 1849, rights, 101
Women, entertainment during the Gold Rush, 96–98, 185–186
Women in 19th century California, 176–178
Women in the Progressive Era, 1900–1920, 219–220
Women in recent California, 1950s–1970s, 291–292
Women poets, in early California, 189–191
Women, Political Equality League, 177–178
Wool, General John, 118–119
Woolwine, Thomas L., 203
Workingmen's Party, 172–175, 224
World War II, domestic consequences, 266–270

Yorty, Sam, 274, 282, 284
Young, Governor C.C., 235, 248–249
Young, Ewing, 73
Yuma Massacre, 34, 37
Yurok Indians, 7

Zamarano, Augustin, 60–61
Zoot-Suit Riot of 1943, 268